Edwin O. Tregelles, Sarah E. Fox

Edwin Octavius Tregelles

civil engineer and minister of the Gospel

Edwin O. Tregelles, Sarah E. Fox

Edwin Octavius Tregelles
civil engineer and minister of the Gospel

ISBN/EAN: 9783337285708

Printed in Europe, USA, Canada, Australia, Japan

Cover: Foto ©Lupo / pixelio.de

More available books at **www.hansebooks.com**

Thy attached father
Edwin O. Tregelles

EDWIN OCTAVIUS TREGELLES

Civil Engineer and Minister of the Gospel.

EDITED BY HIS DAUGHTER
SARAH E. FOX.

London:
HODDER AND STOUGHTON,
27, PATERNOSTER ROW.
—
MDCCCXCII.

BUTLER & TANNER,
THE SELWOOD PRINTING WORKS,
FROME, AND LONDON.

INTRODUCTION.

The following record of one whose experiences and circumstances are not very different from the lives of many who will read this volume, is now published, with the hope that some of these may find encouragement from the narrative of his fruitful faith and consecrated life, resulting in a service for his Lord and Saviour of over fifty years.

To young men his early life speaks of the blessing of true conversion from sin to righteousness through faith in Jesus Christ, followed by a confession of his loving Saviour, and consecration of time and strength to His service.

With all the temptations peculiar to young men, in the workshop, in the great city, as a traveller, and afterwards as a professional engineer, and as an employer of labour, both as farmer and coal owner, the history of his life's experiences will come home to many hearts.

He was very sensible of his own shortcomings, and his diary does not conceal them.

As far as possible the narrative is in his own words, which have been extracted from his papers and diaries.

Whilst the last sheets of this volume were yet in the press, the sudden death of my dear wife has left on me the responsibility of completing the work which we had together so nearly brought to a close.

J. HINGSTON FOX.

Fourth Month 26th, 1892.

CONTENTS.

CHAPTER I.
FALMOUTH.

Birth—Family Records—Childhood's Reminiscences—Mother's Death—Removal to Ashfield—Marriage of eldest Brother—Leaves Home for Neath Abbey—Enters Carpenters' Shop at Iron Works—Visit of Nathan Hunt and Peter Bedford—Bevington Gibbins—First Return Home—His Brother Nathaniel joins him—Camborne—Awakening to Spiritual Life at Barnstaple—Testifies for Christ in Swansea Meeting . . 1

CHAPTER II.
NEATH ABBEY.

Commencement of Journal—Twenty-second Birthday—Visit to London—His brother Samuel's Decease—Dr. Bevan—At Hay Meeting testifies for Christ—London Yearly Meeting—Isaac Crewdson's Ministry at Tottenham—J. J. Gurney—Business Journeys to Brighton, Worthing, and Ireland—Waterford Quarterly Meeting—Edward Alexander—His Father's Illness and Death—Riots and Strikes in South Wales—He addresses Men at Neath Abbey Works—No Strike—Marriage Engagement—Leaves Neath Abbey rather than prepare Machinery for Brewery—Commences as a Civil Engineer—Lights Bridport and Taunton with Gas—Accident—Cholera Epidemic—British and Foreign Temperance Society Meeting—Yearly Meeting—Stephen Grellet—Neath Abbey—Marriage . . 10

CHAPTER III.
BRIDPORT.

With his Wife visits Neath—Bridport—William Forster's Ministry—Sherborne—Anna Price—Quarterly Meeting at Poole—

Newton Tracey Meeting House—Yeovil—Barnstaple lighted by Gas—Journey to Cornwall—Birth of a Daughter—Yeovil lighted by Gas—Upwey—Maiden Castle—Wellington—Attended Long Sutton Meeting alone—Yearly Meeting, 1834—Bideford—The blind Ostler at Barrington—British and Foreign Bible Society Meeting—Bridport—Railway Meeting—Dorchester—Joins his Wife in Ireland and visits Killarney Lakes—Slavery ceases in West India Islands—Takes a House at Neath—Wellington lighted with Gas—Bridgewater Meeting—Teignmouth—Dorchester—Swansea—Birth of a Son—Bridgewater lighted with Gas 26

CHAPTER IV.

NEATH.

Christian Faithfulness—Neath—T. Williams—Barnstaple with Sisters—Clovelly—Honiton lighted with Gas—General Meeting at Brecon—Death of Bevington Gibbins—General Meeting in Hereford new Meeting House—Milford—Thoughts on Business—Gracechurch Street Meeting, London—House of Commons—William Allen and John Barclay at Stoke Newington—W. D. Crewdson and Thomas Shillitoe at Tottenham Meeting—Engineer of Railway, Southampton to Salisbury—A busy Week—Stanley Pumphrey's Experiences when Commercial Traveller—Death of Edward Alexander—Exeter—Birth of a Daughter—Serious Illness of his Wife—General Meeting at Worcester—Fire at Exeter—Yearly Meeting—J. J. Gurney going to America—Peter Bedford—With Edward Ash visits Women's Meeting—Death of King William IV.—Joins his Wife at Youghal—Exeter—Edward and John Pease 43

CHAPTER V.

TORQUAY.

Commencement of Indisposition—Thomas Tregelles—Torquay—Letter to his Sister, R. B. Gibbins—Falmouth—Visits Charles and Sarah Fox at Perran—Apprenticeship of Negroes in West Indies ceases—Scilly Islands—Quarterly Meeting at St. Austell—Unites with Friends in visiting Families—Public Meetings at Falmouth—Goes on Board Vessels and speaks to Sailors—Torquay—William Rouse 63

CHAPTER VI.
FALMOUTH.

Plymouth Meeting—Snow at Falmouth—The Cottage—Visits Ireland with Certificate—Large Public Meeting at Youghal—Visits Vessels in Cork Harbour—Bandon—Newtown School—Brookfield Agricultural School — Lisburn School — Public Meetings at Dublin, and with Miners near Waters-meet—Journey through Wales—Priscilla Hannah Gurney's Memoirs—Meetings at Milford and Neath Abbey—Sidcot School—Interview with Lord Ebrington, Viceroy of Ireland—John and M. Candler go to West Indies—Truro and St. Austell lighted by Gas—Penny Post—Marriage of Queen Victoria—Obtains Certificate to visit Schools connected with the Society of Friends—Croydon, Ackworth and Sidcot Schools—Visits sixty Schools as per List 76

CHAPTER VII.
FALMOUTH.

Yearly Meeting—Sarah Grubb's Testimony—Essex—Brighton—Lindfield School and William Allen—Interviews with Lord John Russell and Daniel O'Connell—Scotland—Meetings with Factory Workers—First Sense of Call to Service Abroad—Liverpool—Wales—Banbury—Plymouth—Meetings at Ilfracombe, Barnstaple and Clovelly—Family Visits at Plymouth and Kingsbridge—John Elliott's Message to his Friends   . 93

CHAPTER VIII.
FALMOUTH.

Monthly Meeting grants Certificate for Service in West Indies—Letter from Jonathan Backhouse—Message from Anna Price—Meetings with Sailors—Quarterly Meeting declines to endorse his Certificate—Professional Duties at Bristol—W. Jay, of Bath—Accompanies his Wife in a Trip to Tintagel—John Allen — Come-to-Good Meeting House — *Lord Beresford*, Steamer, Trial Trip and Storm ; Meeting on Board—Quarterly Meeting grants Certificate for Service in West Indies—Yearly Meeting, 1842, liberates for the Service—Waits for a Companion—Goes to Coverack with his Wife for her Health—Earthquake, Hayti—Bristol—Bradnich, Judith Templeman—James Jesup offers as Companion—Family Visit from Benjamin Seebohm—Kingsbridge—Yearly Meeting, 1843—William Forster at Gracechurch Street—With Maria Fox holds Meetings near Falmouth—Letter from Hannah C. Backhouse 106

CHAPTER IX.

WEST INDIES.

Departure for West Indies—Voyage and Fellow-Passengers—Meetings with Passengers and Crew—Barbadoes—First Impressions of Coloured People—Letter to his Children—Large Meeting in Wesleyan Chapel—Visits Prison at Bridgetown—Moravian Missions at Mount Tabor and Sharon—Byde Mill—Meeting with Upper Class at Bridgetown—Tobago—Pelicans—J. Renkevitz—Progress of Freed Negroes—James Bickford—Wesleyan Missions—Scarborough—Grenada—Call on Governor—Bad Roads—Extinct Volcano—Intercourse with Planters—Meeting in Court House at Mount Alexander—Meeting at George Town—Trinidad—J. M. Phillippo—Port Espano—Yellow Fever at Petit Bourg—Josiah Brown—Convalescence—Dr. Philip—Letters from Josiah Forster—Grenada—Conference of Wesleyan Ministers 134

CHAPTER X.

WEST INDIES.

St. Vincent—Letter to his Wife—Calls on Governor and Macdowall Grant—First Meeting after Illness—Prayers' House—Souffrière Volcano—Death of his Wife—Attends Meeting at Calliaqua—Caribs—Extracts from Journal of James Bickford—Lucia—Letters of Sympathy from Josiah Forster, John Pease and Mahlon Day 164

CHAPTER XI.

WEST INDIES.

Lucia—Meeting in Court House, Castries—Mico Schools—River Dorée—Voyage in Canoe—Tousmassic—Nautilus—Visit to Gaol—Dominica—Call on President—Coasting Voyage—Meetings in Wesleyan Chapels—Mount Wallis—Canoe Building—Visit to Caribs—Mary Dalrymple—Antigua—Earthquake, 1843—Call on Governor Sir C. Fitzroy—Archdeacon Holberton—Meeting in Scotch Kirk—The Moravian Missions—Wesleyan Sunday Schools—F. W. Hougk—Meetings in Wesleyan and Moravian Chapels 185

CHAPTER XII.

WEST INDIES.

Barbuda—Occupations of Inhabitants—Meeting at Governor's House—School—W. Tanner, the Shepherd—Solomon Deazle, Woodman—Antigua—Meetings in Moravian and Wesleyan School-Rooms—Montserrat—Meetings—Poverty—Visits to Gaol—Nevis—Half the Population Wesleyan—Call on Chief Justice Webb—St. Christopher's—Basseterre—Meetings at Wesleyan and Moravian Chapels—Colonial Secretary—R. and A. Inglis and Children—Schools—Gaol—Jesse Pilcher—Grenada—Meetings at Duquesne—Jamaica—John Daughtry—Earl of Elgin and Lady Charlotte Bruce—Scenery at Belcour—Bible Readings with Servants and Neighbours—The Day's Occupations—James Haig—Captain Robert Bruce—Suggests Employment for Prisoners in Kingston Gaol—Draws Plans for a Prison Wall—Humming Bird—Call on Governor—Meeting with Haitien Refugees—Meeting at Wesleyan Chapel, Botanic Gardens—Abraham Hyams—James Ritchie . 201

CHAPTER XIII.

WEST INDIES.

Letter to Joseph T. Price about Anniversary of Liberation of Slaves—Belcour—Shortwood—Cottage Meetings—Stay at Stoneyhill—Oberlin—Low Condition of Education—J. A. Preston—Elliot Station—Meeting at Mount Charles—Tropical Rain—Maroons—Grateful Hill—Myalism and Obeeism—Meeting at Pleasant Hill—School at Mount Fletcher—Richmond Pen—Meeting at Kingston, 2,000 present—Spanish Town—Sligoville—Homes of Freed Slaves—Baptist Chapel, Passage Fort—Meeting at Jericho—Missing Mule—Annatto Bay—Call on two Friends—Mount Hermon—Ascent of Mount Diabola—Phoenix Park—Jonathan Edmundson—Wesleyan School—Waterfall—David Day—Bariffe Hall—Ora Cabessa—William Jamieson—Large Meetings at Beechamville—Ocho Rios—St. Ann's Bay—Beautiful Scenery—Brown's Town—John Clark—Meetings and Schools—Sturge Town—Sunday School Teachers, Brown's Town—James Finlayson and Martial Law in 1832—Dry Harbour—Calabar—J. Tinson—Kettering—William Knibb's House, built by grateful liberated Slaves—Meeting with Teachers—Large Meeting at Falmouth—Earthquake—Prison—Montego Bay—J. L. Lewin, a Converted Jew—Cornwall—H. M. Waddell—

x   CONTENTS.

George Blyth—Meeting at Goodwill Temperance Village—
Moravian Settlement, Irwin Hill—Salter's Hill—Large Meeting, Mount Carey—Thomas Burchall—Lucea—W. H. Hann, Wesleyan Missionary—Savannah-la-mar—Aaron de Leon—Laars Kielson—New Beaufort 218

CHAPTER XIV.
WEST INDIES.

Jamaica—H. G. Pfeiffer and Martial Law—Meeting at New Bethlehem—Schools at Fairfield—Work of Moravians—Meeting with Maroons—Mandeville—Visits Prison—School—Rest at Mount Providence—Old Harbour—Spanish Town—Interview with Earl of Elgin and John Daughtry respecting Prisons—Meeting in Baptist Chapel—Penitentiary—Kingston—Silk-cotton Tree—Morant Bay—Climate—Beauty of Bath—Belle Castle—Port Antonio—Moore Town—Maroons—Fording Rio Grande—Golden Grove—Surrey Gaol—Meeting at Port Royal—Hayti—Arrival at Jacmel with J. T. Hartwell—Climate and Appearance of Town—Call on General Geffrard—Journey to Port Républicaine—Mules—Citrounier—Delmay's Hut a Bethel—Leogane—Port Républicaine—Reminiscences of S. Grellet—Meeting with American Wesleyans—Fabius Day—Prison—Lacahaye—Thomas Williams—Alexis Dupuy—St. Marc—President Guerrier—Desert—Gonaives—James Osler—Coffee Sales 249

CHAPTER XV.
WEST INDIES.

Hayti—River forded Thirty Times—Escalier—Plaisance—Limbe—View of Cape Haitien—Miseries from Earthquake—Visits to Lycée and École Nationale—Prison—Meeting with Europeans and Americans—Plaisance—Gonaives—School—St. Marc—Meeting at Lacahaye—Port Républicaine—Meetings—Incidents on Journey—Haitian Costumes—Miragoane—Aquin—General Lelièvre—Aux Cayes—Meeting—Prison—André Télémaque—St. Louis—Baynet—One of the Horses dies—Jacmel—Voyage to St. Thomas—Santa Cruz—Governor—Visits to Moravian Mission Stations—Schools for the "Unfrees"—Fredericksted—Christiansted—Prison—Meetings at St. Thomas—Return Voyage—Bermuda—Storm—Meeting with Passengers—Southampton—Arrival at Falmouth . . 275

CHAPTER XVI.

FALMOUTH.

Yearly Meeting, 1845—Falmouth—Redruth Monthly Meeting—Goes with Sister and Children to Youghal—Death of Junia Price—Elizabeth Fry—Prospect of Service in Norway—Professional Engagements—Dartmoor—Yearly Meeting—Farewell Gathering at Samuel Fox's—Benjamin Seebohm . . 294

CHAPTER XVII.

NORWAY.

Sets off for Norway with John Budge and Isaac Sharp—Bible Reading on Board *Caledonian*—Hamburg—Emily Sieveking—Copenhagen—Tracts—Crossing the Sound at Midnight—Gothenburg—Meeting on Board the *Tees*, Captain George Brown—Christiansand—Stavanger—Elias E. Tasted—Dussivigan—Two Months' Meeting—Yearly Meeting—Visits to Friends—One who gave up the Trade in Strong Drink—Hund Vaag Island—Crowded Meeting at Stavanger—Stransund—Conference with Elders and Overseers—Letter from E. E. Tasted—First-Day Meeting—Leaves Stavanger—Stagland—Farewells—Meeting at Olen—Bergen—F. A. Putter—Tracts—Letter from Peter Boyesen—Christiania—Gothenburg 302

CHAPTER XVIII.

FALMOUTH.

Return from Norway—Croydon—Prince Town—Meeting on Dartmoor—Anna Price—Distress in Ireland—Dr. Philip—Death of Joseph John Gurney—John Hodgkin—Cornwall Railway—Marriage of his Brother Nathaniel—Samuel Capper and Joseph Eaton hold Tent Meetings at Falmouth—Accident at Railway Works—Depression in Trade—Influenza Epidemic—Meeting with Sailors—Visits Prison 321

CHAPTER XIX.

FALMOUTH.

Meeting with Sailors at Falmouth—Call on Captain B.—French Revolution—Public Meeting in Manor Rooms, Stoke Newington—Funeral of Mary Howitt's Mother—Yearly Meeting

xii   CONTENTS.

—J. and M. Yeardley's Proposed Service in Germany, Russia, and Austria—Disturbances in Paris—J. Lavin—Visits to Vessels in Falmouth Harbour—Neath, J. Rees, C. A. Price—Banbury—Ipswich—Croydon School, Peter Bedford—South Wales Railway—Holds Meeting with Navvies at Neath Abbey—Letter from A. R. Tregelles—Funeral of Elizabeth Fox of Bank House, Falmouth—Conversation with Captain B.—Banbury—Adderbury—Removes to Frenchay—Caroline Fry—Sibford and Sidcot Schools—Barnstaple Meeting—James Veale—Interview with a Swiss—Eliza Allen's Address at Liskeard Meeting—Removes to Derwent Hill, Shotley Bridge—Tin Works—Marriage to Elizabeth Richardson . . . 330

CHAPTER XX.

SHOTLEY BRIDGE.

Derwent Hill—Darlington Quarterly Meeting—London—Scotland on Business—Plants Trees on Wedding Anniversary—Newcastle Quarterly Meeting—Burning of *Amazon* Steamer—Visit from Isaac Sharp—E. O. and Elizabeth Tregelles ride to Winnow's Hill on Horseback—Yearly Meeting—Eli and Sybil Jones—Visits Scotland with Minute—Aberdeen—Lydia A. Barclay—Glasgow—Meetings at Hayden Bridge—Business Thoughts—Address from Jonathan Priestman—John Hodgkin's Address—Endré and Maria Dahl at Derwent Hill—Eli and Sybil Jones—Cholera at Newcastle—Business Changes—Goes with his Wife to Bristol—Mary Ann Schimmelpennick—Falmouth—Illness of his Sister, Anna P. Fox—Camborne—John Dunstan—Visit to his Nephew, S. P. Tregelles, at Plymouth—Family Visits from Ann Eliza Dale and Eliza Barclay—Death of William Forster—Meetings in Cumberland—Harvest Rejoicings—Loss of Mahlon Day—Death of Joseph T. Price—Newcastle Quarterly Meeting—Prospect of Peace with Russia—Death of Emperor Nicolas—Visits the Hebrides with Certificate—Meetings in North Uist, Mull, Skye, and Oban—Capture of Sebastopol—Death of Stephen Grellet—Visits Families with J. Priestman—Colliery Strike—Meeting at Darlington with Young People—Oswald Baynes—George Richardson—Narrative of Preservation from Shipwreck of Dr. R. H. Thomas—Susan Howland and Lydia Congden—Financial Panic—Failure of Bank—Visit of Sarah Squire and Sarah Tatham 347

CHAPTER XXI.

SHOTLEY BRIDGE.

Letters from Oswald Baynes and Caroline Fox—Wet Harvest Weather—Death of Joseph Sturge—Visit of John and E. Clark from Jamaica—Gracechurch Street Meeting—York Meeting and School—Cottage Meeting—Three Colliers killed—Visits Cumberland and Northumberland—Wigton School—Attends Brewster Sessions to oppose Licenses—Marriage of Daughter —Distress from Depression of Trade—Russian Serfs liberated —Commencement of American War—Isaac Sharp goes to Iceland and Greenland—E. O. and E. Tregelles attend Yearly Meeting—With Charles Wilson visits Cumberland and Scotland—Francis Redford—Meetings at Dumfries—Port Patrick— Hebrides—Letter from James Reed of Portree—Wigton School —Exhibition—Extract from Hetty Bowman—Illness of his Sister Elizabeth—Visit of John L. Eddy—Death of Rebecca Gibbins—Letter from Mary Samuel Lloyd 373

CHAPTER XXII.

SHOTLEY BRIDGE.

Visits at Newcastle Gaol a condemned Murderer—Capital Punishment — Matamoros — Answer to Prayer—William Tanner— Yearly Meeting's Committee—Illness of his Wife—Death of his Sister Elizabeth—Goes with his Wife to Scotland—Holds Meetings at Perth and Inverness—Isabella L. Bird—Meeting at Oban—Derwent Hill Harvest Home—Meeting with Navvies —Rebecca Collins—Ann Eliza Dale—Loss of *The London* Steamer—Escape of Sailors from Shipwreck—Sympathy for Sufferers by Financial Failures—Death of W. Tanner—John Henry Douglas and Robert Alsop — David Hunt — Severe Winter—Death of Albert Fox—Yearly Meeting—Slave Children in Brazil set free—Marriage of Son—Sybil Jones relates Experience in the War—Falmouth—Death of John Pease— Amos and Edith Griffith—Accident at Abergele—Meeting at Blackhall Mill 390

CHAPTER XXIII.

SHOTLEY BRIDGE.

Yearly Meeting—Conference at Newcastle—Attends United Kingdom Alliance Meeting at Manchester—Yearly Meeting, Dublin —James Owen—Death of Sarah Richardson—Visits Scotland

—Neath—Public Meeting, Cardiff—War declared between France and Prussia—Appeal for the War Victims—Letter from Robert Alsop—Manchester Meeting—Decease of Abraham Fisher—Marriage of Daughter—Liskeard—Mirfield—Prayer for Recovery of Prince of Wales—Death of Thomas and Jonathan Richardson—Yearly Meeting—Surbiton—Esher—Alabama Arbitration—Visits Northumberland, Cumberland and Westmorland—Attends Aberdeen General Meeting—Inverness, Oban, Tobermory—Joel and Hannah Bean visit Derwent Hill—Yearly Meeting—Neal Dow and Dr. F. R. Lees at Shotley—Meeting at Nenthead—Death of his Sister Dorothy Tregelles—Joins Yearly Meeting's Committee in Oxfordshire—Conference in London on the State of the Society of Friends—Speaks on Temperance at Monthly Meeting, Newcastle—Decease of his Sister Rachel—Proposition on Temperance in Yearly Meeting—William C. Westlake—Deborah Thomas and Mary Haines—Joins Yearly Meeting's Committee in Visits to Ackworth School and Yorkshire—E. O. and E. Tregelles go to Neath, Plymouth, and Penzance—Meetings at Marazion and Mousehole 406

CHAPTER XXIV.
SHOTLEY BRIDGE.

Snow-storm, five Trains blocked—Isaac Sharp goes to Norway, Denmark, and Minden—Death of Dr. Tregelles—Yearly Meeting—Alteration of Queries—Care of Religious Instruction of Youth—Constitution of Meetings of Ministers and Elders—Family Gathering at Surbiton—Ira D. Sankey—At York visits Elizabeth and Sarah Backhouse—Allen Jay—Sedbergh General Meeting—Thomas Handley—Commences First-day Afternoon Cottage Meetings at Templar Terrace—Women Friends' Address to the Queen on Temperance—Kinsey and Caroline E. Talbot hold large Gospel and Temperance Meetings each Night in the Derwent Valley—Yearly Meeting—Rufus P. King, Edward Scull, and Dr. Richard H. Thomas, jun., at Surbiton—Remarkable Dream—Holds Meetings amongst the Northumbrian Colliers—Friends' Temperance Conference at Leeds—Rufus P. King—At Temperance Conference, London, read Paper, "Temperance the Ally of Christianity"—Death of Jane Fisher—Strike amongst his Colliers—Friends' Temperance Union—John Bright on Temperance—Isaac Sharp, Theodore Harris and Langley Kitching depart for South Africa 424

CHAPTER XXV.

SHOTLEY BRIDGE.

Origin of E. O. Tregelles' zeal for Temperance—Letter to *Alliance News* on Local Option—Kars taken by Russians—Dr. Temple, Bishop of Exeter—Business Trials—William Hoyle—Sudden Death of his Wife—Leaves Derwent Hill—Resides at Falmouth and Banbury—Letter of Isaac Sharp from Kuruman—Cornish Sunday Closing Bill 436

CHAPTER XXVI.

FALMOUTH AND BANBURY.

Spends Winter in South of France—Justine Dalencourt—Nimes—Congenies—Lydie Majolier—Quarterly Meeting—Protestants—L. Majolier's Illness—Aigues Mortes and Tower of Constance—Fontanès—Samuel and Clement Brun—Le Vigan—Congenies, Nimes—Returns to England—Resides at Falmouth with his Sister—Temperance Tract Distribution—Encouraged by Temperance Work at Medomsley—Death of Samuel Bowly—Isaac Sharp returns—Removes to Banbury—Dr. Gabriel S. Dobrashian—Meets old Friends from Trinidad—Journal ends—Two Years of Weakness—Letters to his Grandson and Sister—Death—Recollections by Elizabeth N. Capper 443

CHAPTER I.

FALMOUTH.

Birth—Family Records—Childhood's Reminiscences—Mother's Death—Removal to Ashfield—Marriage of eldest Brother—Leaves Home for Neath Abbey—Enters Carpenters' Shop at Iron Works—Visit of Nathan Hunt and Peter Bedford—Bevington Gibbins—First return Home—His brother Nathaniel joins him—Camborne—Awakening to Spiritual Life at Barnstaple—Testifies for Christ in Swansea Meeting.

EDWIN OCTAVIUS TREGELLES, the youngest of the seventeen children of Samuel and Rebecca Tregelles, of Falmouth, was born on the 19th of Tenth Month, 1806. He says:—

My grandfather, Joseph Tregelles, was descended from Nicholas Jose of Sennen, Land's End, who spent a considerable time in Launceston Castle for conscience sake. My grandmother, Sarah Tregelles, was the daughter of Andrew Hingston, of Penryn. My dear mother was the youngest daughter of Thomas Smith, a banker of London.

One of the first occurrences in my life that I remember with sufficient clearness to fix the date was my third birthday. In order to commemorate the day I was taken out in my father's carriage, with my mother and grandmother, when, in returning, the horses were frightened by a boy driving a hoop with pieces of tin on it, making a tinkling; and the consequence was that the coachman was thrown from the box and hurt his shoulder.

In 1811 the health of my valued mother began to fail. In order to keep the house quiet, Henry, Rachel and I were sent to the houses of our relations. I have very lively recollections of our enjoyment whilst staying with them. Much of our time at Grove Hill was spent in a sort of workshop, where we had all we wanted in glue-pot, wood, hammer and nails.

One day, while at Uncle Thomas Were Fox's, our nurse, Maria Thomas, took us to walk "down to Bar." On the bank, just above the lime-kilns, was a white horse grazing, whom I pelted with stones; but, going too near his heels, he felled me to the ground and nearly killed me. I was senseless immediately, and when I recovered, I was in the miller's house three furlongs off.

My mother was devotedly attached to me, and felt most acutely the prospect of leaving me so young. She died in the autumn of 1811. Her deep interest in our eternal well-being was wonderfully supplied by my eldest sister Sarah, then about twenty-five years of age, who endeavoured by example and precept, and by the most watchful care, to lead us in the right path.

In 1815 my brother Robert died. We had gone into the country on his account to Tregenver, a farm near Falmouth, where we children had great enjoyment, spending most of our days in the open air plaiting rushes and straw. The taste we had all contracted for a country life induced my dear father, in 1816, to remove to Ashfield. Joel Lean had carried on a school at this place for many years, but on our going there he removed to Fishponds, near Bristol. All lent a willing hand in laying out the shrubbery near the house, and in the garden my father worked very hard, and soon the ground which had been trodden by schoolboys' feet wore a green and lovely garb. My sisters planted with their own hands most of the shrubs and small trees which adorned that sweet spot.

My brother John becoming ill in 1815, whilst an apprentice to William Prideaux, a chemist, at Wellington, a long voyage to a warmer climate was recommended. Accompanied by his brother Joseph, he sailed for the West Indies in the *Duke of Wellington*. The captain (Williams) was a friend of our father. They had not long sailed before they had cause to regret the step they had taken, which was confirmed by the vessel running aground at the Bermudas. After spending a few months at the Bermudas and Jamaica they returned on one of the Falmouth packets. Though benefited by the voyage, his weakness returned; and in the Ninth Month, 1816, his spirit was released from the earthly tabernacle. This was the first deathbed scene I had ever witnessed, and it made a deep and durable impression on my young mind. I was not then ten years old.

My eldest and favourite brother, Samuel, married early in 1811, Dorothy Prideaux, of Kingsbridge, and great was my joy, at five years of age, when my niece Anna Rebecca Tregelles was born.

In 1819 Uncle and Aunt Price (she was our father's eldest sister) came into Cornwall, and kindly proposed to take me to live with them at Neath Abbey. Arrangements were soon concluded, and on Second Month 16th, 1820, I set out from home with my brother Samuel and two of my sisters to attend the Monthly Meeting at Redruth, in case we should, when at Redruth, learn that there was a vessel ready to sail from Portreath.

In the evening my brother Samuel walked part of the way towards Portreath with me, and, after bending over me in what I believe was silent prayer, he parted from me with the words, "God be gracious to thee, my son!" I pursued my way alone, with childish timidity and simplicity (being only thirteen and a half years of age), unconscious of all that was before me. Of one thing I am now certain, that the Lord has watched over me, He has encompassed my path, He has preserved my going out and my coming in.

On reaching Portreath I was kindly received by William James. The vessel by which I was to proceed was the *Joseph*, Capt. Rees. The wind was not fair the following morning, and learning she could not sail until the evening, I set out to walk to Redruth, feeling very home-sick, and desirous of meeting again some of my friends. In this I was disappointed, and proceeded to Camborne to see my dear nurse. She walked with me a little way towards Portreath, which place I reached just in time to get on board the *Joseph* before she was wafted out of the port by a fine breeze, whilst a glowing sunset shed brilliancy around.

On the 18th we made slow progress towards the Welsh coast, and on that night it came on to blow so heavily that the captain was glad to reach Ilfracombe in safety. My funds being low, I was obliged for the sake of economy to stay in a public room of the White Hart Inn, where I was annoyed with very disagreeable company. I felt very desolate, and as it was First-day I sought a place where I could spend some time in reading my Bible and in worship. This I found on some fine rocks on Hillsborough, and there I passed a blessed season. Several young men spent the evening in drinking and smoking in the room where I was. One of them became intoxicated. I abstained entirely from beer, partly because I did not like it, and this tended greatly to my preservation.

As the *Joseph* was beneaped, the captain, who was kind to me, recommended me to go on by packet to Swansea. On arriving there I went with letters of introduction from my sister Sarah to Robert and Jane Eaton, who at that time lived on the Strand. It was a dismal snowy evening, and I was by no means favourably impressed by the appearance of the town. The following day I remained at Swansea, and with cousin Joseph Tregelles Price attended a peace meeting in the small room at the Friends' Meeting House.

He sent over to Neath Abbey for a pony for me, and on Second Month 24th we rode there together.

Joseph Tregelles Price and his sisters Junia and Christiana were the son and daughters of Peter and Anna Price, who had invited Edwin Tregelles to come and reside with them, and learn engineering at the Neath Abbey Iron Works. He says :—

Cousins Junia and Christiana were absent at Congenies. They returned soon after the yearly meeting. The practice of Christiana A. Price in retiring for meditation during a portion of the evening impressed me with its importance.

In the Ninth Month I went to work in the carpenters' shop in connection with the foundry at Neath Abbey. Here I lost ground as a Christian, being exposed to the rehearsal of vice, though there was not much open sin. True it is that evil communications corrupt good manners; yes, and lay waste the serious impressions of youth. I soon deviated from my habits of piety, but was preserved from descending to the depths of iniquity.

In the spring of 1821 Nathan Hunt, from America, visited Neath. He was accompanied by Peter Bedford. On the evening of their arrival at Neath, cousin J. T. Price and I called on them; and here commenced an acquaintance with my valued friend Peter Bedford, which soon became an intimacy, and a friendship of lasting benefit to me. Nathan Hunt had several meetings, in which he was powerfully engaged as a minister in upholding the cause of truth to my profit, my mind being then in a tender, susceptible state. Several times I rode with Peter Bedford, and before they departed he addressed me in a manner that penetrated my heart. He pressed on me attention and obedience to the swift witness in the soul, reproving for evil and encouraging that which was good. And now as I write, sixteen years afterwards, the recollection is precious to both of us; as my dear friend often now recurs to those early days of our friendship, which I have cause to rank as amongst my highest privileges. After their visit I endeavoured to retire every evening to wait upon the Lord and read the Bible, which I had much neglected. The happiness which followed was of no common kind, and continued until I relaxed my vigilance, and the tempter again succeeded in making the things of time appear preferable to those of eternity.

Bevington Gibbins and Jonathan Rees accompanied Nathan Hunt and his companion to the half year's meeting at Hay on their way to Dublin, and were much impressed and benefited thereby. It was at a meeting at Dolgelly that dear Bevington Gibbins first knelt in public to offer up praise. And at Swansea monthly meeting, soon after his return, I first heard him as a minister quote the words, " The blessing of the Lord it maketh rich, and He addeth no sorrow therewith."

Doubtless the dedication of this young companion must have been very cheering to Edwin O. Tregelles, and especially interesting when in after years he became his brother-in-law by marrying Rebecca Tregelles. E. O. T. writes:—

In the summer I was allowed to visit my home at Ashfield, and a joyful return it was to me. It was my privilege to attend on my dear brother Henry, then very ill. He had returned from his situation at Colchester. I was permitted to remain with him till he died. My stay at home was much marred by my weakness and deviations.

On Ninth Month 15th I again left my father and sisters, and embarked on board the *Calstock*, Captain Lewis, and sailed round the land for Swansea. Off the Lizard we met the Royal Squadron just returning from Dublin, whither they had convoyed King George IV. On arriving at Neath I learnt that my uncle Price had died on the day I left home.

My brother Nathaniel came to the Neath Abbey Iron Works as a clerk in First Month, 1822; this greatly increased my happiness. We afterwards had the privilege of the company of our sister Rebecca as our housekeeper.

In the summer of 1823 I again visited my native place; this time crossing by the *Glamorgan*, steamer, to Ilfracombe. I was engaged in engineering work at Camborne for several weeks, returning to Truro to spend First-days, and was very much at the loose, as it may be termed. If I had not been upheld and restrained by a Hand unseen, I believe I should have sunk in the mire of dissipation. I slept at the house of John Budge, who with his wife proved useful in restraining my follies. They were not aware of the extent of my deviations. I neglected attending week-day meetings, although only three miles distant, until the counsel of my sister Sarah, and a letter from cousin Joseph T. Price, of more than ordinary value, which at his request I destroyed, induced me to resume the practice. It was at the first week-day meeting I attended at Redruth that I was impressed by the address of a minister. I was enabled to relinquish the pursuits I had delighted in; and soon I was liberated from Camborne.

The occurrence which gives me the greatest uneasiness was an excursion to Carnbrae Castle one afternoon with a party of thoughtless young people. Here I threw off the Quaker, and with the Quaker the Christian went, and left the buffoon in its stead. Young as I was, I had nearly formed an unsuitable attachment, of which I should have repented to the day of my death. My faithful nurse, whom I used to visit frequently, saw the vortex of danger I was near, and warned me in such a way that my eyes were opened, and I escaped the snare that was laid for me.

At the conclusion of the year 1824, and throughout the whole of 1825, there was a departure from good previously known. My soul seemed to dwell in darkness. I was, however, much helped by a religious visit from our aunt Sarah Abbot, and Ann Tweedy, who came to Neath accompanied by Dr. Charles Hingston as guide. Nathaniel and I met them in the octagon drawing-room at Glenvelyn, when one of them began her address with the words, "The fool hath said in his heart, there is no God." The message came home to me with blessing, and I was delivered from the paths of the destroyer, though much inclined at times to follow my own devices and delusions. It was marvellous how I was kept from heinous transgression. Towards the middle of 1826 light seemed to force its way to my soul, and I gradually became enamoured with the love and cheered by the hope of the gospel.

I left Neath with my dear Aunt Abbot, and Hannah and Elizabeth Abbot, for Falmouth. We crossed to Ilfracombe, and proceeded to the Golden Lion hotel, Barnstaple. We had our meeting in our sitting-room at the inn. Here my aunt addressed me. And this seemed like the turning-point in my life, a fresh conversion from darkness to light, from the power of Satan unto God. I have ever since regarded Barnstaple with more than ordinary interest, as the scene of my new birth. Thus was answered the prayer of my sister Sarah for my preservation, and that I might give thanks when on the banks of deliverance.

I commenced my present joyous career on Twelfth Month 13th, 1827, having publicly avowed myself as the servant of the Lord at Swansea monthly meeting, when the words were quoted in feebleness, "Wait on the Lord, be of good courage, and He shall strengthen thine heart; wait, I say, on the Lord!"

On this occasion Bevington Gibbins returned a certificate for paying a religious visit throughout

Wales, and writes in his diary, "At meeting I felt there was much encouragement for some, and an unexpected call to one or more individuals then present, when a dear young friend, Edwin O. Tregelles was engaged to open his mouth amongst us."

CHAPTER II.

NEATH ABBEY.

Commencement of Journal—Twenty-second Birthday—Visit to London—His Brother Samuel's Decease—Dr. Bevan—At Hay Meeting testifies for Christ—London Yearly Meeting—Isaac Crewdson's Ministry at Tottenham—J. J. Gurney—Business Journeys to Brighton, Worthing, and Ireland—Waterford Quarterly Meeting—Edward Alexander—His father's Illness and Death—Riots and Strikes in South Wales—He addresses Men at Neath Abbey Works—No Strike—Marriage Engagement—Leaves Neath Abbey rather than prepare Machinery for Brewery—Commences as a Civil Engineer—Lights Bridport and Taunton with Gas—Accident—Cholera Epidemic—British and Foreign Temperance Society Meeting—Yearly Meeting—Stephen Grellet—Neath Abbey—Marriage.

NEATH ABBEY, *Ninth Month* 18*th*, 1828.—Believing that my progress in the christian course may be assisted by the practice of noting the condition of my soul, and recording some of the events which pass around me, I feel encouraged to commence a journal.

The following paragraph refers to his nephew, Samuel Prideaux Tregelles, LL.D., the son of Samuel Tregelles.

Tenth Month 14*th*.—This day dear Prideaux was to leave his peaceful home to commence his career in the world.

Oh that he may be preserved, is the earnest desire of my soul.

15*th*.—Learnt to-day that a small meeting had been established at Barnstaple by William Baker and others, which has my desires for its prosperity, that He who has called them may condescend to be with them, lead, guide, and grant them the refreshing influences of His Spirit.

18*th*.—Have been fearful of becoming too much enamoured by the world. I desire to seek and maintain the correct medium, and to be guided in all things, important, as well as those apparently trivial, by a conformity to my Father's will. I have been tried by adversity in business; may I, when visited by prosperity, keep my ground, and still say, "There is none upon earth that I desire beside Thee." I have had to strive against a quickness in discerning the faults of others.

19*th*.—The twenty-second anniversary of my birth. On reviewing the past twelve months I have gratefully to acknowledge the goodness of my heavenly Father in preserving me through peculiar trials and baptisms. Since the last anniversary I have believed myself called upon publicly to avow whose servant I desire to be. And although of late the consolations of Divine love have been withheld, I am thankful that I have no desire to look back after having put my hand to the plough.

31*st*.—Rose early, and have much benefited by it; have passed this day pleasantly in consequence, without being improperly hurried.

I trust, however deeply I may feel for the interest of my employers, that I shall keep the great end of my life in view.

Third Month 24*th*, 1829.—Left my peaceful home for London with some fear lest I should get off my guard and fall from my steadfastness, but had great satisfaction in the recollection of the apostle's charge, "I commend you to God, and to the word of His grace, which is able to build you up, and to give you an inheritance among all them which are sanctified."

27th.—As I rode in the evening to Tottenham I thought of my precious brother (Samuel Tregelles) as safely removed from the trials of time, and gone to the land where sorrow is not known; cleansed by the blood of Jesus, he is now rejoicing with a joy unknown to men. Earnestly did I crave that I might, through faith in the same atoning sacrifice, eventually join him and others of our dear relatives in singing the praises of the Lamb.

29th.—I took tea at Thomas and Hannah Bevan's. After speaking of the losses I had sustained in our family circle, Hannah Bevan addressed me on the uncertainty of life, "Be ye also ready, for in such an hour as ye think not, the Son of man cometh," and, addressing me as a brother, exhorted me to hold fast that which I had attained, and keep my covenant with a covenant-keeping God.

Neath, Fourth Month 8th.—Completed this day with my dear friend, Joseph Pollard, our engagement for visiting Friends by appointment of the monthly meeting, and feel that I may praise the Lord for the help mercifully afforded to me, who felt very unequal to the work.

9th.—Attended monthly meeting at Swansea. A very sweet testimony concerning Elizabeth Jonathan Rees was read, and affected me with lively feelings of desire for similar preservation to what she experienced. Her blessed spirit now rejoices in the mercies and joys purchased for her by the blood of Jesus.

19th.—I may record many mercies since I last made any notes, and, above all, the goodness of my heavenly Protector for His preservation, having been enabled to declare at Hay, on the 15th, that His is the only name whereby we must be saved.

London, Fifth Month 19th.—The last four weeks that I have spent here have found me so much occupied as to afford but little time for noting much save an extension of the same mercy and goodness of which I have so oft occasion to speak. I feel especially thankful for the sweet feeling which came over me on First-day at Tottenham, when dear Isaac Crewdson expressed his desire that nothing might be withheld, that we might relinquish all the Lord was calling for. I felt my whole soul prostrated in supplication that this might be my happy experience.

E. O. Tregelles was at the sittings of the yearly meeting, and at its close could give thanks for the mercies granted on this strengthening occasion.

24th.—Attended meeting at Plaistow, where in the morning were cousin Sylvanus Fox, Maria Fox, Rachel Fowler, and Joseph John Gurney. In the afternoon J. J. Gurney set forth the offices of Christ, and the necessity of accepting Him as our Saviour.

Neath, Eighth Month 13th.—This day has been one of severe conflict; may I long remember it. In riding towards Swansea, to the monthly meeting, it seemed to be forcibly impressed on me that there must be ability granted by the Lord to endure all His turnings and overturnings. We are very apt to crave that His hand may not spare nor His eye pity until we are made what He would have us to be, and yet when the trial comes, how apt are we to flinch from it, and to desire that our faith may be proved in some other way.

Ninth Month 9th.—Since my last memorandum I have taken a very pleasant journey with my sister Dorothy through Monmouthshire, when much enjoyment was our portion.

E. O. Tregelles, in his connection with the Neath Abbey Iron Works, was frequently employed in superintending work undertaken by them, as well as in securing orders. Thus we find him at Brighton and Worthing, and afterwards at Youghal.

Brighton, Twelfth Month 13th.—With a grateful heart I record the mercies of this day, and desire reverently to ascribe the praise to Him to whom alone it is due for His goodness in enabling me to perform what seemed required at my hands, which was to supplicate on my knees on behalf of those assembled this morning, and peace has followed. Samuel Tuke, of York, afterwards addressed us in language with which I could feelingly unite, and desires were indeed raised in my heart that I might cast my burden on the Lord, pleading for His aid to preserve me from all evil. Oh that I may more and more take up His yoke, which hitherto I have proved to be easy.

Worthing, 15th.—I believe that being here as I am in the line of my business is consistent with the Divine will. May I ever regard this as the correct standard.

Neath Abbey, First Month 1st, 1830.—Have spent this day much as I would wish to spend all my days, in the simple performance of my duty, and occasional aspirations towards the Dispenser of my joys, desiring the continuance of His blessing, to whom I can say, Thy promises are sure, they are yea and amen for ever. Under this feeling I desire a continuance of Thy preserving care, well knowing and firmly believing that none of those, who rightly trust and in humility wait on Thee, shall be ashamed!

Youghal, Second Month 28th.—First-day. Have been favoured this day with quiet confidence in the efficacy of the blood of Jesus to cleanse from sin. I desire thankfully to ascribe praise to the Lord, by whose power I have been kept desirous of serving Him. And also for the favour extended to me yesterday in coming here from Waterford when the coach was attacked.

Neath, Seventh Month 6th.—I was instructed by remembering the case of poor zealous Peter, when he walked on the water to meet Jesus. It appeared to me that he was permitted to sink as an example to us, that we may not be too forward. He had requested his Lord to bid him, had not waited to be called, and had to experience the fears of a castaway. Oh! for passive waiting, willing to run, yet loving to sit at the holy footstool.

Youghal, Ninth Month 22nd.—Have felt sorry this evening for having been rather unguarded in speaking, and was reminded by the unerring Witness of the passage, "If any man offend not in word, the same is a perfect man." I desire to be truly contrite.

Tenth Month 3rd.—It has appeared to me desirable that I should be more careful of an evidence of being sent, than of the fitness of the message with which I may have been commissioned. Freedom from condemnation seems to be the blessing bestowed; may I duly prize it and desire no other reward for obedience than that which the great Master sees meet.

Waterford, 18th.—Kindly entertained by William Peet. It has been my privilege to attend the sittings of the quarterly meeting, commencing by the examination of the scholars at Newtown, and a meeting for worship.

Limerick, 22nd.—On reaching this town we were informed of a melancholy event. A commanding officer in a regiment stationed here was riding alone; he felt unwell, dismounted at the door of a small house, threw off his coat and cap, fell on the bed and expired. I saw the crowd around the door as we passed a few minutes after, and the milk-white steed of the poor man was standing unconscious of his master's fate. It was deeply affecting, and overpowered me.

E. O. Tregelles returned to Youghal by way of Tralee and Killarney. He says:—

Thanksgiving and praise should ascend for the favour

bestowed on me. I bless the Lord who hath given me counsel.

Ashfield, Eleventh Month 20th.—Reached home this evening, and find my dear father better than I had expected.

Twelfth Month 8th.—We have, indeed, a cruel enemy, but we have also an invincible Protector, one who died that we might live through Him. Oh, for continued ability to prize the benefit of His atoning sacrifice.

First Month 8th, 1831.—Have been favoured to keep near to my Leader, who says, "Be thou faithful unto death, and I will give thee a crown of life."

10th.—"I will bless the Lord, who hath given me counsel." At least I desire to do so, and may He, in His abundant mercy, which is new every morning, bless me by strengthening me to endure all His turnings and overturnings, that in sincerity I may say, "Thy will be done."

Youghal, Second Month 10th.—Troubled with sadly wandering thoughts in meeting, so that it appeared to be a very unprofitable time, except it be to make me see the need I have of being kept near to my Saviour, so as to experience His loving care, who said, "Without Me ye can do nothing."

Saw to-day the first purple crocus for the season, a sweet remembrancer of a Christian's triumph.

17th.—My heart rejoices in the belief that my declaration of the Lord's commission this morning was acceptable in His sight. The Lamb and His followers will have the victory. Edward Alexander was at meeting.

18th.—Spent this evening with Edward Alexander at Abraham Fisher's in, I trust, innocent cheerfulness. May he and others who have ranged themselves, or rather, who have been enlisted on the Lord's side, be strong in His might, and in His only.

Third Month 5th.—At the close of this week I feel desirous of gratefully acknowledging the mercy that has been extended to me. May I go forward in daily dependence on the Lord, and deep abasement and prostration of self.

7th.—Have felt a fear of too much confidence, as though I needed not to be led, a feeling arising from prosperity. May this not be the case, but rather let every event in my life tend to drive me closer to the centre, to Him who died that I might live.

Fourth Month 4th.—Much favoured with quietness to-day, though busily engaged in lighting the town with gas, which we did to general satisfaction this evening.

To ABRAHAM FISHER.

Neath Abbey, Fifth Month 14*th*, 1831.

DEAR FRIEND,—

. . . It is very little any of us can do for the promotion of the cause that should be the dearest to us: "Peace on earth, goodwill to men," the fruits of a Redeemer's wonderful love and condescension. Let us then on all occasions seek to be prepared for any service required, and render up our whole selves cheerfully, since the Lord, it is said, loves the cheerful giver.

I have thought very much about thee since we parted, feeling much sympathy in thy situation as it regards the church of which thou art, I believe, a living member; but I think thou mayst be comforted by the remembrance that the cause is not ours, but His who in mercy has called some of us out of darkness into His marvellous light, and into the glorious liberty of the sons of God. . . .

EDWIN OCT. TREGELLES.

Neath, Fifth Month 29*th, First Day.*—Permitted again to enjoy the sweet incomes of a Father's love, and to stand forth as His messenger to declare the purposes of His will in sending His Son into the world. But through inadvertence did not declare the whole counsel of God, did not fashion my work "according to the pattern showed me on the mount," for which I crave forgiveness. Finished reading Mary Dudley's Life.

It was at this juncture, when disturbances and strikes in South Wales obliged E. O. Tregelles to remain at Neath, that his father, Samuel Tregelles, died on Sixth Month 3rd, after he had written in his journal:—

Sixth Month 2*nd.*—Permitted to intercede in spirit on behalf of my precious father.

3rd.—Received tidings of our dear father, which cause us to rejoice, and call for our heartfelt thanksgiving and praise.

6th.—This evening we have received the tidings of my dear father's peaceful close. And now we trust his spirit is returned to God who gave it, presented unblamable at the throne, through the mercy of God in Christ Jesus.

7th.—These are momentous times. Riots at Merthyr. Cavalry constantly passing, and reports of many persons being killed.

This has been a day of considerable excitement. I felt it required of me to address our workmen on adopting the peaceable spirit of the Redeemer, and I feel thankful that I was strengthened to declare the counsel of the Lord. Our men at the Neath Abbey Iron Works were assembled in one of the large smith's-shops; cousin Joseph T. Price, my brother Nathaniel, the clerks and I went to them. Before much was said, I felt a sudden impulse to address them seriously, and taking off my hat, I said, "Christ suffered for us, leaving us an example, that ye should follow His steps; who did no sin, neither was guile found in His mouth; who, when He was reviled, reviled not again; when He suffered, He threatened not, but committed Himself to Him that judgeth righteously."

This was followed by a respectful silence; and from that day forward, never again was any semblance of insubordination apparent. The men quietly dispersed, and we heard no more of the strike.

During his business engagement at Youghal, Edwin O. Tregelles was much with the family of Abraham Fisher, of the eldest of whose seventeen children he writes as follows:—

Youghal, Seventh Month 31st.—One of the most important days in my life. This day my precious Jenepher Fisher concluded to accept my proposal of marriage. Oh that it may tend to increase my love for Him who in great mercy has condescended to guide me.

Eighth Month 7th.—This day has been one of deep wading, having in both meetings to dig deep for the spring, and wrestle hard for the blessing, which was not withheld.

Neath, 29th.—Favoured to perform with comfort my duties as they presented. Had a comfortable meeting, feeding at the Master's table.

This evening the purified spirit of my sister Sarah was liberated from the body, and is now, we may believe, in the joyful presence of her Lord and her God, singing the songs of praise to Him who loved her, and washed her from her sins in His own blood. The close was so peaceful that it could scarce be marked. For myself I am led to crave, "When my heart is overwhelmed: lead me to the Rock that is higher than I."

Tenth Month 19th.—Attended at Glenvelyn Cottage to hear temperance tracts read. May our discussions prove useful, and that I believe they will, if conducted in the spirit that works by love, and desires only the glory of God.

E. O. Tregelles, writing in after years of a crisis in his life, which occurred at this time, says:—

On the 23rd of *Tenth Month*, 1831, a person called at the Neath Abbey Works' office to show some plans, and requested a tender for some machinery. The matter was referred to me as the engineer to calculate the cost and give an estimate. I soon learnt that the engine and machinery were for a brewery at Newport, in Monmouthshire. In a moment I recollected that the liquor brewed at that place had been instrumental in causing murder at Abersychan, which came under my notice when I was there in 1826. I felt that I could have nothing to do with supplying machines for such concerns. I therefore wrote a letter to my kind cousin, Joseph T. Price, telling him that if I had to engage in such work, I should prefer leaving my situation in twelve months. It was no small trial of faith to come to that conclusion. I was anticipating an early marriage to my dear Jenepher, and a house had been selected near the Works. This event completely unsettled me, and in a few months arrangements were made for my leaving; a step I never regretted, though I ever regard my residence at Neath Abbey as a blessed providence in my lot.

Tenth Month 26th.—" Is there no balm in Gilead?" Yes, though my soul may famish and crave the healing influence, it is not any proof of the absence of the good Physician, who may be hiding His face for my good. Oh, may I patiently wait till the day of the Lord comes.

Eleventh Month 29th.—Acting under the advice of my friends, I have thought it best to commence on my own account as an engineer. With this intention I have proceeded to Swansea this morning, on my way to Bridport. Earnest have been my desires for preservation, and I trust that with the blessing of the Lord, which makes truly rich, I shall wish for nothing more than a needful supply for my wants during my continuance in this life which can only be regarded as a state of probation. In all my dispensations, whether of ease or pain, may I keep my eye fixed on my Captain, and if a conquest is obtained ascribe the victory to Him.

For several years the professional duties of E. O.

Tregelles as an engineer obliged him to have no settled home. During this period he was actively engaged in the lighting by gas of many towns in the South of England. He writes:—

Bridport, Twelfth Month 3rd.—Have been engaged to-day in measuring the streets of the town.

Taunton, 12th.—Arrived here this afternoon from Bridport in company with William Forster as far as Crewkerne. After we parted I was rather alarmed by a thunderstorm, which seemed to threaten us with imminent danger. The prospect of being speedily ushered before the Judge of quick and dead produced very serious reflections, and caused me earnestly to crave for mercy. I trust that this circumstance may tend to engage me to devote myself without reserve to Him whose I am.

On arriving here I found immediate employment, which I desire may promote the work of the Lord, and be dedicated to Him.

Bridport, First Month 12th, 1832.—" Thou art careful and troubled about many things; but one thing is needful." May this ever be kept in view. May I by a covenant of love be bound to the Lord, by His power, to serve Him with body, soul, and spirit, that through His grace I may be kept, and experience salvation.

13th.—This is a memorable day, inasmuch as it may be regarded as the first in my career in my profession, being engaged by the Gas Company, at Bridport, as their engineer. The language of my heart has been, " Trust in the Lord with all thy heart, and lean not to thine own understanding." May He who has been with me in trouble still condescend to guide me, if outward ease may be my portion.

Neath Abbey, Second Month 8th.—I crave that I may be strengthened to walk in all the ways of the Lord's requiring, that so His temporal and spiritual blessings may tend to promote the extension of the Redeemer's kingdom.

11th.—At the monthly meeting at Swansea I was comforted by my dear Aunt Price with the language, "But grow in grace, and in the knowledge of our Lord and Saviour Jesus Christ." Also that of Junia Price, "Wait on the Lord, be of good courage, and He shall strengthen thine heart."

Youghal, Second Month 22nd.—"The Lord is good to all, and His tender mercies are over all His works." Therefore none are so low but that they may feel encouraged to hope that they may obtain mercy through Christ, who loved us and died for us, and who by His Holy Spirit shed abroad in our hearts, would lead us to the Father if we would yield ourselves to His sway.

Went to-day, with Abraham and Jane Fisher, and my precious Jenepher, to Castle Martyr. A truly pleasant time.

Bridport, Third Month 12th.—Again at this place with a feeling of peace, as though the blessing of the Lord was with me. Had an accident to-day in Axminster, by the upsetting of the car, but through mercy sustained no injury. This is the first serious accident of the kind I have yet had.

London, Fourth Month 7th.—Arrived here this morning in much fear of the cholera. But when I remember the many preservations I have experienced since I was last here, I may say, "Many, O Lord my God, are Thy wonderful works which Thou hast done, and Thy thoughts which are to us-ward: if I would declare and speak of them, they are more than can be numbered."

Bridport, 23rd.—I had a pleasant ride from Bristol, occupied in reading temperance tracts. I believe I must not keep silence or remain inactive on this subject much longer.

24th.—Have felt bound to devote not only the morning of

my life, but the morning of each day, to the service of my Lord, in reading and waiting on Him.

25th.—Have been led to reflect this morning on the benefit of adversity. David says, "I was brought low, and He (the Lord) helped me. Return unto thy rest, O my soul, for the Lord hath dealt bountifully with thee." Rehoboam did not forsake the ways of the Lord until he was established in his kingdom. Doubtless the prophet Elijah was more comforted by his supply at the brook Cherith, and felt more grateful for it, than Belshazzar at his banquet.

26th.—Finished the book of Revelation this morning; the fourth time, I believe, that I have read through the New Testament. I well remember the anguish of my heart, when ill five years since, in the remembrance that I was so ignorant of the written word.

Fifth Month 10th.—Passed a truly happy day. A sweet feeling was prevalent in meeting, in which I enjoyed the greatest of all joys that I know, communion with the Father of spirits. The meeting was held in silence, and I believe I shall long cherish the memory of this refreshing brook by the way.

London, 22nd.—Attended the meeting of the British and Foreign Temperance Society, at which were present about 4,000 persons, the Bishop of London in the chair. My spirit rejoiced at beholding the evidences of humility and Christianity in his deportment, corresponding with the station he holds as a minister of Christ. Oh that the blessing of the Lord may rest on him and keep him in the way that he should go.

27th.—Spent the day at Tottenham with my sisters Lydia and Rachel. We heard the truths of the gospel ably set forth by the ministers of the Lord, Thomas Shillitoe, Joseph John Gurney and Anthony Wigham. A favoured day: may my heart be led to obey the call and make a full surrender.

29th.—Rose at half past six, and have felt desires that I

may duly prize from day to day the blessing of preservation. The deliberations of this day in the yearly meeting have been truly comforting and satisfactory, very different from those of yesterday. I trust that the labours of a few exercised Friends at the early part of the meeting had a chaining effect. I dined to-day at the Old Jewry, where amongst the guests was Stephen Grellet, who sweetly reminded us of our duty in thanksgiving after meals.

To ABRAHAM FISHER.
4, *Great St. Helens', London.*
Fifth Month 26th, 1832.

MY DEAR FRIEND,—

. . . . I feel a degree of thankfulness not to be expressed, in that it does not appear to me as though the talent was taken from me because I accounted my Master to be hard and hid it. I seem to be favoured with a feeling of rest and peace that the world knows not of.

Let me encourage thee not to be cast down by the apparent pressure of business. I believe thou art bound by a perpetual covenant to serve thy Lord, and His arm is not shortened. God governs, infinite rectitude sits on the throne of the universe, why then should His servants fear? He can and does make a way for us where we can see no way. But then, must we not follow His leading in all things before we shall fulfil His designs? He that followeth Me shall not walk in darkness, but shall have the light of life, the only object of value we can pursue.

E. O. T.

Neath Abbey, Sixth Month 4th.—Once more at this dear spot. May I ever return here with joy, as I do this day, favoured to feel peaceful. And now being amongst my dear friends, who also love me very much, there is great danger of being carried off my guard.

7th.—During the last few days I have had to drink of

"the wormwood and the gall" (Lam. iii. 19), a cup handed me in mercy for my purification. Oh that the work may be fully accomplished, and that I may feel thankful for the cleansing operations.

Barnstaple, 9th.—On leaving that home at Neath, which I have so long enjoyed, and which now ceases to be mine, since my lot will be joined most likely to another ere I return again, I was comforted in retirement a few minutes prior to my departure by the recollection of the passage, "In all thy ways acknowledge Him, and He shall direct thy paths." I craved and do now crave that this may ever be my experience, and that I may be bound to the Lord by a perpetual covenant.

Edwin O. Tregelles met his sisters at Clifton, and they together proceeded to Youghal to accomplish his marriage with Jenepher Fisher. The day before the wedding a large party went up the river Blackwater for an excursion, and a salmon leaped out of the water into her sister Sarah's lap. It was taken home for the wedding dinner.

The marriage was, as he records, "comfortably accomplished on *Seventh Month 5th*, help being afforded to me, an unworthy creature, on this important day."

Milford, Seventh Month 7th.—Left Youghal yesterday, and had a pleasant ride to Waterford. We walked on the pier and enjoyed the beautiful moonlight, and thought of the parting dear Jenepher was so soon to take of her native land. The sea was rough; she exulted in the motion, and quite enjoyed the beauties with me. We remained on deck until half past one, saw the moon set and a small aurora borealis, and the prospect of returning day.

CHAPTER III.

BRIDPORT.

With his Wife visits Neath—Bridport—William Forster's Ministry—Sherborne—Anna Price—Quarterly Meeting at Poole—Newton Tracey Meeting House—Yeovil—Barnstaple lighted by Gas—Journey to Cornwall—Birth of a Daughter—Yeovil lighted by Gas—Upwey—Maiden Castle—Wellington—Attended Long Sutton Meeting alone—Yearly Meeting, 1834—Bideford—The blind Ostler at Barrington—British and Foreign Bible Society Meeting—Bridport—Railway Meeting—Dorchester—Joins his Wife in Ireland and visits Killarney Lakes—Slavery ceases in West India Islands—Takes a House at Neath—Wellington lighted with Gas—Bridgewater Meeting—Teignmouth—Dorchester—Swansea—Birth of a Son—Bridgewater lighted with Gas.

ON reaching Neath Edwin and Jenepher Tregelles stayed at Eagles' Bush, the home of his brother and sister Bevington and Rebecca Gibbins. It was some years before they had a settled home of their own. We find them residing in lodgings at Bridport, and other towns in the south of England, wherever E. O. Tregelles' professional duties as an engineer led them. He writes:—

Eagles' Bush, Seventh Month 12th, 1832. — Attended monthly meeting at Neath. Aunt Price and Bevington Gibbins spoke on the commandment, "Thou shalt love the Lord thy God with all thy heart." Junia Price offered prayer and praise in the same strain, and an impressive meeting we had. Nathaniel read the Epistle from our last yearly meeting. This has been a pleasant day: may I experience dedication of heart to the Lord, renouncing my own will for His, and be led by that grace which brings salvation.

Bridport, 29th, First Day.—"It is good for a man that he bear the yoke in his youth." I have been much impressed with this to-day, and renewedly convinced of its truth. We were addressed in meeting this morning by William Forster in an impressive manner. He first set forth the credibility of the writings of the apostles, and then quoted from their words, "Resist the devil, and he will flee from you. Draw nigh to God, and He will draw nigh to you." He went on to speak of the importance of securing everlasting rather than temporal blessings. "What is a man profited if he shall gain the whole world, and lose his own soul? or what shall a man give in exchange for his soul?" and how dreadful the thought of a man losing his own soul, even if only one among hundreds of millions. After describing the comfort afforded to the Lord's faithful followers in passing through the valley of the shadow of death, having Jehovah to bear up the head above the swellings of Jordan, he said, "And when thus they reach the gate of heaven, they will have nothing to do but to enter in." On taking his seat as he said these words, I desired for him that such may be his blessed experience.

Eighth Month 4th.—Finished this morning the very interesting memoir of Thomas Charles (of Bala). And this evening commenced the perusal of Henry Martyn's life.

I have passed a tranquil day. Oh for more willingness to be made conformable to the holy pattern (Heb. viii. 5), to be brought low and truly humble. Make me what Thou wouldst have me to be!

Bridport, 5th.—I felt as though I was devoted to the Lord as His servant, and that when I was fit, and He needed me, I should be employed in His service. May I be enabled to perform all His requirements, and sing joyfully His praises in the work.

17th.—The cholera increases in this town; two interments yesterday, and two to-day. Feeling it as a duty I called on most of the medical practitioners to lay before them the necessity and propriety of union and concord at this trying juncture. Before I commenced this, I had William Forster's approval, and now I feel relieved.

Ninth Month 13th.—Returned this evening from Shaftesbury monthly meeting, after a pleasant journey. We met with an accident which might have proved fatal, but the merciful care of our gracious Lord prevented any serious injury. The wheel came off. Had the horse kicked or run off, we should probably have been much injured.

20th.—Full of worldly-mindedness! Oh that it were otherwise, that I might daily remember the covenants of perpetual dedication which I have oft times made with my Lord. So eager am I after worldly profit and credit, that my heart seems willing to forget the one thing needful. Oh that I might rightly apply for help to my Redeemer, who died for me and gave this amazing proof of His love; and shall I not trust Him? True it is that "the Lord God is a sun and shield; the Lord will give grace and glory: no good thing will He withhold from them that walk uprightly."

Tenth Month 14th.—At meeting this morning Anna Forster was engaged to supplicate for some present, that when they are tempted they may seek for deliverance, from Him who is a strong tower to those who trust in Him.

Sherborne, Twelfth Month 31st.—Arrived here this evening with dear Jenepher from Dorchester, where I had a satisfactory interview and a prospect of employment. May I be truly thankful to the Father of mercies for His unnumbered blessings, which have been showered on me during the past year.

Bridport, First Month 15th, 1833.—I took tea at Silvanus Stephens' with Lieut. Fabian, who is travelling on behalf of the British and Foreign School Society. He is a zealous advocate of the slaves, having been an eye-witness of their miseries.

Neath Abbey, Second Month 5th.—Have been once more favoured to return to this dear spot. I crave a continuance of the blessing of the Lord my Deliverer, and that I may truly serve Him. After leaving Bristol this morning, per *Glamorgan* steamer, we were in great danger off the sands from thick weather setting in.

Glenvelyn Cottage, 24th.—I have been visiting at this sweet abode for several days, and have much enjoyed the society of my dear aunt Anna Price, and cousins, whose kindness is very great.

27th.—Left the cottage with peaceful feelings after a few words of counsel from cousin Junia Price to keep straight on my course, taking heed of right and left hand errors. Oh that I may rightly seek to be daily kept by the power of the Lord free from evil.

Bridport, Third Month 9th.—On reading "Pilgrim's Progress" this evening, desires were raised in my heart that I may look well for the stepping-stones in the Slough of Despond, and lay fast hold of the gracious promises.

16th.—Called at the Dorchester gaol to inquire respecting the poor boy Wilkins who set fire to some houses in this place, and find he is to be executed this day fortnight.

22nd.—To-morrow we propose leaving for Barnstaple. Often when I am thus going from place to place, the desire arises in my heart, "If Thy presence go not with me, carry me not up hence."

Poole, Fourth Month 4th.—Attended the quarterly meeting. Dear William Forster was remarkably led. He commenced by reminding us that the early Christians used great plainness of speech. And truly he dealt closely and plainly with us, laying before us the necessity of attending to internal reproofs, which convince of sin, and lead us to look for deliverance to Him whom God hath exalted to be a Prince and a Saviour to give repentance to Israel and remission of sins. Anna Forster added her testimony very acceptably. And then William Forster supplicated for mercy, although our sinfulness is so great that we are unworthy to lift our eyes to the sacred footstool.

Dorchester, 5th.—Let me not, in days of fulness of bread, forget the timely relief this day supplied by a friend paying me my account.

Barnstaple, 27th.—What a favour that a Sabbath is allotted us. May I prize this privilege, and seek for help truly to benefit by it.

Honiton, Fifth Month 6th.—Had precious comfort at the little Coplestone Inn, where the Lord was pleased to make Himself known. Oh that I might at all times feel that my daily support and guidance is of the Lord's abundant mercy. May my dear wife also be visited by the messenger of the covenant in her seasons of retirement, and may these seasons be blessed, is the sincere desire of my soul.

Barnstaple, 24th.—Much interested in the perusal of Alexander Jaffray's diary, and I trust benefited by it.

29th.—Spent this day pleasantly, and without much to condemn me, except needless petulance at the Gas Works. Oh, how at times I long for a meek and quiet spirit.

Bridport, Sixth Month 5th.—Left Barnstaple this morning, intending to reach Dorchester this evening. But on arriving here it appeared best to remain over meeting to-morrow, and in this I have been comforted by reading the "Selection of Advices" on attendance of meetings,[1] and have remembered with some satisfaction the promise of the Lord to Israel, when they were absent at their sacrifice, that no man should desire their land.

Yeovil, 9th, First Day.—Blessed with near and comfortable access to the throne of grace during part of meeting-time. Felt encouraged by the language, "Trust ye in the Lord for ever; for in the Lord Jehovah is everlasting strength." A friend addressed me at the meeting-house

---

[1] See "Book of Discipline," of the Society of Friends.

door, saying that he supposed I was there on business, and that even in temporal things there was nothing like the wisdom from above to direct.

11*th.*—I was favoured this day with the appointment of engineer to the Yeovil Gas Company. I feel thankful for the help which has been granted me. The language of my heart is, "I will bless the Lord at all times; His praise shall continually be in my mouth: the humble shall hear thereof and be glad."

Barnstaple, 16*th.*—Went to Newton Tracey meeting this morning, and sat there alone without any friend joining me. It was a comfortable time, and I was led to reflect on the changes which had taken place since I was last there, nearly seven years ago. Since which time some of my relations have been gathered to their eternal rest, and I have been called to work in the Lord's vineyard. May this be my lot until time to me shall be no longer.

19*th.*—In the near prospect of soon leaving this part of the country I am led to inquire whether I have performed the purpose for which I came here. And though surely I have done but very little, yet the answer of peace is as balm to my soul.

27*th.*—Comforted by the remembrance of the promise, "Ask of Me, and I shall give thee the heathen for thine inheritance, and the uttermost parts of the earth for thy possession." As to temporals, I desire it not, but I would fain know a fulfilment of the promise as to spiritual things; that I may possess the land of the heathen, if it be my heavenly Father's will, through me as His poor instrument, to make known to those who sit in darkness the glad tidings of the gospel. Oh for close communion with Him, and fitness in all things for the service of my Lord.

Yeovil, Seventh Month 10*th.*—Slept last night at Dorchester, whither I went intending to return here in the evening; but between Weymouth and Dorchester the horse fell under the gig with such force as to throw dear

Jenepher and me out. It was a great mercy that neither of us was materially hurt. It should teach us that we are indeed very dependent for all our favours on our heavenly Father.

Barnstaple, Eighth Month 11th, First Day evening.—Spent a pleasant day with James Veale. Sat with him alone this afternoon in our little meeting in Joy Street, which was a season of some comfort to me, more than has latterly been my portion.

Yeovil, 13th.—Attended Bridgewater monthly meeting to-day. The meeting for worship was held in silence, and a blessed meeting it was for me. The Lord by His Spirit gave me to see that the all-important object of my life is to reach the goal which appeared before me in glory, with a narrow straight path leading to it, in some parts slippery.

Bridport, Ninth Month 1st.—To-morrow we are to set out for Cornwall. I crave simple dependence on the Lord, that He may in all things order our steps aright.

"How are Thy servants blest, O Lord!
How sure is their defence!
Eternal wisdom is their guide,
Their help omnipotence!"

After E. O. and J. Tregelles reached Falmouth, professional engagements called him away, and he left his wife there with his relations. He writes:—

Barnstaple, 9th.—Through the condescension of my Holy Guide I have this day been preserved from giving much vent to hasty feelings, though I have been fully occupied, and rather hastened to-day, in the arrangements for lighting this town, which was accomplished this evening to my satisfaction.

Dorchester, Tenth Month 9th.—Attended monthly meeting at Yeovil yesterday. I may truly say that the things of time had such hold of me that I could scarcely look towards the Lord's holy temple. But just at the conclusion I felt cheered by the remembrance of the blessing pronounced on the poor in spirit.

Okehampton, 11*th*.—I was favoured to reach this place this evening from Axminster. The journey was performed in our own phaeton drawn by Nimrod.

Falmouth, 14*th*.—Reached this dear spot at half-past three, rather late, but went to meeting and had a favoured time. I find my precious Jenepher well, which is a great mercy, especially now cholera is visiting this land.

In the morning meeting at Truro I seemed somewhat drawn to declare the things of the Lord to those assembled, but not so clearly as to warrant my proceeding. Before the close, Ann Tweedy spoke to my state, advising a single eye, and a keeping close to the witness within, waiting only on the Lord. Attended the preparative meeting, at which no representatives were appointed, in consequence of the cholera at Falmouth, where the monthly meeting is to be held. At the preparative meeting I heard the new Queries and Advices read for the first time, and like them much.

19*th*.—This day I am twenty-seven. Though my faith has been at times very low during the past season, yet I can see that some good has been accomplished by my many trials. And now my language would fain be, Courage, my soul, thou art one year nearer to an eternity which, through the mercy of God, will be of enduring bliss to those who through faith and patience inherit the promises.

Barnstaple, 26*th*.—Permitted to reach this place safely, with my dear Jenepher. Poor Nimrod has performed well. I felt tried on my arrival here to see some remarks in a newspaper, about the Gas Works, to my prejudice. I must now put in practice what I have found to be beneficial heretofore, not to notice aught that may be published in this way concerning me, be it praise or blame.

L. T.

Milverton, 29th.—Left Barnstaple this morning. Read in sister Sarah's diary to my comfort and I hope, instruction. Reflecting this evening on the degrees of happiness in this world, and the most ready way of procuring it, it has forcibly appeared to me that simple obedience to the righteous will of the Lord is most essential.

Dorchester, Eleventh Month 13th.—Arrived here from Yeovil this evening, bringing dear Jenepher by Holy Well and Stratton. From the high ground we had a fine view of the scenery near Bridport, and saw the sun sink to his rest in magnificence, so that we thought ourselves well repaid for taking that route.

It appears to me that the Christian may be compared to the moon; all the light he can show is reflected from the beams of the Father's face. Oh that I may ever feel that of myself I am nothing.

27th.—Blessed this day by the safety of my dear wife after giving birth to her first-born, a daughter. I crave the merciful regard of my heavenly Father, who has again shown His great goodness towards us. May we all be dedicated to Him and His service.

Twelfth Month 14th.—I had a pleasant visit from William Forster to-day, during which he counselled me as to a more settled residence. Sincerely do I desire to be led aright, and wish to have no will of my own. "The steps of a good man are ordered by the Lord," "None of his steps shall slide."

25th.—This day should not pass without serious consideration of the benefits which have been bestowed on fallen men by the incarnation and propitiatory sacrifice of the Son of God; and indeed every passing day we ought to be impressed with thankfulness for the blessings bestowed on us by our Redeemer. Him first, Him last, Him midst, and without end.

26th.—This evening the moon was totally eclipsed, but it was so cloudy that we saw little of it. I have seldom felt more impressed with the infinitude of the wisdom which directs the planet's course, so exact, so regular, and wonderful.

28th.—It is a great favour that the Lord leaves me not without a witness, that His Spirit continually strives with me, reproving me for evil. Oh, grant that I may be enabled to maintain the warfare against my soul's enemies, and ultimately to triumph in a glorious deliverance.

Tonedale, First Month 17th, 1834.—Nathaniel and I left Bridport, after attending the week-day meeting yesterday, and were favoured to reach Taunton in safety, late in the evening. Our ride was particularly pleasant, though rainy, our minds being at ease, and we enjoyed sweet converse together. Truly it may be said, "Behold, how good and how pleasant it is for brethren to dwell together in unity."

Yeovil, 25th.—Spent this evening at John Slade's. I think I see the dawning of a Temperance Society here. May the Lord's work prosper.

31st.—I have been impressed lately with the impropriety of calling the Scriptures " the word of God," having been led to reflect on Luke v. 1. and also on the passage, " And this is the word which by the gospel is preached unto you."

Second Month 10th.—Dined to-day at John Slade's, where way was opened for declaring the peaceful sentiments of Friends. and those connected with the Peace Society. I feel thankful that I was helped to avow my confidence in a faithful prayer-hearing God.

11th.—Favoured with help to get through the cares of this day without much anxiety, and to accomplish the lighting of the town of Yeovil with a good degree of satisfaction, for which I desire to acknowledge the mercy shown me.

Upwey, 14th.—This day I have been peevish and uncomfortable; though I had a pleasant time of retirement before breakfast. Had I not endeavoured to live too long on this feeling, it might have been better for me.

20th.—Left Wellington at three, and reached Yeovil at

ten in safety. My ride was most pleasant, peaceful and cheerful. I rode along, my mind in no way dismayed by fear of attack.[1] This feeling has very much subsided since I was led to avow unequivocally my sentiments of non-resistance.

Third Month 21st.—Reached Wellington this evening, though my poor Nimrod fell with me at Hammill, but did not hurt himself much.

Upwey, 30th.—Walked to see Maiden Castle: a surprising earthwork fortification which took us forty minutes to go round, though we walked on the middle bank.

Fourth Month 8th.—A day of carefulness: being engaged on an arbitration at Weymouth about a Roman Catholic chapel. I was strengthened to maintain consistency with regard to not having the oath tendered to the opposite party.

13th.—I feel a degree of comfort in remembering the passage, "The Lord is nigh unto them that are of a broken heart, and saveth such as be of a contrite spirit." Had much satisfaction this evening in distributing some tracts, of which if only one does good I shall greatly rejoice.

16th.—Have had a busy and a trying day. May I be helped by Him whom I desire to serve, who wills not that "any should perish, but that all should come to repentance."

Wellington, 22nd.—This afternoon, at Tonedale, we were addressed by our cousin, Sylvanus Fox, on the importance of walking in the light, both for our own good and that of others. Oh that my dear Jenepher and I may cleave fast hold to the anchor of faith.

Neath Abbey, 29th.—To-day has been one of much comfort and enjoyment amongst my dear relatives in this part. As I saw swallows skimming joyfully in the air, I thought it was not unlike my condition. I, like them, have great enjoyment whilst in pursuit of my subsistence.

30th.—I called to see Edward Powell, my fellow-draughts-

---

[1] Highway robberies were not uncommon in those days.

man at Neath Abbey Works, who seems rapidly sinking to the grave. An affecting interview it was. I endeavoured to point out to him that his allotment was to be preferred to ours, seeing that he is about to enter the mansions of bliss, whereas we are left to struggle on.

Wellington, Fifth Month 22nd.—I have to record the mercy shown me in my lonely sitting at Long Sutton meeting, where I went expecting to meet with Friends, but none came. My heart seemed full of love, gratitude and praise. I do not remember having before felt such holy joy. Blessed, for ever blessed, be the Lord most high!

London, 26th.—At the yearly meeting, under a sense of duty, I ventured to speak on the subject of oaths being required of others by those who object on strict conscientious grounds to use them themselves.

28th.—The meeting for worship at Devonshire House was a most memorable season. John Pease was engaged at length in very comforting strains, and the language of my heart at the end was, Shout, for the Lord thy God hath triumphed!

Bideford, Sixth Month 5th.—Favoured to reach this place safely, and settle quietly and pleasantly in lodgings.

At Barrington we had a blind ostler, who was quite clever with the horse. He had been injured by an explosion in a lime-stone quarry twenty years since, and lost his left thumb as well. I could not but admire the industry of a man who is maimed to a degree that would render most persons a burden to their relations.

10th.—A quiet, busy day, but not free from temptation. It behoves me at all times to be on the watch, and to guard against every approach of the enemy of all righteousness. This evening, on hearing the clock strike eight whilst a person was preaching on the quay, I was reminded that the day will come when I shall hear the clock strike for the last time, and then all the petty things of time, which now excite and engross my attention, will dwindle into utter insignificance when compared with the interests of eternity.

Bridport, Seventh Month 1st.—I was taught a useful lesson yesterday in ascending a ladder at the Gas Works. Whilst I kept my eye on objects above me my head was not dizzy, but the instant I looked down and saw the height to which I had attained I felt in danger. May I long remember this feeling when I am ready to think that I have attained to a point above my fellows.

14th.—Attended this evening a meeting of the British and Foreign Bible Society, and had to take an active part in it, at which I rejoice, although the effort to me was considerable. I cannot but feel that my dear father would have encouraged my labours.

Dorchester, 17th.—This day was the first railway meeting here, and now at midnight I proceed to Bridport on my way *via* Liverpool to meet my dear wife in Ireland.

Limerick, 27th, First Day.—I was taken very poorly after breakfast at the house of my uncle, Edward Alexander, and was unable to attend the meeting in the morning; but was favoured in the afternoon meeting with ability to stand as on the Lord's side.

Killarney, 28th.—Have had a pleasant day in riding to this place with dear Jenepher, and have felt some drawings of Divine love. May I be kept near this power.

29th.—We have been engaged to-day in visiting the various spots of interest in this delightful neighbourhood, and I have felt a care, whilst we have enjoyed this fine scenery, that we might endeavour to do all the good in our power in our intercourse with our fellows.

Springfield (Youghal), Eighth Month 1st.—This day the West Indian slaves are to be set free! Oh, how delightful it is to live at such a time; when the cruel shackles are broken which have been imposed on an unoffending set of beings, by nations professing Christianity. Those who may come after us will scarcely credit the stories which may be handed down, of the enormities that have been practised in the wars encouraged by Europeans in Africa for the capture of slaves. Chained together they were driven to the shore, and stowed closely in small vessels, to convey them to the sugar plantations, where they suffered corporal punishment at the caprice of their fellow-men; some of these by no means their superiors, but claiming authority because of the difference in the colour of the skin. And oh! now that they are thus liberated from their bonds, may they also be freed from their spiritual fetters, and partake of the glorious liberty of the sons of God.

Bridport, 24*th*.—A day of much conflict. Sat both meetings with very little comfort. In the morning my heart was engaged to petition for the blessing of the Lord to descend on my dear child and her precious mother. The remembrance of my obligations on their account seemed to draw my heart to renew my covenant of allegiance.

Bridgewater, 27*th*.—A busy day has passed satisfactorily. How greatly do I desire not only to appear as a Christian, but to be one.

Melyncrythan, Neath, Ninth Month 1*st*.—This day we enter on our new abode, and commence housekeeping for ourselves. Truly pleasant is the prospect. May it be our chief concern to serve the Lord.

9*th*.—I have this morning, in mercy, been led to see that I have not enough of the fear of God before my eyes. The language of my heart has in sincerity been: Teach me Thy way, O Lord, that I may walk in Thy path; strengthen me in the way of holiness, and unite my heart to fear Thy name. Oh, purify me inwardly and outwardly. Create in me a clean heart, and renew a right spirit within me. Sanctify me wholly by Thy truth, that I may be purged and made meet for Thy use.

Tenth Month 14*th*.—Attended an appointed meeting this evening, where was William Gundry, who rose with the language, "In quietness and in confidence shall be your strength," which impressed me much. I have derived comfort, and I trust some spiritual strength, from the labours of our dear friend.

19*th*.—This day I have reached the end of my twenty-eighth year, and the impression on my mind has been of a more serious cast than on any former anniversary that I can remember. It has appeared to me to be indeed high time to be in earnest about eternal things, seeing that it is probable that more than half of my life is past. Greatly do I desire to allow Christ Jesus my Lord to reign and rule in my heart.

Wellington, 22*nd*.—Fully occupied to-day preparing for lighting the town, which has been accomplished this evening to my satisfaction.

Melyncrythan, Eleventh Month 1*st*.—Had this evening an agreeable visit from my cousins Robert W. Fox and his daughter Anna Maria, also cousins Joseph and Junia Price.

Feel calm and quiet at the close of one of my busy weeks, and greatly desire that though the world may smile on me, I may ever prefer Jerusalem above my chief joy (Psalm cxxxvii. 6).

Bridgewater, 5*th*.—Was at meeting here to-day, and felt better for the time of waiting, wherein I was enabled to lay my all at the feet of my Lord, and was comforted by the remembrance of the passage, "Gather My saints together, those that have made a covenant with Me by sacrifice."

Teignmouth, 7*th*.—This day has passed with some care, in consequence of my peevishness, the result of rising late this morning. Whilst dressing I saw a small vessel in distress, which tried twice to enter the port, and then bore away to leeward towards Exmouth. I felt much for the sailors. I was behindhand with an appointment that I had made, and in consequence was led to reflect on the vast importance of being prepared for the summons of my righteous Lord.

Dorchester, 14*th*.—Arrived here at three o'clock this morning per *Herald* coach, having left Exeter yesterday evening at five. The night was very cold, and my heart was grieved by the sad conduct of a drunken man on the coach.

Twelfth Month 11*th*.—Monthly meeting at Swansea, which I attended with my dear wife. It is the anniversary of the day when I publicly avowed myself to be on the Lord's side, seven years since. My heart was then made to rejoice, and to-day I have felt bowed in thankfulness for the mercy afforded me in having been kept hitherto, I trust in degree steadfast in the faith.

Neath, 17*th*.—Through unmerited mercy I have been permitted to pass another peaceful day. Oh, that my soul may grow deep in the garden of the Lord during this season of His visitation and watering.

19*th*.—Some of our cousins took tea with us this evening, and I have been exercised with a fear lest I have used lightness to the injury of, what shall I say, the truth, or my character?

25*th*.—When I rose this morning I was favoured to come near to the fountain of holiness, to draw water as from the wells of salvation. As I walked towards our meeting, being Fifth-day, my mind was led into silent exercise, and after we were gathered the visitation was renewed, constraining me to offer a petition on behalf of those assembled, which I again crave may meet with acceptance at the Lord's holy altar.

Cardiff, First Month 10*th*, 1835.—Am now kindly entertained in this place by our friend Thomas Lloyd, whose wife has joined in profession with us. In the prospect of spending to-morrow with them, I feel concerned lest I may injure the growth of the pure seed in those who are led to adopt the views of our Society.

11*th*.—Still at Cardiff. I trust that the Sabbath has not been spent unprofitably. Much exercise has been my portion throughout the day, and now at the close of it I am led to petition for my dear wife and child and self, that we may be rich partakers of the salvation which is freely offered us of God, through faith in His beloved Son.

16th.—Have read this evening with chastened, yet thankful feelings, the memorandum I made when about to leave the Neath Abbey Works, and have to adore the power and help which have been afforded me. May all I possess be laid at the feet of the Giver of every good and perfect gift.

25th.—This morning Jenepher gave birth to a boy, to my great joy. May I dedicate him to his Maker, placing him in the hands of Him who gave us this additional treasure, with the heartfelt prayer that he may find favour with God and man.

26th.—Had this evening an interesting visit from my dear brother Nathaniel. He mentioned a narrow escape he had from a piece of casting flying off from under the ball. Surely this is a great mercy. The piece of iron, of twenty pounds weight, flew by him with the force of a cannon shot, and broke some cast iron behind him. Let this teach us that we are still under the kind and merciful protection of a Providence infinite in wisdom as in power.

30th.—Felt disposed to be angry to-day, but through the aid of the Holy Spirit, the remembrance of the absolute nothingness of all worldly things compared with the awful realities of eternity served as a check.

In reading the Memoirs of John Fletcher I have met with a passage that has appeared peculiarly instructive. "Absolute resignation to the Divine will baffles a thousand temptations, and confidence in our Saviour carries us sweetly through a thousand trials."

Bridgewater, Second Month 3rd.—I have had much satisfaction in hearing persons speak approvingly of the gas in the town, which was lighted last Seventh-day.

CHAPTER IV.

NEATH.

Christian Faithfulness—Neath—T. Williams—Barnstaple with Sisters—Clovelly—Honiton lighted with Gas—General Meeting at Brecon—Death of Bevington Gibbins—General Meeting in Hereford new Meeting House—Milford—Thoughts on Business—Gracechurch Street Meeting, London—House of Commons—William Allen and John Barclay at Stoke Newington—W. D. Crewdson and Thomas Shillitoe at Tottenham Meeting—Engineer of Railway, Southampton to Salisbury—A busy Week—Stanley Pumphrey's Experiences when Commercial Traveller—Death of Edward Alexander—Exeter—Birth of a Daughter—Serious Illness of his Wife—General Meeting at Worcester—Fire at Exeter—Yearly Meeting—J. J. Gurney going to America—Peter Bedford—With Edward Ash visits Women's Meeting—Death of King William IV.—Joins his Wife at Youghal—Exeter—Edward and John Pease.

Falmouth, Second Month 16th, 1835.—This day fifteen years I left my dear home for Wales, and lodged at Portreath, whither I walked from Redruth lonely and desolate. Oh, how much have I passed through since! May no child of mine ever be exposed to the trials I have had to encounter; and yet I can acknowledge "out of them all the Lord has delivered me."

Exeter, 22nd, First Day.—Have been much pained to-day by seeing a young man in the coffee-room engaged in painting some sketches. After deep searchings of heart I took up my candle, believing that it was not required of me to express my feelings, but unexpectedly it seemed laid on me to express my regret at seeing him thus employed, which I endeavoured to do in a christian-like kind spirit, and the hint was well received, though he sought to vindicate his conduct. "In the morning sow thy seed, and in the evening withhold not thine hand: for thou knowest not whether shall prosper, either this or that, or whether they both shall be alike good."

Neath, Third Month 1st.—I read this evening in John Fletcher, "No religion will in the end do us and our people any good, but that which works by love, humble, childlike, obedient love. May that religion fill our souls, and influence all our tempers, words, and actions."

22nd.—Have been blessed to-day with greater desires after an increase of holiness than for some time past. Both meetings, though silent, were profitable seasons. May my soul be clearly engaged in attention to the leadings of my spiritual Guide.

Merthyr, Fourth Month 12th.—Called this morning on Thomas Williams, who seems to be sinking fast into his everlasting rest. May his sun set peacefully, and may his soul partake of the unseen glories which are to be revealed to those who love God. Had a precious season with him after reading the eleventh and twelfth chapters of Isaiah. Both in going to his cottage, and in returning, my mind was overflowing with peace and joy, which still continues, blessed be the Father of mercies, and the God of all comfort. He lay in his bed in a small upstairs chamber, with his head bound up with a blue handkerchief. His mind in a sweet state, only waiting for the message to go forth. "It is enough, gather My saints together, those that have made a covenant with Me."

Bristol, 17th (The day called Good Friday). May I ever be deeply impressed with the benefit I have derived from the coming and the sacrifice of my Redeemer; and by the remembrance that, as an Intercessor with the Father, He is my all-sufficient Surety. As my Comforter, He cheers the otherwise at times sorrowful path; as my Guide, He by His Spirit leads me.

Fifth Month 9th.—At Bideford met my dear sisters Elizabeth, Lydia, and Rachel, and accompanied them to Barnstaple.

10th.—I was much pleased to see an increase in the numbers at meeting, both in the morning and evening. I feel peace in the retrospect of my engagement there this morning.

11th.—We visited Clovelly. A sweet spot, where I should like to take my dear wife and spend a week. The people appear to be in a very simple, open state. The grounds of Clovelly Court, the seat of Sir James Hamlyn Williams, are very beautiful. The cliffs are grand. My sisters were also much gratified by the school supported by Lady Williams.

Wellington, 12th.—Left my sisters at Barnstaple. Called at Castle Hill, driving through the beautiful grounds. I had Lord Ebrington's company in the coach from Tiverton very agreeably.

Honiton, 13th.—Spent this evening with William Wright, the Independent minister, who, in his prayer before supper, pleaded on my behalf, that I might experience the God of Abraham, Isaac, and Jacob to be my God, and that I might be permitted to return to my family in peace.

15th.—Favoured to reach Bridport in safety, though we came with great speed over the hilly road between Honiton and this place; twenty-one miles in two hours and twenty-five minutes; a sad rate for the poor horses.

16th.—Thankfulness covers my mind for the preservation witnessed this day in keeping me from evil. Though I have to lament my wandering of mind in both meetings, I had intervals wherein I was able to relinquish myself and all I have into the hands of Him who orders all things well.

22nd.—This evening the town of Honiton was lighted to my satisfaction.

Neath, Six Month 3rd.—I heard this evening of the prospect of work at Bath, and desire that all my movements may be in accordance with truth, that I may fulfil in all things the will of my heavenly Father, and of Him I crave help, ability, and preservation, to run in the way of His commandments.

9th.—Spent the day very pleasantly in visiting the waterfalls of the valley, and much enjoyed the lovely scenery. Thirteen years had elapsed since my former visit with Robert and Rachel Howard.

28th, First Day.—I was led this morning, whilst dressing, to crave that I might be permitted to abide patiently in the watch-tower throughout the day, and greatly have I been favoured in this respect.

Brecon, Seventh Month 15th.—This day the general meeting has been held here. It has proved to be a time of renewed favour. We have had the company of John Barclay, who was engaged to declare the way of self-denial, the way of holiness, the way of truth, with clearness, and boldness, and great simplicity. I was made thankful that the spirit of prophecy was afresh poured forth, and that judges were raised up as at the first, and counsellors as at the beginning.

Bridgewater, Eighth Month 2nd.—I have been tried of late by apprehensions as to the continuance of supplies of the needful for the support of my dear wife and family. May all things tend to draw me nearer to my heavenly Father, depending on His mercy and goodness; and may I, in seasons of more hopefulness, not forget the impressions of the day of carefulness, but be led to receive all my blessings with a thankful heart, and be at all times able truly to sympathise with the depressed. It has felt to me far better to know a temporal poverty, wherein the heart is inclined to seek after God, rather than to have abundance and forget God.

4th.—Received to-day the mournful tidings of the decease of my precious brother Bevington Gibbins, which has plunged me into greater mental distress than I ever remember to have experienced, partly in consequence of the suddenness, and partly because of the intimate intercourse we have recently had. But in the midst of my distress I can rejoice on his behalf, that he is removed beyond the reach of trial, and has entered, I firmly believe, on the joys prepared for those who love their Lord.

Neath, 13th.—Monthly Meeting at Swansea. When the burial note for the remains of our dear brother was read, many tears were shed. William Moyse testified his belief that he was partaking of the blessing of "that servant whom his Lord, when He cometh, shall find watching." Cousin Joseph T. Price also bore testimony to him. Surely the remembrance of his having so recently been amongst us, as to have been on an appointment at the last monthly meeting, was enough to impress the minds of many.

17th.—I had a refreshing visit from my dear Aunt Fox to my soul's comfort. After reminding me of the text, "I will never leave thee nor forsake thee," she took my hand at parting, and repeated the promise, "Fear not, I am with thee." How I cling to her! I crave her help by prayer, though I have an ever present and omnipotent Helper, Mediator, and Intercessor with the Father.

19th.—Returned from Merthyr in five hours, with Nimrod and the four-wheeled gig; roads very stony and bad. Found my dear mother-in-law here to my satisfaction. I feel thankful for the peace which has been my portion. May I remember a remark of John Newton, that "Satan is like a foot-pad who does not rob a man when going to a bank, but when returning with full pockets."

20th.—Felt a fear lest I had omitted to declare the message that ran in my heart in meeting this morning; but I believe I was not required to stand forward. Oh, when shall we be willing each one to be taught of the Lord, to know Him for ourselves, and to be instructed by Him? How far better than any instrumental ministry!

28th.—We had a pleasant visit from my brother Thomas. He was the means of saving our precious little girl from being run over by a horse which passed our gate, where she had been standing before her uncle caught her out of the way.

Ninth Month 12th.—Have completed the perusal of my brother Bevington Gibbins' memoranda, which are instructive and interesting. How blessed is his state! I am impressed with the beauty and joy there is in having everything consecrated to the service of the Most High, who knoweth our frame, and remembereth that we are dust.

Bridport, Tenth Month 3rd.—May I remember that my heart is like tinder, ready to kindle and consume away with the least spark of flattery; of which I had lamentable proof twelve years ago, when I sadly retrograded after I had overheard some praise bestowed on me. May my heart be as ready to kindle with the rays of Divine love, and blaze until all is consumed that is contrary to the Divine will.

Hereford, 8th.—This day, for the first time in the new meeting-house, was held our general meeting: only Jonathan Rees, Robert Eaton and myself in the men's meeting from our part. After Ann Dickenson had made allusion to casting the net on the right side, I was strengthened to pray for a renewing of the covenants made by young, middle-aged, and those in the decline of life; for which service peace is my portion.

Hirwain, 14th.—Left Merthyr late this evening with a cheerful heart, having passed through a severe ordeal with the Gas Committee, in consequence of a letter having been written to them informing them of my inefficiency. May I be truly thankful for the kindness which has been shown me in being yet more firmly placed in their esteem. May I conduct myself to all as becomes one professing godliness.

19th.—Yesterday I spent most pleasantly at Milford, whither I walked after breakfast, just in time for meeting, which was to me a season of comfort, in the feeling that those who were met with me preferred Jerusalem above their chief joy. This I felt ability to express, to my own comfort. I dined and spent the afternoon at Gayer Starbuck's, where I also slept, and much enjoyed my visit.

Melyncrythan, 27th.—This morning while sitting in my chamber at Merthyr, earnestly desiring to be redeemed from the corruptions of the world, I was impressed with the language as if spoken by the Lord to my soul: "I will crucify every lust, if thou wilt love and serve Me; not only the lust of the flesh, but also the lust of the world, and the pride of life."

28th.—It is a high privilege to be dealt with as the Lord is now dealing with me, filling my cup with blessings to overflowing, my heart with gratitude, and my lips with the praises due to His high and holy name.

Eleventh Month 4th.—How peaceful and thankful are my feelings this evening on the receipt of a letter from Teignmouth desiring me to proceed with my engagement there. Truly I feel more than I can express of gratitude for this fresh proof of my heavenly Father's providential care. May it engage me to a closer walk with Him, and to a watchful obedience to all His commands.

10th.—A day with scarcely a cloud inwardly or outwardly. May my soul praise the Lord for His great goodness to me, and may He still preserve me by the manifest extension of His holy hand. Oh, how do I desire at times complete dedication to His will of all I have or may have. May the increase of wealth not induce increase of expensive habits, but rather tend to liberate me the sooner from the engagements of business to attend more exclusively to other pursuits.

Plymouth, 25th.—I rejoice that I was made willing to bear my testimony at cousin William Collier's to the love and mercy of our heavenly Father, often revealed under the semblance of affliction. I have a comfortable letter from my dear Jenepher. May the Lord carry forward His work in her soul.

Neath, Twelfth Month 31st.—Oh for ability and steadfastness in serving the Lord more closely than I have ever yet done. Whilst I write, the prattle of my babes, restless though at midnight, reminds me of my ties, of my blessings, of my obligations. And greatly do I desire to perform my part to them and their dear mother as may be acceptable in the sight of my heavenly Father. Keep us, O Lord, all as under the shadow of Thy wing.

First Month 3rd, 1836.—This has been a truly pleasant day, except that I rose very late this morning, and had hard work to get to meeting in time.

Exeter, 8th.—I had a very narrow escape of a serious accident in Bridgewater, in consequence of standing on the wheel, which on moving caused me to fall with violence on the ground. It is well I did not fall before the wheel. Very serious for me would be any accident that prevented me from earning my daily bread.

Neath, 24th.—My desires this morning were that I might this day praise the Lord by my actions. And great have been my seekings after the arising of His good presence in the meetings to-day. On closing the Bible at the family reading my mind was sweetly clothed with the feeling: "Thou hast given me my heart's desire, and hast not withholden the request of my lips." In a deep sense of my own blindness I may say, Not as I will, but as Thou, Lord, seest meet for us.

25th.—This day my precious boy is one year old. How do I crave for him preservation in the path of life.

I have been very busy to-day, yet able to look towards the object of my hopes, my ultimate aim, the Lord of peace and never-ending joy. May I ever regard this life as merely a passage, and deal with the things of time, as the circumstances amongst which I have to pass, but amongst which I must not take up my rest.

Second Month 7th.—We had a precious time in the morning meeting, which cousin Junia Price was constrained to acknowledge, in the language, "It is good to be here!"

On sitting down in meeting, I felt it to be an especial favour, and a sound truth, that in worship we were not dependent one on another, but each for himself had ability granted to obtain access to the Father through the way He had sanctified and appointed.

18*th*.—This morning, whilst sitting in meeting, I was led to crave that I might keep singly in view the object of my life; that it is not for amassing this world's goods, but to fulfil the will of my heavenly Father. May I be careful that the riches which He bestows are all appropriated as seemeth good in His sight.

London, 25th.—Yesterday attended meeting at Gracechurch Street to my comfort, although we had little in the way of ministry to cheer. But it seemed as though I could sit and derive comfort from thus waiting to partake of the blessing which, in His own time, the Master of our assemblies may bestow.

26*th*.—Visited the House of Commons this evening. Amidst the pleasure I had, there was a mixture of pain, in a sense of the very perverted judgment of most present. The war in Spain was the subject.

Third Month 5th.—Attended this day the interment of our valued friend, Mary Stacey, of Tottenham. The assembly was very large. Thomas Shillitoe's voice was heard at the grave. On entering the Meeting House I felt that the language of thanksgiving might go forth, and I was constrained to acknowledge my feelings in a few words. After meeting I walked to Stoke Newington, and dined with William Allen and his two nieces, and afterwards called on John Barclay.

Neath, 23rd.—Melted this night into tears of tenderness whilst leaning over my precious little girl in sweet sleep, and poured out my soul in prayer on her behalf. O Lord, keep those whom Thou hast given me, as in the hollow of Thy holy hand.

Neath, Fifth Month 8th.—Comforted in meeting this

morning by the renewed visitations of the Dayspring from on high, and in the ability given, I was enabled to enlarge on the words, "The dead shall hear the voice of the Son of God, and they that hear shall live." Cousin Junia Price followed in a most forcible and convincing manner, on the words, "Satan hath desired to have you, that he may sift you as wheat," and commented powerfully on the errors into which some of our members are now falling, who are resting in the outward belief of what has been effected for them by the sacrifice of our Saviour. "The devils also believe and tremble," they believe and know that Jesus died on the cross to save sinners. This outward belief will avail nothing, unless there be a corresponding obedience.

Tottenham, 15th, First Day.—Saw the eclipse of the sun in the afternoon through William Allen's telescope. Took tea at William Ball's. In the evening meeting William D. Crewdson alluded to the glad tidings of the gospel, and to the unsearchable riches of Christ, which was known only by a belief in Him. Soon after he sat down, Thomas Shillitoe said that we must not stop short with a belief in Christ our Lord and Saviour as our Redeemer, but that we must know Him to rule in our hearts, and to operate with us. Whilst writing the foregoing I have heard the nightingale singing most sweetly.

Southampton, 19th.—Went yesterday to Romsey to sleep, and again this morning walked to Salisbury over the line of railway for which I was this day officially appointed the engineer.

Bristol, 22nd.—Attended both meetings, to my comfort. Very soon after we sat down the language arose in my heart, "Unto you first God, having raised up His Son Jesus, sent Him to bless you, in turning away every one of you from his iniquities:" but dwelling under a state of waiting to know the will of my heavenly Father, the expression of it did not appear to be required, nor yet in the evening, when it again came before me. Very tender have been the dealings of my God, whilst I have this day been seeking to renew my covenants for an increase of holiness. Oh, that I may keep them, and in the day of prosperity remember those of adversity.

> "O Lord! increase my love for Thee,
>   Let me not wander from Thy way,
> Strengthen me to Thy cross to flee,
>   And give me bread from day to day!"

Neath, 23rd.—My mind has often turned towards my precious little girl. She has had a narrow escape from sudden death, owing to being thrown out of the carriage; her head fell between the wheels on the off side. The horse stopped instantly, or her head would probably have been crushed. Dear child! I desire to hold her as the gift of One in whose hand is the breath of every living thing. "Oh, give thanks unto the Lord, for He is good, for His mercy endureth for ever."

30th.—I have been very hasty in my spirit to-day, which I desire may not occur again. Poor and frail indeed I am. Lord, help Thou Thy poor weak unworthy servant.

Sixth Month 9th.—I have been able to enjoy this stanza:

> "To Thy saints while here below,
>   With new years new mercies come;
> But the happiest year they know,
>   Is their last, which leads them home!"

Exeter, Seventh Month 9th.—I stopped at Bridgewater to settle the accounts there, and was gratified by being appointed by the disagreeing parties to settle the matter for them, which I believe I accomplished to the satisfaction of all concerned. Thus has the promise made to me two nights ago been confirmed, "I will make darkness light before thee, and crooked things straight." I close a busy week, having travelled in three nights a distance of 320 miles, attended to several matters of importance at home, as well as four committees at Haverfordwest, and one at Bridgewater, a Bible meeting at Haverfordwest, and my own meeting at Neath.

14th.—Prevented to-day from attending the mid-week meeting by another pressing engagement, which I much regret. It is the first time that I have thus acted since I have been engaged as an engineer. I trust I may not repeat the practice. I feel that there is great danger of allowing the smallest inroad on good practices. No man falls into open sin at once.

Haverfordwest, 21st.—General meeting at Swansea. George Jones pointed out in a very clear manner what it was to live the life of the righteous, enforcing the necessity of yielding obedience to the manifested will of the Lord, through the operation of the Spirit of our Lord Jesus Christ in our hearts. Ann Jones beautifully set forth the state of a redeemed soul, liberated from the shackles of mortality, and after receiving the sentence, "Well done, good and faithful servant!" being clothed in white, and singing high praises to his Deliverer.

Exeter, Eighth Month 7th, First Day.—Spent chiefly in the company of my valued friend Stanley Pumphrey. He related to us a circumstance that occurred to him in early life on the first day he started as a commercial traveller. A steady respectable traveller saw that he was young and inexperienced, and called him to the window, and addressed him thus: "I see that you are a young traveller; allow me, as an old traveller, to advise you to stick to your principles as a Friend. Many inconsiderate persons will jeer you at first, but the respectable part of the community, whose opinion you should value, will respect you the more." And surely, in Stanley Pumphrey's case, the plan completely answered.

Teignmouth, 8th.—I have passed a cheerful day; well in body and mind, free from condemnation, joyful in the ability to commune with my heavenly Father in secret, animated by His mercies shown me on behalf of my dear wife and family, whom I crave the Almighty to guide by His counsel.

Hereford, Tenth Month 13th.—This day attended the general meeting at this place, which has been a day of rejoicing, a feast of fat things, of wines on the lees well refined. My soul has been made glad in the Lord. Notwithstanding the heavy rain and inclement weather, the attendance was large. We had very acceptably the company of Ann Tweedy, cousin Maria Fox, and Lucretia Crouch, with certificates. My dear cousin Junia was liberated to pay a religious visit to Friends in Ireland, much unity having been expressed.

Neath, 15th.—Had this evening the painful intelligence of the decease of our uncle, Edward Alexander, of Limerick, who died after a short illness. Thus are we deprived of a dear relation, and our Society of a zealous and highly approved labourer, who is now gone to reap the reward of well-doing.

Southampton, Eleventh Month 6th.—This day I heard Alfred Mordaunt's voice in meeting for the first time. He addressed us, reviving the language, there is a "Fountain opened for sin and for uncleanness"; and again in the afternoon, on the parable of Dives and Lazarus. My tears fell whilst I remembered the sweet feeling that was my portion on the day of my first dedication.

Exeter became for a while the home in lodgings of Edwin O. Tregelles and his family. In connection with his profession as engineer he was often called to Southampton and other places.

Exeter, Eleventh Month 15th.—Arrived here this morning from Salisbury. I rode with a most agreeable gentleman, Captain Hawker, of Plymouth, a captain of a man-of-war. He is an advanced Christian, I believe, though not yet convinced of the unlawfulness of war for a Christian. May the Lord open his eyes that he may see, and when sight is granted, may he, like blind Bartimeus, rise up and follow his Redeemer whithersoever He leads.

Romsey, 31*st*.—Half-past four in the morning. Closely engaged all of yesterday, as well as three preceding days, about railway plans, and have been busy at it all night. In the midst of this, my thoughts have been turned towards the Source of all good, with desires that the blessing of the Lord may rest upon me.

Exeter, 31*st*.—Read this evening the 13th chapter of Genesis, containing an account of the separation of Lot from Abram. A sweet example of the benefit of forbearance, and the exercise of the principles of peace.

Second Month, 1*st*, 1837.—Though much occupied by my concerns, which have to-day required me to walk with peculiar circumspection, I have felt a sweet calm. In all the arrangements I have made for my employers, I have with much care studiously observed their interests, and have sought to act uprightly towards those whom they employ. I crave the aid of Him whom I seek to serve, to enable me to walk as a Christian in the world.

2*nd*.—I was impressed this morning, on rising, with the recollection of my covenants of dedication, on this wise—

> "My life, if Thou preserv'st my life,
> A sacrifice shall be,
> And death, if death now be my doom,
> Shall join my soul with Thee."

18*th*.—This day my dear wife gave birth to a little girl, and mercy being again shown us I desire to be duly thankful for the favour.

The journal contains details of the very severe illness of Jenepher Tregelles, of which he writes:—

Third Month 4*th*.—I have made no note since the 18th of

Second Month. Deep indeed have been the trials I have had to pass through, and bitter the cup which was handed me to taste. Words fail me to describe what my feelings have been.

12th.—To-day I sat both meetings in silence, and had refreshment therein. In the evening I read a letter I had received from my cousin Christina A. Price, from Neath, which to my surprise I found contained an account of the proceedings of the last monthly meeting, when she felt bound to propose to the consideration of Friends that I should be acknowledged a minister, with which the meeting united, and she was desired to apprise me thereof. On reading it, my soul felt bowed in thanksgiving for the mercy which has hitherto upheld my feet from falling, and desires were raised that I might walk worthy of my high and holy calling, esteeming the work of the Lord as my chief delight.

13th.—This day my father and mother-in-law left us, and sweet was our feeling of thankfulness for the mercy which has been shown us. My heart seems overflowing, and able publicly to acknowledge, " Thou, Lord, doest all things well ! "

19th, *First Day.*—In the evening meeting I expressed my belief that nearly all present had heard the language, " Son, give me thine heart," and set forth the benefit of entering into unconditional covenant with the Lord on His own terms. I also expressed a hope that none would be found kicking against the pricks, nor crucifying the Son of God afresh, but that we should turn unto the Lord, from whom we have deeply revolted ; turn unto the Lord that He might have mercy upon us, and to our God, for He would abundantly pardon.

Worcester, Fourth Month 19th.—The general meeting was held to-day, and has proved to be a memorable time to me. I came empty, and return empty, yet rich with favour, and full of the blessing of the Lord. The meeting closed under a solemn feeling. During the second meeting my mind was under much exercise whilst the Queries were answered, on account of the deficiencies which were acknowledged. I reminded Friends of the language of Holy Writ: "All thy children shall be taught of the Lord; and great shall be the peace of thy children"; desiring that we might individually seek to be led by the Spirit of the Lord, and then we should attend to the language, "I am the Lord thy God, which teacheth thee to profit, which leadeth thee by the way that thou shouldst go." "Open thy mouth wide, and I will fill it."

Exeter, Fifth Month 19th.—I was preparing to retire to rest at ten o'clock when I smelt fire. On opening the back door the smoke entered, and assured us that an extensive fire was near. In ten minutes I heard the crash of a falling building, and awful indeed was our situation. The thatch at the back of our house caught fire several times, but was quickly extinguished. The roof of our dwelling was in a flame for a few minutes. The fire raged for several hours, and at length was stayed, so that at two we retired to rest.

London, 21st.—Arrived here this morning with dear sister Lydia from Bristol, where I left Jenepher and the children on board the *Express* steamer for Cork. Although I had travelled two nights successively I felt sufficiently fresh to go to Gracechurch Street meeting this morning, where we had the company of George Richardson and Jacob Green.

23rd.—At the adjourned meeting of ministers and elders Joseph John Gurney laid his concern before Friends for visiting the continent of North America, some parts beyond the limits of any yearly meeting, and also some of the West Indian Islands on his return. The matter was spread before the meeting by J. J. Gurney in a very weighty manner. He commenced by saying, "In the fear and dread of Almighty God I venture to lay before you, my friends, a concern which has rested on my mind for many years past, almost from the earliest period when I believed myself called to the ministry, to pay a visit to Friends in America."

26th.—The yearly meeting this afternoon was attended with more exciting circumstances than any former sitting; but truth prevailed, to my humble admiration, and I desire to confide yet more and more in Him who is the Leader and Commander of His people.

Croydon, 27th.—Came here this evening to visit Peter Bedford. We have both been able to rejoice in the retrospect of the day when we met sixteen years ago. I regard it as amongst the special mercies of the Most High that I became acquainted with this dear servant of my Master.

28th.—This has been a precious day spent at Croydon. The Lord manifested Himself by the breaking of bread amongst us in a marvellous way, enabling Thomas Frankland to bear noble testimony to the truth.

30th.—During the sitting of the yearly meeting this morning I felt constrained to yield to an impression that had rested on my mind, that it would be required of me to go and visit the Women's Meeting. I felt great peace in leaving the matter to the decision of my friends. Edward Ash, of Norwich, had been liberated previously, and we went together, accompanied by Edward Pease and Joseph Marriage. Whilst Edward Ash was delivering his testimony I was waiting for instruction, which was granted, to my thankful and humble admiration.

31st.—Attended Devonshire House meeting this morning. William Forster ministered very powerfully, in a way not very pleasing to those who believe themselves to be righteous, and despise others.

Sixth Month 4th.—Breakfasted with William Allen, and went to Stoke Newington meeting, where I had to speak on true worship, and to call off from dependence on man.

Joseph John Gurney had a parting meeting with young Friends in Devonshire House this evening.

Exeter, 7th.—Left London this morning at a quarter past

five, and came here 175 miles in 17¼ hours by the *Telegraph* four-horse coach, which we now think is very fast, though in a few years it may be deemed slow.

Thankfulness covered my mind, as I returned to the scene where I had experienced so much mercy, at the recollection of the favour shown in preserving my going out and my coming in.

18*th, First Day.*—Oh, how deep are my desires to be wholly given to the Lord! Strengthen me, Lord, for all the baptisms Thou mayest see needful. Give me patience to endure, and give, oh, give to my dear wife and children, hearts to love and serve Thee.

20*th.*—Closely and pleasantly occupied all day. I heard this evening by the guard of the *Telegraph* coach, that King William IV. died last night at Windsor.

24*th.*—The proclamation of Queen Victoria took place to-day. It was a gaudy pageant. I have no wish to see another.

25*th.*—This has been a blessed day to me. A Sabbath of rest and instruction. We had the company of George Richardson, of Newcastle, who is travelling with a certificate, accompanied by Thomas Robson. John Dymond broke the silence of the meeting: soon after which I was led to express my belief, that the Lord Himself was at work in the hearts of many present, who were querying, "What wilt Thou have me to do?" I desired that we might follow the Lamb, the Lord Jesus Christ our Saviour, whithersoever He leads.

Seventh Month 19*th.*—Was much disturbed last evening, anticipating an unpleasant interview with my employers to-day. But on retiring to rest this language gave me comfort, "All things work together for good to them that love God." I rose this morning refreshed, and earnestly desired that my feet might be upheld from falling. To my surprise to-day, my employers seemed quite altered in their bearing, and disposed still to place confidence in me.

23*rd.*—Sat meeting this morning in a condition of

wandering; was assailed by business thoughts and apprehensions that I should be involved in a chancery suit, for doing my duty conscientiously. I was encouraged after meeting by the recollection of the passage of Scripture, "The Lord that delivered me out of the paw of the lion, and out of the paw of the bear, He will deliver me out of the hand of this Philistine." I trust I may rely alone on the Lord, and be led on step by step in His way.

Bideford, 28th.—Have passed a pleasant day, endeavouring as opportunity was afforded to plead the cause of the poor apprenticed negro in our colonies.

Exeter, 31st.—Rose this morning with the intention of remaining at Barnstaple, and returning *via* Ilfracombe to Swansea, but on considering the matter, and desiring best direction, I was permitted to see that my safe course was to return here. I am thankful that I came, as many things had occurred that required my attention.

Bristol, Eighth Month 11th.—I read this evening an instructive valuable letter of counsel I received from Peter Bedford, dated 16th of Eleventh Month, 1827, about four weeks before I yielded to the necessity laid on me to stand as an advocate on the Lord's side.

Exeter, 30th.—The desire of my heart on rising this morning was, that I might be so kept by the power of the Holy Spirit during the day, as that I might retire to rest with feelings as peaceful as those I had when I rose. This has been fulfilled to my admiration; for, although I have had to pass through a somewhat severe ordeal to-day in the way of my business, I must acknowledge with thankfulness that the Lord sustained me.

Ninth Month 5th.—Attended this evening the monthly meeting of ministers and elders, held at Sarah Wilkie's, Heavitree. A time of renewed and unmerited favour to me.

9th.—This evening closes peacefully a busy week. May the blessing of the Lord rest on my labours to serve Him; and on my labours to procure food and raiment.

10th.—Took leave of our dear little babe to-day with no small degree of interest, not knowing whether I shall again see my precious child, who is left in charge of a nurse at Heavitree. Thou, Lord, who knowest me and lovest me, condescend to love, watch, care for, and preserve my child.

Springfield, Youghal, 14th.—Favoured to reach this place in safety, and to find my dear Jenepher and the children well. On my voyage I was accompanied by Charles Fox; we experienced very rough weather, and were forty hours in going from Bristol to Cork.

Exeter, Tenth Month 1st, First Day.—We had the company of our friends Edward and John Pease at our meeting this morning, to the edification of many, I trust. During this sitting I felt that John Pease would be led to appoint a public meeting in the evening, which he mentioned at the close, and it was acceded to. It was largely attended. Before I went I read to the children when they were in bed, and afterwards bent the knee by the bedside, and supplicated the Lord on their behalf, that He would be pleased to take them into His especial keeping. At the conclusion —— said, "Papa must not say that again," fearing, I believe, that I had asked the Lord to take them away. But I renew my petition that Thou, Lord, wilt be pleased to preserve them and me by keeping all of us under Thy peculiar care.

8th.—Dined at Henry Sparkes', where my interest on behalf of the oppressed negroes was renewed, and I consented to become an advocate for them.

Ashburton, 10th.—I deemed it desirable to come to this place to endeavour to establish gas works, and though I do not succeed, I am not disappointed. If it were the Lord's will that I should be engaged here, He would make way for me. All I desire in such cases is to be found every day doing that which is acceptable in the Lord's holy sight. Guide me, O Lord, by Thy counsel, and afterwards receive me to glory.

CHAPTER V.

TORQUAY.

Commencement of Indisposition—Thomas Tregelles—Torquay—Letter to his Sister, R. B. Gibbins—Falmouth—Visits Charles and Sarah Fox at Perran—Apprenticeship of Negroes in West Indies ceases—Scilly Islands—Quarterly Meeting at St. Austell—Unites with Friends in visiting Families—Public Meetings at Falmouth—Goes on board Vessels and speaks to Sailors—Torquay—William Rouse.

In the spring of 1836 Edwin O. Tregelles caught a cold, from the effects of which he suffered for some years. The death of Thomas Tregelles, the last survivor but one of his seven brothers, which took place after a severe illness, was to him a touching sorrow. He had the inexpressible comfort of being able to minister to the peace of his brother's soul as he lay on his bed of suffering. Doubtless the experience he passed through at this time had something to do with his own increased feebleness. He spent the following two winters at Torquay.

Falmouth, Tenth Month 28th, 1837.—For several days I have been nursing on account of my cold, which I believe is not thought seriously of by those around me; but I have been engaged to consider the probability of my life being drawn to a close, and a future state has occupied much of my attention.

Exeter, Eleventh Month 8th.—Since I made the last memorandum my weakness has increased, and all my friends unite in proposing that I should proceed immediately to the south of France. This morning, before I dressed, my cough was troublesome, and there were other signs of the seriousness of my illness; but this did not appal, for I knew that He in whom I believe has power to slay and make alive; that He sees the end from the beginning; He knows what is best for me, His way has always been found by me to be better than my own way, and I crave ability to keep so close to His light, to His word written in my heart, as that my feet shall not slide.

16th.—My dear cousin Joseph T. Price, and brother Nathaniel arrived here on the 11th. After seeing the medical man, they came to the conclusion that it was best for me to remain in this neighbourhood. My sister Lydia and brother Nathaniel being unable to procure lodgings here, proceeded to Torquay, and having secured a house, we go there to-morrow.

Torquay, 17th.—In the prospect of continuing here through the winter, my heart craves that the blessing of the Lord may rest on us.

19th, First Day.—Have passed a truly pleasant day, in frequent communion with my God and Redeemer. My thoughts turned to the consideration of a visit to the Scilly Islands, in case I should recover. "Cause me to know the way wherein I should walk; for I lift up my soul unto Thee."

27th.—I trust that in this seclusion I may improve every way, to the glory of Him with whom I have entered into a covenant of allegiance.

To REBECCA B. GIBBINS.

> 2, *Lower Terrace, Torquay,*
> *Eleventh Month 29th,* 1837.

MY DEAR SISTER,—

. . . Thy kind notice of me in my present unexpected situation is particularly precious to me. I have had to pass through deep waters, but should this be a subject for lamentation? Let me rather speak of the mercy that upheld, of the power that was near to support, and kept my head from sinking beneath the waves. . . . How is it that we speak of being "willing to die"? If we had attained that state which we all should strive for and press after, we should regard the change as an entering into a safe port to go no more out, after having encountered storms and perils. It was not that the future—that eternity—appeared dark to me, but there was a degree of uncertainty that made me crave for a lengthening of the time of preparation, that I might know my peace to be really made, and myself prepared for an entrance to the regions of spotless purity.

. . . I am thy much attached brother,

E. O. T.

He continues his diary as follows:—

30th.—I have had sweet communion this evening in my closet, and been engaged to lay all I possess of estate of strength of body and intellect at the feet of my Lord, that He may dispose of me as He sees meet.

Twelfth Month 20th.—Impressed to-day with the recollection of Elizabeth Dudley's address to me, at Glenvelyn Cottage, six years ago. "Abide in Me: as the branch cannot bear fruit of itself, except it abide in the vine, no more can ye, except ye *abide* in Me." Oh, may it be my care to dwell low at the root of the Vine.

22nd.—This day I am privileged to have my darling youngest child with us. I desire, if it be the Lord's will, that she may be blessed with health, and may long continue to cheer us.

26th.—Last evening I was led to consider intently my present critical position, balanced as it were between an extension of my mortal life and the speedy commencement of an eternity. My only resource was to seek for ability to commit my all, whether for life or for death, to the care of my unslumbering Shepherd, to Him with whom I made a covenant for preservation during life, and who will not forsake me in the hour of trial.

First Month 1st, 1838.—Thus am I permitted to see the commencement of another year, and to enter on it with joy. How it may be with me in the termination is known only to the Searcher of hearts, the great Disposer of events, who sees the end from the beginning.

Second Month 5th.—Have this day been again employed in my profession, which feels strange to me after my long seclusion. Fully did I anticipate being admitted within the pearl gates of the glorious Kingdom to go no more out, instead of which I again return to the busy scenes of this life, to the pursuit of temporal things. This evening I was surprised by receiving a letter from Falmouth, informing me of further employment there, for which I feel thankful.

12th.—I have again been laid low, and have had to regard the prospect of the near approach of death, which was not attended with anything like alarm. I do believe that the Lord is watching very closely over me, and moulding me to more conformity to His will.

28th.—Favoured, through unmerited mercy and goodness, with the refreshing influences of the Lord's Holy Spirit, especially in our little meeting this evening, for which my soul renders thanksgiving and praise.

Third Month 20th.—To-day my dear father, Abraham Fisher, arrived from London, and brings me interesting tidings of many of my dear friends there; also a letter from Hannah Bevan, in which she addresses me with:

"Happy christian brother! thus early to hear the sound of release from the field of battle. Thy glorious Captain hath done great things for thee. He made thee willing in the day of His power, subdued thy foes for thee, and opened thy mouth to tell of His wondrous acts, and to declare what He hath done for thy soul, that so others might be invited to come, taste, and see how good He is." This cheers me, whether the rest of my days be few or many.

29th.—This night, probably at this hour, the House of Commons is discussing the slavery question. Oh that Thou, Lord, would deign to interfere, and direct their councils; give to those who have to decide, ability to see the right path, and make their hearts willing to render to the slave the justice so long delayed. Thou, Lord, canst do it. Make bare Thy holy arm, and give to the negro's friends wisdom to direct them in those things which will fulfil Thy counsels.

Falmouth, Fifth Month 7th.—This day has been delightfully warm and summer-like. We went on the water round the Black Rock, and enjoyed it much. My cough is lessened to-day, and I feel stronger. Cheered this evening by a visit from Aunt Fox.

16th.—Sarah Squire has visited me nearly every day. On First-day evening she addressed dear Jenepher and me with the language of Holy Writ: "I will never leave thee nor forsake thee," which had occurred frequently to my mind during the morning, being a promise on which I had firmly relied since the spring of 1833, when we were at Barnstaple, and it has often supported me in trials since.

Sixth Month 3rd.—My strength continues so to increase as to give me at times cause to expect that health may yet return to me.

5th.—My mind feels the weight of the prospect of having a religious interview to-morrow afternoon with some of Lovell Squire's pupils. I feel the matter very serious, seeing I take upon me to speak on behalf of Jehovah.

8th.—Finished to-day the perusal of my dear sister Sarah's journal, which has interested me deeply. I did not know before how closely she was exercised, and how large was her experience. My belief is strengthened that she was indeed qualified to take of the things of God, and hand them to others, of which in her life I had many times abundant evidence, for her service was blessed to me, especially when I left my home in 1826. That was a memorable evening, when she craved on my behalf that I might eventually give thanks on the banks of deliverance.

Falmouth, 17*th, First Day.*—I went to meeting this morning, desiring simply my own refreshment, but soon after I took my seat a state of conflict was my portion, feeling engaged to express a few words, but restrained by the fear of being injured in health. Soon, however, it was given me to feel that I was safe in the Lord's hand, and trusting in this, I stood up for the first time in a meeting for seven months, and revived the promise of our Lord, "Blessed are they which do hunger and thirst after righteousness, for they shall be filled."

Perran, 30*th.*—To-day we received accounts of Queen Victoria having been crowned on the 28th.

I have enjoyed exceedingly a stroll in some of the older shrubberies which I assisted cousin Charles Fox to thin out about fourteen years ago. In cousin Sarah's garden I sat awhile enjoying the beautiful flowers and the lovely scenery, improved by the water being full in the river: but sweet and attractive as was the scene, I was led to prefer the glories of the unknown world, believing that if permitted to enter that state of bliss, it will far exceed in delight every earthly joy, although my comforts and enjoyments in this life are very abundant.

16th.—Have felt to-day overcome by the kindness of my friends, loading me with benefits, and yet we receive the daily gifts, the daily blessings of the Lord, often without a thought of the mercy which is shown us: they are repeated daily, and we receive them as things of course, not as mercies renewed every morning.

19*th*.—Instead of repining at my allotment, I am ready to rejoice at the Lord's dealings with me. I believe that my illness has been blessed to me, and that it will be still further blessed if I am preserved from frustrating, by my own willings and runnings, the Lord's gracious designs respecting me.

Eighth Month 1*st*.—Whilst I write the sun is just rising on the hundreds of thousands of poor West Indian slaves, who are to be this day liberated from the galling bondage of the apprenticeship system. Thus have the labours of their friends been crowned with success: but the language in my heart this morning is, "Not unto us, O Lord, not unto us, but unto Thy name give glory." We give Thee thanks for directing our steps and our labours in such a manner as to have accomplished Thy will.

10*th*.—This day twelve years I spent the day at Plymouth, and was so impressed by the earnest call of dear Hannah Abbott to forsake my foibles, and turn with full purpose of heart to the Lord, that I became in earnest for the salvation of my soul, and rejoice that I was thus made willing to submit to the guidance and teaching of God's Holy Spirit.

11*th*.—Nathaniel arrived this evening, bringing with him a certificate from the monthly meeting at Swansea, liberating me to visit the Scilly Islands. The prospect feels mountainous, but I desire to be solely under the guidance of the good Shepherd of the sheep, as expressed in the document. Truly I have no strength of my own.

20*th*.—This evening my dear brother Nathaniel has taken leave of me, after having been kindly engaged in investigating my affairs, and arranging them. Marvellous, indeed, it is to me to find that the Lord in whom I have trusted has not suffered the barrel of meal to fail; but that it is even considerably increased since this time last year, when I was working vigorously. What a lesson is this! May it increase my faith and love, and cause me to acknowledge the Lord yet more fully in all my ways, craving and trusting that He will direct my paths.

St. Mary's Island, Scilly, 30th.—Arrived here last evening, having had a fine passage of eleven hours and twenty-five minutes from Falmouth, the little cutter, the *Rose-bud* of Plymouth, being a very good sailer. Among our party were cousins Robert W. and Charles Fox, Jenepher, and sister Lydia. The sun set with peculiar beauty in the ocean just as we tacked to enter the Sound to come in here.

This morning, being again fine, it seemed best to take one of the most distant islands first. We arranged to go to St. Agnes, and dined amongst the fine rocks on the south-west side. The meeting at half-past four was tolerably well attended. Help was granted me to relieve my mind, and I left the island, feeling clear, and thankful that I had been thus helped to set forth the gospel message.

Hugh Town, 31st.—At eleven o'clock we proceeded to St. Martin's, rather more than three miles distant, and were met as we walked towards the village, by Catherine Harris, a Bryanite, who kindly received us, and asked if we were going to have a meeting there. Our intention being made known, she took measures to inform her acquaintances. The meeting was held at half-past four, and again I was helped to deliver the message, which I believed I had received to convey.

Ninth Month 1st.—Left our quarters at ten o'clock this morning, proposing to have meetings at Sampson and Bryers; but on our way we met with the inhabitants of Sampson coming hither to market. We concluded, therefore, it might be better to give notice at Tresco for a meeting to-morrow afternoon; and at the two former islands at ten in the morning.

Whilst some of our party were giving notice, we spent

the time in cruising on the calm and lovely sea, dining on a small rocky island between Tresco and Bryers. On this island were a number of very large spiders, and a beautiful vein of agate on the south-west side.

2nd, First Day.—Cheered this morning by the return of lovely weather. Soon after nine we started for Bryers Island, and extremely interesting it was to see the strings of persons moving from various directions to the simple School-house which served us for our meeting. It was fully attended, and I left this island with peaceful and thankful feelings.

We crossed to Tresco to dine, and were kindly accommodated at the house of a Methodist named Ellis. The meeting was held in the Methodist Chapel, which though large, was crowded, and many stood at the door. I had to lie very low and broken before the Lord in order to discern what He would have me do; but thanks be to His name, He manifested His will, and gave me ability to deliver what appeared to be given me to hand to others.

5th.—The day before yesterday, accompanied by my cousins R. W. Fox and Charles Fox, I called on Augustus Smith at Tresco. I feel a hope that the care which he as Proprietor extends may be blessed, though his conduct now appears harsh.[1]

After tea at Francis Banfield's we went to the Methodist Meeting-house at Hugh Town, where a considerable number were gathered, and it was a very satisfactory time. After the meeting I seemed like one set free. Yesterday we went on board the sailing packet. When becalmed off

---

[1] As the Islands could only support a limited number of inhabitants, all above a certain number in each family were expected to leave, and get a living elsewhere.

Twenty years later, a visitor to the Islands says, " When the present proprietor first came, he found his tenantry living miserably and ignorantly. He has succoured, reformed, and taught them, and there is probably no place in England where the direr hardships of poverty are so little known as in the Scilly Islands."

the Islands I examined myself to see if it were desirable to return for further service, but I felt clear, and great peace was my portion.

St. Austell, 12*th*.—Quarterly meeting. A committee was appointed to visit the families of Friends in this county. After the reading of my certificate in the men's meeting, I expressed a wish to unite with this committee, which was approved of.

Trewirgie, Redruth, 27*th*.—Had a delightful walk with Charles Fox towards Carnbrae. We shall both long remember it. Our subjects of conversation were varied and interesting. The weather delightful.

Falmouth, 29*th*.—Went yesterday to Burncoose, where, in carrying out our quarterly meeting appointment, we had an interesting sitting; we then proceeded to Trewirgie and Camborne, sat with John Budge and family, and slept last night at Camborne. The language of my soul as I lay in bed was, Sing praises unto God, sing praises; sing praises unto God, sing praises!

Falmouth, Tenth Month 6*th*.—Impressed this morning, very unexpectedly, with the requirement to have a meeting with the inhabitants of Falmouth to-morrow evening, which I have laid before my cousin R. W. Fox, who gives me encouragement to take measures for its accomplishment.

7*th*.—Strengthened to attend the meeting, which was appointed for this evening, and there to deliver the message which seemed then to be committed to my charge. All the work is Thine, O God, and to Thee do I render thanksgiving and praise.

19*th*.—Another of my years has passed, bringing me to the age of thirty-two. I may truly say, With new years new mercies come. The Lord has dealt very bountifully with me during the past year, and I can trust Him for that which is to come. Lord, into Thy hands I commit my all; lead me and guide me by Thy counsel, and afterwards receive me to glory.

21*st.*—We had a meeting for sailors in the Sailors' Room, which was well attended, and I believe that the Spirit of the Lord was amongst us. The meeting was addressed by William Hoskins, cousin Maria Fox, and me. Praise and prayer were offered in conclusion. Gratitude and thankfulness and peace is my portion, in that the Lord helped me to deliver His messages.

28*th.*—On entering the meeting this morning, my mind was impressed with the words, "Keep thy foot when thou goest to the house of God, and be more ready to hear than to give the sacrifice of fools." Hear what? To hear the still small voice of the Lord; which I sought to wait for, and very soon felt commissioned to revive the ancient promise, "They that seek Me early shall find Me." A blessed meeting we had, concluding in prayer and praise.

It was at this time that Edwin O. Tregelles, accompanied by Robert Were Fox, and others, visited some of the vessels which made Falmouth their port of call, and held meetings with the sailors, especially on First-day afternoons. The crews generally assembled in the captain's cabin, and in some cases were disorderly at first, but they often had good times with them, so that the captains thanked them for their efforts to benefit and reach the sailors, who were then a much neglected class. The Journal continues:—

Eleventh Month 9th.—For some time past I have been distressed by a fear of falling, of becoming as the apostle Paul says, a castaway; but to-day it was shown to me that we must not fancy ourselves safe. We must throw ourselves altogether into the arms of Jesus, and rely on the power of our Emmanuel. Then shall we know what it is to be born of God, and to be free from sin, according to the doctrine set forth 1 John iii. 6-9.

14th.—Now I seem longing to return to my winter abode at Torquay that I may be sheltered from outward storms, and strengthened, if bidden of the Lord, again to go forward next spring. It seems to me now that I must visit some of the schools in this country, and afterwards proceed to Ireland.

At this time there was no Friends' Meeting at Torquay, but E. O. Tregelles assembled his family, and any friends who chose to join with them, for worship on First-days in his parlour, as they valued the privilege and liberty of gathering in the name of Christ, to realize His promised presence, whether words were spoken or not.

Torquay, 23rd.—Our little meeting this morning was held in silence. It was a season in some degree owned by a lifting up of the light of the Lord's countenance upon me. Secret prayer was offered on behalf of my wife and children, as well as for myself. Feeling that I was brought very low, I was ready to derive comfort from the belief, almost amounting to assurance, that the Lord would guide me continually.

First Month 9th, 1839.—I have been led to compare my present condition with my state this time last year, and certain it is that I am not so strong in health as I was then. What the design of my great Master may be, I desire not to know before He chooses to reveal it. May I rather seek daily to perform His will, as revealed in the secret of my soul.

Second Month 28th.—Finished reading Daniel. I never enjoyed my Bible so much as in the present perusal.

Fourth Month 7th.—I experience that it is more difficult to bear the trials that come from the creature, than those which have been sent more immediately by the Divine hand. May all tend to my further refinement.

13th.—Oh, that the Spirit of Jesus, lowliness, meekness, and humility were more the covering of my spirit. I fear that I am too hasty with my dear children, and other members of our household. Lord, make me what Thou wouldst have me to be.

I had a pleasant call from William Rouse, of Torre, who seems to be a sincere Christian, desirous of doing good in any form that may present. He acts as minister to the Independent Chapel. I rejoiced to observe his sentiments as to war, oaths, and a paid ministry. He is not paid.

Fifth Month 1st.—Called before meeting on Dr. P., and felt my mind led to speak to him of his practice of visiting the public News Room on First-day; and to allude to the uncertainty of his life, which might be taken in a moment. He expressed himself much obliged for the visit.

3rd.—We had this afternoon another call from William Rouse. After sitting some time engaged in serious conversation he became silent, and then expressed a desire to engage in vocal prayer. After a short pause he knelt in prayer, asking for blessings to be poured forth upon us, and for a lengthening of my life, and that the children might walk in the fear of the Lord. After he had concluded I felt engaged to address him, encouraging him to follow the manifestations of the Spirit of truth, not querying where it leads, and not to go forward groping in the dark, but to wait for the light of the Lord's countenance, and thereby he would go from strength to strength.

8th.—We had again an interesting visit from our friend, W. R., who acknowledged that a tract I had given him had convinced him of the unlawfulness of paying tithes and other ecclesiastical demands, and that he saw it to be his duty to refuse and suffer. He also stated that he could not swear, or be the occasion of another person taking an oath.

CHAPTER VI.

FALMOUTH.

Plymouth Meeting—Snow at Falmouth—The Cottage—Visits Ireland with Certificate—Large Public Meeting at Youghal—Visits Vessels in Cork Harbour—Bandon—Newtown School—Brookfield Agricultural School—Lisburn School—Public Meetings at Dublin, and with Miners near Water's-meet—Journey through Wales—Priscilla Hannah Gurney's Memoirs—Meetings at Milford and Neath Abbey—Sidcot School—Interview with Lord Ebrington, Viceroy of Ireland—John and M. Candler go to West Indies—Truro and St. Austell lighted by Gas—Penny Post—Marriage of Queen Victoria—Obtains Certificate to visit Schools connected with the Society of Friends—Croydon, Ackworth and Sidcot Schools—Visits sixty Schools as per List.

PLYMOUTH, *Fifth Month* 12*th*, 1839.—I entered with joy the Friends' Meeting House, from which I had been cut off for six months: but as to any service required of me, I felt as empty as ever I did in my life. After a time the spirit of prayer seemed raised in my soul, and I yielded to apprehended duty. Catherine P. Abbott followed; after she sat down, I felt it right for me to allude to the words of the Apostle, "This is a faithful saying, and worthy of all acceptation, that Jesus Christ came into the world to save sinners." Aunt Abbott set her seal with the language, "Thanks be to God, which giveth us the victory, through our Lord Jesus Christ."

Falmouth, 15*th*.—It commenced snowing at eight this morning, and continued for three hours, so that the fields and trees in full leaf were white with snow. At Torquay I saw a field of hay cut on the 8th.

16*th*.—Engaged this afternoon in seeking for a house.

Sincerely do I desire that we may get into our right house, and not into one where we should be out of the place designed by our heavenly Father for us to fill.

17th.—My mind has been a good deal impressed to-day with a sense of my situation, which, since my late interviews with Dr. Hingston, at Plymouth, I am convinced is very critical.

26th.—Retired to rest last night with very comfortable feelings, being led to query, Will the Lord forsake me now, seeing He hath led me hitherto? Immediately I had the peaceful answer—

> "He who has helped me hitherto,
> Will help me all the journey through,"

and I felt encouraged to confide in the oft-remembered promise, "I will never leave thee nor forsake thee." May I carefully refrain from resting on this promise, as though the Lord required on my part no co-operation with His holy will as manifested in my soul.

Sixth Month 13th.—To-day I engaged to take "The Cottage," recently occupied by the late John Carne.

15th.—Another day has passed, claiming my heartfelt acknowledgment for the favours shown, both as to spirituals and temporals. I received to-day a supply of the latter in the way of payment on account of my services in this place. This renewal of business engagements seems strange to me, as I imagined last year that I should scarcely engage in business again. Let me ever feel that my times are in Thy hand, O Lord!

Impressed this evening with the perusal of the passage in the Epistle to the Hebrews referring to Jesus as He who tasted death for every man. This being the ground of my hope of eternal life, what a call it is for gratitude.

Seventh Month 3rd.—Attended the quarterly meeting at Liskeard, and was strengthened to lay my concern to visit Ireland and other places before Friends, who very feelingly united with it, and a minute was added to the certificate granted me at the monthly meeting at Truro.

Falmouth, 8th.—This day we have had some of our furniture removed to our new abode, "The Cottage," which is intended to be my sheltered residence for the ensuing winter, and in which home our sisters join us.

9th.—Our dear children are better, and were removed to-day to "The Cottage" in a sedan. Dear Jenepher and sisters are lodged there to-night.

13th.—I felt grateful for the mercy shown me in enabling us to obtain such a sheltered nook. Enjoyed sowing some seeds with the children this afternoon in the initials of their names. We also gave them a small spot for their gardens. Cheerfulness and enjoyment marked the day, and thanks to Thee are raised in my heart, O God, in that Thou hast led me about and instructed me, and made me willing in the day of Thy power.

Cork, 16th.—Through the continuance of unmerited mercy I reached Cork comfortably this evening in company with my sister Lydia and cousin Robert Were Fox.

17th.—I was led to apprehend that it was my place to see Captain S., who is in permanent confinement in the lunatic asylum for murdering his crew some years since, when under the influence of monomania. Way was kindly made by Thomas Beale, who is one of the governors. We had an interview which has quite relieved my mind, and I trust may be helpful to a poor fellow-mortal who is justly and patiently enduring a sentence which he regards as mild. He had to me no appearance whatever of being insane. Before we parted I handed to him a few tracts, memoirs of John Woodman, William Edmundson and others. These he gratefully received, and expressed himself obliged for the visit.

Youghal, 24th.—A meeting was held here which was largely attended. I was told afterwards that many Roman Catholics were present. At first I found it hard work, and it seemed as though I should be obliged to go away burdened, but seeking after ability to give myself up entirely to the Lord as His messenger, I was enabled to declare with freedom the whole counsel committed to me; and for this I was humbly thankful under a sense of my great unworthiness.

27th.—Called at Passage on the way to Cove [now Queenstown] to see William and Sarah Lecky, an aged couple bowed down with grief, as their daughter Mary was lying at the point of death. She was taken ill with consumptive symptoms about four weeks since. R. W. Fox and I visited her. On entering the room the language arose in my heart, Now "thanks be to God which giveth us the victory, through our Lord Jesus Christ," to which I felt bound to give utterance. We learn that she died this morning.

When we reached Cove we called to see the wife of Captain S., who seemed obliged for the visit, and expressed her willingness to allow her children to read the tracts we gave her, though she is a Roman Catholic.

At seven we went to a meeting held in the Columbine Assembly Rooms, Cork, where a ball had been held the previous evening. The meeting was largely attended, and after a time of deep wading, proved relieving to me.

Next day, with cousin R. W. Fox, my father-in-law, and brother Joseph Fisher, I proceeded to visit two vessels in port. Our first visit was to the *Hindoo*, bound for New York from Cardigan. The crew and passengers were invited below, and we had an agreeable time. On our suggesting to the captain that he should to-morrow commence the practice of reading the Holy Scriptures to his crew, he intimated that he should do so. The cook on the other vessel asked us for a Prayer-book, but our views on this were explained, and a Bible promised instead, which was sent off, Joseph giving up his own, as none could be procured in the whole of Cove.

Bandon, 29th.—The meeting at seven o'clock in the Wesleyan School-house was exceedingly crowded, and not so quiet as that at Kinsale; but both felt to me to be precious seasons, favoured with the presence of the Lord. According to the ability granted I laboured in my work, and it is sweet to feel free from condemnation.

We had a fine ride in this place, most of the road being near the river Bandon, which is beautifully wooded, in many parts reminding me alternately of the Blackwater, the Wye, and Neath Valley.

Mayfield, Eighth Month, 9th.—Parted from my dear father-in-law and brother. I desire long to remember and profit by my father's parting words: "Mayest thou be preserved every way." Oh for an increase of humility that the Lord's name may be exalted and self laid low in the dust! Called at Anner Mills, and on Barclay Clibborn and family.

10th.—Accompanied by Eliza Malcomson we reached Waterford at twelve o'clock. After dinner at Richard Allen's we went to Newtown School, and had religious interviews with the boys and their teachers in five companies.

11th.—I went to meeting this morning in a depressed state, seeking after ability to do my Master's will. The language, "Instruct and strengthen me" seemed the breathing of my soul. Soon after we were gathered I felt engaged to supplicate that bread might be broken amongst us (which was granted in no ordinary degree), and that our hearts might be softened and laid open to receive the Holy Spirit, which was also experienced, for it seemed to me as though incense ascended from very many hearts—more than half of the large company.

New Ross, 13th.—I met the members of the Waterford meeting of ministers and elders at Joseph Strangman's, together with the overseers, and a truly precious time it was. Robert Were Fox handed counsel and encouragement to those Friends who have been closely tried.

We called on Samuel Ely; he is above eighty years of age, and is probably the first person who signed the temperance pledge in Europe—the first Society having been formed here, and he signed first.

Ninth Month 4th.—Went to meeting at Lurgan, where Sarah White was engaged in testimony, and I also. I did not quite feel clear on leaving the meeting; and concluded to communicate what rested on my mind to the individual for whom I believed it was intended. I rose up quickly and followed him to the grave-yard, whither he went that he might weep. I found him in deep distress. On giving him my hand he said, "I am the poor prodigal," and smote his breast in an agony. I communicated what impressed me for him, and called the attention of Thomas Christy Wakefield to him, as he wished to see him. I trust he will be restored and preserved. He has been a great sinner.

William Edmundson settled first at Lurgan, and the meeting-house bears the date 1696.

Lisburn, 6th.—Left Moyallen accompanied by Samuel Haughton as our guide. Reached R—— in good time for meeting; but what a meeting! Three members of that place came, besides J. and A. Malcomson from Liverpool. The house was wretchedly out of repair. On sitting down I felt ability sweetly to confide in my Redeemer: a greater evidence of His love and approval I think I never remember; and I needed it, for it was heavy work to labour for the souls of those who are reckless about the work for themselves.

13th.—Went with John and Harriet Richardson to Brookfield Agricultural School, which pleased me much. The boys work on the farm and garden; by this means they are supported and educated at £5 per annum. I had a sitting with the boys to my comfort.

14th.—This afternoon I went with John Richardson to visit the Provincial School, and sat with the boys and girls separately: afterwards with William and Anna Bellows and M. A. Kenway, the present caretakers.

Dublin, 22nd.—Attended meeting to-day at ten and two o'clock. I felt the Lord's power near to support, and His Spirit to instruct me to do His work, which I endeavoured to do, and left the meeting this evening poor yet peaceful.

23rd.—After breakfast went with my sister Lydia to the "Shelter" for females liberated from prison. We met Mary J. Knott there, and had a satisfactory meeting with about forty young persons. Made some calls, and dined with Dr. Harvey. The public meeting which followed was not very numerously attended; after a season of deep prostration of soul I felt ability to declare the glad tidings of the gospel; to God be ascribed the praise. Gladly would I spend and be spent in His service.

Avoca, 25th.—A meeting was appointed here at seven o'clock, to which were invited the men from the mines near Avoca. We assembled in the schoolroom, which was quite full, and perfect silence soon prevailed. After I had been speaking about five minutes, a number of young men, who I presume were Papists, left the room shouting and trying to disturb the others, who however kept their seats, and listened with fixed attention whilst I continued speaking, and after I sat down profound silence prevailed.

Dublin, Tenth Month 2nd.—Went to Monkstown meeting this morning. Henry Perry kindly conducted me on board the *Crescent*, bound for Australia. The crew, nearly thirty, met between decks, and were very orderly and well conducted. I found comfort in the visit.

3rd.—Went to Claremont to dine with Joseph and Mary Humphries, and saw the Deaf and Dumb Institution with 120 children. Felt very calm and peaceful at the prospect of leaving this land to-morrow evening.

Aberystwyth, 9th.—It was my privilege to have the perusal of the memoirs of Priscilla Hannah Gurney. It seemed as though she being dead yet spake to me; but more than this, I had most precious intercourse with Christ as my Redeemer and Deliverer from the power of Satan, who was assaulting me, and I entered into a fresh covenant of allegiance to my Lord and my God, who granted me an evidence that He would never leave nor forsake me, if I did but cleave closely to Him. The joy and peace which is my portion this evening, seems like a new birth; and I can say, "the life which I now live in the flesh, I live by the faith of the Son of God, who loved me, and gave Himself for me."

Milford, 13*th, First Day.*—Attended meeting this morning, and had a truly satisfactory and comforting sitting with the few of our Society living here. At six this evening we had a meeting in the Wesleyan Chapel. It was large and satisfactory, much liberty being given me to declare the free mercy of God, through our Lord and Saviour Jesus Christ.

Glenvelyn, 18*th.*—I attended a public meeting with the Neath Abbey workmen this evening, in the Chapel at the Abbey, and was enabled to relieve my mind of the load I have been bearing for them for months past. Help was near. I entered the meeting under much exercise, and was helped to express all that was laid on me.

Sidcot, 27*th.*—I have had much comfort in spending this day in this interesting school. In the morning meeting William Tanner was engaged sweetly in prayer. I spent some time this afternoon with the children, whilst they were questioned in Scripture, and in the evening, whilst the Bible and the memoirs of E. F. Brady were read.

28*th.*—We had a pleasant ride to Exeter, arriving about three o'clock. I had been much exercised on the way, querying whether I should be able to meet Lord Ebrington (Viceroy of Ireland), who was to be in Exeter to-day, but intended leaving soon after receiving a deputation in the city. John Dymond met us at the coach. I inquired whether I could by any means see Lord Ebrington, and learned that his carriage was ordered out for his departure, and that he was taking refreshment with other noblemen. We ascended the stairs of the New London Inn, and sent in the waiter to inform him that John Dymond wished to see him in a private room, where he soon joined us, saying as he entered, that he was much limited for time. John Dymond introduced me as a minister of the Society of Friends who had recently travelled through Ireland. Lord Ebrington stood by the fire, and listened attentively and kindly, whilst I laid before him the importance of ruling over men in the fear of the Lord; of acting on sound Christian principles, rather than those of expediency; of encouraging morality at his court as a means of checking inconsistencies in other ranks; and of seeking to secure for himself the crown of glory laid up in store for those who love and serve the Lord. He thanked me, giving me his hand at parting. Thanks be to the great Preserver of His little ones, I feel at liberty to return to my home, which I do, with the full reward of peace.

Falmouth, 30th.—This evening John and Maria Candler arrived, prior to their departure for Jamaica.

Eleventh Month 3rd, First Day.—Yesterday Barnard and Samuel Dickenson arrived here, the latter being on his way to Jamaica on business. John and Maria Candler and Samuel Dickenson left us this morning at nine, intending to embark on board the *Magnet* packet for Jamaica; but on reaching the Meeting House we found them, and sat with them in precious union of spirit as worshippers. Cousin Maria Fox knelt in prayer for those who were about to make a sacrifice of their home comforts for the sake of spreading a knowledge of the Truth. We parted hastily after meeting, and my sisters Elizabeth and Lydia saw them into the boat.

Truro, 12th.—Pleasantly engaged in my business pursuits, and able to have my thoughts often turned towards the better country.

Falmouth, 13th.—Was refreshed by the time of waiting on the Lord in meeting this morning: towards the close I felt engaged to bow the knee with thanks for the bread and the water that had been dispensed to the refreshment of hungry and thirsty souls. Lucretia Crouch and Maria Fox both spoke on the subject of Mary going to the sepulchre to seek our Lord. My heart now seems full to overflowing, as though my cup of happiness was full. Rest and peace have taken possession of my soul.

Truro, 19th.—I have been more than commonly engaged to-day, and very painfully so, in dismissing the men at the Gas Works for improper conduct. Sad indeed was the lament made by the wife of one of them. I could wish that all who do wrong could see the consequence of sin, entailing as it does, misery on all around.

Twelfth Month 13th.—Came to St. Austell to-day, and have been closely engaged in attending to gas business. Met my partner, Francis Fox, who went to Charlestown. Have enjoyed being with cousins William and C. T. Browne.

Truro, 18th.—Attended quarterly meeting here. It was a highly favoured meeting, the Lord's power being evidently over all; and to Him be ascribed the praise.

31st.—How different are my prospects now from the beginning of the year, when I had no expectation of living to the end. Surely in Thy hand, O Lord, is the breath of every living thing! Many of my friends who seem girt round with strength for many days, have been cut down, and my frail tabernacle has been strengthened and renewed. May every remaining day be more and more dedicated to Thy service.

Falmouth, First Month 10th, 1840.—I am impressed this evening with the importance of redeeming the time, and spending each day as though it were my last, as if the mandate were to go forth, " This night thy soul shall be required of thee."

To-day the penny postage system commences.

12th, First Day.—Owing to the state of my health I remained at home, having my sister Rachel's company, as well as that of the dear children. We had a season of worship together, for I believe the Lord was amongst us in our little gathering. I hope that this day has been spent profitably; my care has been that it should be so.

Second Month 9th, First Day.—Stayed at home again to-day. Sought for a season of retirement this morning; but little —— being poorly, she was obliged to be in the parlour with me, and in some degree interfered with my quiet; but it brought my mind into sympathy with those who are much encumbered with a family, and with the cares of life, and perhaps limited to two rooms. How little opportunity can they have for secret retirement before the Lord: but doubtless " the soul's sincere desire, uttered or unexpressed," is accepted as sweet incense at the throne of grace.

10th.—This day Queen Victoria has, I suppose, been married to Prince Albert of Saxe Coburg. I have had an unusually busy day: surprising it is to myself that I am able to do so much.

26th.—Lieutenant Symmons called; he is the agent of the Naval and Military Bible Society, which was established fourteen years before the British and Foreign Bible Society.

27th.—Lieutenant Symmons took breakfast with us, and gave me an authority whereby I may be able to supply gratuitously, any vessels I may visit, with Bibles and Testaments. This I esteem a privilege.

Third Month 12th.—I trust that He to whom I have committed myself is carrying forward the work of grace in my soul, though there is but little evidence of it. May I be preserved from admitting, or in any way countenancing the idea, that outward sacrifices of my time and talents in the service of the Lord—that running to and fro as His messenger—will be accepted instead of personal holiness.

26th.—Barclay Fox called this evening, to take leave of us prior to his departure to Neath. My heart yearns over him, with desires for his preservation. O Lord, keep him as in the hollow of Thy holy hand, from every snare.

Falmouth, Fourth Month 7th.—Attended monthly meeting here. Early in the meeting Philippa Williams rose with the language, "I am Thy shield, and Thy exceeding great reward." Soon after which I expressed what had previously presented, "Them that honour Me I will honour, and they that despise Me shall be lightly esteemed." At the close of the meeting I felt strengthened to lay before Friends my prospect of visiting the schools connected with the Society and some other service, which was most feelingly united with, and a committee appointed to bring a certificate to the next meeting. Much excellent counsel and encouragement was handed, and Philippa Williams knelt in prayer for my preservation.

8th.—Attended the quarterly meeting. I felt strengthened at the close of the second meeting, to relieve my mind of what it has long felt against the practice of Friends requiring others to take oaths on their behalf.

16th.—I attended a meeting gathered at the request of Samuel and Sarah Rundell, who, with Ann Tweedy, were well engaged in preaching the gospel: "Christ in you the hope of glory." My place seemed to be to sit still, and wrestle for a blessing on the word preached; that the condemnation of those present might not be increased, seeing that their responsibility was greater by having the privilege of hearing such gospel truths.

The following memoranda of E. O. Tregelles' visits to Croydon, Ackworth and Sidcot will be read with interest by those who still remember his earnest words of exhortation and prayer for them.

Sixth Month 13th, 1840.—I attended Croydon meeting. In the afternoon, accompanied by John Finch Marsh, I sat with the children and the various officers of Croydon School whilst they read the Memoirs of John Pemberton; I afterwards addressed them, and had a separate interview with the boys of the first class.

14*th*.—I went again to the school and sat with the remainder of the boys, in four companies, and with the girls, in three companies. I took tea with John Sharp; and afterwards sat with the teachers of the girls. I was mercifully helped, and felt that the work was not mine but my Master's, and that He is all-sufficient for His own work.

15*th*.—We had an interview with the boys' teachers, and a searching time it was.

25*th*.—At the close of the monthly meeting for business, I felt that it was my place to ask that the school children should withdraw, and the women Friends rejoin us, when I was led to express a desire that each member of the meeting might feel a religious concern for the well-being of the dear children of the school.

27*th*.—Though feeling unwell, I thought it best to continue my engagements at the school. We had the orphans collected together, and on coming into the room found many of them in tears; it was a profitable season which I desire ever to remember. Peter Bedford, John F. Marsh and I afterwards saw the teachers all together, and then the whole establishment of superintendents, teachers and scholars.

Ackworth School, Seventh Month 24*th*.—I attended the educational meeting, which was extremely interesting.

27*th*.—Soon after breakfast I commenced my sittings with the girls of the school, dividing them into four companies, beginning with the youngest. This occupied the day until tea-time; since which we have been with them at their Bible reading.

28*th*.—I was engaged this morning in sitting with the female teachers and the governess, Hannah Richardson, of North Shields. It was a memorable season. Most of our party of twelve were in tears.

29*th*.—Yesterday I attended the boys' evening reading, and to-day sat with the two upper classes of boys.

30*th*.—I am called upon to commemorate the extension of the Lord's goodness to me this day, directing and aiding my movements.

Eighth Month 1*st*.—This morning I was presented with several gifts of their own handiwork, from the dear girls of Ackworth School, with a sweet note, and a copy of the hymn, "The Time for Prayer," which they had repeated, and to which I had alluded when addressing them. This was a tendering preparation for sitting with the orphans, ninety of whom were collected, and a most touching time it was.

Gratitude was the covering of my spirit in the remembrance of the mercy and lovingkindness and condescension of my Lord during the visit to Ackworth. Water, preserve, and render fruitful the seed which Thou, O Lord, hast sown; and give me to see that in myself dwelleth no good thing.

Sidcot, Tenth Month 25*th*.—I sat with the children of the school after breakfast. In the afternoon I met the orphans in the school—about thirty—a deeply affecting time. I joined the children and family at their evening reading.

Thus has closed my present engagement in visiting schools. I may thankfully acknowledge I have been helped on my way from day to day, in a manner I little expected when, in much weakness in every way, I commenced my work at Tottenham.

THE TIME FOR PRAYER.

When is the time for prayer?
  With the first beams that light the morning sky,
Ere for the toils of day thou dost prepare,
  Lift up thy thoughts on high;
Commend the loved ones to His watchful care:
Morn is the time for prayer!

And in the noontide hour,
  If worn by toil, or by sad cares opprest,
Then unto God thy spirit's sorrows pour,
  And He will give thee rest;
Thy voice shall reach Him through the fields of air;
Noon is the time for prayer!

When the bright sun has set,
  Whilst yet eve's glowing colours deck the skies,
When with the loved at home again thou'st met,
  Then let the prayer arise
For those who in thy joys and sorrows share:
Eve is the time for prayer!

And when the stars come forth,—
  When to the trusting heart sweet hopes are given,
And the deep stillness of the hour gives birth
  To pure bright dreams of heaven,—
Kneel to thy God—ask strength life's ills to bear:
Night is the time for prayer!

When is the time for prayer?
  In every hour while life is spared to thee;
In crowds or solitude—in joy or care,
  Thy thoughts should heavenward flee.
At home, at noon, and eve, with loved ones there,
  Bend thou the knee in prayer!

GEORGINA BENNETT.

SCHOOLS VISITED.

Thomas Binns, Grove House School, Tottenham.
Sarah Sweetapple, Girls' School, Stoke Newington.
Richard Abbatt, Boys' School, Stoke Newington.
Thomas Uzman, Boys' School, Croydon.
John Sharp, Friends' School, Croydon.
S. and M. Palmer, Girls' School, Croydon.
Sarah Cudforth, Girls' School, Berkhampstead.
Anne Keckwich, Girls' School, Maidenhead.
Sarah Day, Little Boys' School, Epping.
Isaac Pain, Boys' School, Epping.
Isaac Brown, Boys' School, Hitchin.
Ann Knight and Sisters, Girls' School, Woodbridge.
Ann Lockwood, Infants' School, Woodbridge.
Edmund W. Watt, Boys' School, Colchester.
Mary Gopsill, Girls' School, Chelmsford.
C. E. and E. Dix, Girls' School, Haverhill.
Anne and Eliza Rickman, Girls' School, Rochester.

LIST OF SCHOOLS VISITED.

Benjamin Abbott, Boys' School, Lewes.
Thomas Pumphrey, Friends' School, Ackworth.
Martha Cooper, Girls' School, Pontefract.
  Friends' First-day School, Highflats.
W. Rothway, Friends' School, Rawden.
Samuel Marshall, Boys' School, Kendal.
Jane King, Girls' School, Kendal.
James Hunter, Boys' School, Ulverstone.
John Ford, Friends' School, York.
Hannah Brady, Friends' School, York.
Lucy Waterfall, Girls' School, Leeds.
Louisa Cooper, Girls' School, Leeds.
Jane Thurnham, Girls' School, Leeds.
Jane Procter and Sisters, Girls' School, Selby.
Martha and Hannah Wragg, Girls' School, Selby.
Sarah Harrison, Girls' School, Doncaster.
H. and R. Brady, Girls' School, Sheffield.
Sarah Bleckley, Girls' School, Manchester.
Lydia Graves, Girls' School, Manchester.
Charles Cumber, Boys' School, Manchester.
J. Barret Young, Boys' School, Manchester.
  Friends' School, Penketh.
Martha and Jane Bellis, Girls' School, Nantwich.
Maria and Eliza Peacock, Girls' School, Chester.
J. Jackson, Boys' School, Warrington.
E. and M. Sanders, Girls' School, Warrington.
Hannah Puplett, Girls' School, Layer Breton.
Priscilla Coare, Girls' School, Tottenham.
Joseph Sefton, Boys' and Girls' School, Liverpool.
Abraham Isherwood, Boys' School, Liverpool.
Richard Batt, Boys' School, Preston.
Joshua Kelsell, Boys' School, Wyersdale.
Tabitha Eveleigh, Girls' School, Southport.
Elizabeth Alderson, Girls' School, Blackburn.
J. Harrison Smith, Boys' School, Preston.
Mary and Esther Stickney, Girls' School, Preston.

George Edmondson, Boys' School, Blackburn.
    Camp Hill School, Worcester.
Lucy Marshall, Girls' School, Worcester.
William Palmer, Boys' School, Charlbury.
Eliza Grey, Girls' School, Charlbury.
John Frank, Boys' School, Thornbury.
Harriet Hoare, Girls' School, Bath.
Mary Ann Dymond, Girls' School, Bristol.
Thomas Ferris, Boys' School, Sidcot.
    Friends' School, Sidcot.
    Friends' School, Wigton.
    Friends' First-day School, Newcastle.
    Friends' First-day School, Shields.
Deborah Smith, Girls' School, Sunderland.
Lucy Marshall, Girls' School, Birmingham.
Letitia Impey, Girls' School, Worcester.

CHAPTER VII.

FALMOUTH.

Yearly Meeting—Sarah Grubb's Testimony—Essex—Brighton—Lindfield School and William Allen—Interviews with Lord John Russell and Daniel O'Connell—Scotland—Meetings with Factory Workers—First Sense of Call to Service Abroad—Liverpool—Wales—Banbury—Plymouth—Meetings at Ilfracombe, Barnstaple and Clovelly—Family Visits at Plymouth and Kingsbridge—John Elliott's Message to his Friends.

BETWEEN the intervals of visiting the schools, E. O. Tregelles attended London yearly meeting and travelled through Scotland, holding public meetings. The following extracts refer to these engagements.

Stoke Newington, Fifth Month 21st, 1840.—Left Croydon yesterday morning and attended the opening sitting of the yearly meeting, the commencement of which felt to me a low season until we were visited by Sarah Grubb and Priscilla Green. The latter cautioned us to wait on the Lord for counsel and wisdom to direct the proceedings aright. Sarah Grubb's testimony was clear, searching, and long; several states were addressed, amongst them those who though they may now occupy the foremost rank among us, will be laid low if there be not a digging deep for the rock on which to build; that unless this be the case, they will not stand when the storms arise. This came very close home to me, and I have been led to examine whether my heart is most set on the service of the Lord or of Mammon;

whether I do not love the praise of men more than the praise of God.

23rd.—Josiah Forster proposed the appointment of a committee to visit schools. This proposal had much approval, but it seemed best to postpone the matter. To me the expression of sentiment from many friends was very interesting and encouraging.

26th.—Cousin Mary Sylvanus Fox and Hannah C. Backhouse came into the men's yearly meeting. The former addressed us very acceptably, quoting the words of Jesus: "If ye believe not that I am He, ye shall die in your sins: whither I go ye cannot come."

28th.—With the help of the Lord, which was mercifully afforded, I laid my prospect of visiting the women's yearly meeting before my brethren. George Crosfield and Joseph T. Price accompanied me. I went under a sense of deep poverty and inability to do any good thing, but I have cause to believe that my great and good Shepherd went before and supported me.

31st.—Yesterday I attended the yearly meeting of ministers and elders, which was a very interesting season. William Allen and Elizabeth Fry gave interesting accounts of their visit to Holland, Prussia and Belgium, encouraging faithfulness in others, saying, that they had found the door open and had left it open.

Sixth Month 5th.—Attended the monthly meeting at Sudbury. I quoted the text, "Great is the Lord, and greatly to be praised." Sarah Grubb was sweetly engaged in supplication, manifestly on my behalf, that my eye might be kept singly fixed on my great Master.

9th.—At the quarterly meeting at Chelmsford, met William and Ann Tweedy, Lucretia Crouch, Margaret Richardson, Katherine Backhouse, George and Ann Jones, John and Philippa Williams, and Stanley Pumphrey. Ann Tweedy broke the silence with the language, "Give unto the Lord, O ye mighty, give unto the Lord glory and strength." We had not much silence. The call went forth to many of the strong and willing-hearted. A young man named Isaac Sharp also spoke, to my comfort. I expected to maintain silence, but very soon felt bound to express the language, "Woe unto them that are at ease in Zion." I never had such a sense of riches being possessed, both spiritual and temporal, of which there was so little occupation.

19th.—Went to Brighton to meeting, feeling poor, yet confiding. I knelt to implore that the Spirit of the Lord might descend on those present who had not called upon His name. John Finch Marsh and Maria Fox spoke, and I had, to my surprise, to allude to those who were laying up treasure for themselves and are not rich toward God.

Lindfield, 20th.—Accompanied by Daniel Pryor Hack, I had a lovely ride, and sweet converse with a brother beloved in the Truth. After dining at William Allen's cottage, we went to the school, where we found about nineteen boys, boarders, who were addressed by William Allen, John Finch Marsh, and myself. We also saw the master and mistress. Besides these boys a large number of day scholars receive instruction.

21st.—To my surprise this morning cousin Joseph T. Price came from London to spend the day with us, travelling through the night. At meeting I revived the language, "Children, have ye any meat?" I felt peace in the apprehension that I had been preserved close to my Guide. This was also my favoured experience after the afternoon meeting, which was largely attended, and in which I was led to pray that the Spirit of the Lord might be poured forth upon us. Now, whilst I write, I feel earnest prayer arise from my soul on behalf of those who may have been visited by the Spirit of the Lord this day, desiring that they may patiently abide the complete operation of Divine grace.

Croydon, 23rd.—We left Lindfield yesterday morning, and proceeded to Worthing for a meeting at six o'clock held in the Assembly Rooms, Steyne Hotel. The Lord was pleased to bless us, and enabled Daniel P. Hack, John F. Marsh and me to give full and free expression of gospel truths. The room was quite full of the class of persons I wished to meet. A sweet feeling came over me before we went into the meeting, to which I gave vent in prayer at the tea-table. At the meeting the subjects adverted to were, man's condition in the unregenerate state, and the means and necessity for his redemption by the alone Way.

Tottenham, 28th.—George Stacey and John Hodgkin called, and the latter sweetly addressed me, expressing his belief that my service in seeking to instruct dear children in the way of truth would lead me to confide my own to the care of the Church when I was taken from them.

30th.—Attended the quarterly meeting of London. William Forster queried of me whether any service rested on me yet to perform in London, and I avowed that I felt required to visit Lord John Russell. John Kitching, Peter Bedford and himself, all encouraged me to proceed.

It was doubtless to relate some of the experience gained by his visit to Ireland, and to plead for peaceful measures, that E. O. Tregelles had interviews with Lord John Russell and Daniel O'Connell, as previously with Lord Ebrington, Viceroy of Ireland. He writes:—

Seventh Month, 3rd.—Went with William Allen to the Meeting for Sufferings at ten, and in half an hour we left, to go to Lord John Russell's house, Wilton Crescent. He soon joined us, and after calmly offering us his hand, sat quietly down and gave me a full opportunity to relieve my mind. He seemed to pay attention to the subjects brought before my view to communicate. It was to me a deeply interesting time, and I feel thankful for the opportunity.

After this, William Allen and I called with the same object on Daniel O'Connell, who also received us very kindly.

When I had expressed all I had to communicate, he addressed us at some length, giving full expression of thanks for the visit. He invited us both to visit him at his Seat in Ireland.

5th.—This evening I was at a meeting at Devonshire House, appointed at my request, chiefly for young persons. It was very well attended. I felt required to commence with the words, "The Lord upholdeth all that fall, and raiseth up all those that be bowed down." Cornelius Hanbury, William Allen, and Sylvanus Fox followed. At the close I felt constrained to supplicate specially for the children of our ministers. A solemn meeting it proved.

Edwin O. Tregelles had received a certificate for service in Scotland from his monthly meeting. He was accompanied by his cousin, Charles Fox, of Falmouth, and his sister Rachel Tregelles. He describes the journey as follows:—

Eighth Month 6th.—We went this evening to Swarthmore Hall and Meeting House. In the latter place, after walking in the graveyard, I asked my companions to assemble in the House, where I felt constrained to supplicate the Father of mercies. It was a solemn season.

Edinburgh, 13th.—My feelings on coming into Scotland were of a very peaceful kind, and I trust it may be given me to see what to do and say, and what to leave undone.

Aberdeen, 14th.—A fine smooth voyage of twelve hours brought us safely to this granite built city, where we are kindly entertained by Anthony and Mary Wigham.

16th.—Went to the General Meeting under a sense of great poverty of spirit, and thus I sat for some time waiting on the Lord. After Jonathan Backhouse was engaged in prayer, my soul seemed set at liberty to declare the glad tidings of the gospel freely.

17th.—In the business meeting I asked for an evening meeting to be held. I had to speak on the words, "There is therefore now no condemnation to them which are in Christ Jesus, who walk not after the flesh, but after the Spirit." The meeting ended well. To the Lord may praise be ascribed.

Kinmuck, 19th.—Had a crowded meeting. The heat and crowd was so great that one young woman fell down faint. We are staying at the house of John and Elizabeth Cruickshank, who occupy a well-cultivated farm. Jonathan Backhouse and his daughter Jane are with us.

Aberdeen, 20th.—We had a very full meeting for the spinners and others of the labouring class; ability was given for declaring the truths of the gospel.

Edinburgh, 22nd.—The meeting at Stonehaven was held to my comfort. Jonathan Backhouse and Anthony Wigham were enabled to minister with power; and it was granted to me also to have the privilege of preaching Christ crucified. Parted from the Backhouses to-day, after having much enjoyed their society.

Kinross, 25th.—Attended a meeting here this evening in a small schoolroom. It was crowded, many standing; I suppose 150 persons were present.

27th.—Yesterday we left Kinross for Perth, and met there Joseph McIntyre who had walked seventeen miles to be with us. In the afternoon we had a call from M. G., of Perth, a young woman who was led to follow her Redeemer much in the same track as that in which Friends walk. She attended some of Hannah Backhouse's meetings, and encounters much opposition from her mother. William Gray, who was our companion, conveyed a parcel of books to M. G.'s home, and was told by her mother that she wished Friends and their books were burned. She was prevented by her mother from being at the meeting we had last evening, but her two brothers were there; they came to seek their sister.

We had a precious time of worship with Joseph McIntyre and M. G. yesterday afternoon, such as I trust I may long remember. We also saw at Perth, Andrew Fenwick and his family. His son James accompanied us to Crieff. May these and many others be watered as by heavenly dew. The meeting at Perth was large and comforting; about 700 present. Favoured with a precious time this evening at a meeting with a large company in the Mason's Lodge at Crieff. Many were ready recipients of the doctrine that was declared, and knew, I believe, what it is to feel the strivings of the Lord's Holy Spirit. I was greatly distressed before I went to meeting, sinking low indeed, so as to bring tears of anguish; but I was brought low, and then the Lord comforted me.

28th.—On reaching Stirling at noon to-day, I found that no place could readily be obtained for a meeting. But on going with David Howison, we soon procured the upper part of the Guildhall, where we had a good meeting this evening. The company was not so quiet as at Crieff, but many were, I believe, very attentive to the word inwardly, as well as outwardly spoken. Thankful do I feel for the help which has been afforded me for the work of this week.

Glasgow, 29th.—Received a letter from Henry Tuke, informing me that Jonathan Backhouse had been seized with paralysis, as he was retiring to rest after a public meeting at Montrose.

31st.—Yesterday I received the following note from Edward Richardson, dictated by Jonathan Backhouse, encouraging me to faithfulness:—

"MONTROSE, *Eighth Month* 28th.

"My uncle, Jonathan Backhouse, requests me to answer thine to him. Thou called your band a 'youthful one.' Can our youth or strength be better or more honourably employed than in the cause of our dear Redeemer? or are we more fitted for it at any period of our lives than when there is ability of mind or body for the performance of the work? Some of us find that feebleness of both very soon ensues. . . . How important is the call to work while it is day! I am laid up from infirmity."

On this letter E. O. Tregelles comments as follows:—

Truly I needed all the aid I could obtain, both outwardly and inwardly; but the arm of the Lord is the best support; and it did strengthen me to rise above the many things that oppressed me. It is good to be depressed, that we may know how to comfort the mourners.

We had a meeting in the Secession Chapel, Cowcaddens, with the persons engaged in factories: about 400 were present, and it was held to my comfort. Ability was given me to declare some gospel truths.

Ninth Month 1st.—At Paisley we had a large meeting at the Trades' Hall; about 600 persons were present, and a peaceful blessed meeting it was; such a calming influence seemed to spread over the whole company. At first I was somewhat disturbed by seeing a man by my side taking notes; but I was raised above everything of this sort.

2nd.—We went to Kilmarnock, where lives J. Mathie, a weaver, now too infirm to earn his livelihood in that way; he can only wind thread for the weavers. He is a bright example of patient suffering. Cousin Charles Fox and I were interested by our visit to him. He spoke with much pleasure of the works of Isaac Pennington, which had often solaced him. This poor man, almost a cripple, rode to the gate of the Meeting House, and was carried in on a man's back. It was a favoured meeting, crowded, but very quiet; between 600 and 700 people were present, and many went away for want of room.

Glasgow, 4th.—We returned here yesterday, and attended a meeting where about 800 persons were assembled. Ability was renewed to me to preach the gospel. The company was remarkably quiet, and left with seriousness. I retired to rest with peaceful feelings, relieved of the weight of exercise which for months past had rested on me respecting the working class of Glasgow.

This morning, whilst I was dressing, I felt impressed with the apprehension that I must visit America. No rebellious feelings arose, though my spirit sank within me. May I be instructed by my testimony in Glasgow meeting yesterday morning. "O thou of little faith, wherefore didst thou doubt?" "I will make darkness light before them, and crooked things straight." "Trust in the Lord with all thine heart, and lean not unto thine own understanding. In all thy ways acknowledge Him, and He shall direct thy paths."

5th.—We had a meeting at Lanark last evening. It was long in gathering, and consequently unsettled. I trust the message delivered was fruitful. It was not until after we had left the meeting that I was reminded that infidelity abounds.

Dunfermline, 7th.—Came here this afternoon to attend a meeting, where I was helped to hand some of the things of the kingdom to some inquirers for the road to Zion.

I was much impressed, as we entered the town and saw the remains of ancient grandeur, with a sense of the misery and ruin which were consequent on the vices and enormities of the Court in former days.

Kelso, 10th.—Yesterday morning we sat with Friends at Hawick, which was a close searching time, when I had hard things to say. The evening meeting was large. I was very unwell throughout the day, and glad to retire to rest. This morning I was engaged in distributing books which had been forwarded by the Meeting for Sufferings for several of the persons we had met with.

We had a delightful ride to Kelso, where a large and quiet meeting has been held in the Town Hall. May it be to the praise of my great Master, whose voice I have sought to hear and obey in my movements. Now I believe the work designed for me in this visit is finished.

Stockton, 14th.—Had this evening the privilege of sitting in the meeting of ministers and elders, which was to me a season of unusual favour. I felt that I was indeed amongst my brothers and sisters in the gospel. Ability was given me to recommend others to lengthen their cords and strengthen their stakes, and I desire to know this to be my own practice, having entered into a covenant of unconditional allegiance not to limit the Holy One of Israel.

York, 16th.—Last night my mind was turned with parental fondness towards my dear children, for whom and for my dear wife my prayers ascended that they may be saved with an everlasting salvation, and rejoice in the presence of their Redeemer.

17th.—Cousin Charles Fox left us to-day, after a season of deep interest in travel together. Before he left, Thomas Pumphrey came to engage in the work. Sweet is the unity of spirit with this dear friend.

Liverpool, 26th.—We are kindly received at the house of Isaac and Tabitha Hadwen.

27th.—Went to meeting much depressed, but the Lord sustained me, and helped me to do what seemed to be His will. After meeting we saw the teachers of the First-day school; they seem to me vigorous young men. The public meeting this evening was a large one, in which I trust ability was given to make known the will of the Lord. In the retrospect of the day I thank my God and take courage.

Hindwell, Herefordshire, Tenth Month 10th.—This day has been spent quietly in this sweet spot, which derives its name from the hinds coming to drink at the large pool. It abounds with coots, dab-chick, and moor-hens, as well as ducks and swans.

Rhayader, 11th, *First Day.*—Accompanied by Edward P.

Southall I attended Pales meeting at eleven, and had another at three, to which the neighbours were invited. Calm and delightful have been my feelings this evening. I may say my soul is joyful in the Lord, and my spirit rejoices in God my Saviour.

Banbury, 19th.—This day I am thirty-four years of age. May increase of days bring an increase of dedication. Let everything be made subservient to Him, whose are the cattle upon a thousand hills: then all care will be taken from my mind, except that of seeking to know His will, and fearing to offend against His law. Found a kind welcome from our dear friends Joseph Ashby and Martha Gillett. Our kind friend, J. A. Gillett, went with us to Chipping Norton. He was very acceptably engaged to minister.

Bristol, 23rd.—Dr. Ash offered prayer at meeting this morning. At the conclusion I asked permission to have a meeting with the men Friends alone. It was fully attended, and help given in the needful time, so that I now feel clear. Called on Joshua and Sarah Wheeler at Clifton.

Plymouth, 27th.—How different is my state of health from what it was when last here, eighteen months ago! Oh, that all my strength and every energy may be dedicated to the Lord's service.

28th.—Called on James Gent, who engaged our services about a slip for vessels. It seems as though the Lord was indeed regarding me, thus to provide employment for me in summer and winter; to proclaim His unsearchable riches during the season favourable to my being absent from home, and to work for my support during the cold months.

Ilfracombe, Eleventh Month 3rd.—Notice was given by Charles Fox, who arrived this morning, and by James Wadham, for a meeting in the Wesleyan Chapel, which was crowded, and a good meeting it was. I know not that I ever felt the Spirit of the Lord nearer. To Him be all the praise, and to the Lamb for ever.

Barnstaple, 4th.—Busily engaged after meeting here this morning, in giving notice of a meeting in the Wesleyan Chapel, which was attended by 600 persons, who were attentive to what I had given me to communicate.

6th.—Went to Clovelly yesterday, and had a meeting at two o'clock with the fishermen and their wives. Many came, and one poor man seemed sensible of deep transgressions. At Bude we arranged for a meeting, which was largely attended. We took tea at the house of John Newton Coffin, who welcomed us, as did Samuel Brown, after he learnt that we were not Papists, of which he had at first been suspicious, expecting a Romish priest to come there to advocate teetotal principles.

Wadebridge, 8th.—Went to Padstow to have a meeting in the Wesleyan Chapel, which was crowded, and a blessed time it was.

And now the service for which I left my home being accomplished, I return with a heart grateful for the help afforded me by the Lord, and for the kindness shown me by friends. Rejoicing as I do in this blessed work, I feel ready to be again held, or still retained, in the bonds of the gospel. Not unto us, but unto Thy name give glory!

Falmouth, 18th.—Attended monthly meeting at Redruth, where Ann Tweedy spoke on the language, "Cleanse thou me from secret faults," making an impression on my mind which I hope will be durable. Cousin Maria Fox and I returned our certificates.

21st.—Thankfully performing my business duties, and surprised to find on making up my accounts this evening, that my property has increased considerably during the past ten months, although I have been away for six months attempting to do my Master's bidding.

Plymouth, First Month 5th, 1841.—This evening we completed our visits to the Friends, and attenders of meetings; having sat with about forty families and individuals. I trust I have profited by the counsel of Richard Barrett, my companion. I feel thankful for the help afforded, and that the Lord made me willing. May all the praise be ascribed to Him.

8th.—Dined pleasantly at Aunt Hingston's, and conversed with her and her daughter, Susan Anna, on religious topics.

Kingsbridge, 10*th, First Day.*—In the morning meeting both Elizabeth Sarah Prideaux and I had vocal service. In the afternoon meeting I had to bear my testimony again to the importance of following Christ, and knowing Him to cleanse and purify the heart. Our kind cousins George and Rachel Fox hospitably receive us.

Falmouth, 19*th.*—May I be able to discern the pointings of my good Shepherd, and follow Him nothing doubting.

I called at Liskeard to see John Eliott, who seems to be very near his journey's end. He gave me a message, which I delivered to Friends at Plymouth monthly meeting, to this effect: "Give my dear love to the Friends of that monthly meeting. I love my friends much. I love all mankind. I have had of late many conflicts, but now not a cloud is in the way, all is peace. Had I been more faithful I should have done more good, but I believe these omissions are forgiven."

21*st.*—A meeting was held this evening, which from the state of my health I felt excused from attending. I was afterwards told that Richard Barrett spoke on the words, "Wherefore seeing we also are compassed about with so great a cloud of witnesses, let us lay aside every weight, and the sin which doth so easily beset us, and let us run with patience the race that is set before us, looking unto Jesus the author and finisher of our faith." It is remarkable that whilst they were at meeting, I wrote this text in the Bible of my dear son for his instruction in after years. I wish that he and my other children may have these important subjects constantly before them when my eyes may be beholding Him whom not having seen I love.

CHAPTER VIII.

FALMOUTH.

Monthly Meeting grants Certificate for Service in West Indies—Letter from Jonathan Backhouse—Message from Anna Price—Meetings with Sailors—Quarterly Meeting declines to endorse his Certificate—Professional Duties at Bristol—W. Jay, of Bath—Accompanies his Wife in a Trip to Tintagel—John Allen—Come-to-Good Meeting House—*Lord Beresford*, Steamer, Trial Trip and Storm; Meeting on board—Quarterly Meeting grants Certificate for Service in West Indies—Yearly Meeting, 1842, liberates for the Service—Waits for a Companion—Goes to Coverack with his Wife for her Health—Earthquake, Hayti—Bristol—Bradnich, Judith Templeman—James Jesup offers as Companion—Family Visit from Benjamin Seebohm—Kingsbridge—Yearly Meeting, 1843—William Forster at Gracechurch Street—With Maria Fox holds Meetings near Falmouth—Letter from Hannah C. Backhouse.

FALMOUTH, *First Month* 22nd, 1841.—I was strengthened to-day to communicate to my aunt Elizabeth Fox my belief that it would be required of me to go to the West Indian Islands and America. She encouraged a patient abiding under the exercise, seeking after a state of simple submission to the Divine will, that that will, and not mine, may be done. To this state I desire to attain, and believe that it will be my portion, if I seek the aid of our great High Priest, who is touched with the feeling of our infirmities, and who ever liveth to make intercession for us.

26*th*.—How easy it is for us to praise our pilot's skill, when sailing with a fair and pleasant breeze; but how apt we are to doubt His power when angry storms arise. May my present dispensation prepare me, under the hand of the great Master, to compassionate those who now may be in suffering consequent on the alteration in the post office arrangements to-day made known, which will be likely to involve many in this place in deep distress.

The mails had been carried by swift sailing packets which made Falmouth their port of arrival and departure. Henceforth they were to be carried by steamers, which, from facility of railway communication, were despatched for the most part from Southampton. His journal continues:—

27th.—The meeting this morning was held in silence to my refreshment. It is very important for each member to keep his place, and not to suppose that because on former occasions a revelation of the Lord's will has been our portion, which we may have been required to communicate to others, that therefore such would be continued.

31st.—After meeting, whilst walking with cousin Charles Fox in the rope walk, I communicated to him my prospect of going to the West Indies and to America. Lord, confirm it, if it be Thy will and Thy work; disannul it, if it be the work of the enemy.

Second Month 5th.—Read with much interest the experience of George Fox in the year 1657; his full recognition of Christ as his Redeemer.

8th.—Yesterday was First-day, but I was precluded by the stormy weather from venturing to meeting. It blew a gale from the east, and such was the violence of the storm, that a large brig on the roads drove from her cables. She would have gone ashore and been wrecked, but for a cutter which afforded assistance.

Plymouth, Third Month 2nd.—I am impressed with a sense of the great amount of interested prejudice that there is to be overcome in the matter of war and ecclesiastical establishments. So many well-informed and well-intentioned persons without consideration become involved in the support of these things, which are I believe both, though no equally, opposing the spread of true Christianity.

Falmouth, 17th.—I attended the monthly meeting at Redruth, when I was strengthened to lay before Friends my views as it regards visiting the West Indian Islands and North America, in which many sweetly concurred, and a committee was appointed to prepare a certificate. Edward Richardson of Sunderland returned with us to be our guest.

21st.—Alfred Burlingham arrived from Penzance last night to commence his visit. He brought me from Edward Richardson a present of a beautiful Bible as a travelling companion. I know not when I have had a more valued gift.

JONATHAN BACKHOUSE TO E. O. T.

Polam Hill, Darlington, Third Month 21*st*, 1841.

MY DEAR FRIEND,—

The intimation conveyed in a letter from Falmouth to-day, of thy intention of crossing the Atlantic, seems to call for the expression of my unity with thy concern, which I am prepared to give from having had thee so much in my mind for many weeks past. . . .

I have often reflected with satisfaction on the willing-heartedness manifested in thy letters, that it was not only thy meat and drink, but thy delight to do the Divine will. A wise choice I may truly say, for in contemplating my cousin James Backhouse, and other servants, after their long and arduous travels and preservations in a wilderness land, I am constrained to acknowledge, "How are Thy servants blest, O Lord!" and the disciple yet knows it to be true that no man is sent on a warfare at his own charges, but he is abundantly accoutred for whatever service he is called into, and enabled thankfully to acknowledge when the query is put forth, Lacked thou anything?—Nothing, Lord. And though at times there may be fasting and poverty, yet how richly is the servant made to partake at times of the dainties of His table, even the feast of fat things.

My heart is with the willing in Israel, and would say, "Go, and the Lord be with thee." I hope thy dear wife will cheerfully give thee up, and be made a rich partaker of the blessing. My love to her, and thy sister Rachel and thyself, in which all my family unite, who are much interested in thy prospect.

Thy very affectionate friend,
JONATHAN BACKHOUSE.

The journal continues :—

29th.—In recounting the mercy of this day I may say, "I was brought low, and He helped me. Return unto thy rest, O my soul, for the Lord hath dealt bountifully with thee."

This morning I received a summons from my kind friend Richard Fry to go to Bristol on professional business, which I am disposed to regard as an answer to prayer, and I trust I may now be able to lay by a little for the expenses of my family in my contemplated absence. During the past few days I have more than ever felt that all I have—talents of every kind—and all my worldly estate, are dedicated to the Lord.

Fourth Month 9th.—A few days since I received from my Aunt Price (now eighty-two years of age) an interesting message, which is as follows:—

"I am pleased to find that Edwin will not be likely to go to the West Indies till towards winter, when I hope that that climate will be more genial than injurious to his constitution; but however that may be, these lines of Addison can be appropriated by him, which have frequently occurred to my mind when thinking of him, as respects his present prospects:

> 'My life, if Thou preserv'st my life,
> Thy sacrifice shall be,
> And death, if death should be my lot,
> Shall join my soul to Thee.'

"And as I lay awake one night, ruminating on his religious prospects, in adition to the above, these few lines of dear Sarah R. Grubb revived:—

> 'Thus through the few succeeding steps
> Appointed me to run;
> Thy honour may be all in all,
> Thy praise alone be sung.'

"I also thought of dear old William Rickman's prophetic testimony in the yearly meeting (I believe the last he attended) respecting the liberation of the poor slaves, that it would be done, and also that messengers would be sent among them who should preach the gospel of Christ. I was led to desire that these people, as they advance in civilization, may not live to themselves, but to Him who died for them and rose again. May they understand the nature of the cross of Christ, and, taught by the Holy Spirit, guard against indulging a spirit of resentment towards those who have been their oppressors.

"I wish my dear love given to dear Edwin, and a copy of the above as a proof of my interest in the welfare of the African race. May they prove their gratitude to the Lord who has wrought marvellously for them, and, by abiding in the Heavenly Vine, be enabled to bring forth much fruit."

E. O. T. writes in his journal:—

11*th, First Day.*—During the past week I have been led to consider the disadvantages attending long vocal prayers, often wearying to some, who, if they cannot unite heartily in the engagement, become disgusted, and injury to the progress of religion in their soul is the result. In all our movements we should seek to know and follow the mind of Christ. From remarks recently made to me, I fear that too many allow the seed of the kingdom to be choked by the cares of this world, indulging in the unlawful pursuit of lawful things. The end and object of their existence here seems to be the gathering together of outward substance, things that perish with the using.

Falmouth, 14th.—At the quarterly meeting, a joint meeting of men and women Friends, I laid my prospect of service before them. The subject was deliberated on for some time, and finally concluded to be postponed to next quarterly meeting.

The language of my heart was,

> "What Thy wisdom sees most fit
> Must be surely best for me."

24th.—One of my children ran to me in my office to show me some shells. I felt that she interrupted me, and discouraged her. I was led afterwards to reflect that we may at all times approach the throne of our heavenly Father with our joys and sorrows without being repulsed, and that our great High Priest ever liveth to make intercession for us.

Fifth Month 2nd.—As I went to the afternoon meeting I said to cousin Charles Fox in reference to the scattered members of Christ's fold in Scotland, "Let us bear them in remembrance." Thinking over these words after I was seated, I remembered how favoured the condition of poor sinful man is, in being borne in remembrance as on the breastplate of the great High Priest, who ever liveth to make intercession for us: "who His own self bare our sins in His own body on the tree, that we being dead to sins should live unto righteousness."

Exeter, 8th.—In the afternoon meeting I asked the Lord that I might be enabled to commit myself and my cause into His hands. It was a season of renewed favour, and I felt called to say a few words on the text: "Behold, I stand at the door and knock; if any man hear My voice, and open the door, I will come in to him, and will sup with him, and he with Me."

Bristol, 13th.—Unworthy as I feel, the Lord condescends to bless me by accepting my offerings of silent homage in my seasons of retirement, and at intervals of my busy day, when my soul turns to its best Beloved.

Newport, Isle of Wight, 15th.—Enjoyed my ride and voyage to this sweet retired spot. I had a precious season in the coach, taking a retrospect of the past, and glancing at the future. I felt calm in the assurance that I might leave all in the hands of Him who hath hitherto wrought for me marvellously.

Falmouth, Sixth Month 12th.—Another day of unalloyed peace. I went to all the vessels in the harbour, to give notice of a meeting to be held at the request of Catherine P. Abbott. Met with a pleasing reception in every vessel, and some tracts which I gave were apparently very acceptable.

13th.—At our meeting this morning Maria Fox was sweetly and powerfully engaged in prayer on behalf of the boys of Lovell Squire's school. The meeting at six o'clock, by appointment of Catherine P. Abbot, was crowded, and proved a solemn season.

Southampton, 19th.—Met Joseph John Gurney, Samuel Gurney, Josiah Forster, Rachel Fowler and Hannah Gurney unexpectedly to-day, on their way from Paris, where they have been to advocate at the French Court the cause of the oppressed negro in the French colonies.

20th.—Rose this morning impressed with a desire to be kept on the watch throughout the day, that I may be found amongst those willing and qualified to serve. Towards the close of the morning meeting I had to allude to the benefit of silent worship; to the need for true brotherly love as a preparation for and an accompaniment to worship; to obedience to our Good Shepherd; to the call that is still going forth as to laying aside every weight.

Liskeard, Seventh Month 7th.—Attended the quarterly meeting to-day, at which was considered the subject of my visit to the West Indies and America. After mature deliberation, friends concluded that they could not liberate me for the service. On this occasion I felt constrained to go more into the definition of the line of service in prospect, and although it was not in any way beyond the limits granted in the certificate of the monthly meeting, yet it was again referred to me, and removed from the books of the meeting.

Although I feel bound to submit to the judgment of the Church, and gladly do so, yet I am ready to question the propriety of requiring too much exactitude in describing the prospect of service, and that it is not in the spirit of gospel liberty. If I have erred in my steppings in any way, I desire to see my mistake and to avoid it in my future course. Whilst I regard it as my duty to submit to the judgment of the Church, I crave I may be preserved from turning away from the service of Him whose right it is to reign, to the pursuit of the world and its fading fascinations.

Falmouth, 12th.—A day of special trial and conflict. Pained by my own deviations, and the transgressions also of some of my children, for whom I feel sympathy, inasmuch as they with myself yield to the tempter.

14th.—Felt cheered by the belief that the Lord Jesus Christ would take possession of and fill my heart, if I would yield it to Him. If this were the case, I should have nothing to glory in, or to be proud of, any more than I should merit commendation for accepting an invitation to a scene of great enjoyment. Lord, strengthen my faith in Thee, and my desires to follow Thee.

18th.—I was impressed before I went to meeting, with the language, "Thou art weighed in the balances and found wanting." This presented again and again in meeting, as also the fulness of the remedy that is to be found in Christ. But fearing lest it was the working of imagination only, I let in discouragement, and kept silence. William Ball was engaged in prayer in a striking manner, making reference to Jesus as our Redeemer. Since the conclusion of the meeting I have learnt that a stranger, a decided Unitarian, was present; and I feel condemned for having allowed the reasoner to have the ascendancy in my heart. May I profit by the lesson, and learn humble obedience.

Bristol, 21*st*.—On my journey here I maintained a care to adorn the doctrine of the gospel, and had sweet communion with my Lord by the way. I trust I have renewed my covenant of unconditional allegiance. When I felt that His finger pointed to continued service, and renewedly to the Western World, the answer of my inmost soul was, "Be it unto me according to Thy word."

Eighth Month 1*st*.—As soon as I took my seat in meeting the language arose, "Oh give thanks unto the Lord, for He is good; for His mercy endureth for ever. Who can utter the mighty acts of the Lord? who can show forth all His praise?" to which I gave utterance, after Dr. Ash had sweetly poured forth his soul in praise and prayer. It has been a day of renewed favour, and I feel thankful for the help afforded both to worship and to minister.

Received from Henrietta J. Fry some lines much in unison with my feelings, on the words, "The Lord will guide thee continually" (Isa. lviii. 11).

> "Thou faithful follower! whosoe'er thou be,
> Thou who art true to Him who died for thee;
> Oh! let the words of sacred promise dwell
> Deep in thy heart with joy ineffable.
> Thou like a watered garden shalt be found;
> Within thy borders all is holy ground.
> Jesus the source, the centre, and the spring
> From which the saints their living waters bring;
> There they may drink, and find a large supply
> Of faith and love, and joy and charity.
> From that blest fount the Christian graces flow,
> Which cheer and fertilise this vale below.

>   Mark the believer,[1] let the Saviour's word,
>   Afresh, a soul-sustaining strength afford.
>   And oh! to us may His salvation be
>   A tide of bliss to all eternity!"

Bristol, Ninth Month 9th.—Left Falmouth on the 7th by the *Beresford* steamer, and had a nice cruise to Southampton. In continuing my journey I had for my companion William Jay, a minister at Bath. He spoke of John Newton of Olney, with whom he was well acquainted.

17th.—Arnée Frank addressed us this morning, alluding to the Query, "Is there among you any growth in the Truth?" After which ability was given me to express a few words on holiness, and on the importance of fighting the good fight of faith. The day has been very peaceful and enjoyable, thanks be to the Father of mercies, and God of all consolation.

22nd.—Attended the quarterly meeting, at which we had the company of Sarah Grubb, who was engaged at much length. She alluded to the sifting which had taken place, and which would yet take place, but that not one grain of solid wheat would be lost. Lucy Aggs was engaged powerfully and sweetly in supplication this morning, also in testimony on the words, "Except the Lord build the house, they labour in vain that build it." This helped me to wrestle for the victory, and induced me to seek to commit my whole self to the keeping of Israel's Shepherd.

Tenth Month 9th.—Have been comforted during my worldly duties by sweet incomes of Divine favour, so that I can say, "In the multitude of my thoughts within me, Thy comforts delight my soul."

11th.—Felt much annoyed by a letter which I received to-day, and whilst I was engaged in preparing a reply that should return a large portion of the odium on the writer, I felt uncomfortable; and though I could have written so as to condemn the party, yet I felt most easy to pen a simple

---

[1] John vii. 37, 38.

moderate reply; and thankful am I that the enemy did not succeed in this quarter. I greatly pity those who take pleasure in backbiting, and who, as it were, feed on the mistakes and frailties of their fellows. It would be well for us all to adopt Lavater's suggestion, and place ourselves in the picture when we begin to criticize. Better still to obey the injunction of our Redeemer, "Judge not, that ye be not judged."

24th.—Went to meeting under a sense that the Lord was at work in my heart, fitting me for His service, to which I yielded, and much peace has since been my portion. I now feel clear of Bristol meeting, and thankful that I was made willing and strengthened in the day of the Lord's power.

Falmouth, Eleventh Month 8th.—Returned home this evening in much comfort, after a very nice trip with dear Jenepher to Tintagel, Boscastle and Delabole, lodging at Gonvena, where we spent yesterday with our bereaved cousins, who feel much stripped by the removal of their mother, Mary Fox.

When at Tintagel we went to see King Arthur's castle, a very interesting ruin, indicating the ravages of time, for it had evidently once been an extensive building.

28th, First Day.—Went to meeting under much exercise of spirit, and had strength and ability given me to hand to others the message that rested on my mind. Oh that some then present would bring their gold, their myrrh and frankincense, and lay them all at their Redeemer's feet: then would He restore to them again the full measure of abundant blessings to the satisfying of their souls.

Lucretia Crouch had spoken on the handwriting on the wall that was seen by the sinning monarch. After she sat down I felt engaged to remind my friends that He who blotted out the handwriting of ordinances was the Lord Jesus Christ. Maria Fox prayed that all might avail themselves of this redemption.

Twelfth Month 3rd.—Received some verses from Henrietta J. Fry, on the words "Trust and follow," having allusion to a circumstance that occurred to me many years ago in London, when I was much cast down. As I walked along the street I glanced at a baker's man carrying a basket with the letters T and F marked on it. The words, "Trust and Follow" passed through my mind, and I went cheerfully on my way.

  Trust and follow! cheering word!
   To the Christian fitly spoken:
  O ye servants of your Lord,
   Be your faith in Him unbroken!

  Weak and wavering, faint and few
   Though the prayers your hearts are sending,
  Oh may grace your souls renew!
   Grace with streams of mercy blending.

  Trust and follow! Christians, go
   Where your gracious Lord is leading;
  There His own disciples know
   Him for sinners interceding.

11*th*.—Returned home yesterday from Plymouth with aunt Fox and cousin Charlotte. We had a truly pleasant ride. On reaching home I received a letter from John Allen, which proved as water to a thirsty soul. I could desire that he might participate in the rich feeling of calm peace which has been my portion since the receipt of that letter; an evidence to my own mind of the rectitude of the prospect before me. But, oh, at times it feels fearfully important, and almost overwhelms me. May I keep my eye steadily fixed on Him who, I believe, calls for my dedication to leave all and follow Him, although the professional prospects before me are more glittering and promising than I ever remember them before.

25*th*.—I have been led to consider to-day by what means the largest portion of happiness is to be obtained in this life; and it has felt to me that, concurrent with the Divine approbation, we derive the truest and greatest pleasure by seeking to increase the enjoyments of others. How many are retiring to rest this night, at the close of a day of ease and leisure, surprised that they have not been able to feel so happy as they had fondly expected.

Falmouth, First Month 8th, 1842.—Returned this evening from St. Austell, where I had a satisfactory and busy time. My ride alone from Truro was very enjoyable, as my heart seemed attuned to praise. I saw many persons walking towards Tregothnan, to attend the funeral of Lord Falmouth. In my walk from Restronguet two days ago I called at Kea Meeting House. As I looked at the neat interior through the open window, my mind was turned to the subject of the sweet seasons which I doubt not valued Friends have had there; some of whom have gone to their rest, others are yet on their pilgrimage, not yet summoned to partake of the joys of their Lord, and to sleep with Jesus. A belief prevailed in my heart that that meeting-house will again be regularly occupied by a body of faithful disciples of the Lamb, who will worship there, and thereby grow in grace.[1]

Bristol, 23rd.— I desire to record for the instruction of my dear children, that many a time I have been brought low, and have had cause to acknowledge that the Lord, and the Lord alone, hath helped me. Often has He supplied my temporal wants, enabling me to provide for the necessities of my family in a manner surprising to myself, so that I have been ready to say, This is the Lord's doing, and it is marvellous in my eyes.

I have sought by insuring my life, and by a careful investment of the payments I receive for my exertions in business, to lay by a suitable provision for my family. This has cost me much toil and some anxiety at times; but I

---

[1] A meeting is held in this ancient meeting-house at Come-to-Good, four times in the year, which is largely attended by the surrounding residents.

have acted from a sincere desire to do right, and not from the love of accumulation.

Falmouth, Third Month 6th.—Heard to-day of the decease of Robert Barclay, jun., who was married about six months ago to John Backhouse's daughter. When we last met at Croydon in 1840, he was vigorous, and I an invalid! I believe he is taken in mercy, and that in the same mercy my life is lengthened, though trials of my faith are permitted.

10th.—Returned this evening from Restronguet, where, during the past four days, I have had the most arduous service I was ever engaged in as to engineering duties, in attending to the *Lord Beresford* steamer.

16th.—Went to-day to Redruth monthly meeting, where my mind was sweetly comforted by the renewed favour of the Lord, which seemed as an earnest of the approval of my heavenly Father in the step I felt engaged to take, of informing my friends of my continuing to feel bound to visit some of the West Indian Islands.

Charleston, 22nd.—On the 18th I went to Plymouth in the *Beresford* steamer for a trial trip, and left Plymouth on Seventh-day for Falmouth; but it blew so tempestuously that we could not get beyond four miles west of the Rame Head. The sea was awfully grand, and I felt thankful when we were safe in Cawsand Bay, where we anchored, and remained until First-day at twelve o'clock, when we again proceeded towards Falmouth, and reached comfortably that evening. I had on First-day morning, whilst lying in bed, felt that it would be my duty to ask the captain to collect the crew and passengers in the cabin, to which he readily assented. At about half-past ten o'clock we collected together, when I read to them the eleventh and twelfth chapters of John, also the fifty-first Psalm, after which I was led to say a few words on the nature of true worship, regeneration, redemption by Christ, and freedom from sin. Almost immediately after we separated, the captain came to tell me that the weather was moderate, and he should start. I expected it would be so, and felt thankful that I had yielded to a sense of duty. "Great peace have they which love Thy law, and nothing shall offend them."

23rd.—May I long remember the awful sense I had of a speedy prospect of death last Seventh-day off the Rame Head, when two tremendous waves seemed following to engulf us, and I thought that in less than five minutes we might be in eternity. For myself, I may say that I had no ground on which to trust but the Rock of Ages, Christ Jesus; that every work comparable to a work of righteousness was but an evidence of discipleship, not a warrant of redemption.

25th.—Took a pleasant walk on the cliffs with Alfred Burlingham and Silvanus W. Jenkin, and was led to consider a little on the many ways in which professing Christians spend this day (Good Friday), regarded as the anniversary of our Saviour's propitiatory sacrifice. May a sense of the mercy shown, by what He has done and suffered for us, and what He would do in us if we allowed Him to do His own work, ever remain prominent in my view.

Fourth Month 3rd.—Snow fell about nine o'clock, rendering it difficult for dear Jenepher and me to get from Charleston to meeting at St. Austell. This brought me into sympathy with some who live at a distance from their ordinary place of worship, and on the days of assembling may find it difficult either to convey or to leave their young families. I could not but regard the belief of our Society as peculiarly well suited for such persons, seeing that worship may be as well performed at home, and in small companies, with the presence of the great High Priest, as in large gatherings at a distance. It is however best to meet with our fellow professors at regular and stated seasons.

Falmouth, 12th.—The monthly meeting concluded to liberate me by certificate to visit the West Indies. At the quarterly meeting of ministers and elders this evening Samuel Rundell was engaged to counsel us to be very watchful in the present state of declension. John Allen handed encouragement to those who felt poor and feeble, possessors of only one talent; calling attention to the fields white already to harvest.

13*th.*—To-day the quarterly meeting was held. I was enabled to lay before it my prospect of going to the West Indies. My friends united without the expression of any dissent, and now I am liberated by my monthly and quarterly meetings. Oh, I do sincerely desire that if this measure be not of God, and according to His will and time, it may come to nought, and that I may be restrained from pursuing any matter of my own contriving. But, on the other hand, if it be of the Lord, as I now believe is the case, may nothing turn me aside; but may I go as with my life in my hand, and be made cheerfully willing to leave my dear family and friends with the probability of not seeing them again in time. Oh, may the language of my heart constantly be, I am Thine; save, counsel, and direct me.

London, Fifth Month 27*th.*—Had the privilege of attending the last two sittings of the yearly meeting, and listening to the excellent epistles which have been prepared for America, Ireland, and Great Britain. The meeting closed under sweet feelings, shortly after we had had a precious address to fathers, young men and children, from Jacob Green.

28*th.*—On waking early this morning I was led again to prove the fleece as to whether it was right for me to bring my concern before the meeting of ministers and elders; desiring earnestly that the Lord would make His will clear before my view. After which I felt most easy to proceed, whilst the prayer of my heart earnestly was, "Hold up my goings in Thy paths, that my footsteps slip not." Under this feeling I went to meeting, and in a remarkable manner felt that the Spirit of the Lord was around me, making way before me amongst my friends, enabling me to give expression to my feelings, and causing their hearts to sympathise and unite with me fully on the occasion. For all which I reverently desire to magnify the Lord. May I long remember the varied counsel extended to me, and be engaged to keep very close to the Guide of my youth.

To have received the approval of Friends in that to which he felt called was doubtless a great comfort to Edwin O. Tregelles, but it was long before he was able to commence the work for which he was liberated, as no suitable companion offered to accompany him; and although his wife cheerfully gave him up for the service, the state of her health was such that it was difficult to feel it right to leave her. Thus he missed the season when it would be safe to go to the West Indies, and waited till the autumn of the following year before setting off.

Coverack, Cornwall, Sixth Month 4th.—Came here to try change of air for dear Jenepher. She spoke to me of the dear children, saying she feared she had been too earnest to make them understand every part of the Holy Scriptures, and feared it might lead to scepticism if they were taught to expect to understand before they believe.

10th.—At Kynance Cove, where we much enjoyed three hours amongst the magnificent rocks in that extraordinary place, dear Jenepher requested me to write in my pocket-book some lines that had impressed her when she looked at me whilst I was sketching:—

> "The Lord can change the darkest skies,
> Can give us day for night,
> Make drops of sacred sorrow rise
> To rivers of delight."

Falmouth, 20th.—During the past few days a report has prevailed, that a serious earthquake has occurred at Hayti, which has destroyed the greater part of the town of Cape Haytien, with many thousand inhabitants. I have been greatly impressed with this calamity, and I feel thankful that my steps have been guided as they have been during the past fifteen months; that I did not withhold offering to go there last year, and therefore that I am by no means, I trust, chargeable with the blood of those who may have perished, nor can I be unconscious of the mercy of having been preserved from being among the sufferers in that awful calamity.

Seventh Month 14th.—Took a pleasant walk with my sister Lydia and the children to Swanpool. We saw a large shoal of porpoises taking a westerly direction, and keeping within half a mile of the shore. In their gambols they leaped completely out of the water, rising about four or five feet above it, and entering about twelve or fifteen feet from the place where they emerged. We heard the sound of their blowing very plainly.

Bristol, 23rd.—I am now pleasantly quartered at Richard Fry's. As I walked to his house on this lovely evening, I was led to consider that my joy in the restoration of my dear Jenepher may in some slight degree compare with the hallowed pleasure that was the portion of Abraham, when he returned with his precious son Isaac from Mount Moriah.

Falmouth, Eighth Month 21st, First Day.—This has been a day of peculiar conflict. I know not when I have been helped to endure such a fight of affliction as has been my portion. The effect was to drive me to the stronghold of the tribulated ones. Truly I can say, "Thou hast considered my trouble; Thou hast known my soul in adversities." I believe I should this day have fallen if the Lord had not made bare His holy arm for my defence. When my heart was overwhelmed, His Spirit led me to the Rock that is higher than I, giving me to believe that His grace is sufficient for me, and that His strength will be made perfect in my weakness. I was cheered by the invitation,

"Come unto Me, all ye that labour and are heavy laden, and I will give you rest."

Ninth Month 27th.—Last First-day I spent at Plymouth, where I had a sweet season of religious communion with my dear aunt Abbott and cousin Elizabeth Abbott. The former addressed me with the language, "In all thy ways acknowledge the Lord, and He shall direct thy paths." The latter encouraged me with the words, "As poor, yet making many rich;" adding, "Why art thou cast down, O my soul?" And now I am able to believe that the many causes of trial which are permitted to attend me, are in mercy to my soul, to humble and instruct me, and to qualify me in some degree to comfort others.

Spiceland, Tenth Month 8th.—Have enjoyed a sunset ramble amidst lovely scenery, and been sweetly reminded of a walk I took about five years ago in this district, when my dear Jenepher was in Ireland. How much has passed since! much of trial, more of joy, and that too, of a kind wherewith the stranger cannot intermeddle. There is no strength given for anticipation, but there is permission to pray, "Hold Thou me up, and I shall be safe." Into Thine hand I commit my spirit, and all I have is surrendered to Thee for Thy keeping: enable me to serve Thee faithfully.

Bristol, 13th.—Have been very kindly cared for by my friends Francis and Matilda Fry. I find business matters here working smoothly, which is a favour, whilst at other places they seem unusually pressing and painful. May all I am passing through tend really to humble me, and draw me from taking delight in the perishing things of time. I desire really to pray for the present and eternal happiness of all those who cause me distress of mind.

17th.—Yesterday was a day of spiritual refreshment. At the morning meeting Elizabeth Dudley was engaged in a striking manner, on the words, "I am come that they might have life, and that they might have it more abundantly."

Bradnich, Eleventh Month 3rd.—During the past few days I have been staying at this place under much outward trial and inward peace. Cheered yesterday morning on waking, with the language, "Oh, how great is Thy goodness, which Thou hast laid up for them that fear Thee, which Thou hast wrought for them that trust in Thee before the sons of men!" This and other texts cheered me through the day, and helped me to bear many trials of patience.

In the afternoon I called to see Judith Templeman. Her sympathy seemed overflowing, and she poured out much encouragement, so that I felt refreshed by the widow's cruse, and went on my way rejoicing, the better prepared to encounter a dispensation in a matter of business wherein I was nearer at my wits' end than I ever before remember; but out of all I was helped, and now the language of my heart is, "Return unto thy rest, O my soul, for the Lord hath dealt bountifully with thee."

Falmouth, 9th.—Pleasantly surprised on entering the meeting to see Samuel Tuke there. He was engaged to minister to us on the unity of the flock of Christ, on following the voice of the true Shepherd to the neglect of the stranger, and on the necessity of honestly following this Leader, and taking up our cross to the world and the flesh, which are at enmity with God, and are not subject to the law of God.

25th.—Engaged to-day in the delightful employment of distributing Testaments to the foreigners now in port. Many of them are here from stress of weather.

28th.—A tranquil day. Able to look upward for help to maintain the warfare.

Twelfth Month 10th.—Through much tribulation we shall enter the kingdom, if ever such a privilege be ours; and, if it be, it will be only by our availing ourselves of the mercy of God through Christ Jesus, who suffered for us, for me, the Just suffering for the unjust, that He may bring us, the unjust, to God. Oh to be brought close to Him, to know Him to be encompassing our path, our lying down and our uprising.

30th.—Received this evening, very unexpectedly, a letter from an unknown Friend, James Jesup, offering himself as my companion for the West Indies, which looks to me very pleasant, and the desire of my heart is, that if right in the sight of the Lord, it may be owned by Him, and promoted by our friends.

First Month 6th, 1843.—Went to-day to the prison, and there saw the prisoners, all of whom would fain represent their condition as blameless, except having been indiscreet, but none of them admit being very guilty. Such is the proneness of the human mind to extenuate its own misconduct. Presented a Spanish prisoner, who is charged with smuggling, with a Spanish Testament.

19th.—Benjamin Seebohm paid us a family visit, to my comfort. Our several states were, I believe, addressed very correctly, and it was sweet to me to observe the genuine tenderness of the dear children. Oh, how earnest do I feel that they may be the Lord's, and be acknowledged worthy, through the blood of the Lamb, to partake of the joys of eternity.

Exeter, Second Month 19th.—I went with some difficulty through the snow to meeting. The day has been greatly blessed to me, not only in my seasons of worship with others, but alone in my lodgings. I have read, to my profit, Isaiah li., every verse of which is replete with counsel. With gratitude I feel able to receive the language of the last two verses as a token of good, and desire to dedicate my all to the service and disposal of Him, whose are the cattle upon a thousand hills, who can open rivers in high places and fountains as in the midst of the valleys.

Kingsbridge, Fourth Month 1st.—I arrived here yesterday, having attended, to my comfort, the meeting at Modbury on the way; and thus I have been enabled to attend all the meetings in Devon and Cornwall, east of Falmouth.

whilst on this business journey. In all I have believed myself called on to serve as a minister. The Lord has been my gracious Helper; to Him be all the praise.

2nd, First Day.—Had a precious season in the arbour in cousin George Fox's garden this morning before breakfast, when I was led to remember the time spent at Bridport ten years ago, when I used to sit and read Henry Martyn's Memoirs before breakfast in the garden. The remembrance of the mercy and goodness which has since followed me, flowed sweetly through my mind, and the word of the Lord arose freshly, "Call upon Me in the day of trouble; I will deliver thee, and thou shalt glorify Me."

Clapton, London, Fifth Month 27th.—During the past few days I have been a quiet listener to the proceedings of the yearly meeting. I was instructed by remembering that the nautilus spreads his sail when the sea is calm and untroubled, but when winds and storms arise, he draws in his sail, takes in ballast, and sinks into deep water. May I also so sink into the ocean of Divine love when trials and storms arise.

28th, First Day.—In the family reading this morning words to the following import were expressed in prayer by Mary S. Lloyd: "Seeing Thou hast promised to grant the prayer of faith, we venture to ask that our joy may be full. Be pleased, therefore, to grant unto the heads of this family Thy wisdom, which is profitable to direct, so that they may occupy with Thy talents and gifts to their own increase in wisdom, and their own enlargement. And seeing that Thou hast granted unto us the spirit of supplication, we would entreat Thee, on behalf of a dear brother, bound by the ties of the gospel to serve in a foreign land; grant that his feet may be directed in Thy paths, and that the angel of Thy presence may encompass him about."

Sixth Month 2nd.—The yearly meeting closed this day. Most of the sittings have been to me seasons of favour. The pause at the close was accompanied with such a sweet sense of spiritual communion with the Father of lights as I have rarely experienced. My mind has often been closely exercised, but in dwelling under it, I have found that expression has been given verbatim to my feelings by Friends of deeper experience.

London, 17th.—Attended Gracechurch Street meeting on Fourth-day. Was silent there, and sweetly refreshed by the language poured into my soul: "Who His own self bare our sins in His own body on the tree, that we being dead to sins should live unto righteousness." William Forster addressed us, to my comfort. I felt as though I could have wished that all who passed by in Lombard Street could have heard it.

18th.—This evening a large meeting of young Friends was held at Devonshire House. Never did I feel greater inability of myself to preach the gospel, than when I rose with the words, "If any man think that he knoweth anything, he knoweth nothing yet as he ought to know." For the help afforded I desire to give thanks.

Falmouth, 26th.—Went with dear Jenepher to Penzance, and yesterday attended the funeral of William Dymond, at Marazion. On our return we were informed of the serious illness of John Hodgkin. I feel that this sickness is not unto death, but for the glory of God.

30th.—Whilst dressing this morning my heart was sweetly turned towards the God of my life; and His Spirit brought to my remembrance the many mercies which He has granted me, and the belief was given that all that has happened to me, according to the will of God, is really for my good, though I may not at all times be sensible of it.

Seventh Month 1st.—My heart is often clothed with gratitude for the prolongation of the life of John Hodgkin. May I pray for his preservation, and that the residue of his days may be given up to his Lord, whom he has already served to the blessing of others.

Spiceland, 16th.—William Fry, in meeting to-day, said

the desire of his heart for the friend on his right, just about to go to distant lands, was, that the Lord may go with him, be around and about him, and bring him back again to his friends in peace. My heart was before satisfied with favour and full with the blessing of the Lord, so that it then overflowed, and the language passed through my mind, "Thou anointest my head with oil; my cup runneth over."

Falmouth, Eighth Month 19th.—At the monthly meeting on Fourth-day cousin Maria Fox and I were liberated to hold some meetings in the neighbourhood of Falmouth. This service was commenced yesterday at Mylor Bridge. For the people residing there I have felt a lively interest since I passed through this place so repeatedly in my visits to Restronguet about the *Beresford* steamer. The attendance was large, and the meeting very comforting to my mind. Cousin Maria spoke of the praise that was due for the rich harvest.

20th.—This evening I attended a meeting at Budock with Maria Fox and James Jesup. The former spoke on partaking of the living bread, and on following Christ the Good Shepherd; also on silent worship. James Jesup spoke on obedience to the manifested will of God. I arose with the words, "I will bless the Lord, who hath given me counsel."

23rd.—Went to Glendurgan yesterday, where Maria Fox, James Jesup, and I had a meeting in the chapel to my comfort. M. Fox alluded to the perils of the deep, and the importance of preparation for the uncertain call to stand before the Judge of quick and dead.

Ninth Month 5th.—On First-day we had a meeting at Coverack in the Independent Chapel, and a precious season it proved: the house was crowded. The company were invited to another meeting in the Wesleyan Chapel in the evening. This house was larger, and still more crowded. Again gospel truth was communicated freely and effectually by my dear cousin Maria Fox.

Yesterday we went to Mawnan; where the gospel was freely preached to my comfort. Lodged at Trebah, and walked home.

Plymouth, 10*th*.—Whilst dwelling under a sense of the things that hinder my way, I have been ready to say, "All these things are against me," just as W. Batkin, the poor soldier whom I saw at William Matthews', might have said, when he had to wait eighteen days in suspense, in the East Indies for the signature of his commanding officer for his discharge. The *Conqueror* sailed without him, and he had to wait for another vessel, in which he safely reached England; but the *Conqueror* was lost, and nearly all on board drowned. How does this teach, "Commit thy way unto the Lord."

St. Austell, 12*th*.—The meeting of ministers and elders was one of refreshment. Just at its close John Allen called the attention of Friends to the probability that one of our number would soon be departing from our shores. He expressed a hope that my speech and my preaching might not be in the wisdom of men, to gratify itching ears, but in the demonstration of the Spirit and of power. Joel Lean said he hoped that my eye would be singly kept to the object before me. He instanced the example of Daniel Wheeler in this respect. Cousin Maria Fox said, "If Thy presence go not with me, carry us not up hence;" she believed the Lord would appear to me as He did to Moses. Alfred Jenkin revived the language, "He led him about, He instructed him, He kept him as the apple of His eye." Philippa Williams said, It was only as little children we could know the Lord's will, adding, "I thank thee, O Father, Lord of heaven and earth, because Thou hast hid these things from the wise and prudent, and hast revealed them unto babes. Even so, Father, for so it seemed good in Thy sight." Aunt Fox desired I might be kept dependent on the Lord day by day. John Foster knelt in prayer for my preservation, and that the Lord would be pleased to bless the labour which He might assign for me, and bring me home in peace, if consistent with His will. Thus ended a blessed and memorable meeting; at the close of which dear Samuel Rundell waited for me in the cloak-room, and expressed a hope that I should mind the putting forth of the great Shepherd; that our principles are different from those professed by any other people.

In addition to the spoken words of cheer, he received the following letter from his kind friend Hannah C. Backhouse:—

Wednesbury, Ninth Month 22nd, 1843.

MY DEAR FRIEND,—

I must send thee a salutation of love before thou leavest our shores. I know something of the vastly mingled sensations that are the portion of those who leave everything they hold dearest on earth, to follow their Lord in the obedience of faith, and the sweetness of the enjoyment of His presence, even when we are undergoing feelings heart-rending to nature.

I believe that thou will be favoured with the sense of its being full time to go, and that peace will go with thee, and that in taking leave of thy beloved wife and children, and sisters, thou wilt be able to commend them to the care and keeping of the unslumbering Shepherd of Israel, and feel as if thou couldest now, for a time, do no more for them.

I do crave thy preservation and prosperity; and by dwelling close to the Lord, thou wilt probably be much enlarged in thy gift, and preach with more authority than thou ever hast known before. Thy heart, too, will in all probability be greatly enlarged in love, and find at times that this love is an ocean to swim in. I know also thou wilt have thy deep baptisms, thy heart enlarged both to suffer, as well as to enjoy. Oh, mayest thou be preserved both in heights and in depths. Keep thy heart with all diligence. Be not allured by pleasant things or pleasant people. Seek only to fulfil thy calling, and return unspotted of the world; then indeed I believe it will be a peace that passeth understanding again to resume thy place amongst thy family and friends, with renewed vigour to fulfil and enjoy all the relationships of life. . . .

We are now at the truly kind and hospitable house of Samuel and Mary Lloyd, and expect to be engaged in holding meetings for about ten days longer in Staffordshire. Thy cousin Junia Price is with me. I was much interested in hearing of thine and my cousin Maria Fox's meetings in your neighbourhood; an engagement apparently very seasonable and agreeable, affording thee a very pleasant opportunity of being with thy friends, and also an illustration that "His ways are ways of pleasantness;" that, by a patient submission to all His dispensations, thou mayest continue to find them so to the end of thy pilgrimage, is the fervent desire of thy very affectionate friend,

H. C. BACKHOUSE.

Falmouth, 17th.—Yesterday my brother Nathaniel arrived to stay with us until I leave these shores. To have his company is truly pleasant. Cousin Maria Fox and I attended a meeting at Constantine to-day, which was a large one.

28th.—The important day has arrived, when I must bid farewell to my dear family and home pleasures, to pursue the path of duty in the West Indies, in accordance with the language often heard in my heart, "Ye are not your own, ye are bought with a price."

Last evening, when greatly humbled, I bent my knees at the bedside of my dear boy, and silently renewed my covenant of allegiance with Him who is almighty to save, to guide, guard, redeem, and glorify. And then it was given me to see and to feel that in the condition of a simple child I should be safe.

Lord, bless and sanctify and redeem my precious wife and children. Guide them by Thy counsel, and afterwards receive them to glory. And if I see them no more, enable them and me in Thy mercy and goodness to say, "Thy will be done."

CHAPTER IX.

WEST INDIES.

Departure for West Indies—Voyage and Fellow-Passengers—Meetings with Passengers and Crew—Barbadoes—First Impressions of Coloured People—Letter to his Children—Large Meeting in Wesleyan Chapel—Visits Prison at Bridgetown—Moravian Missions at Mount Tabor and Sharon—Byde Mill—Meeting with Upper Class at Bridgetown—Tobago—Pelicans—J. Renkevitz—Progress of Freed Negroes—James Bickford—Wesleyan Missions—Scarborough—Grenada—Call on Governor—Bad Roads—Extinct Volcano—Intercourse with Planters—Meeting in Court House at Mount Alexander—Meeting at George Town—Trinidad—J. M. Phillippo—Port Espano—Yellow Fever at Petit Bourg—Josiah Brown—Convalescence—Dr. Philip—Letters from Josiah Forster—Grenada—Conference of Wesleyan Ministers.

SOUTHAMPTON, *Tenth Month* 1st, 1843, *First Day.*—Whilst James Jesup, and Nathaniel and I were at breakfast, Robert Forster and John Candler arrived, and we read together 2 Peter ii., after which we went to Southampton meeting, where ability was given to James Jesup, John Candler and me to hand to others of the things that pertain to godliness and everlasting life.

2nd.—Samuel Gurney and J. H. Glaisher accompanied us on board the *Forth*, steamer, Robert Forster, John Candler,[1] Peter Bedford and George Stacey having preceded

---

[1] John Candler, writing to his wife, says, "At noon we proceeded to the steamer, which lay at anchor a short way down the river. E. O. Tregelles was in tears as he gave the last shake of the hand. He told me that he felt as calm as if he were going to his own home at Falmouth, and thanked us all for handing him more than 'a cup of cold water.' Samuel Gurney said to me and Peter Bedford, as we returned by train, 'I am only sorry I did not bring down my dear sister Bessie (Elizabeth Fry); she would have enjoyed it.'"

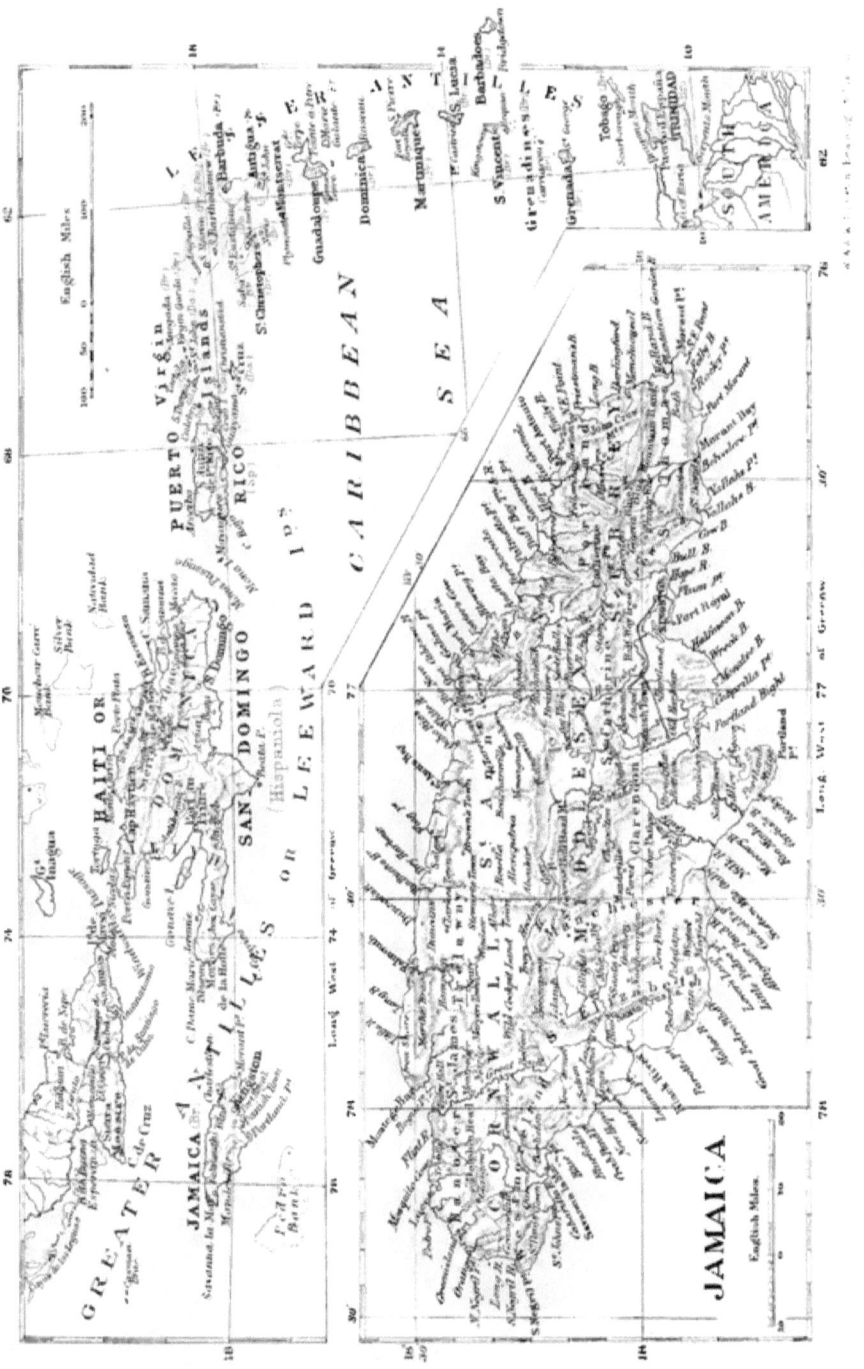

us. After remaining a short half-hour, they left us for the shore.

4th.—Have had much satisfaction in my association with some of my fellow-passengers. James R. Douglas, a young man from Edinburgh, going to the island of St. Vincent, interests me deeply. He goes to become a planter. He seems to be preciously visited, and if he keeps his place, he will, I believe, be a blessing to many.

With the permission of the captain, a chapter in the Bible was read after tea. Captain Chapman assembled the company in the saloon, and I read Romans viii., after which I felt constrained to speak on the language, "If God be for us, who can be against us?" I felt much openness to address the varied group around us, consisting of some from Scotland, England, Germany, France, Hayti, Chili, Columbia, Mexico, and various islands in the Antilles.

14th.—Mentioned to Captain Chapman our wish to have a meeting to-morrow morning with the passengers and ship's company, to which he consented.

15th, First Day.—James Jesup and I sat down in his cabin for our time of worship together soon after ten o'clock; and after the captain had read prayers to the crew, we went on deck, and found a large company seated in a most orderly manner on the quarter deck. After a short time of silence I made allusion to the importance of knowing a spiritual waiting on the Lord, in seasons of worship, consonant with the words, "Search me, O God, and know my heart; try me, and know my thoughts; and see if there be any wicked way in me, and lead me in the way everlasting." A precious covering was felt, and manifestly the power of the Lord was over all. Not a sound was to be heard but the flapping of the sail as the vessel rolled in the swell of the ocean, or the rushing of the water by the paddle-wheels. J. Jesup soon followed, commenting on the way everlasting, and on the merciful Guide who is given to all in that path. After which I spoke on the words,

"Eye hath not seen, nor ear heard, neither have entered into the heart of man, the things which God hath prepared for them that love Him. But God hath revealed them unto us by His Spirit." Many of the sailors were present, and I felt much drawn out towards them. There are few persons for whom, as a body, I feel more interested. Much peace was our portion when we retired to my cabin.

19*th.*—My birthday. Cheered this morning by the perusal of a note addressed to me by my dear sister Elizabeth, which was not to be read till to-day. It is a happy thing for me that I have such sisters.

Much of what follows of the account of Edwin O. Tregelles' visit to the West Indies is extracted from his letters as well as from his journal.

Barbadoes, Tenth Month 22nd, First Day.—James Jesup and I withdrew to his cabin after breakfast, where we sat together to the refreshment of our spirits. It was permitted to me to rejoice that I had not excused myself when I heard the call to this service, but that the answer of my heart was, "Here am I, send me." The peace which has this day been my portion is worth enduring all the trials and perils of crossing the deep to enjoy.

James Jesup went on deck to distribute the tracts we had selected for the stewards, the enginemen, and the seamen. He soon came to inform me that land was in sight; but I felt so happy where I was, selecting books for my fellow passengers, that he could not induce me to quit my occupation.

When I went on deck we were within ten miles of the island of Barbadoes, and truly pleasant it was to gaze on the pale green cane fields, and on the white villas scattered numerously over the country, like the Isle of Wight. The land is low, and in regular gentle undulations. At three o'clock we dropped anchor in the bay a short mile from the quay. We landed in a boat at some wooden stairs, and there we found a small cart ready to take our luggage. I let our black boatmen and porters have their own way, that I might judge of their capacity: and certainly this example proved to me that Cowper was right when he said, in his poem entitled "The Negro's Complaint":—

> "Deem our nation brutes no longer,
> Till some reason ye shall find,
> Worthier of regard and stronger
> Than the colour of our kind."

One of the men took the shafts, and another pushed by his side. Our head boatman did not put his hand to help his brothers till I set him the example, to show him that I was not above lending a hand to my black brethren.

Very soon after our arrival we had a call from John Daughtry, a special justice of the peace of Kingston, Jamaica, well known to Peter Bedford. He heard that two Friends had arrived, and immediately called to give us the right hand of fellowship. He is an inspector of prisons. We drove with him to the house of Sir Charles Grey, the Governor, who received us kindly. I presented my certificate.

LETTER FROM E. O. T. TO HIS CHILDREN.

Bridgetown, Barbadoes,
Tenth Month 25th, 1843.

MY DARLING CHILDREN,—

. . . James Jesup and I are now lodging at the house of Thomas Harris. On going to my chamber I was followed by a little black boy carrying my luggage. I said to him, "How old art thou?" "I can't tell." His master tells me he is eight years old. Finding that he could not read, I gave him a lesson on a piece of paper, making several letters of the alphabet. This morning he awoke me soon after six o'clock, bringing a cup of coffee. I read to him part of the first chapter of Genesis. He could not tell me who made the world, or who was the first man. This little John lays the table and waits most expertly.

Mount Tabor, Eleventh Month 1st.—Since the first part of my letter we have been at several places. I will endeavour to describe some of the objects which have particularly attracted my attention.

Throughout the southern and eastern parts of Barbadoes we have seen very few hedges; the grounds of sugar cane, millet, or Indian corn are therefore open to the roads, but clothed with green of a beautiful bright colour, where the canes are young and growing.

I cannot attempt to describe the trees and plants that abound here. Our choice hot-house exotics grow as common weeds. The manioc, from which tapioca is obtained, is a beautiful weed, with a rich assemblage of leaves, somewhat like a fine lupin, with a deep lilac or puce stem; the flower is bell shaped, of pale sulphur, with a rich eye. The ipecacuanha grows as a weed, somewhat like mint, with a rich cluster of small yellow and orange flowers, about fifteen inches high. Water-lilies also grow wild.

In consequence of the absence of hedges, almost all the cattle, sheep, goats, pigs and fowls are tethered. The cattle are very small; full-grown cows are the size of our yearlings. I have seen several teams of oxen of this size yoked to carts.

All the carriages are light and flimsy, with high wheels, and, as we should say, crazy in consequence of the hot weather shrinking the wood. They are mostly phaetons, the hinder seat having a head, with an opening behind, to allow of a current of air.

The horses are nearly all imported from America, and are of a light elegant make with long tails. The sheep, goats, dogs and cats are similar to ours, only very thin.

The birds are numerous, turkeys, guinea-fowls, ducks and fowls and pigeons are plentiful. A black bird abounds in great numbers, much like the starling, and I am inclined to think it is the starling. This bird is regarded as sacred by the peasantry. The dove is about the size of our thrush. It cooes very pleasantly, seated amongst the feathery crest that surmounts the bare stalk of the cocoa-nut trees, which are sixty feet high.

Yesterday I saw a beautiful bird amongst the sugar-canes, like our tom-tit, with black back and bright yellow breast, with a patch of white over each eye. But the bird of all birds that I have seen is the humming-bird. Whilst looking at some beautiful flowering shrubs, I saw a dark purple bird hovering over the flower of the guava, and immediately recognised it as the humming-bird. It was rather large, three or four inches from bill to tip of tail. The flying fish and this humming-bird interested me more than any other objects of the kind I have seen. The humming-birds plague the starling and similar birds. They fly faster, and are quicker in their movements, and prick the bigger birds, so as quite to torment them.

Land crabs abound, of different sizes and colours: when near the sea-shore they are nearly white, like the coral sand; when they dwell inland, they are more the colour of dead leaves, amongst which they scramble in a ludicrous manner.

The peasantry who work in the cane-fields dress very peculiarly. The men wear slouched straw hats, and often have the head bound round with a handkerchief; their dress is a blue check shirt and blue striped trousers, mostly no stockings or shoes.

The women also often wear large straw hats over the kerchiefs which bind their heads, a neat gown of printed cotton of large pattern, lilac, pink or blue, rather short; a printed cotton handkerchief over the shoulders, and a striped apron. In this attire they work in gangs of twelve or fifteen women in the fields, both men and women using hoes very dexterously.

In one walk we took, the road was lined on each side

with beautiful flowering shrubs and fruit trees; the banana or plantain and lemon; the wild coffee looking a little like finely grown privet, with a delicate-looking flower like the jessamine, only much larger and deliciously scented. The most striking flowering shrub is that called " the pride of Barbadoes," growing a little like the mountain ash, bearing a profusion of rich orange-coloured flowers. The delicate mimosa, which grows so well in our staircase window, here forms hedges by the road side. The cactus also, with its formidable prickles, is the most common effective fence. E. O. T.

* * * * *

Walmar Lodge, Tenth Month, 27th.—Having received a kind invitation from Thomas P. Robarts and his wife, we arranged to come to their house, Walmar Lodge.

A ride this morning on one of his horses has benefited me. I started at six, and rode along the coast towards Speights Town. The coast is very low, and landing is easily effected. Our ancestors deemed it important to defend themselves by erecting small batteries at intervals. One of these I passed, where the cannon lie half buried. I hope the day will come when all cannon will be not only half buried, or sold for melting, but the hatred which causes their construction be exchanged for the love that thinketh no evil.

We enjoy being here. The house is very comfortable, in the midst of pretty grounds reaching to the sea, distant about two hundred yards. The grounds contain a great variety of trees—mahogany, cocoa-nut, bread-fruit and banana.

The house is surrounded by a deep verandah, the rooms spacious and airy, no windows in the first floor; but the drawing-room in which I write has six large doors, three opening into the entrance hall or into a passage, and three into the deep verandah. It is about twenty-two feet long, fifteen feet wide and ten feet high, with a capital red pine floor without carpet; a sofa table at which I write occupies the centre; near it is a mahogany couch, covered with printed cotton, and chairs with cane seats. A bracket clock stands on one of the several tables against the walls, which are papered. I should have said that the doors have all of them jalousies or venetian blinds instead of glass, and every opening has shutters to be closed when hurricanes blow. I have attempted a description of this house, that some idea may be formed of the usual style; they vary very little.

Yesterday after breakfast we went to see some of the Bridgetown schools.

On retiring to my chambers last evening I was surprised to see on the dressing-table a copy of Josiah Forster's edition of "Piety Promoted." On opening it, the first name my eye rested on was Joseph Tregelles. The records of my dear brothers and sisters which it contains are deeply interesting, and stimulating to me to work while it is day.

On the 28th T. P. Robarts drove us in his carriage from Walmar Lodge to Locust Hall in the centre of the island. Whilst the horses rested we were conducted over the sugar manufactory by the manager. Every estate has a windmill, the sails of which are taken down when not wanted, and they are only wanted in crop time.

Going on from thence we went to Malvern to breakfast with Josiah Heath, an intelligent planter and magistrate. His garden abounds with beautiful shrubs and many English plants and flowers.

On leaving Mount Tabor, J. Heath and T. P. Robarts took us to the edge of a cliff of great elevation above the plain, over which we had an extraordinary view, much like the Undercliffe in the Isle of Wight, but chiefly interesting to us from the number of scattered cottages occupied by the descendants of English people, who have sunk low in the scale of society, but who keep themselves remarkably distinct.

29th, *First Day.*—In the prospect of service now opening

before us, my soul craves that we may seek only to know the will of the Lord, and to move in His fear, doing heartily whatsoever our hands may find to do, as in His name, not easily dismayed because of the dangers that may beset our path; but keeping our eye fixed on the Captain of our salvation, confide in the assurance that we shall be made more than conquerors through Him that hath loved us.

In the evening a meeting was held by our appointment in the Wesleyan Chapel; J. Fidler, the minister, having kindly consented to give up their usual service. The house, which was large, was crowded, probably 1,700 being present. After a short time of silence, the language was brought before me, "Wherewith shall I come before the Lord? . . . He hath showed thee, O man, what is good; and what doth the Lord require of thee, but to do justly, and to love mercy, and to walk humbly with thy God?" It arose freshly, and with that sense which is better understood than described, that it was required of me to give expression to it. With these words I stood up, and alluded briefly to silent worship, expecting soon to take my seat, but was led on to speak of other points of Christian doctrine. Jesus Christ was pointed to as the Refuge for the sinner, for the traveller Zionward, and for the experienced Christian. James Jesup followed with "Other sheep I have, which are not of this fold; them also I must bring, and they shall hear My voice; and there shall be one fold and one Shepherd;" after which I offered prayer.

30*th*.—We went to Bridgetown to visit the gaol, having an order from the Governor. We found 210 prisoners, much needing classification. The chief causes for imprisonment are debt, petty thefts, and breaking of the peace.

At seven we had a large meeting at the Moravian Chapel, about 500 present, to whom the gospel flowed freely, and, I am comforted in believing, to some effectually. Allusion was made to the qualification some of them would experience, if they would give up their hearts to the Lord, to become His ministers; when they would probably be commissioned to carry the glad tidings of the gospel to the land from whence their fathers and their mothers were stolen, and to declare the unsearchable riches of Christ to those who are now in darkness.

31st.—We came to the Moravian settlement at Mount Tabor in Thomas Harris's phaeton, a drive of about twelve miles in a north-easterly direction. We met with a cordial welcome from J. G. Zippel and wife, and lost little time in repairing to the school. After hearing some of the boys read, and examining their writing, I produced the map of Barbadoes for them to try and copy, and truly was I surprised at the map one of the boys drew on a slate. Two have produced very fair copies on paper, which I hope to forward my cousin Charles Fox, at whose suggestion I took these maps. The boys were well pleased with the gift of a penknife each, added to the little map which they had copied. In the evening the large Moravian Chapel was quite filled, and a comfortable meeting it proved.

Eleventh Month 2nd.—A young man, Alexander Rous, from Clifton Hall, called on us. He had attended the meeting here, and being interested by it, he came to inquire if there was to be another. His countenance bespoke deep seriousness, and in conversation we learnt that he feels earnest to be employed as a teacher in Africa. I doubt his being altogether suitable, having feeble health. We encouraged him to give his heart up to the Lord in the matter, and then he might help others to go if he could not go himself.

We had a season of spiritual refreshment with J. G. Zippel and wife, when I read a Psalm, and he addressed us sweetly in the language of blessing. We left Mount Tabor with the reward of peace.

4th.—We went to Sharon, another Moravian station, nine miles distant, where lives the bishop, John Ellis. For a description of him I would refer to 1 Timothy iii., except that he, poor man, is a widower, and is in expectation of soon receiving a bride elect from England, in accordance with the express will of his Church. We dined with the bishop in beautiful simplicity on roast mutton and potatoes, and boiled rice pudding, waited on by a black girl.

The meeting in the evening was large, and I have rarely known more of a solemn sense of the object of our gathering in such a company, to whom silent waiting is a novelty. We returned by the light of a lovely moon. Our driver, black John, is a nice serious man, who comes to all our meetings that he can, and gets the carriage immediately after.

7th.—We went by invitation to dine at White River, the estate of Matthew W. Cromartie, the manager of the Colonial Bank. We visited a school of thirty-five boys and girls, kept on the estate by an intelligent young black woman, whose talents are far beyond what are usually found in the class of labourers from whence she sprung. She teaches the children advanced lessons in arithmetic, and they read remarkably well.

We felt disposed to have a meeting with Matthew W. Cromartie's negroes, and those of the adjoining estates, for which he was kindly willing to arrange. It was held at Byde Mill, another of his estates. We found the sugar-boiling house densely crowded with 700 persons, chiefly negroes. I felt it right to speak of the great uncertainty of time. "Thou art weighed in the balances, and found wanting." Christ was pointed out as the sinner's Friend. Prayer was offered for a blessing on all, but especially on the master and his household. It was a closely uniting season.

We inspected one of the old burying-grounds belonging to Friends, which is about fifty yards north of St. Philip's churchyard. From thence we went to Providence Chapel, where the Wesleyans have a station. The meeting was crowded. Our coming together was blessed by Christ, the great Head of His Church. W. Perkins, manager of Byde

Mill estate, rode eight miles to attend this meeting. He seems to be seeking durable riches.

10*th*.—We were much interested by the Wesleyan school at Speight's Town. The children are taught by Francis Church, once a soldier, now a local preacher. The master said to the children, "Well, now, perhaps whilst we are gone, you will put down on your slates what you would like to say to those kind gentleman." On our return in ten minutes, we found eleven boys and girls had written nice letters to us.

Francis Church told me that one of the Testaments, presented on the emancipation of the slaves in 1834, was blessed to a whole family in consequence of a child learning to read in it. On taking it home, all the family became earnest to know its contents, and, knowing them, to lead different lives.

A meeting was held, attended by 300 persons, and was not so much to my comfort as some others, there being much unsettlement, and a drum beaten at an adjoining house to disturb us.

Philip T. Goodridge and his sisters kindly lodged us at their house. They are people of colour, intelligent and serious. As we sat together in their drawing-room before retiring to rest, he proposed we should read a Psalm; and then prayer was offered on their and our behalf, that the Lord would be pleased to lift up the light of His countenance, and grant us peace; that we all might be followers of the Lamb, and be engaged to dedicate ourselves more fully to the service of the Lord.

11*th*.—After breakfasting with F. Church, I felt bound to see an aged man who attracted my attention at the meeting. We called on him at a small huckster's shop kept by his daughter, a mulatto. He received us kindly, and avowed the enormity of his sin. He stated his intention to make atonement for his sins by leading a very different life. After listening to him for some time I endeavoured to set before him that nothing that he could do would atone for past transgression. The sacrifice of Christ was the atonement for past sins, through the obedience of faith. If in future he would receive Him as his Redeemer from sin by obeying His laws, he would know Him to become the Author of his eternal salvation. His heart was contrited, and we wept together.

We left Speights Town with peaceful feelings for Scotland, and had a fatiguing journey, having to walk many miles, part of it in heavy rain that made the road very slippery.

Parade House, 13th.—Our meeting yesterday morning at Scotland was numerously attended. I felt thankful that I yielded to apprehended duty, again to encounter the hills and roads to meet with that interesting people, to whom the gospel flowed freely, so as to cause some to acknowledge it was good for them to be there. I saw the moistened cheek of some who appeared obdurate when they first sat down. To the Lord be ascribed all the praise.

Scotland is a beautiful district. The Mission House stands on the north side of Mount Hellaby. We ascended this hill, which is 1,147 feet above the level of the sea, and from its summit we had views of the sea on all sides, except where obstructed by a hill four miles distant.

Bridgetown, 15th.—We went to the gaol at eight o'clock by appointment, and had to wait nearly an hour, whilst the chaplain, who was late, was performing his service. As he objected to our using the chapel, the prisoners were assembled in the hall, all standing. We sat on the stairs. Freely did the language of sympathy flow towards the poor victims of iniquity, many of whom were much broken in spirit, and were, I believe, glad to receive the message, " This is a faithful saying, and worthy of all acceptation, that Jesus Christ came into the world to save sinners."

21st.—On the 18th we had a breakfast visit from W. Fidler and E. Branstone, Wesleyan ministers; James

Titherington, Moravian minister; Joseph Hamilton, a black local Wesleyan preacher; Joseph Thorne, a serious Episcopalian; Charles Ellis, son of Bishop Ellis, and Edgehill, a promising young man. W. Fidler was engaged in prayer, and I felt bound to remind my friends that One is their Master, even Christ, and all they are brethren. We had much conversation, chiefly on the past and present condition of the peasantry. The remarks of our friends confirm the impressions made on our own minds by what we had heard and seen, that their present condition far exceeds the past: both masters and men are benefited by the change; and if a word would revoke the law setting free the slave, that word would not be heard from any except a few subordinate overseers, who lost their influence over their fellows when the whip was taken from their hands.

On First-day we breakfasted with M. W. Cromartie at White Water. He and his family accompanied us to Byde Mill, where a meeting had been appointed in his mansion. Three or four lower rooms were crowded, and many seated at the doors and windows and on the stairs. The people brought their chairs and stools on their heads. We had a nice meeting with them in the morning, and again in the afternoon—James Jesup having much to communicate. A sense of Divine favour prevailed. Very interesting was it to watch the crowd, as they moved away in large companies by different paths through the trees that surround the house. Many had come several miles.

Yesterday we took measures to have a meeting with the more affluent class, and 500 notes of invitation were printed and freely circulated. A large company assembled in the Wesleyan Chapel, where we had held our first meeting; and a comforting time it proved, though attended with a deeply humbling sense of weakness. If there was any strength it was the effect of His aid who "giveth power to the faint; and to them that have no might He increaseth strength."

It was pleasant after the meeting to recognise our friend

Peter Milne, Provost Marshall, and some others of his class. We now feel at liberty to leave this island, and expect to go to Tobago to-day.

Before we left Bridgetown I felt very low, and desirous of again proving the fleece (Judg. vi. 29), to see if it were right to depart. Under this exercise of spirit I withdrew twice to my chamber to seek the Lord in retirement of spirit. Peace was my portion each time, but it flowed like a river at the last, when the whole of our intended route through these islands seemed illumined by a ray of Divine approval; and under this I felt more than a liberty to move forward.

Tobago, Eleventh Month 25th.—Whilst dressing yesterday on board the *Medway*, to my surprise I saw the verdant mountains and valleys of Tobago. At ten o'clock we landed in Courland Bay. Our boat passed within two yards of a turtle that was floating on the water, but it soon disappeared. On approaching the shore we observed a number of large birds. They appeared like herons, but we soon discovered that they were pelicans. They plunged nearly vertically about fifteen feet for fish, and made sure work of every plunge. No sooner were they fairly up again after a great splash, than they were surrounded by five or six gulls, which seemed to grudge the noble bird the prey that he had procured. A gull would often perch on the back of the pelican.

Tobago reminded me, as we approached it, of the scenery of Killarney, the hills green to the water's edge, and the ground thrown about fantastically, as it always is in volcanic districts. We had to land on the backs of the sailors through the surf which broke on the sand.

On our way to Montgomery, mounted on a horse and a mule, we met two horses sent for us by our friend Julius Renkewitz, under care of Charles, a trusty negro of fine character.

J. Renkewitz, the minister of the Moravian establishment,

and his wife seemed glad to entertain us with their spare chamber and simple accommodation. Our bed has for its foundation four forms from the chapel. It is well for me that I was "brought up hardy."

Montgomery is a mission station of the Moravians, named after the father of the poet. The situation is beautiful, being on one of the thousand hills of which this lovely island is composed.

Julius Renkewitz is a pleasant and intelligent person. His wife was born in Greenland. She has two sisters, one the wife of Lars Kieldson, of Sharon, Barbadoes. They once met for an hour on shipboard a few years ago, when, on their way from Jamaica, they stopped off Barbadoes. Does not this look like renouncing the world? The other sister she has never seen. This renouncing our sisters would not suit me!

J. Renkewitz and I are very good friends. As soon as I entered the house, my appearance reminded him of a "Brother Zoon," of whom he was very fond, who died this year in Jamaica. After a few days' acquaintance, J. R. handed me his birthday book for me to write my name; and strange to say, my name came immediately under that of his dear "Zoon," who was born exactly ten years before me.

So far as we have been able to form a judgment, we should say that this island is far behind Barbadoes. The peasantry are not so well clothed or instructed. They speak English less distinctly, and their cottages are of a very inferior description. The land is much richer than Barbadoes, but only a small portion is cultivated. Instead of manuring highly, as in Barbadoes, they change their cane ground every three years, and the land remains idle, and soon it becomes a tangled brake of luxuriant exotics. The growth of vegetation is very rapid, the result of intense heat, with a rich soil and moist climate. But what promotes vegetation is prejudicial to European life; the usual number of deaths of white men is one in six. There are only 208 whites by the last census. The total population is about 11,000, as against 100,000 in Barbadoes.

The question having reached me from home, What do we think of the coloured folk with whom we associate? I may premise my answer by saying that I feel well satisfied in having made the sacrifice to come amongst them, great and costly as that sacrifice indeed is. From the little I have seen of the negroes, I regard them as still in a transition state; but they are making great strides in civilization, and I trust steady progress in Christianity. How important it is that new populations and new districts should have a right direction given to their energies. An early right training greatly facilitates the progress of truth. Hence I feel earnest that these people, who are easily trained, should be rightly instructed in the things that belong to their own everlasting peace, and the welfare of future generations.

Some persons, who have ample means of coming to a correct conclusion, are of opinion that the negro is not capable of the high education that may be given to the descendants of Shem; that the minds of the black children cannot grasp abstruse subjects. For my own part, I consider it too much to expect that the son of a slave should have that high degree of intelligence which would be found in the child of a professor of one of our universities. But let education be duly applied to successive generations, and the distinction will become less and less marked.

Some of the men are delightfully intelligent, especially those who have allowed their hearts to be opened to receive the truth. I do enjoy talking with them, and observing the brightness that passes over their faces when anything particularly pleases them.

These remarks chiefly apply to the labouring class. Those who are more educated, with whom we have associated, are able to discuss various matters as well as their white brethren. Probably their minds are not as well balanced as those of the same class in England; more impulsive and rash, but very interesting.

Mount Moriah, 30th.—The meeting here was worth going a long way to attend. We retired to rest with thankful hearts, after a season of prayer in the family of J. G. Munzer, the Moravian minister, on behalf of those whose hearts had been touched in the meeting.

Montgomery, Twelfth Month 1st.—We went yesterday to Scarborough, and dined with James Bickford and wife, at the Wesleyan Station. They came from Kingsbridge, Devon.

Whilst visiting the gaol we saw the tread-mill standing idle, and another was lying in the yard in parts, not put together. It had been procured from England that they might be prepared to punish the negroes, in case they became more vicious after they were set free. At the same time they erected two new prisons. Both are now unused, I am glad to say.

We walked out on the sands of the lovely bay of Plymouth, and enjoyed seeing the noble pelicans plunging for their food. Sweet was the sense of Divine favour spread over me as a canopy, bringing to my remembrance the language, "The Lord shall preserve thy going out and thy coming in"; and, again, "There shall no evil befall thee." Such support is unspeakably precious in this land, which seems beset with dangers, where the mind looks tremblingly towards those distantly absent, whom we may at times be led to believe we shall never meet again.

5th.—Yesterday morning several persons called, so as greatly to hinder our preparations for departure, but I trust we were even then in our right allotment, though it was trying to our patience.

In the evening a negro from Mount Irvine called on us. His mind seems enlarged beyond many others to receive the truth as it is in Jesus, but his power of conveying his ideas is limited. His visit was just before the time of our evening meeting, and it felt to me very encouraging in the belief that the Lord is at work in the way of inward revelation of His power. The meeting was largely attended. A few overseers and managers were present. James Jesup alluded to the value of silence for self-examination and reverent worship. I spoke of the need of parting with all our sins, not keeping any vestige of them which would act as a leaven, and would cause a continuance of the warfare. It was a close searching time, in which I felt that the power of the Lord was reigning. Prayer was offered that those present, as well as others in this island, might know the fulfilment of the language, "There is therefore now no condemnation to them which are in Christ Jesus, who walk not after the flesh, but after the Spirit."

After meeting, two persons called on us with whom we had a deeply interesting conversation. They are far from yielding their hearts unreservedly to the Lord. One of them acknowledged himself to be a great sinner, of which there is no doubt. He was urged not to put off the day when he would seek the Lord. James Jesup spoke of the importance of total abstinence from intoxicating drinks. The result was that both signed a pledge before they left us at half past ten.

George Town, Grenada, 7th.—We were roused at midnight with the cry of the steamer being come. We left Courland Bay, Tobago, at twelve o'clock, by the light of a lovely moon, which we had watched with much interest when eclipsed four hours before.

9th.—I had to endure strong temptation as regards temper. I feel thankful for the supply of preserving and delivering grace.

We called to pay our respects to the Governor, Carlos Joseph Doyle, who received us courteously, and after reading my certificates, expressed his readiness to promote our object. Ministers are not allowed to preach without licenses.

We did not deem it needful to wait for this kind of license, but arranged for a meeting at the Wesleyan Chapel at Woburn.

10*th*.—We went to Woburn to-day, and had a meeting as arranged. Though but a small company, it was a good meeting. When allusion was made to the deliverance they had experienced from bondage, one negro, named Cuffee, ejaculated, "Praise the Lord!" Richard Walker, who is a coloured local preacher, told them it was no common occasion to have a visit from members of the Society of Friends, who had so nobly espoused their cause. He said the visit seemed like that of Paul and Barnabas, going into the dark corners of the earth with tidings of the unsearchable riches of Christ.

On our return we had our season of retirement together before the Lord, and found refreshment in waiting again upon Him. I felt impressed with the preciousness of the gift committed to our trust, and it was accompanied by a sense that we have the treasure in earthen vessels.

11*th*.—Carriages are not used here, any more than in Tobago, the roads are so bad. Our luggage is conveyed on the backs of mules. For my own part I enjoy horse-back exercise, and it suits me. The roads are sometimes soft spongy grass, stiff clay, marly slippery rock, or large round stones. It was surprising to see how my horse, when left with a loose rein, would pick out a path for himself.

We went to Constantine, where the Wesleyans have a school, where we had appointed a meeting at four o'clock. The room was nearly full, and I was glad to meet there with many of the agents of estates. It was a season of renewed favour when my heart felt drawn out largely and sweetly towards some of the young men who were present. I felt—

> "I'd preach as though I ne'er should preach again,
> Would preach as dying, unto dying men."

The school was under the care of Ishmael Mainwaring, a man of colour. We heard the children read in the New Testament. One of the little boys attracted my attention from his distorted form, his pleasing style of reading and calm, steady eye bespeaking peace and rest. His name is Celestine. A fall in infancy caused an injury to the spine. He is now twelve years old. He goes to read to those who from infirmity cannot read to themselves. Nor does he confine his efforts to reading only; he speaks to them also. I felt sure the boys of Falmouth British and Foreign School would wish one of their Testaments given to this dear child.

Near Constantine, about 1860 feet above the sea, is an extinct crater filled with water, called "Le Grand Etang." Accompanied by William Bannister, we went to see it. The ride was up a rugged road, cut in the sides of the steep slopes, overhung by climbers and trees of many kinds. We looked down into deep ravines, filled with luxuriant plantains, tree-ferns, and bamboos. From our road, some 2,000 feet above sea-level, we looked over conical and ridged hills between us and George Town, and from near the "Grand Etang" we saw Grenville Bay on the opposite side. The air was cool, as low as 64°. The hills and mountains are all green with luxuriant forest trees to their summits, like Surrey hills in their richest season. Nearly all this land would produce canes if the trees were cleared away. Only a portion of a fringe along the shore is in culture, with patches here and there in the interior under the care of settlers who have a "bit of their own."

George Town, 19th.—For our meeting at Goiave we had a cocoa loft. It was largely attended by the inhabitants of the town, as well as by the agents and labourers on estates.

On the 15th we went two miles to Mount Alexander to breakfast with W. McEwen, from Perth, a planter, magistrate, and member of the House of Assembly. He accompanied us to Sauteur, and introduced us to Henry

Patterson, in the same position as himself. They granted us the use of the Court House, and gave notice to the estates around by one of their constables.

We had a good meeting, I had looked to it with more than usual fearfulness, partly because our way had been made easy by those whom we had least cause to expect would facilitate our object, and partly because some of these are not such as those to whom we can offer the right hand of fellowship. Many of the leading class, and many labourers were present, so as to crowd the room.

After the meeting we met, at the house where we stayed, some of the wives of the planters. They were very cordial, and I am ready to doubt whether we ought not to have endeavoured to see them again before we left that district; but we intend sending them some books and tracts, which they said they should gladly read. Seldom have I met with any persons more earnest for deliverance from the thraldom entailed on them by the sins of others than they were. It is not all gold that glitters in this land, any more than other lands. The husbands lead some of the wives sorry lives. One of the planters was evidently a slave to intemperance. A brother planter said to him after the meeting, "Mr. ——, we must join the Temperance Society." To this the wife and mother joined their earnest heartfelt pleadings, so as really to call forth my sympathy.

On our way to Sauteur we deviated two hundred yards from our course to look at a precipice over which a remnant of the Caribs leaped to escape the sabres of the French when they were pursuing their cruel work of extirpation.

We passed Lake Antoine, which is the crater of a volcano, and is very deep. We had a beautiful view of the Grenadines in the distance, the ever interesting ocean, the aspiring sugar loaves of Grenada, covered to their summit with tropical trees, and the curved and verdant ridge which forms the basin for the peaceful lake. In the foreground are magnificent aloes in full bloom, throwing up their stems nearly thirty feet high. I was reminded frequently of Brecknockshire. There were the beacons, and the peaks, affording shelter to the negro insurgents of 1723, just as the Brecknockshire beacons did to Caractacus in his struggles for freedom; the rushing streams, the pasture slopes, and brakes of uncultivated ground, grazed by herds of horned cattle, mules, and sheep.

We spent the morning of the 17th quietly together at Grenville Town. In the midst of much to depress, it was a time of rejoicing and refreshment to our spirits. We had a small and unsatisfactory meeting there, though I may acknowledge that we felt glad to be found in our allotment, in giving up our wills, and enduring much discomfort.

It was with more than ordinary joy we turned our faces towards George Town on the 19th. We started early and reached the police station house, at the "Grand Etang," to breakfast. The seven miles of ascent occupied us two and a half hours. Such roads, boggy, rocky, slippery, stony, narrow, steep, undiscoverable except by the sagacity of our horses, our guide, a running footman, having given us the slip, and gone by a footpath.

On our arrival I could not refrain from asking James Jesup to give up a little time with me to waiting on the Lord, during which an Ebenezer was again raised, and an acknowledgment made, "Hitherto Thou, Lord, hast helped us."

We prepared printed notices of the meeting which we believed it right to appoint in the Wesleyan Chapel, George Town. It was largely attended. J. Jesup spoke of the importance of waiting on the Lord for spiritual help, refreshment, and strength. The subject on which I spoke was that of Elijah on Horeb (1 Kings xix. 12), when the still small voice instructed him; I went on to show the importance of paying regard to the teachings of the Lord as set forth in the description of the houses built on rock or sand (Matt. vii. 24-29). All classes were represented in the meeting, from the chief justice to the black labourer. A person who has a yard near the chapel caused some riotous people to collect, so as to create a great noise by way of diversion, but his scheme utterly failed; indeed, I think it contributed rather to the furtherance of the gospel.

On the 21st we met an interesting company of 150 labourers, who were assembled in a rum distillery at Caliving. This meeting may class amongst the best that we have attended. The silence was deep and impressive, and the company drank in the counsel given as those who thirst after the truth.

23rd.—We went to the gaol, where we found about thirty prisoners in a wretched place. I called alone on the Governor to take leave, and represented to him as strenuously as I could the bad condition of the gaol.

J. Miller, superintendent of the Normal School in Antigua, where youths prepare for missionary service, visited us. He sat with us in our little meeting on First-day. After a season of refreshment together, we all went to the prison, where we saw twelve of the thirty prisoners. The fifty-ninth chapter of Isaiah was read, and prayer was raised for those present, as well as for the absent inmates.

27th.—We left Grenada for Trinidad last evening. Our companion on the voyage was J. M. Philippo. From him and another planter we heard of Dr. Robert Kalley, who is in confinement in Madeira for disseminating doctrines at variance with the established religion. Peter, Paul, Silas and others suffered for the same reason about eighteen centuries ago. The authorities are desirous of Dr. Kalley leaving the gaol, as the magistrates were who incarcerated Paul, but he is unwilling to escape before his time. Many come to him daily for instruction, and in consequence he has a great opportunity of diffusing his views. He has distributed 16,000 tracts since he has been in prison.

28th.—I feel thankful for the way in which our work has been promoted, particularly by Arthur White, the colonial secretary.

Through the introduction of the Colonial Secretary Edwin O. Tregelles became acquainted with the Hon. Louis Philip, a retired medical gentleman, who resided at Corinth, one of his sugar estates, of which he had 900 acres.

Corinth, Trinidad, First Month 29th, 1844.—A considerable time has elapsed since I penned any memorandum, during which time I have had a serious fever.

We left Port Espano on the 29th of Twelfth Month, and reached Petit Bourg at 11 p.m. I had to lie on the floor at the Naparino Hotel, and on waking in the morning of the 30th I found I was very unwell, which proved to be yellow fever. We called in Dr. R. Johnson, who recommended that I should be moved to the house of Josiah Brown, where I was most kindly nursed, and well attended by Josiah and Martha Brown of the Wesleyan Mission House, and their American negro, Talbot Hayes. Besides the regular attendance of Dr. Johnson, I had very frequent visits from Dr. Louis Philip. Their skill and attention were blessed for my relief, though I passed through a time of much mental and bodily suffering. I was conveyed to Josiah Brown's, Twelfth Month 31st, in a hammock slung on a pole, and carried by two men. For ten days and nights I scarcely slept, except for a short time when overcome by weakness. I was in one constant chase after rest, which seemed to elude my pursuit.

On the 8th of First Month, 1844, I was so ill that James Jesup deemed it right gently to apprise me of my danger. I was strengthened to receive this information without much dismay, my mind having been kept, by the power of the

Lord, remarkably stayed on His will, which I found to be a precious anchor of the soul. For many days I felt that my recovery was very doubtful, and for one day I believed that I should soon stand unveiled in the presence of Him whom I have long loved. For the calm acquiescence in the Divine will which was then granted me I desire to be truly thankful.

I was most mercifully dealt with, so that whilst I live I feel bound to dedicate all I have to Him who has made bare His holy arm on my behalf. If He had not supported me I could not have held fast my confidence during the ten days and nights that I passed without sleep and food; but it pleased the Lord to restrain the fever.

I was able to write to my dear wife on the 16th and 17th, and to resume my practice of reading in my Bible before breakfast. I enjoyed reading the hundred and forty-fifth Psalm.

On the 18th I felt the bed shake under me, and felt convinced that it was an earthquake. A sharp shock was felt at Port Espano, thirty miles distant.

The next day Dr. Philip called to convey me in his gig to his house, where we have been most kindly cared for by him and his widowed sister Marianne Corsbie. The fever returned intermittently till the 26th.

I have been sweetly comforted, the language of Isaiah cheering me, "I will trust and not be afraid; for the Lord Jehovah is my strength and my song: He also is become my salvation." But there were seasons when I felt it difficult to say, "Thy will be done."

In after years Edwin O. Tregelles said that at this time he could have made the language of the following hymn his own:—

> "My God, Thy service well demands
> The remnant of my days;
> Why was this fleeting breath renewed,
> But to renew Thy praise?

> Thine arms of everlasting love
>   Did this weak frame sustain,
> When life was hovering o'er the grave,
>   And nature sunk with pain.
>
> Back from the borders of the grave,
>   At Thy command I come;
> Nor would I urge a speedier flight
>   To my celestial home."

We see him carrying out his renewed covenant of service, for he writes:—

28th.—We had a meeting with Dr. Philip, his sister Corsbie, and his children and hers, also several of his managers and overseers; besides these, several of his retainers about the house quietly collected in an adjoining room. Before the close of the meeting one of the overseers in a simple pleasant manner bore his testimony to the strivings of the grace of God in his heart. I felt thankful at the conclusion that we had had this opportunity, limited as it was, of setting before our fellows the importance of not resting on any outward performances or rites, but of knowing their hearts to be changed, and Christ to become their only hope of glory.

Deeply, indeed, was this impressed on my mind during my serious illness, when I had nothing to depend on for acceptance but that one great offering whereby "He hath perfected for ever them that are sanctified."

JOSIAH FORSTER TO E. O. TREGELLES AND JAMES JESUP.

Tottenham, First Month 1st, 1844.

MY DEAR FRIENDS,—

. . . The brotherly desire arises while I write, that you may be increasingly united in the bonds of the gospel, and may, from time to time, be permitted to take refreshment from the presence of the Lord when reverently presenting yourselves together before Him. And that waiting in humility, faith, and love for the fresh putting forth of His Spirit, you may experience qualification for the work of the day, and may your desires to walk before men as becometh the gospel be blessed. Thus do I, in brotherly sympathy, give expression to these unpremeditated thoughts which come before me. . . .

Our interest on behalf of these coloured people is such, that we shall be glad to receive any information which you may incline to convey, both as regards morals, intellectual advancement and religion, and also the local advantages of the labouring population. Of Trinidad I should expect a very different account from that of Barbadoes. A Roman Catholic people speaking a different language from ours, much virgin soil, many immigrants recently brought thither, an island increasing in commerce, present to me, who know so little of it, many peculiar features. . . .

It may be no surprise to you to hear that our dear and honoured friend William Allen is released from all the cares and sufferings of time. He died the evening before last at Lindfield, where he has been for the last two or three months. His kind watchful attendants, Lucy Bradshaw and Cornelius and Elizabeth Hanbury, have been with him uninterruptedly for many weeks, also Anna Pease, of Darlington. It may truly be said his sun has set in brightness. You would hear of the death of Elizabeth Robson, of Liverpool, after a short illness, just when she was about to leave for religious service in this quarterly meeting. Thus you see we have many warnings, many lessons of instruction. May we wisely profit by them. . . . In the renewed feeling of warm brotherly interest in you, and in your religious engagement,

I am your affectionate friend,
JOSIAH FORSTER.

George Town, Grenada, Second Month 5th.—I was well enough to leave Corinth on the 31st of last month, and, accompanied by Dr. Philip, we went by steamer from Petit Bourg to Port Espano, where our kind friends, T. B. and Eliza Darracot (from Kingsbridge), received us most kindly. Our voyage hither was pleasantly accomplished, and I felt much benefited by the change.

Yesterday (First-day), as I was going on deck with James Backhouse's journal in my hand, one of the sailors said to another, for me to hear, "I say, Sam, have you got any book you could lend us?" I quickly said, "I shall be very glad to supply thee, and any of your company, if thou wilt hand out those tin boxes." Whilst he was uncording the box, I said to him, "Would you like us to go forward, and read a chapter in the Bible?" "Yes, sir," he replied, "we should like it very much." I went and told J. Jesup how the way had opened for us. We read Matthew v. to the few who had the courage to stand near us; they were attentive, and great stillness prevailed; soon more of the men came quietly up from the forecastle and sat down. After a short pause at the conclusion of the reading, I addressed them on the need that all have of being true followers of Christ; not in name only, but in heart renouncing the devil, and laying hold of the grace of God which bringeth salvation; so that sudden death, which is the lot of many sailors, might be to them sudden glory.

7th.—On reaching George Town we made known to each other how our minds had been respectively exercised concerning the Wesleyan ministers, who were in conference at Grenada.

8th.—We met sixteen regular ministers from the different islands, and three or four local preachers. Deep silence prevailed for some time after we were seated, and then ability was given me to express the desire I had felt, that in their councils the Spirit of the Lord might so direct them as that their movements might be to His glory; that by them the gospel might be preached in its simplicity as the Holy Spirit may direct; expressing my belief that if in this way Christ crucified were set forth, apart from rites and ceremonies, that the Redeemer's kingdom would rapidly extend. After I sat down, William Moyster rose and said, that on our gathering into silence, the language arose in his mind, "Behold, how good and how pleasant it is for brethren to dwell together in unity:" that he could truly say, "It is good to be here." James Jesup then gave expression to his concern, that rites and ceremonies and plausible modes might have no place in their proceedings. After which praises and prayer were offered to the Lord. It appeared to me that the Spirit of the Lord was amongst us, and much unity was felt when we dispersed.

CHAPTER X.

WEST INDIES.

St. Vincent—Letter to his Wife—Calls on Governor and Macdowall Grant—First Meeting after Illness—Prayers' House—Soufrière Volcano—Death of his Wife—Attends Meeting at Calliaqua—Caribs—Extracts from Journal of James Bickford—Lucia—Letters of Sympathy from Josiah Forster, John Pease and Mahlon Day.

Whilst Edwin O. Tregelles was ill of fever in Trinidad, his beloved wife died suddenly on the 16th of the First Month, 1844. The following letter was addressed to her four weeks after her decease, while he was still ignorant of his great loss.

Calder, St. Vincent, Second Month 15th, 1844.

Dear Jenepher,

When I finished my last letter at Grenada on the 9th, I fully purposed commencing another at once, that I might detail to thee some of the things left untold in my hastily concluded packet. Three hours after I posted it we went on board the *Teviot*. The navigation of this route is somewhat dangerous from the great number of rocks that lie as a chain connecting Grenada with this island (you will see them on the map), well known by the name of Grenadines. Many of them are very pretty, on some the cultivation of cotton is carried on, and in former times sugar was made in one or two, but this I believe has ceased for want of labourers.

We arrived at Kingston, St. Vincent, at 3 p.m. of the

10th. The harbour is much larger than that at George Town, but, being more open, it is not so safe.

The agent of the steamers showed us much kind attention, and conducted us to Flemming's Hotel, where we took up our quarters, dining at the public table. There we met with a special magistrate named Edwin Polson. He welcomed us cordially and invited us to visit him, offering to accompany us in our visits to schools. He mentioned to us the name of Hay Macdowall Grant, a gentleman of known philanthropy, who would be glad to see us.

As the day after our arrival was First-day, we remained quietly at our quarters, excepting that we enjoyed a few strolls for exercise on the high ground at the back of the town. We had our morning sitting as usual. Read portions of our letters to each other; and filled up the interval with Samuel Fothergill's Memoirs and James Backhouse's Narrative.

We were much impressed by the quiet and orderly proceedings throughout the town, and at our inn. It was a day of rest, and I hope of spiritual refreshment to many besides ourselves, which it is pleasant to contemplate, especially if contrasted with some other districts which we have visited. Moreover, I believe it to be the result of Christian principle, here grown into practice. We were told by a police magistrate, named Ross, who called on us, that when he came out in 1810, the only place of worship in the island was a small and poor Wesleyan Chapel in Kingston. Now various denominations have good chapels there, and we learn that they are numerously scattered over the cultivated portions of the island.

On Second-day we called on the Governor, Sir Richard Doherty, to whom we were introduced by letter from Sir Charles Grey, Governor of Barbadoes. Our reception was most kind. He invited us to stay at his cottage; this we did not accept, but engaged to dine with him the following day.

On returning to the inn we learnt that James R. Douglas,

of Colonarée (my young friend with whom I became acquainted on board the *Forth*) had arrived with a gig and two saddle horses to convey us to the residence of Thomas McIntire, with whom he resides. This did not accord with our previous arrangements, and we felt constrained to postpone availing ourselves of the kindness.

It was refreshing to see the nice schools. Sir Richard Doherty went with us, and at the Episcopalian School we met many members of the committee, some of whom had received their education in that school, which was established for the coloured class in 1822.

Fever was very prevalent, so that we felt well pleased to leave Kingston yesterday morning. We started after breakfast, on horseback, accompanied by a special magistrate named Struth, having a man to carry our luggage on his head. In passing through the seaport village of Calliaqua we stayed to see a school of sixty children under the care of the Episcopalians.

After we had arrived and lunched at Calder, the residence of Hay Macdowall Grant, we went with him to see a school on his property, of ninety boys and girls, under the care of the Wesleyans. H. M. Grant seemed quite at home amongst the children.

We have believed it right to appoint a meeting in the schoolroom; and this morning James Jesup and I have been riding amongst the adjoining estates to ascertain whether the notice was duly spread, and also that we might converse a little with the labourers. We are pleased with their intelligence. It is premature to give any opinion of their character and condition, but the little we have seen of the people in this island pleases us much, and tends to cheer and encourage.

Though I have not alluded to my health, thou wilt conclude, and correctly so, that it is much improved. I feel as if I had nearly regained my former standard. I am not unmindful of the mercy shown me; daily do I rejoice in my portion, and can feelingly unite in the language, "Oh, that men would praise the Lord for His goodness, and for His wonderful works to the children of men."

Hay M. Grant is an advocate for free independent villages for the negro labourers. He has one in the midst of his estates, which at its formation, and in the early stage of its establishment was a great annoyance to him; his labourers left him to build their own cots, and till the ground which they had purchased. Now, however, he reaps the benefit, for whilst some planters are losing their labourers, who roam as they please, and without tie, he has a large population of persons bound to the spot by their interest in their own houses and land, who prefer working for him rather than go to a distance to labour. This free village is called Victoria; it is within half a mile of Calder, and forms a pretty object from the windows of the drawing-room in which I now write. Victoria does not belong to Hay M. Grant, or rather, the land did not; but he is so satisfied of the policy and benefit of the measure, that he is about to appropriate a piece of ground on a distant estate to the same object. Within three miles of this place another of these villages is to be met with.

16*th*.—Our meeting at the school-house or chapel on this estate was numerously attended, although the evening was wet and the paths very dirty, the building, which will seat six hundred persons, being nearly full. We felt thankful that we had been able to meet this interesting company, and also that the Lord by His Spirit had been amongst us. The prospect of this meeting had felt formidable to me, it being the first we have appointed since my illness, so that there has been a lapse of two months, the last being at Grenada before we left for Trinidad.

George Town, 19*th*.—We called at Colonarée, on Thomas McIntire, who is the manager of John Sterling's estate. Here I met with my young friend James R. Douglas. He is at this estate as an overseer, learning the duties of a planter. It was interesting to me to see the spot where J. and S. Sterling had resided whilst in this island, amid scenery of unusual beauty and grandeur; and to see the house that replaced the one which was blown away over their heads in 1831. . . .

In coming from Calder to this place we had to cross an almost endless number of little valleys, and our road has in consequence been very tortuous, sometimes at the edge of a precipice fifty to a hundred feet above a roaring sea, with one hundred feet of soft vertical rock above us, and then suddenly turning up a valley four or five hundred yards. The cliffs and deep cuttings reminded me constantly of the road between Charmouth and Lyme. . . .

21st.—Two days ago we rode out before breakfast to see several estates situated at the back of George Town. We saw many of the labourers busy at work. Some of the gangs had task work which could be completed by eleven o'clock. Sometimes they begin their task at five, and finish at nine o'clock. They have all the rest of the day for their own grounds. We arranged to have a meeting that afternoon at Rooabacca estate, in a building appropriated for meetings for worship, commonly used by the Wesleyans about once a fortnight. We gave notice of the meeting at several estates.

After breakfast we paid attention to a nice school of ninety boys and girls, conducted by James Ogilvie. They do not read as well as children of the class in other schools we have seen, but spell well and answer questions agreeably.

In the afternoon we kept our appointment; and, on going to the building to attend the meeting, found that it was quite empty. However, I felt best satisfied to go and take my seat, and had a precious season of comfort before any of the labourers arrived. These soon filled the place to overflowing, so that some stood outside, and there they were as well circumstanced as if they were inside, for the construction of the building is simple, the sides being formed of upright posts wattled half-way up, and the roof thatched with cane tops.

Yesterday we started after an early breakfast to visit a settlement of Caribs who are located near Sandy Bay. We were two hours going there, walking our horses. Our road lay for half the way over very rough and steep ground, across deep, stony, dry ravines, and by a narrow path under thick brushwood. In some places the descents and ascents were so precipitous as to oblige me to dismount, though I had been accustomed to some very bad roads in Wales.

We made our way to the school, of which we had had accounts that led to our expecting something capital; but instead of this the room was empty, and the master, Thomas Laurain, was absent. Our companion blew the shell, and soon the master made his appearance with cutlass [the tool for gathering in the canes] in hand. He only keeps school two days in the week, for which he receives 3d. per week from each child, and I believe he has an allowance from some society in England. He and his wife are Caribs. On asking how many scholars he had, he said, "Not many"; and at last I screwed out that he had about twelve. Not more than three or four could be collected at first. I heard one of these, a nice little girl of eight years old, read in the New Testament; and then opened my treasures of workbags, thimbles, pictures and tracts for her to choose from, to her delight. This gave an uncommon impulse to the scene. Sukey and Jack and many others were called, and the shell again blown lustily, and soon we were surrounded by old and young. Only three could read in the New Testament, and other children could manage to read words of one syllable. The Carib children are really beautiful, with a lovely expression, such as I have not seen in any other children since I left England.

We had a comforting meeting in the schoolroom with about thirty adults, to whom gospel truths were preached, and prayer was offered for the increase of joy and peace in believing and obeying that gospel. We should probably have called on some of them in their huts, which are scattered numerously amongst plantains and palms and bread-fruit and cocoanut trees, on the sides of precipitous slopes and rich ravines, but rain fell copiously while we were there, and rendered it unfit to go amongst so much foliage and "bush," as the low scrub is called, which is very wetting even when passing through it on horseback.

Our companion in this visit was Samuel Crichlow, manager of Orange Hill estate, and coroner of the district. We were introduced to him, and being unable to proceed with us when we called, he followed, and overtook us when within about a furlong of the place where we needed his guidance. He was educated by Benjamin Gilkes at Nailsworth, and spoke of him with lively interest.

In the afternoon we met an interesting company in the "prayers' house" at Lot 14 estate. This erection was similar to the one we used the day before, only larger, and situated in a thicket of palm and bread-fruit trees. The meeting was crowded, many outside standing; we had the company of some of the managers and overseers. Help was again afforded to take of the things of God and to hand them to others; we left with grateful and humble feelings, which were renewed in our sitting together this morning, when an Ebenezer was afresh raised, where we could acknowledge that "hitherto hath the Lord helped us," and that we had lacked nothing.

The eruption of the Souffrière, which took place in 1812, was attended with serious consequences to this island, as well as to Barbadoes, which, though eighty miles to the eastward, was on that occasion covered for four or five inches deep with the ashes of this volcano. This is the more remarkable, seeing that Barbadoes is to the windward. Though thus deluged with dust the island will be ultimately benefited, as it has proved an enricher of that exhausted soil.

Many estates in this island were injured by having their fertile lowland destroyed by the streams of lava and scoria which overwhelmed vast tracts. We passed, in going from George Town to the Carib country, the dry beds of five or six occasional streams, down which water used almost constantly to flow; but now some of them are full, nearly level with the banks, of black stones, gravel and fine sand. One of these is about 150 yards wide, and another about eighty yards; they have a remarkable appearance. Thirty years have passed away, and yet not a blade of any green thing varies the blackened plains. We were told that the river pursues its way under the surface on which we rode. The trembling of the earth was so evident during a portion of the days that the mountain was pouring out its treasures of darkness, that many persons believed, or apprehended, that the whole island would sink or be swallowed up in the ocean. . . .

This island affords us a deeply interesting field for labour. We prefer it to any we have yet visited. A large proportion of the people avow their fondness for religious instruction, but of course many of these are professors only.

I feel disposed to complete my letter by my signature now, leaving space for addition if opportunity admit, and remaining with much love to the dear circle and friends around,

Thy very affectionate husband,
E. O. TREGELLES.

The Journal continues :—

George Town, 18th.—We had a large meeting at eleven o'clock in the Wesleyan Chapel, when much liberty was felt in preaching the gospel; the need of repenting of sin and forsaking it, and of belief in and obedience to our Lord and Saviour was much dwelt on. We had another meeting at four, which was attended by the inhabitants of the town, but not many negroes.

During this day my mind was often occupied in the sweet remembrance of the mercies showered upon us seven years since, when my heart was sorely tried by the serious illness of my precious Jenepher. In remembering these things I can say, "Surely goodness and mercy are still following us, and may we dwell in the house of the Lord for ever!"

Kingston, 28th.—As soon as I had penned the foregoing, many pressing duties prevented me from proceeding with the narrative of our engagements, and at five o'clock on the afternoon of the 26th inst. a packet of letters arrived for me, which contained the afflictive intelligence that my ever-precious Jenepher had been taken from me, having, I firmly believe, fallen asleep in Jesus on the morning of First Month 16th; and thus have my prayers for her, and hers for herself, that she might be kept from falling, and be of the number of the redeemed, been answered.

It cheers and animates me in my pilgrimage, especially in the work now before me in this portion of our Redeemer's heritage, that her heart was strongly bound to it, and I now rejoice that she so much promoted my entering on this field of labour.

A fresh sense was also given me, more than I have ever felt before, of the mercy of God in Christ Jesus in providing for her and all mankind a means of reconciliation with God and admission to the glorious condition of the redeemed, which I doubt not is now her happy portion. Already have I heard the whisperings of her sweet earnest spirit, "My Edwin, if thou continuest to love me, feed my lambs which I left in thy charge." Renewedly do I bless the Lord for these treasures, and I crave that I may be instrumental in leading them forward in the paths of peace, and effectually showing them the Lamb of God who taketh away the sin of the world, according to the desire and endeavours of their blessed mother.

In reference to my union with my precious wife, whom the Lord has seen meet to withdraw from me, I can in sincerity express my belief that the Lord gave, and for this I bless His holy name; and seeing that He has also taken, I crave ability so to abide in the dwelling-place of the Lord, as that I may see His mercy in this also, and eventually join her to celebrate the praises of the Lord God and the Lamb in her pure and joyous dwelling-place for ever.

In one of her last letters she says, "I feel interested in everything thou writes. I have not written half what I want to, but it would not be good for me to write much more. May the consoling language be spoken to me, 'Let her alone; she hath done what she could.'"

The morning of the 27th was occupied in reperusing the last notes I had received from my darling Jenepher, and those of my dear sisters. I had a kind sympathetic call from James Nibbs Brown, who engaged in prayer on my behalf.

We went in the afternoon to Calliaqua to attend a meeting which we had appointed before we received the letters; 700 persons were present. May the blessing of the Lord rest on our endeavours. Before I concluded to proceed with that engagement I waited for best counsel, and believed it was the will of the Lord that we should pursue our object.

29th.—We attended a meeting in the Wesleyan Chapel, where we met 1,700 persons. Much of the labour devolved on James Jesup, as at Calliaqua. He spoke of the object we had in view in coming amongst them. I addressed them on the importance of each knowing his heart to be changed. Reference was also made to John the Baptist, who came as the forerunner of our Lord to prepare His way, baptizing with water, which was to give way to the baptism of the Holy Ghost and of fire. That John made Jesus known to his own followers as the Lamb of God that taketh away the sin of the world. That all present had felt the strivings of the Lord's grace in their hearts. He had given warning too, and that recently, for when He made their mountains to tremble, had He shaken them a little more, none would have escaped to tell the tale. They were pleaded with not to delay for another visitation, but to give up their hearts to the Lord, and know Him to rule in them and to become their Redeemer, seeing that "other foundation can no man lay than that is laid, which is Jesus Christ."

Prayer was offered that we might become the temples of the Lord, and that laying aside our own righteousness as filthy rags, we might be clothed with the pure robe of Christ's righteousness, and thus stand at the awful tribunal with acceptance.

When allusion was made to the earthquake, as a proof of the Lord's power to prove His cause, a thrill of assent, "Yes, yes!" passed through the vast assembly, which was preserved in much solemnity the whole time.

Baronallie, Third Month, 2nd.—Yesterday rode twelve miles to this place, where we had a meeting in the Wesleyan School Chapel; 400 were collected. I had to speak on the language, "He that cometh to God must believe that He is, and that He is a rewarder of them that diligently seek Him."

Château-belair, 3rd.—Arrived here yesterday and met with a truly kind reception from our friends James and Fanny Bickford, whom we had previously met at Tobago.

I have felt low and much tried to-day, feeling my state of strippedness more than I have before realized. At times panting to be going forward with our work, that I may the more quickly join my precious children and sisters, but have felt restrained from this, lest I should do the work of the Lord deceitfully.

Baronallie, 4th.—Our meeting at Château-belair last evening was largely attended. Many of the upper classes of that district were present, to some of whom the doctrine of the cross and the consequence of sin was very unpalatable, so as to induce a few to behave badly; but this did not prevent honesty and faithfulness on our part.

After breakfast this morning James Bickford, J. Jesup

and I set out for Morne Ronde, the Carib settlement near the foot of the Souffrière. We were accompanied by two men on foot, and were met near Walliboo by John Lewis, the captain of the Caribs, who came to aid us in passing a perilous portion of our road, where the sea washed up close to the cliff, and rendered it dangerous to pass, the waves being unusually high. We were favoured to get along safely, though not without much alarm. We left our horses about half a mile from the settlement, and walked over the rocks and masses of basalt that covered the shore, and up a beautiful, well-cultivated ravine.

We found an interesting group of fifteen children at the school, five of whom could read in the New Testament. About fifty adults sat down with us, and a precious meeting we had; a more solemn silence I never felt, and ability was given to speak of the work of regeneration as essential to redemption.

It was interesting to meet thus with the intelligent remnant of a race who have been cruelly oppressed by our ancestors; but now they and we, by obedience to the law of the Lord, have come into the condition of fellowship.

The black Caribs raise great quantities of provisions and fruit for sale, build canoes, make baskets, and catch fish. It is a rare occurrence for a Carib to be brought before the magistrates.

The following extracts from the "Autobiography of James Bickford" refer to the intercourse he had with Edwin O. Tregelles and James Jesup.

"It was our happiness once more to entertain Messrs. Tregelles and Jesup in our humble home at Château-belair. They visited the plantations that they might see for themselves the condition of the field labourers. I accompanied these worthy men to the black Carib settlement along the sea-coast, about seven miles from Château-belair. We passed through Fitzhugher, Richmond, and two other plantations on our way thither, that our friends might watch the process of cutting, carting, and crushing the sugar canes at the mills. The crop season is one of a cheerful character to whites and blacks alike. Extempore songs in the cane fields, and willing co-operation at the works, mark the recurrence of every day's engagements. At that time so well did the planters and labourers understand each other, that a large return was a mutual satisfaction. 'Plenty of sugar good for Buckra and nigger too,' was the expressed belief of employers and employed equally.

"Arriving at the fort Morne Ronde, the head man, John Lewis, met us and conducted us up along the rocky steeps to the solitary and mountainous home of these sons of the forest. The shell was blown, and the people came to the house of prayer. Mr. Tregelles conducted the service. Every word he uttered was full of dignified courtesy, whilst his references to the terrible struggles of their forefathers with those Europeans, who had reduced their once powerful tribe to a mere remnant, were cautious and pathetic. The prayers offered by these christian Englishmen before parting were such as could only be uttered by men accustomed to ponder over the misfortunes of aboriginal races with tearful regrets and burning shame."

After this visit to the Carib Settlement E. O. T. and J. J. returned to Kingston, from whence he wrote :—

Kingston, 10*th*, *First Day*.—Whilst at breakfast we had a call from four women of the Wesleyan Society, who wished for a little talk with us. They seemed to be aware of the importance of a change of heart. They told us that if any Quakers came again to this island they should not want accommodation. As soon as this party left, we went to the gaol, accompanied by John le Gall, the Governor's aide-de-camp. Our interview with the prisoners and their keepers felt relieving and comforting to me.

We retired to my chamber, where I had to keep silence before the Lord, desiring that my eye might be kept single to Him in all my movements, that I may really be able to teach transgressors His ways, and that sinners may be converted unto Him. In the afternoon we were at a meeting in the Wesleyan Chapel at Layou, where both of us received help to minister to those assembled. And now we feel at liberty to leave this island. I am thankful for the mercies shown me. I have had deeper plunges than I ever before experienced. I came here in great bodily and spiritual weakness, and have been refreshed in body, and strengthened in spirit for the Lord's service.

Castries, Lucia, 14th.—We left Kingston on the 12th by the *Thames* steamer; on which I was accosted by a boy, who called me by my name, and I found that he was James Gillingham, who had been a scholar at the British and Foreign School, Falmouth. I was also spoken to by a Spaniard whom I had supplied with a Testament in Falmouth gaol. We landed at eleven o'clock at night. On going to the first house we were promptly told that we could not be received. I was taken to another; there also the hostess said "No," but I pleaded, "Canst thou not make up beds for us on sofas?" Then she relented, and prepared a bed on the floor. We preferred arranging our luggage in front of a sofa, so as to raise the mattress from the ground, and thus had six hours of refreshing sleep.

In our time of waiting on the Lord after breakfast, James Jesup was engaged to give thanks for past favours, and to pray for a continuance of Divine regard, even if it might be to the humbling of the creature. In silence I was comforted by the language, "My God shall supply all your need according to His riches in glory by Christ Jesus," on which I desire to lay hold, and to have my faith strengthened by the Lord's power, knowing His grace to be made perfect in my weakness and strippedness.

The letters I received yesterday from home had the effect of probing my recent wound very deeply, though the cordial was attempted to be administered, but how vain in such cases is the help of man. I seemed destitute of that sustaining power which had before been granted for my support in my extremity, perhaps because I did not sufficiently seek it, trusting too much to past experience, and in degree depending on myself, so that I proved that " he that trusteth to his own heart is a fool," and the result was that I had more of conflict than I have known for a long time past.

Josiah Forster to E. O. Tregelles.

Folkestone, Third Month 20th, 1844.

My dear Friend,—

It has been a great favour that thy mind has been kept so calm and so trustful during the time thou wast on a bed of sickness, and that thou wast in the way of good medical advice and kind helpful friends. May the Lord be pleased during the remainder of your journey, and to the end of your pilgrimage, to supply all your needs through the riches of His mercy in Christ Jesus.

Before this reaches thee I apprehend thou wilt have heard of thy heavy loss in the death of thy dearest earthly friend. . . . Whilst I doubt not thou felt the peculiar uncertainty of your meeting again here on earth, the intelligence will have very acutely awakened the tenderest emotions. . . . It is a remarkable coincidence that thou and thy dear cousin Samuel Fox were deprived of those most dear to you just about the same period of time. He has been amongst us a striking example of Christian submission. We feel our loss not a small one, but we ought to rejoice with thankfulness in thinking of the gospel labours, the bright example, and the pleasant, instructive society which has been ours in having Maria Fox amongst us the last few years. . . .

The devotedness of our dear friend John Hodgkin, jun., is striking. He has been pursuing his religious engagements in Suffolk. Peter Bedford is gone with him. . . .

I write this, expecting in two or three hours to go across to Boulogne in company with Joseph John Gurney and his wife, who, after spending a little time in Paris, are proposing to travel southward as far as Bordeaux and Toulouse. J. J. Gurney goes out to complete the visit which he had in prospect when abroad last summer. . . .

I should be glad of those observations which thou art kindly intending to send, on the general working of the freedom of the slaves in those islands which you have visited. May the Lord be graciously pleased to bless your labours of love, and to keep you in safety, humility, and trust, before Him, replenishing your hearts from day to day with a sense of His goodness and providential care, and giving you to feel the sweet incomes of His love, and the guidance of His blessed Spirit.

Thy sincere friend,
JOSIAH FORSTER.

JOHN PEASE TO EDWIN O. TREGELLES.

Salem, Ohio, Eighth Month 26th, 1844.

MY BELOVED FRIEND,—

. . . My heart turned towards thee with much emotion as, from one source or another, I learnt the great bereavement, and I apprehend the consequent trial of thy faith permitted by the All-wise Disposer of events; it now appears that in His own time He hath condescended to prove to thee that He wounds to heal. He alone knows how much is requisite for the purpose of teaching the full meaning of the truth, that the trial of your faith is much more precious than of gold that perisheth. He alone can tell how much either flesh or spirit can bear when such reduction of self is going forward. . . .

During my four or five weeks' sojourn in Virginia and Carolina, I had some opportunities of seeing what slavery is. Together with a solid concern amongst Friends here for its extinction, there is a measure of that indifference, by a yielding to the assumed difficulties attending its extinction, which is the natural result of living more or less in contact with the evil. I love to have the opportunity of informing them of your visiting coloured people, thy being attended by physicians of that class, and the results of emancipation generally. On this account, and for my own comfort, may I hope to hear from thee soon again.

I salute thee and thy dear companion in the love of the everlasting gospel, desiring that the presence of Him through whom its blessings are brought to light may be largely with you, your wisdom, strength, and joy; that your labours may be abundantly blessed, and your peace flow.

Thy brother in the tribulations, consolations, and hope of the Gospel,

JOHN PEASE.

P.S.—I have met with uniform kindness, I think I may say openness, everywhere.

MAHLON DAY TO EDWIN O. TREGELLES.

New York, Ninth Month 5th, 1844.

ESTEEMED FRIEND,—

The enclosed letter from our beloved friend, John Pease, I forward with much pleasure, and I wish to add that I feel a good deal of sympathy with thee and thy dear companion in the visit you are now performing in the West Indies, having been over much of the ground myself with my beloved friend, Joseph John Gurney. There was much that enlisted our feelings in our progress: nothing more than the readiness of all classes, more particularly the coloured population, to receive our visit, and the order and solemnity of the people in the vast assemblies which upon short notice convened.

May your labours of love be blessed to many, and you receive the blessed reward of the faithful labourers in the Lord's vineyard. I trust you will be preserved every way in your travels and exercises among the West Indian Islands, and I cordially invite both of you, if you should think best to return to England by way of the States, to accept of our house, No. 52, Henry Street, as a resting place while in New York.

With feelings of sympathy and love,
                    I am, thy assured friend,
                                MAHLON DAY.

THE WANDERER AND THE SWALLOWS.

    Bright birds of summer, have ye seen
        My home, my native land?
    Oh, could ye tell, ye would I ween,
        News of that distant strand.

    The dear ones, are they grouping still,
        Around the evening fire,
    With hearts that fond affections fill
        For me, their absent sire?

    Are all still there? the unbroken chain—
        The mother with her three?
    Or must we never meet again
        Till in Eternity?

    Stranger! if all thy joys were flown,
        All in their youthful bloom,
    Still must thou say, "His will be done,"
        Who gave and may resume.

    Oh, stranger! by the distant hearth,
        Thy stricken children weep
    For that dear form which gave them birth,
        Now couched in dreamless sleep.

Fond words for thee the last she strung,
　For thee the prayer at night.
Almost thy name upon her tongue,
　She took her painless flight.

Stranger, farewell! an unseen Hand
　Hath led us from thine isle,
The same restore thee to thy land,
　And to thy children's smile.

ANNA P. FOX.

CHAPTER XI.

WEST INDIES.

Lucia—Meeting in Court House, Castries—Mico Schools—River Dorée—Voyage in Canoe—Tousmassic—Nautilus—Visit to Gaol—Dominica—Call on President—Coasting Voyage—Meetings in Wesleyan Chapels—Mount Wallis—Canoe Building—Visit to Caribs—Mary Dalrymple—Antigua—Earthquake, 1843—Call on Governor Sir C. Fitzroy—Archdeacon Holberton—Meeting in Scotch Kirk—The Moravian Missions—Wesleyan Sunday Schools—F. W. Hougk—Meetings in Wesleyan and Moravian Chapels.

LUCIA, *Third Month* 17*th*, 1844.—A meeting with the inhabitants of Castries was held in the Court House. This was probably the first ever held by Friends in Lucia. In much weakness I went to the meeting, which was fully attended, many of the wealthy class being present. Ability was given to preach Jesus as the Sanctifier, Redeemer, High Priest and Intercessor. I have seldom known the increase of the Lord's power spreading over all as on that occasion. Many were talking, and almost jesting, when we commenced; all were calmed down before the close, and I believe some left with the intention of thinking on these things. The Governor and his daughter were present, and he renewed his invitation for us to visit him on our return from the southern part of this island.

River Dorée, 19*th*.—Yesterday we left Castries for this place, accompanied by James N. Gordon, agent for the Mico Schools. These schools (so called from the lady who endowed them) were established for the coloured people. We hired a pirogue, a large canoe, to convey us twenty-five miles to Souffrière for forty-eight dollars. We sailed gaily out till we reached the open sea, and then our hearts quailed with apparent danger of an upset, so that we agreed with the men to take down the sail and row us with five paddles on being paid two dollars more. They were satisfied, and worked well. We quite enjoyed our cruise, passing many small bays which are the mouths of deep ravines and valleys. The cliffs also were beautiful, showing sections of volcanic *débris;* sand, basalt and boulders lying in strata in some places, and in others, large masses of basalt were exhibited in a fine variety of its conchoidal fracture.

We reached Souffrière in four hours, and were met on the beach by the Episcopalian minister of this district, who, hearing of our approach, came to greet us kindly, and to conduct us to the special magistrate, Johnston, who had prepared horses for us at the request of the Governor, and sent forward our luggage under charge of a policeman. Such is the reception given to Quakers now-a-days!

We are now staying at the residence of some ladies, named Alexander, who are owners and occupiers of two sugar estates, on one of which, the River Dorée, they live. Their labourers are chiefly Protestants, and these sisters use continued efforts to check Popery and spread their own opinions. At their family worship twice a day many of their people attend, besides some of the children of the Mico School.

After dinner, at six, we met a large company in their dining-hall. At the close of their usual service I gave expression to my feelings freely, partly in French. Prayer was also offered for the growth of the good seed, for the sanctification of those present, and for the spread of the gospel in this land by their means.

This morning we visited the Mico School; fifty-six on the list, forty-two average attendance. The labour of the estate was lessened to set a larger number at liberty to meet us than otherwise would have come. Our kind friends gave us breakfast at six, at the close of which I read the 118th Psalm, and addressed the sisters and their schoolmaster. It was a uniting season, and a satisfactory close of a visit of no common character.

We left them at seven, and proceeded a quarter of a mile to the mouth of the River Dorée, where a canoe was waiting for us. We took our seats in the canoe whilst it was aground, and were launched by the men into the water. They skilfully managed to avoid the billows that rolled in, and, watching their opportunity, pushed off. Our friends assure us that these canoes are safe, for if they do upset, you only lose your luggage; the canoe always floats, and by laying hold of it, all the passengers are supported. The negroes soon bale out the water, and in half an hour are ready to encounter further dangers.

Castries, 23rd.—Our visit to the south has been accomplished to our comfort. At Canelle we had a meeting with many of the labourers on the estate. The manager sat by us, and interpreted sentence by sentence what we expressed. He is a Roman Catholic, but performed his part with fairness, I believe, though many things he expressed were at variance with the doctrines of his Church. We heard afterwards that the people were well satisfied with the meeting. I believe it would not be difficult to induce many of these negroes to renounce Popery for a spiritual religion, though it may not be easy to induce them to relinquish one set of forms for another set of forms.

Next morning we proceeded to Tousmassi, which, as well as Canelle, belongs to W. Muter, who has possessed himself by purchase of many estates at prices far below their real value, as the climate and political condition of the island is repulsive to Englishmen.

At Tousmassi we called together a few persons who were disposed to meet us. They were Protestants, mostly Scotch. We felt sympathy with them as sheep having no shepherd, never visited by their own pastors. We directed their attention to our great High Priest, whom they would prove would be all-sufficient for them.

From Tousmassi we returned on horseback to Vieux Fort, where we lodged in the simple wooden dwelling of the Mico schoolmaster, who kindly gave up his bed and home to us.

Vieux Fort is under Romish influence. On a hill near the town a large cross has been erected, bearing an image of our Lord. Such is the superstition and idolatry of these people that on most headlands which we passed along the coast, which are the points of danger in canoe navigation, they have erected small sentry boxes of stone, containing images of Mary, the mother of our Lord, to whom they make their cross in passing, in token of their dedication. Anything but the real thing.

Yesterday morning we embarked in a pirogue for Castries, accompanied by J. N. Gordon and several of his Mico teachers, who meet in town to discuss their matters. We passed a nautilus with his gay sail set, fringed with purple. When storms and dangers arise, this wise creature draws in its sail, and finds safety in sinking deep. So would I do.

24th.—Yesterday we went to Vielle Ville to breakfast with John Reddie, the Chief Justice, and his wife. We had interesting conversation, and they were addressed on the importance of being disciples of Christ in heart as well as in name.

25th.—Yesterday being First-day, we went at ten o'clock to the gaol. We saw all the prisoners in their cells. Some small cells had five prisoners in each, and very close, smelling like the den of wild beasts. We remonstrated, and were told that they could not give more space. Afterwards the prisoners were assembled in a long open gallery, where they were addressed on the concerns of their never-dying souls. The Friend of sinners was pointed to as their refuge at all times, especially in times of trouble. The Inspector kindly interpreted. One poor woman had been a prisoner more than thirty years, having been convicted in 1813, under

French law, of poisoning a child. She showed me her rosary of black beads and little silver cross. I assured her that such things are ineffectual in procuring salvation; that if she truly repented of her sins, God would forgive her and love her freely for the sake of Jesus. I called again to give her a pair of the spectacles kindly supplied by cousin R. W. Fox.

On our return from the gaol we had our time for worship, when J. Jesup prayed for the blessing of the Lord on the seed sown through our efforts to serve Him in this island.

We afterwards visited the hospital, where about twenty persons diseased in body and mind are cared for at the expense of the colony. Thence I went to the Sabbath school, where twenty children were assembled. Then to the gaol again, where I found men at work, which I took measures to prevent, and they ceased, for the time at least. At the close of an interesting day we read a portion of Samuel Fothergill's Memoirs.

De Bernard, the prison inspector, called on us. On giving him some tracts, he avowed himself to be a Catholic, and expressed regret at the errors and bad practices of their priests, believing it to be an error that payment should be made for gospel labour. On leaving, I urged him to read his Bible to himself daily, and to begin this day with the Psalms.

26th.—My health has greatly improved, and we have endured a bronzing heat. In our late journey southward we have given away large numbers of French and English tracts.

Mon Répos, Dominica, 30th.—At twelve o'clock at night of the 26th we embarked in boats for the *Acteon* steamer. A stiff breeze caused a tumble, out of which we were glad to get safely on board. We reached Roseau on the 27th, and called on Maria Dalrymple with a letter of introduction from Joseph John Gurney. She could not receive us, but provided lodgings at the house of a worthy Wesleyan, named

Elizabeth Jones. When I heard her familiar name, I could not but revert to the mercies that attended me nineteen years ago, when cared for at Neath by another Elizabeth Jones, sharing her simple apartments with my brother, when we were young men.

Though weak and weary, ability was given me to rejoice in meeting with the Wesleyans assembled in regular course that evening. I reminded them of their first love, and of the need of watching unto prayer, that they might grow in grace.

On the 28th we called on the President, Dugald Stewart Laidlaw, who is acting for the Governor in his absence. He received us kindly, inquired what our plans were, and furnished us with letters for his managers on several estates, to afford us facilities by horses.

On the 29th we left Roseau in a canoe for the north of the island, attended by J. Horsford and C. Fillan, a man of colour. We were rowed by four able negroes, using proper oars, and a coxswain steering with a paddle, with which he urged forward as well as guided the canoe. We had interesting converse with our companions on leading points of doctrine. We enjoyed our row exceedingly, and were interested by the fine scenery along the coast. We met a number of canoes heavily laden, going to Roseau with plantains and other vegetables.

On reaching Portsmouth Joseph Phillips soon called with two horses, which he placed at our disposal to convey us to his house, and to be at our service when we proceed. Having been associated much with Friends when he was an active agent of the Anti-Slavery Society, his reception of us has been most cordial.

Castle Bruce, Fourth Month 4th.—We had two good meetings last First-day, in the Wesleyan Chapel at Mount Wallis. The hearts of the people were opened in a remarkable degree to receive the message we had to deliver, directing them to the Lamb of God who takes away the sins of those who are willing to receive Him as their Light, Guide, High Priest, Sacrifice and Intercessor.

On returning from our morning meeting I extended my ride for the sake of exercise, and had agreeably the company of a manager who had been at the meeting. He is young, and bids fair to choose the right path, if not already walking therein.

Next morning we took leave of Joseph Phillips, after a season of precious access at the throne of grace. I was cheered by his brief testimony that he believed the Lord had sent us among them, and that His ways are inscrutable. He is a Moravian, but commonly attends the Wesleyan Chapel.

I must not pass away from Mount Wallis without giving a brief sketch of its origin. Many years ago a planter died, leaving considerable property to a trustworthy woman-servant named Wallis, an African of the Foulah tribe. She could neither read nor write, but her heart was open to receive the gospel, and she became a serious Methodist, after which she gave liberty to all her slaves, though they remained on her property and worked for her as before. She required all to speak English, promoted religion among them; and at her death gave some land to the Wesleyans for a chapel, which they have called after her own name. I wish there were more of such Lydias.

Leaving Mon Repos we had a beautiful ride (amidst scenery which in many respects reminds me of the coast of North Wales) on two long-tailed, sure-footed ponies, excellent mountaineers, that scrambled safely up and down extraordinarily rocky roads, with their reins as slack as we could hold them.

We reached the Hampstead estate, and had a precious meeting in the negroes' prayers' house, situated in the midst of a plantain grove. It was a season of renewed favour, and I trust will tend to comfort and cheer the faith of some veteran servants of the Lord, who are become grey in His service.

In one of the many beautiful, woody, rocky and foaming bays which we passed, we saw the process of canoe making. The tree had been hewn, and shaped and hollowed as near to the size as it would admit of, and then, in order to make the canoe wider, a fire was lighted at each side, so as to heat and expand the wood; whilst a quantity of stones were placed in the interior to force out the sides.

At La Soye we met with T. M. Chambers, the Wesleyan minister. We had a meeting in the Wesleyan Chapel, with the labourers of the neighbouring estates. It was interesting afterwards to hear T. M. C.'s impression respecting silent worship. It was the first meeting held by Friends he had ever attended; he was much impressed by the silent part of it, and felt that in a condition of true silence the soul could draw nigh unto God.

Accompanied by J. L. Walsh we went to the Londonderry estate, where by some means the people had heard of our approach. The manager had reduced their work that day. On our arrival the shell was blown heartily, and in a very short time an interesting company was assembled in their prayers' house.

Leaving Londonderry for Melville Hall we there met with the same reception. Alexander Black, the manager, had the estate bell rung; and very soon we had a large gathering in their prayers' house, when such a solemn silence prevailed as is rarely met with in such meetings; not a sound was to be heard, and I felt it to be a serious engagement to disturb that solemnity by any vocal exercise. In the evening I had all the young persons collected, and proved their powers in reading Matthew ii., making small presents to each.

Next morning we started for Hatton Garden on two mules lent by Alexander Black. We had a meeting with the people before breakfast, to their comfort and ours, for we have our full reward as we pass along, and much enjoyment.

We left Hatton Garden at eleven o'clock, and proceeded through a district called the Carib country, by an Indian path. We had heard of the difficulties, and had been advised to avoid them; but those who knew the district well, said we were safe in proceeding.

We gained the summit of the first ascent by a steep zigzag path, a great exertion to our mules. We had to descend down paths beset with large loose stones, or tangled and bare roots of trees, and to find a way across mountain torrents whose beds were strewn with large masses of rock. Our mules were unshod, and seemed as sure-footed as goats; in this unshod state they are well adapted for such scrambling work over paths sometimes grass or clay, or rough stones or greasy clay-rock. My mule was delightfully easy; it was like riding in a sedan.

Our path during the past few days has been near the coast, and often have I looked over my left knee on the foaming waves which have dashed at the foot of the cliff some hundreds of feet beneath me, and felt such security in the safety of my mule, and comfort in the belief of being in my right allotment, that I have feared no evil; though sometimes, when my beast has been proposing a serious move downward, his ears have seemed a long way off. Our path was repeatedly obstructed by fallen trees, both living and dead. The weather was peculiarly favourable.

In passing through the Carib country we saw a few of their huts, and called at one. The man was out hunting in the forest, the woman was seated at the door, sewing a blue check shirt. Several children were about, and the younger ones ran crying to their mother. The eldest girl was preparing castor oil from the seeds which grow plentifully. I gave the woman a thimble and bodkin; she was reserved. They have little or no religious profession, and no school.

A large population in the northern part of this island is lamentably deficient in schools. If I were free from strong ties at home, and understood medicine, I believe I could be made willing to settle down in this quarter, and act the double part of doctor and schoolmaster. Both are much wanted, and the people interest me more than any we have seen in these islands. Their hearty thanks and blessings when leaving our several meetings have caused my heart to overflow.

At the table of W. Davis we have partaken of crapeaux in soup and in hash. The crapeau is a large frog. I thought the soup excellent, and praised it, ignorant of what it was made, until I discovered the minute and beautiful vertibræ of the animal. Lizards, I believe, we have not yet eaten, nor am I ambitious to do so. They and the crapeaux keep up a brisk concert every evening, the lizards whistling like partridges at sunset, and the crapeaux croaking gaily.

Buckingham, 8th.—It was the day called "Good Friday" that we left Rosalie, and the priest had come there to attend to his flock on that day. Amongst other privileges, he granted them small phials of water which he said he had made holy, and sold them to the credulous at a dollar each. I felt it right to speak to a few who gathered around us, and assured them of the folly of depending on such hopes for eternal bliss. Our road to Roseau took us through fine mountain scenery, consisting chiefly of a zigzag of nine miles to the summit level, where lies a beautiful lake, surrounded by the wooded peaks of many mountains. This lake is fully 3,000 feet above the sea, and it supplies a few of the rivers which empty themselves on either side of the island.

We accomplished our mountain ride of eighteen miles to Roseau in five hours, thankful for the favours extended to us during the whole of this journey of thirty miles by canoe, and seventy miles by horses and mules without accident.

The meeting in the Wesleyan Chapel at Roseau on First-day evening proved to be an occasion for thankfulness for the fresh ability given to take of the things of God and hand them to others; declaring some of the unsearchable riches of Christ. We had been in the morning to the gaol, and visited the prisoners in their respective cells, and afterwards saw them collectively. They were addressed by both of us, the gaoler standing by to interpret into *patois*, most of them being French. The gospel truths seemed to find entrance to their hearts. We found one man engaged in making a net, notwithstanding the day. This we spoke against, and it was given up. In order that the poor man might have the void rightly supplied, I took him some books in the afternoon. Amongst them was one of the little spelling books with which my dear Aunt Fox kindly supplied me. I spent a little time with him, going over A, B, C, D; and discovered a fellow prisoner who could instruct him.

I heard the women from the hospital, seventy yards off, calling for English tracts. The only one I had was that precious one, "The Stone Breaker," the last of two given me by my sister Elizabeth on leaving. I felt I could not spare it, as I wanted to read it to Mary Dalrymple. After reading it to her I said I could spare it to her on one condition only, and that was that she should read it to the prisoners, and translate it into French as she proceeded. This she promised, and that promise she fulfilled yesterday, going with a young Methodist—Frances Hazel. They had the prisoners assembled, and after reading it and talking to them, proceeded to do the same at the hospital, a place of refuge for the old and infirm. I hope their visits will be continued. The prisoners hitherto have had no outward religious instruction.

Roseau, 10*th*.—Yesterday we saw a Mico school at Souffrière. After school I asked a cluster of boys, whom I had heard read Luke vii., whether they all had Testaments. I found six had not. I had with me only one of the Testaments sent by the Falmouth boys, and therefore told the children they must cast lots for it. The lot fell on a fine black youth, named William Gabriel. As I wrote his name in it, I reminded him that Gabriel was an angel, and I hope he would become a good angel also. He said he wished to be. This scene took place on the sands of Souffrière Bay, just as we were about to embark in a canoe which brought us back to Roseau.

St. John's, Antigua, 14th.—We left Roseau on the 11th by the *Medway* steamer. John Horsford and C. Fillan accompanied us to the ship.

In passing Guadaloupe we saw marks of the earthquake of 1843. The damage in that island amounted to more than £1,000,000, besides a fearful loss of life. The effects of that shock are to be seen in every quarter of Antigua, so that as I rode along from English Harbour to St. John's I was repeatedly reminded of the language, "Come, behold the works of the Lord, what desolations He hath made in the earth."

J. Millar, whom we had met at Grenada, heard of our arrival, and invited us the first morning to breakfast. At his house we met a large gathering of the Mico teachers, assembled at their quarterly meeting. We listened to their remarks on the various subjects brought forward by J. Millar. A Psalm was read, after which we addressed them. This is a class for whom I feel much interest, believing as I do, that the welfare of thousands depends in a large degree on the zeal, faithfulness, and dedication of the hearts of these young labourers in the Lord's work.

We called on the governor, Sir Charles Fitzroy, who was courteous and kind in his reception. He expressed his readiness to serve us in any way we might point out. We also called on Archdeacon Robert Holberton, pastor to a numerous and much attached flock. His wife is a pleasing Creole, educated in England. They both bear the impress of devotedness of heart to the best of services. He took us to see the daily meal institution, where a number of destitute persons are well cared for in food, clothes, and lodging, and much attention is paid to their religious instruction. We saw a new ward which had been recently erected, consequent on a gift of £50 from Joseph John Gurney. Some shipwrecked English sailors were inmates.

18*th*.—We had a call from the Polytechnic deputation, who informed us that we were elected honorary members of that institution, and asked me to give them a lecture; I declined because I deem it inexpedient to devote any talent I may have entrusted to my care for speaking in public, to any other than religious or moral purposes.

We had a meeting in the Moravian Chapel of Five Islands. Deep conflict was my portion during the day, and truly I might say that I cried unto God with my voice, and wept before Him; when I was cheered by the remembrance of the sufferings of our great High Priest and Sacrifice, He who is touched with a feeling of our infirmities. And laying my cause on Him I was comforted, and ability was given at the meeting to speak on the language, "I will bless the Lord, who hath given me counsel." After the meeting, an aged and almost blind negro, named Samuel, came to us, and taking us both by the hand, said, "Dear brothers, Christ has sent you here to feed His sheep; I feel thankful for what I have heard this night, and believe I shall know more of the Lord's will."

We were accompanied to St. John's by James Heath, a Moravian, who has the care of several schools. We visited one with about fifty boys and girls, fairly taught by a young coloured woman. We heard them question each other on Scripture history. All the children except one sat in the gallery, and that one stood on the floor of the room to be questioned by any child, who must lift up the hand as a token of the wish to speak. If the child cannot give the answer, it is supplied by the questioner, who then changes places and is questioned in turn. One boy, who was sharp, bid fair to maintain his ground amid a host of little examiners, who sent their darts thick and fast upon him. At last he was brought to a stand by a little black girl, who asked, "What did Reuben say when he came to the pit and found Joseph gone?"

20th.—We called on Bennett Harvey, at Spring Gardens, who showed me at the Moravian station their chapel, which was built in 1769, chiefly by the labour of the negroes on First-days. They used to bring a large stone on their heads when coming to their "praise" on that day; and after "praise" they would set to work diligently and labour. This chapel was afterwards enlarged, and now forms about one fourth of their present building, holding 1,200 people.

21st, First Day.—We went to Parham, through an open country like Dorsetshire. We were kindly welcomed by William Waymouth; and at eleven, met a large company of nearly 1,000 persons in the Wesleyan Chapel. Under a fresh call I knelt in prayer that our hearts might be humbled, broken, healed, and raised up by the Lord.

At four o'clock we went to the Scotch Kirk at St. John's, where we met about 150, chiefly of the wealthy classes. To these I had to speak on the need of receiving Christ in the heart as our Redeemer from sin, Instructor in righteousness, Sanctifier and Sacrifice. J. Jesup quoted the words of our Lord, "Blessed are the poor in spirit; for theirs is the kingdom of heaven."

22nd.—We spent the morning pleasantly at Buxton Grove, a Normal school for training teachers. A young black man was exercising his powers of teaching by giving a lecture on wading birds to an intelligent class of boys.

In the afternoon we went to Lebanon, a Moravian station. After visiting their school we had a good evening meeting with about 700 persons. I set forth the ability all have to be saved, if they are willing to submit to the terms of becoming a disciple of the lowly Jesus.

23rd.—We passed on to Gracefield, a Moravian station occupied by Brother and Sister Baum, to see their school. A meeting of over 400 people in the evening. Pastor Baum expressed much comfort at our visit, which he said was providential. He seems to have a sweet spirit, to which I found myself much bound in the love of the gospel.

24th.—Proceeded to Zion Hill. Visited the Wesleyan day-schools, and attended a very crowded meeting in the Wesleyan Chapel; 100 outside, and 700 inside. My heart was cheered with the language which I quoted: " My soul doth magnify the Lord, and my spirit hath rejoiced in God my Saviour."

Newfield, 25th.—This evening we were present at a crowded meeting at the Moravian Chapel. For myself it was not a very lively time, though I was helped to encourage some present to a growth in grace. I enjoyed the rest and refreshment in being here.

The Moravian Mission was commenced in 1750 by Samuel Isles. In 1788 their numbers were 6,000. They now number more than 10,000.

27th.—Yesterday W. Byam Herbert took me in a gig to Freetown, where we had a crowded meeting. The commencement was disturbed by dogs. I spoke to the people on the impropriety of bringing dogs with them when they come to worship. Afterwards the meeting proved to be a favoured one, a desire being expressed that the word of the Lord might have free course, and that His grace might not be received in vain. Towards the close I felt that many present were with me as in a flowing river of love, of which Christ was the fountain.

After the meeting we came to Bridgetown, a Wesleyan station on Willoughby Bay. A good stone chapel was destroyed here by the earthquake last year. I have much enjoyed the quiet of this retired spot, and spent the afternoon in reading.

The exertions of the negroes in clearing ground for their settlements, and promptly repairing the damage done by the earthquake, go far to prove that they are not that idle, indolent people which it was said they would be unless they were flogged to their labour. On the day that the Lord shook these hills and convulsed these plains, more than fifty of the windmills and boiling-houses and chimneys fell. By the free compensated labour of the negro nearly all have been rebuilt, besides numberless houses. The masons and carpenters have had a busy, profitable harvest. I believe all the Episcopal places of worship suffered; many I have seen prostrate, not touched since they fell, whereas the Dissenting places have all been repaired, or rebuilt by means of the voluntary principle.

Gracehill, 29th.—We left Bridgetown, accompanied by L. Railton, of Barnard Castle, Durham, for Bethesda, where we met a crowded assembly. The simplicity, obedience, and early dedication of the youthful Samuel was the subject of my comments. The same results would be experienced by the youth of the present day, if like Samuel they would listen to the voice of God in their hearts.

From Bethesda we went to English Harbour and dined with George Black and his wife. He is a magistrate and a local preacher. In the afternoon I met about sixty children at their Sunday School. The parents were there also to express their wishes, whether their children should continue in that school, or be led off, by renewed vigorous efforts of a youthful curate, to attend his school and services. Several serious black women calmly arose and without effort said, "All the good that has come to my soul was given me by the blessing of the Lord in coming to this school, and I do wish for my children" (some said grandchildren) "to continue to attend here."

The meeting at English Harbour was fully attended by about 400 persons. Hilton Cheeseborough, the superintendent of the Antigua Wesleyan Circuit, in giving notice in the morning of our meeting, had mentioned our practice of silent worship; that they must not suppose themselves at liberty to gaze about whilst we sat in silence, as worship had commenced, and they should rather seek to approach unto God in prayer. He had read Daniel Wheeler's Journal, which he much enjoyed, and he saw that the drift of our mission was to lead people to a more spiritual view of religion, and from a dependence on man in religious matters. I felt comforted in this, for truly I do desire to direct all with whom I meet to the Lamb of God, who taketh away the sin of the world.

There is a capital school at the Moravian station of Gracehill. The boys were questioning each other. A jet black of thirteen asked, "How many inches long was Noah's ark?" This was too hard for the other. I was surprised with what spirit and feeling they asked and answered such questions as "What text begins with B?" "Behold, how good and how pleasant it is for brethren to dwell together in unity!" "What with R?" "Remember now thy Creator in the days of thy youth."

As we went down the romantic Fig-tree hill, a happy group of scholars, all black, were overtaken by us. As we passed them they sang, and made the woods merrily ring with the greeting, "We make our obeisance to you, sirs, as children ought to do." The effect was sweet and thrilling. We enjoyed seeing them and their happy comrades soon after in their school, Grace Bay, and gave them fifty little books, such being the number out of one hundred who could read Luke xiii. and xiv.

F. W. Hougk and his wife welcomed us kindly. He was educated as a Unitarian in affluence at Leipzig, but when the name of Christ became precious to him as his Deliverer, he was obliged to leave his home. He went to Sarepta, a Moravian colony on the Volga, and thence came to Antigua.

Our visit to Grace Bay was more than commonly interesting. Its situation, aspect, character, and the impression made on my mind well accord with its name.

The meeting was crowded: 600 present. We had a precious season, as comforting to me as any on the island, though there have been not a few when it was evident that the presence of the great Master was felt amongst us.

After the meeting several of the labourers came to speak to us; they were evidently amongst the number who have been taught of the Lord, and who have profited by the teaching. They said, "When will you come again?" "We do not expect to come here again, but I hope that some other Friends will visit you before long." "Hope so too." "But we desire you may go to the Fountain for refreshment. Who is the Fountain? You know who." "Yes," one replied, "Jesus Christ."

> "Oh, Christ, He is the fountain.
> The deep sweet well of love!
> The streams on earth I've tasted,
> More deep I'll drink above."

Such comfort and joy was my portion when meeting that company that I could willingly go there again, if right, but the language seems to be, "Go rather to the lost sheep."

St. John's, Fifth Month 1st.—We proceeded by gig over a bad road along the coast, skirting beautiful amphitheatres of hills and savannahs, to Cedar Hall, a Moravian station, occupied by Brother and Sister Coates from Brighouse, Yorkshire.

I was deeply interested, whilst speaking in the large evening meeting, by hearing several children near me repeating text after text that I used, in a low tone, simultaneously with me, proving at any rate that they do not come to school for nothing. I felt that the seed was falling on well prepared ground—ground on which the great Husbandman had been at work.

2nd.—In the afternoon we started on horseback to find our way to Sawcolts without a guide. The road is intricate, but, by studying a good map, there was no difficulty.

There, again, we met a crowded company in the Wesleyan Chapel. We were thankful that we had made the sacrifice. We rode home at a walking pace by the light of a full moon, with a chorus of lizards. On arriving at our lodgings we learned that some one had called to say that the vessel would be ready for Barbuda the next morning.

CHAPTER XII.

WEST INDIES.

Barbuda—Occupations of Inhabitants—Meeting at Governor's House—School—W. Tanner, the Shepherd—Solomon Deazle, Woodman—Antigua—Meetings in Moravian and Wesleyan School-Rooms—Montserrat—Meetings—Poverty—Visits to Gaol—Nevis—Half the Population Wesleyan—Call on Chief Justice Webb—St. Christopher's—Basseterre—Meetings at Wesleyan and Moravian Chapels—Colonial Secretary—R. and A. Inglis and Children—Schools—Gaol—Jesse Pilcher—Grenada—Meetings at Duquesne—Jamaica—John Daughtry—Earl of Elgin and Lady Charlotte Bruce—Scenery at Belcour—Bible Readings with Servants and Neighbours—The Day's Occupations—James Haig—Captain Robert Bruce—Suggests Employment for Prisoners in Kingston Gaol—Draws Plans for a Prison Wall—Humming Bird—Call on Governor—Meeting with Haitien Refugees—Meeting at Wesleyan Chapel, Botanic Gardens—Abraham Hyams—James Ritchie.

BARBUDA, *Fifth Month 4th*, 1844.—We left Antigua yesterday morning per *Spray*, a schooner of about 110 tons, sent purposely for us. The captain and crew were very civil. The wind was barely fair for us, so that we made the island far to leeward of it, and had to beat against wind and current, until we cast anchor at 9.20 p.m., too late to land.

At seven o'clock next morning we were cheered by tidings of a boat coming to us across the lagoon. We landed on the narrow bank of sand, and were met by J. W. H. Gore, the agent for the island, who conveyed us across the lagoon in his boat. This lagoon is ten miles long, and a mile and a half wide; separated from the ocean by a narrow bank of sand about a hundred yards wide and three to four feet high.

We were soon seated at the breakfast table of J. Gore, and partook heartily of tea, yams, toast, and venison chops. After breakfast we walked with him over his somewhat extensive premises for doing a little at tanning the hides of the wild animals they take in hunting, and saw the carpenters' and smiths' shops for the estates. Neither sugar, nor coffee, nor cotton is grown here. Five hundred persons exist by the chase, raising provisions, burning charcoal and coral-lime, and cutting firewood to supply Antigua.

Before we quitted Antigua, and whilst on the passage, I was engaged in close searching of heart, feeling it to be a serious, and if wrong, a dangerous undertaking, to come to this low island, so difficult to find, and so beset with sunken reefs, reminding me that in this, as in other things, "danger may be at an hour when all seemeth securest to thee." Whilst waiting before the Lord in secret prayer my cry was, "Leave me not, neither forsake me, O God of my salvation." He spake peace in the words of His ancient covenant, "I will never leave thee nor forsake thee."

5*th*.—At an early hour we saw Samuel Deazle, the schoolmaster and clerical teacher, an intelligent, lame, black man. He queried whether we had any authority from the Archdeacon on coming here, without which he could not grant the use of the chapel. J. Gore said that the chapel was not under the control of the bishop, but under the proprietor of the island, Sir William Codrington.

However, we felt best satisfied that we should have a meeting in the hall of the mansion. This was readily agreed to, and J. Gore and his overseers promptly prepared the room after dinner. At five o'clock the large hall was filled, as well as the spacious porch and a platform at the back door and windows, with about 150 adults. Our message seemed to fall on prepared hearts, like water on thirsty ground, and after the meeting there was a full and free expression of gratitude for the visit. Samuel Deazle sat by James Jesup; by my side sat a venerable yet athletic stock-keeper, who seemed as if he had in the course of his life checked the course of many a wild "bullock unaccustomed to the yoke." Near him sat Robert Teague, a vigorous young man, black as jet, with a refined aspect. His greeting to me was, "God bless you indeed, sir."

6th.—We found about 120 in the school; twenty of these read in the Testament fairly. To those who had not a Testament I gave one, believing that my young friends at the British and Foreign School, Falmouth, would approve of their gifts being thus bestowed. I gave them an earnest exhortation to read in them daily, and spoke of the blessing which would, I believe, rest on those who did so.

In the afternoon we had interesting conversation with young and old. Some vigorous men expressed their wish that we would stay with them. They are remarkably healthy and long-lived; we saw several above eighty. Frequent wrecks on the coast inure them to danger. Cousin R. W. Fox's present of spectacles came into requisition very acceptably. They have no shops, therefore no rum is sold. Their houses are wattled and plaistered, and covered with sedge-grass. Some of the women are so fleet and vigorous that they will run down and catch a wild sheep.

We took a strolling ride on horseback for an hour or two amongst the herds of tame cattle and sheep, getting glimpses of the wild bullocks and horses as they galloped away and hid themselves in the brushwood that abounds over the island.

We met with William Tanner, a fine young shepherd, having the care of 520 sheep. His greeting on the previous evening after the meeting had been, "Well, if we never meet again in this world, I trust we may meet above!" We had also some conversation with Solomon Deazle, a woodman. It was precious to listen to the outpouring of his heart, bearing witness with my spirit as to the rectitude of going amongst them, preaching peace by Jesus Christ. "I could have listened till sun down to the blessed truths;

without one book; all true; your blessed headpiece; may God in heaven bless you, send you safe home. I wish you stay with me."

St. John's, Antigua, 8th.—Yesterday morning we crossed to Parham, Antigua, and were kindly welcomed, and brought to this city by Charles Thwaites in his gig.

10th.—About 900 were present at a meeting in the Moravian Chapel, Spring Gardens. James Jesup alluded to the joy felt by one of the elders of Israel at the birth of our Lord as his Deliverer. Whilst J. J. was speaking, it was laid on me to follow with a comparison of the stages in the dispensations of Jehovah. Adam, Noah, Abraham, Moses, and lastly the accomplishment of full and free deliverance from sin, by the coming and due reception of Jesus as the well beloved Son of God, whose language was, "Come unto Me, all ye that labour and are heavy laden, and I will give you rest."

12th.—We held our last meeting in the Wesleyan Schoolroom. It was attended by 1,200 persons. We had had seventeen meetings in this interesting island, and were "ready to depart on the morrow"; when to our surprise a person called to say that his little schooner was going to Montserrat, and that to-morrow. At seven we were on board the *Ocean Bride*, once a yacht of thirty tons.

Plymouth, Montserrat, 17th.—We had a rough passage to this island, rendered disagreeable and dangerous by the crew being the worse for liquor, and quite unfit to have the care of life and property. Through the continued mercy of the Lord we were permitted to reach in safety this small town.

Our reception has been kind and cheering. We had a letter for Henry Loving, who took us to the house of a widow Chalmers, where we are accommodated very comfortably. James Harris, an active stipendiary magistrate, spent an hour with us and invited us to his house to dine. Henry Loving is a Wesleyan, once the editor of a leading paper in

Antigua. He visited England as a delegate for the people of colour some years ago, was unexpectedly selected a chief of the police, and is now Colonial Secretary for this island for life, also a magistrate. He was born a slave!

Yesterday evening we met a full gathering in the Wesleyan Chapel at Cavalla Hill. It was attended by some who seemed able to receive the truths that were handed to them, and we felt at the close of the day that although we had nothing to glory in, we had not come hither in vain.

This morning the funeral service took place for a young woman who died suddenly. As I was dressing at six I heard the sound of hymn-singing. After the burial service was concluded it seemed right for me to address the bystanders.

This is a beautiful island, but it has more the appearance of poverty and abandonment than any we have before visited. It is greatly injured by the departure of the labourers to other more flourishing islands. The whole population of this little spot is doubtless below 10,000; those that remain seem inert and listless. Most of the inhabitants of Plymouth were present at a large meeting in the Wesleyan Chapel this evening.

20th.—The wind was so boisterous as to delay our departure. Yesterday we breakfasted with Christopher Skerritt, a young coloured local preacher, at Bethel; we met a large company who seemed more strangers to the work and fruits of righteousness than many whom I have recently seen. I do indeed pity those who are taught to depend on a perishing fellow-creature for the breaking of the spiritual bread, which is dispensed freely by the great High Priest of our profession. The more I see of other sections of the Christian Church, the more do I value the truths which I was taught.

We visited the gaol, and I read Psalm li. to the five prisoners, and also repeated the words, "Seek ye the Lord while He may be found; call ye upon Him while He is near.

Let the wicked forsake his way, and the unrighteous man his thoughts; and let him return unto the Lord, and He will have mercy upon him; and to our God, for He will abundantly pardon."

Had a pleasant call this morning from James Delvin, who seems to see the need of increased spirituality amongst the Wesleyans. Our conversation has been cheering and interesting. His father was a slave, but valued education for his son, and placed him at school, where he remained till he could read words of two syllables. At twenty years of age he felt strong convictions for his sinful life, and before he was thirty he joined the Wesleyans. He was made a leader, afterwards a teacher in the Sabbath School, and fourteen years ago he was appointed a local preacher. He is one of the most intelligent of the deeply-coloured class I have met with.

On leaving Montserrat, Thomas Dyett, a fisherman, conveyed us and our luggage in his boat to the vessel, and refused compensation. He is a hearty, kind man, very black. His house stands near the shore, and when he took us to it he said, "See, Massa, the place my Father provide for me." His grateful heart often acknowledges the goodness and mercy which have followed him.

Charlestown, Nevis, 21st.—We left Montserrat by the *Industry*, a small sloop of twenty-seven tons. I esteem it no small favour to have reached this island in safety, notwithstanding the raging sea we have this day passed over, of which I had much fear.

22nd.—We called this morning on Jesse Pilcher, and looked over his interesting little garden of choice plants and shrubs. We also examined the new handsome chapel, now erecting, to hold 1,400 persons. The Wesleyan hearers number 6,000 out of a population of 12,000.

After breakfast we visited their school, where 250 boys and girls are daily taught. The master had been a slave, and was very intelligent and very black.

Our meeting in the old Wesleyan Chapel was attended by 700 persons. James Jesup spoke on true spiritual worship, and I had to quote the words, "Let My people go, that they may serve Me." The children of Israel knew not what they must sacrifice unto the Lord, until they had reached the place in the wilderness. I turned the attention of the people to ask themselves what they thought of Christ. Some children of Belial tried to interrupt our meeting by noise outside; but truth had the dominion, as it ever will; whilst the servants of Satan will have an awful recompense.

24*th*.—Yesterday we called on the Chief Justice; he is a son of the late George Webb, of Flushing, near Falmouth. I encouraged him to persevere in well-doing, using the language, "Fear ye not the reproach of men, neither be ye afraid of their revilings."

We had a meeting at noon in the Chapel Schoolroom, at Clifton, when the presence of the Great Master was felt, and ability given to declare some of His counsel, encouraging those gathered to yield their hearts now to do His will.

From Clifton we proceeded four miles to Newcastle. I spent a few hours in much depression of spirit, feeling no ability to do the work of the Lord; but on going to the Wesleyan Chapel, I was enabled to labour amongst the people to the relief of my mind. We enjoyed our ride home by moonlight.

Basseterre, St. Christopher, 25th.—We came from Nevis in a small sloop, the *Ebenezer*, a well found craft of twenty tons. The channel between the islands is very little wider than the entrance of Falmouth Harbour. It also has its black rock, called Boobie Island: it is used by boobies and pelicans as a resting and probably a nesting-place. Although the channel between these islands is so narrow, yet it is more dangerous than most other parts of these seas, owing to the puffs off the mountains. Our captain and crew, who were all black, had to stand by and promptly shorten sail as the squalls came. The distance, by the course we took, was fifteen miles; and the view, as we came across, was beautiful of the sugar-loaf, slope lands, and low lands of Nevis; the rugged outline of St. Christopher's, with its lofty and cloud-capped Mount Misery, forming a magnificent bay. Both islands appear to be in high sugar cultivation. The sides of the mountains are brilliantly green, from the extensive patches of cane. Monkey Hill is prominent and conspicuous behind Basseterre. We asked our boatmen whether monkeys were plentiful, "Plenty in the mountains, but not much caught now." "Why not?" "People got something better to do now than catch monkeys."

27th.—Yesterday evening we attended a meeting in the Wesleyan Chapel, at Basseterre; about 1,000 persons present. The meeting was rendered somewhat uncomfortable towards the close by the haste of the collectors handing round the boxes for contributions. We explained fully that this collection was not for our benefit, believing as we do that the gospel should be freely given.

Before breakfast we walked to the Moravian settlement, and arranged for two meetings; which, with those arranged for in the Wesleyan Chapels, will be all that will, I believe, be required of us ere we turn towards Grenada and Jamaica. Before I had yielded full submission to the appointment of these meetings I had much conflict, since then, peace in the midst of poverty of spirit.

28th.—We had an interesting call from Robert Murray Rumsey, the Colonial Secretary, who conversed freely on the leading doctrines of Christianity, on which we agree, and also on the points on which we differ. We presented him with our last copy of Dymond's Essays.

There was a meeting of about 600 persons last evening at Old Road. A deep feeling of spiritual poverty and bodily infirmity was my experience before we entered the chapel; but as the people gathered, strength was granted to give utterance to the words which arose in my heart for them. I found it right to call their attention to the silence of all fleshly and creaturely feelings, every thought being brought into subjection to the obedience of Christ, in order that true worship may be known. The youthful wanderers, who have strayed from the path of peace, were exhorted to turn away from the deceiver of their souls, and to give their hearts to the Lord Jesus, that they may be created anew by Him.

This evening we went to Cayenne, and had a meeting in the Moravian Chapel at Bethesda, 500 present; with whom I laboured as ability was given, but it proved to me a low season, and very heavy. The cause is yet hidden from me.

29th.—James Jesup and I had our meeting together, a season of renewed dedication, when a sense prevailed that if we were faithful, neither heights nor depths would be permitted to separate us from the love of God which is in Christ Jesus.

We went along the coast through gardens of "tous-les-mois," bearing their brilliant scarlet flowers. The roots are ground as arrowroot, only it is a much more delicate food. It is sold here at twopence per pound. We reached Sandypoint in good time for a four o'clock dinner, on fish, kid, and guava tart, at the house of Robert and Anne Inglis. They have four children. I enjoyed a morning stroll with the dear little trio, after my mind had been relieved by a large and satisfactory meeting of about 1,000 in the Wesleyan Chapel.

30th.—We left Sandypoint after breakfast, and continued our drive round the northern part of the island. Whilst rounding the furthest point I could mentally enjoy that hymn:—

> "How are Thy servants blest, O Lord!
> How sure is their defence;
> Eternal wisdom is their guide,
> Their help omnipotence."

31st.—We visited the capital school of 280 boys and girls under the care of the Moravians at Basseterre. In the evening we had a meeting in their chapel, attended by 1,200 persons.

Sixth Month 2nd.—We visited the gaol, a poor place, very full. Seven soldiers were there, besides twenty-four of the usual class; a large number in a population of 20,000. We had a profitable interview with the seven soldiers; they acknowledged their guilt, and declared that rum had been their ruin.

After a time of worship in our room, when feelings of thankfulness arose in our hearts, we embarked for Grenada. The little *Acteon* steamer laboured heavily, but when under the lee of the islands we had very smooth and delightful cruising; and thus we had thirty or forty miles of rough and smooth alternately.

At Nevis we were joined by J. Mortier. He handed us a cordial letter from his colleague, Jesse Pilcher. I felt whilst with him, and others of kindred spirit, that it was pleasant, thus as it were, to shake hands with fellow pilgrims at the low places of the fences which distinguish our paths; for I do esteem it a privilege to be able to discover good in others, whilst I believe the path in which Friends profess to walk is a more excellent way. A recently increased experience of the ways of many others tends to confirm me in this opinion.

I felt thankful for our preservation as we glided safely into the sweet little harbour of George Town, Grenada, after an absence of four months.

Duquesne, 7th.—We left George Town yesterday, and had a squally sail and row in a large canoe, reaching Goyave, where horses awaited us, sent by H. F. Fairclough. We rode most of the way in the dark by a dangerous road; much of it on a precipice over the sea, or under precipices on the sea-shore, where large stones impeded our path.

At seven this evening we attended a small meeting at Duquesne; and had conversation with several persons living in sin, who promised amendment.

9th.—Still at George Town. I had a pleasant stroll this morning in my favourite walk round the Fort. Read in Waring's Melodies, "Moonlight and Sunshine." Faith was sweetly given me to believe that if I am faithful to my covenant with a covenant-keeping God, that I shall experience my path to "bloom as it ne'er bloomed before." Under these feelings I remembered the sweet language I heard in my soul when ill at Naparima, "I will make thy way perfect." My thoughts turned sweetly towards my dear children, who were then probably at meeting, and my prayer arose on their behalf, that they might be truly engaged in worship.

Kingston, Jamaica, Sixth Month 15*th.*—We arrived here yesterday, per *Forth* steamer, having had a safe and pleasant passage from Grenada of five days. I had much satisfactory intercourse with several of the passengers. Amongst these was ex-president Boyer of Hayti. He declared that the present unhappy condition of that island was the result of the absence of religion amongst the people.

When abreast of that low dangerous ground called Morant Point, and seven miles off, a black pilot came off in a canoe, made out of a single tree. It seemed an absurdity for this uncultivated youth to supersede the authority of our Commander Chapman, but the insurance laws require this regulation. As we threaded the coral rocks and banks that guard the harbour of Port Royal, it was evident that local knowledge was important, if not essential. We were soon cheered by the sight of John Daughtry, who conducted us to the lodgings kept by Grace Blundell.

16th.—On awaking this morning I remembered that it was this day five months that the spirit of my darling Jenepher left its earthly tabernacle for one of those buildings of God, an house not made with hands, eternal in the heavens. Whilst I mourn my bereavement, I can unfeignedly give thanks unto Him, who I believe redeemed her soul, and gave her the victory over death, hell, and the grave.

In our morning meeting J. Jesup quoted, "Whatsoever He saith unto you, do it." I was forcibly reminded of the words, "He brought me into the banqueting house, and His banner over me was love." It was a precious season.

In consideration of his recent illness and bereavement, Edwin O. Tregelles was advised to rest for awhile during the hot season. They had engaged for this purpose a house called Belcour, about nine miles from Kingston, before John Daughtry made the kind offer recorded in the following entry.

20th.—John Daughtry called, and invited us to his house at Richmond Pen. So at sunset we went thither. He goes to New York next week to examine the result of prison discipline in America, and has most handsomely offered us the use of his dwelling-house, and ample accommodation during his three months' absence. We had a time of worship together, when John Daughtry's family were collected, and John i. was read, after which I spoke on the character and importance of true worship, and on the blessings we enjoy in having the revelation of the Divine will.

21st.—I went to Craighton to breakfast with the Earl of Elgin. My reception was kind and cordial from him, and his brother Robert Bruce, and sister Lady Charlotte Bruce. He is a widower, having been bereaved of a lovely superior wife, a few months ago. She left a sweet little girl, now two years old. After breakfast I proposed our having a chapter in the Bible read, which was most cheerfully complied with; and eight or ten servants assembled with the family in the drawing-room. I read Psalm ciii., and afterwards addressed them on the necessity of walking as children of the light; that we may know the blood of Jesus Christ to cleanse from all sin.

23rd.—I have of late, from various causes, been led to

dwell on the joys and blessedness of heaven. The happiness of the redeemed is complete; they have no ungratified desire, and every joy is hallowed, according to the language, "They hunger no more, neither thirst any more." I am ready to believe that one source of their continuous bliss is the unceasing addition of other redeemed spirits, that swell and increase the ranks of those whose harps are tuned to the praise of their Redeemer.

27*th*.—We have succeeded in securing a suitable carriage and horses. The carriage is light, with a head to the back seat. We have a pair of grey ponies that run well in harness, and carry us well on saddles, which is a needful arrangement where good level roads prevail in the large savannahs; and then among the mountains the roads suddenly change to bridle paths. We cannot approach our new residence, Belcour Lodge, with any carriage, and goods must be conveyed on men's heads or mule back, a mile by a steep narrow path.

Belcour Lodge, 30th.—We came yesterday to our snug, peaceful retreat. The valley in which our house stands is so tortuous, and the sides so steep, as to limit our view in front, though at the back we can see the tops of many hills, two miles off and 2,000 feet high. We dwell in the midst of a coffee plantation, and in a thicket of shaddocks, forbidden fruit, oranges, lemons, guavas, mangoes; and at the back the hill is planted with pines. Any of these fruits that are ripe we may have on our table daily without charge. The profusion of mangoes surprises me; the tree grows as large as an ash. There are 1,000 mango trees loaded with clusters of fruit which yields a delicious odour, but tastes of turpentine. This flavour is dissipated by heat, and it is excellent baked or stewed. Quadrupeds, birds and insects feed on it abundantly.

At half past ten this morning we met for worship, having the company of our house-keeper Sophia Nicholson, her little *protégée* Elizabeth, and our man James Harris. I spoke on the words, " Where two or three are gathered together in My name, there am I in the midst of them." James Jesup knelt in prayer. We had previously collected our servants and neighbours together at our Bible reading after breakfast, when Hebrews i. was read. I alluded to the value of such a testimony to the divinity of our Lord, and the importance of avoiding the error into which the Jews fell, of rejecting our Redeemer because He came not with the pomp and ceremonies they expected; that it is needful for us to receive the Spirit of Jesus into our hearts, as the Guide into all truth, which, if followed, will lead from darkness to light, and from the power of Satan unto God.

Seventh Month 17th.—I enjoy our snug retreat, and hope I may profit by the retirement; every hour seems fully occupied. I rise at half past six. After an early cup of coffee and an American cracker, we have an hour's walk, unless we prefer using our ponies; we return to breakfast, after which our housekeeper, and servants and some of the people residing near come to our usual reading. Writing occupies much of the morning. About noon I give a writing lesson to two little girls, and hear them repeat hymns. A lunch of fruit refreshes us, writing again until four o'clock, when we dine. After this we read together. A walk about sunset. A lesson in writing and reading to our man Harris, and Ritchie, a boy worth cultivating, from a neighbouring cottage. About seven we all are collected again for the family Bible reading.

A few days ago I was led to the shop of a shoemaker in Kingston, named James Haig. He knew John Candler, and valued some books received from him when they met at Port au Prince. He is a total abstainer, having formerly drunk freely. One day he attended the deathbed of an acquaintance, a surgeon, who fell an early victim to intemperance, and his dying advice was, " Refrain from the course which has led me to destruction." From that time J. Haig has relinquished strong drink, and now objects to have any in his house.

Some may think our lives do not exhibit much of the missionary character, but that we are living too much to ourselves. To this I plead guilty, though I do not feel that it is sinful. We are, I hope, pursuing a means for the sake of the end.

One evening, as J. J. and I were preparing for our sunset walk, we were surprised by the appearance of a caller approaching the house on horseback. It proved to be Captain Robert Bruce, brother of the Earl of Elgin. He came and spent a short time with us. I enjoy his society, believing that he possesses the "oil of gladness" beyond most of his class.

23rd.—I may with much thankfulness acknowledge the condescending mercy which attended me to-day on leaving this place on horseback, when my horse, being somewhat restive, threw me, but I was marvellously preserved from injury.

Whilst walking with John Daughtry in his grounds one evening, I suggested he should offer a price per hundred weight for all the bones that might be brought to the Penitentiary, where some of the convicts might be employed in breaking them for manure. He took the hint, and offered 2s. per hundred weight. When I went with him to the Penitentiary two weeks after, the place was crowded with poor old black women, and with children, bringing baskets of bones. They are thus turned to good account, and the revenue of the Penitentiary increased by their conversion and re-sale. I have given some hints about the foundation of a new boundary wall that they are building on bad ground.

As we crossed the stream one evening, a mile above our dwelling, J. Jesup's pony, Whitefoot, lost a shoe, which induced us to turn back and call on Wiles. He is quite a character, full of vigour, and, though about eighty, took delight in showing us his English plants—geraniums, roses, dahlias. An exquisite humming-bird chose that moment for extracting sweets from the flower of a shrub above my head. The general colour of the bird was a dark green approaching to black, but varying to purple and gold. Its chief beauty lies in two feathers about six inches long, that formed an elegant forked tail, waving in the wind; its whole length nine inches.

25th.—After our meeting in the morning, which was held in silence, we rode up to Craighton, to call on the Governor, the Earl of Elgin. After conversing on general subjects, allusion was made to the departure from Jamaica of several missionaries to Africa. This seemed to open the way for me to relieve my mind of the load I had been bearing on behalf of the Governor, who received my message of counsel and sympathy with much feeling, and thanked us for our visit. I returned home with a light and peaceful heart, believing that it was a right commencement of our labours in this land to encourage the representative of our beloved Queen to be just in his conduct: "He that ruleth over men must be just, ruling in the fear of the Lord." I reminded him that his conduct would greatly conduce to, or check, the spread of the Lord's work in the earth.

26th.—We went to Kingston to meet at the house of Charles Lake such of the Haytian refugees as might be inclined to attend. About seventeen assembled. After a solemn pause I gave expression to the words, "Live in peace; and the God of love and peace shall be with you." I reminded them that true worship was not that of the mouth or the hands, but of the heart; this must be cleansed during our lives, or we shall suffer consequent punishment: as the tree falls so it lies. I encouraged them to the diligent perusal of the Holy Scriptures, with a desire to be instructed by the great Teacher. Prayer was offered on behalf of the people of Hayti, that they may be brought to a knowledge of the truth.

29th.—Yesterday we ventured to commence the work for

which we came to Jamaica, by appointing a meeting at eleven o'clock in the Wesleyan Chapel at the Botanic Gardens, kindly offered by Abraham Hyams. We went to his house to breakfast. He told us very modestly: "I was once of the same faith as the Apostle Paul [had been], but mine eyes have been opened." Now Jesus Christ and Him crucified is the theme on which his heart delights to dwell, as well it may. The meeting-house was well filled with about 250 persons—black peasantry, coloured dealers and jobbers, and some of the white planter class. The words given me to stand up with were, "For ye know the grace of our Lord Jesus Christ, that though He was rich, yet for your sakes He became poor, that ye through His poverty might be rich." Counsel, warning and encouragement flowed freely whilst preaching Christ crucified, as the hope of glory for those who walk in the light which He gives.

It it not probable that we shall proceed much in our work yet, although I do not see the necessity for lying by. I do not feel the heat more oppressive than in other places where we have been. The peace, which is the result of yesterday's engagement, is so sweet, that we trust we may soon feel liberated to proceed.

My poor friend, James Ritchie, whom we have often visited, seems sinking. It is deeply affecting to me to watch him weakening almost day by day. I felt well repaid for the labour bestowed when I saw the expression of his sable countenance as he said, "I can neber be thankful enough to you." To-day he said to us under a sense of accumulated transgression, "Sometime my sin so big as de house, and I can't get rid of any part of it, not a morsel, and sometime it seem divided. Oh, if I could but crawl once more, I'd serve God with ebery vein in my body!" He was reminded that those thick clouds between him and God would be removed, and his sins blotted out by the blood of the all-sufficient Sacrifice, if he would but give his heart unto the Lord in covenant.

CHAPTER XIII.

WEST INDIES.

Letter to Joseph T. Price about Anniversary of Liberation of Slaves—Belcour—Shortwood—Cottage Meetings—Stay at Stoneyhill—Oberlin—Low Condition of Education—J. A. Preston—Elliot Station—Meeting at Mount Charles—Tropical Rain—Maroons—Grateful Hill—Myalism and Obeeism—Meeting at Pleasant Hill—School at Mount Fletcher—Richmond Pen—Meeting at Kingston, 2,000 present—Spanish Town—Sligoville—Homes of Freed Slaves—Baptist Chapel, Passage Fort—Meeting at Jericho—Missing Mule—Annatto Bay—Call on two Friends—Mount Hermon—Ascent of Mount Diabola—Phœnix Park—Jonathan Edmundson—Wesleyan School—Waterfall—David Day—Bariffe Hall—Ora Cabessa—William Jamieson—Large Meetings at Beechamville—Ocho Rios—St. Ann's Bay—Beautiful Scenery—Brown's Town—John Clark—Meetings and Schools—Sturge Town—Sunday School Teachers, Brown's Town—James Finlayson and Martial Law in 1832—Dry Harbour—Calabar—J. Timson—Kettering—William Knibb's House, built by grateful Liberated Slaves—Meeting with Teachers—Large Meeting at Falmouth—Earthquake—Prison—Montego Bay—J. L. Lewin, a Converted Jew—Cornwall—H. M. Waddell—George Blyth—Meeting at Goodwill Temperance Village—Moravian Settlement, Irwin Hill—Salter's Hill—Large Meeting, Mount Carey—Thomas Burchall—Lucea—W. H. Hann, Wesleyan Missionary—Savannah-la-mar—Aaron de Leon—Laars Kielson—New Beaufort.

E. O. TREGELLES TO JOSEPH TREGELLES PRICE.
Belcour, Kingston, Jamaica.
Eighth Month 3rd, 1844.

MY DEAR COUSIN,—

Thou wert so frequently my companion mentally last Fifth-day, the 1st inst., that I feel as if I could do no less than attempt to give thee an outline of the day. After an early breakfast on Fourth-day we were seated in our carriage, which remains at the mouth of our glen because we cannot bring it nearer. I drove most of the way to Spanish Town, eighteen miles distant, our man being somewhat timid, the horses lively, and the first two miles more dangerous, narrow and precipitous than any I have met with in my peregrinations at home. We stopped to bait at a tavern seven miles from Spanish Town.

Our reception from J. M. Philippo and his wife was truly kind. They usually reside at Sligoville, a thriving negro settlement, on land purchased by J. M. P., which has accomplished an important object in carrying out the freedom of the people. It is thirteen miles north of Spanish Town, and J. M. P. came down to his former station, as being the most central, and best adapted for the celebration of the tenth anniversary of partial, and sixth of complete, freedom of the slaves.

At seven o'clock that morning we met the teachers of their First-day and other schools, about twenty young men and women, chiefly coloured, and partook of tea, coffee, and chocolate, which was elegantly provided in a spacious entrance hall that separates the boys' and girls' schools. Cakes, biscuits and fruits of various kinds were freely enjoyed. After tea, an opportunity was afforded to hand counsel and encouragement to this important class. We left them soon after nine, with a caution not to become too much excited by their hymn-singing, with which they meant to usher in the new eventful year.

James M. Philippo tapped at our door the next morning before five, and invited us to witness the doings of the company who were assembled in the yard. They had a standard chandelier supporting a dozen candles burning in the tranquil air, by the light of which they read the hymns they sang. At 5.30 a.m. they assembled in the large chapel, where the people had long been collecting, from whence we heard the sounds of prayer and thanksgiving, arising from the lips, and, I trust, from the hearts of the liberated.

My heart ascended with desires such as David used: "Oh that men would praise the Lord for His goodness, and for His wonderful works to the children of men!" To this language I gave expression when opportunity was kindly afforded by J. M. Philippo of meeting a large company at eleven. They were reminded that although their freedom was apparently accomplished by the efforts of their friends, yet it was evidently the Lord's doing, and marvellous in the eyes of many. One of the most striking features was, that it was effected without bloodshed: very different, indeed, from their neighbours in Hayti, of whose state a brief sketch was given, and they were told that if in any evil hour they should be induced to take up carnal weapons to obtain what they may consider their rights, they would in that hour forfeit the esteem of their warm steady friends in England. And more than this, they would depart from their allegiance to Jehovah; no longer the servants of the Prince of peace, they would become servants of Satan. When they were charged never to stain their hands with the blood of a fellow-creature, and take away life, we heard the response of "Never, massa: oh, never!" This coming simultaneously from about 2,000 persons would have warmed thy heart.

Amongst the other subjects brought before the meeting were those of intemperance, the right education of children, avoiding cruel beatings, a relic of slavery. Several black men who had been slaves took part with J. M. Philippo and ourselves in giving this advice; and last, but not least, was Richard Hill, a man of colour, highly cultivated, intelligent and pleasing: we have met him repeatedly, and I have never been five minutes in his company without instruction.

After a fruit lunch at J. M. Philippo's, in company with J. M. P. and R. H., J. Jesup and I had a conference with about twenty of the leaders, deacons and assistants, mostly black; when some subjects were brought before them not fit for more public discussion. In connection with these was the subject of suitable dwellings for their people.

At the close of this conference we went to the Wesleyan Chapel, where we found 150 little school children dining on roast beef and plum pudding, with the liberal addition of as much mango and pine-apple as was good for them. They were nearly all black, clothed in white dresses, and as orderly as children at home. At the close of their handsome and much enjoyed repast, opportunity was afforded us to address them and their parents, many of whom were present. We then dined with the teachers and helpers at the house of H. B. Britton.

After a short interval, we again assembled in the Wesleyan Chapel, which was soon crowded. It proved a good season of worship, for which I felt thankful, though cast down at the commencement, when I was ready to question the rectitude of our having appointed that meeting. Now I believe it was in right ordering. We returned to our pleasant quarters at J. M. Philippo's under the feeling, that although we might have been weak and unprofitable we had not that day been slothful servants.

We left early next morning, and reached home in safety, travelling one hour with a nearly vertical sun, which caused me to feel more heat than I have often done before, but not more than I can easily endure.

Often have I been reminded of thy many late rides, to Swansea and back, labouring in the cause of peace and freedom, when I was thy occasional companion. Now I see that my manner of life in long fatiguing rides, finding out places and people before unknown, enduring various vicissitudes of temperature, change of place and employment, was in degree favourable for my present varied experience, of which I should like for thee to partake.

Thus much I believe I may safely state, that if all the labour thou and thy colleagues endured, if all the expense you incurred, and if all the apocryphal compensation money were multiplied by ten, the sacrifice would not have been too costly to obtain all the blessings which are now possessed, enjoyed and appreciated by the objects of your efforts.

I am not disposed to pen on this page some of the benefits which have resulted, and which will increasingly result, from the change from slavery to freedom; but I should like for thee to know that the former condition of degradation and misery exceeded any idea I had formed previous to coming here. The wrongs of the slave, though often exhibited in dreadful description at home, did not equal what I have since heard and believe to have been true.

Now, I fancy I hear thee say, "So much for cousin Edwin, and his *couleur de rose*." Well, make all the allowance thou likes, and yet I believe all I have written is true.

Farewell: believe me to be thy very affectionate cousin,

E. O. TREGELLES.

Belcour, Eighth Month 4th.—We met at half-past ten this morning in company with seven of our attendants and neighbours. It proved a refreshing season. Life-giving bread was, I believe, broken amongst us, and thanks were given at the conclusion for the evidence afforded that where two or three are gathered together in the name of the Lord, there will He be in the midst of them.

11th.—At 8 a.m., after a thunder-storm, we started for Shortwood, a settlement of negro huts seven miles to the west of us, which we reached soon after ten, and at eleven met an interesting company, chiefly blacks of the labouring class. It was a good season, though the meeting was small. Rain, lightning and thunder again detained us after meeting, and admitted of our partaking of cold dinner without loss of time. We were much pleased with F. W. and M. Wheeler, a dedicated juvenile pair, whose minds seem open to the truth. They appear to walk with much simplicity and singleness of purpose.

The storm was over in time for us to proceed homewards, taking on the way a meeting at four o'clock in the house of Thomas Gibbert, a leader amongst a sect known as native Baptists. His simple cottage was crowded by about fifty persons, to whom plain counsel was handed by J. Jesup. They wished to be allowed to visit us, which we promoted.

Stoney Hill, 13*th*.—We are at the house of our friend S. Oughton, a Baptist minister of Kingston, where he has a large chapel. He went to Kingston last Seventh-day, and left instructions that we were to have the range of this place. This sort of easy understanding suits us. We wanted a resting place in this quarter, and here we find a good house, boarding ourselves.

Oberlin, 16*th*.—Charles Stewart Renshaw has built a neat chapel and dwelling-house here, so combined as for the chapel to be used at meals. He is an American missionary, and with his wife, a young Friend from Philadelphia, gave us a most cordial welcome.

19*th*.—Accompanied by C. S. Renshaw, we proceeded eight miles to Brainard, another American Missionary station, where we met with a kind reception from Julius O. and Jane Beardslie. Here we saw a good school of eighty boys and girls, taught by Charles B. Venning, from Kent, on the British and Foreign school system,—the first we have visited in Jamaica. It is grievous to see schools going to decay in districts where rum shops are increasing.

About 500 persons came to the meeting at half-past four, chiefly of the labouring class, and some of their masters. At the close, J. O. Beardslie said a few words to the people as to a notion they had that we came to "give them free of the land." They had heard, he said, that day, what was far better, the means of redemption and how they might become heirs of the kingdom of heaven.

20*th*.—We proceeded five miles farther north to Elliott station. On our way we called at Lewisburg, an estate of 2,000 acres, once a fine sugar estate, but in the year of freedom the owners declined giving wages to the labourers, and allowed the canes to rot on the ground. Now it is changed into a pen where cattle are raised. The manager attended the meeting last evening, and sat opposite to me. I felt that his mind was under conviction, and accepted his invitation to call. He received us courteously. After a short time I asked him to take a walk with me in his garden ; as he was deaf we went to a distance from the house, when I told him that I believed he had yesterday felt the power of the Lord at work in his heart. "Yes," he said, " more than I ever felt before." I encouraged him to keep under the feeling, and to follow the teachings of the Lord, who would show him His will. "How long are you going to stay in the island? You should stay; we require to be told again and again." I sought to direct him to Christ as the foundation of his hope. After a while he said, " I have made up my mind to alter my mode of life."

At Elliot station James A. Preston and his wife live in a very simple thatched cottage, forming part of the meeting-house, which was similar to the prayers' houses on the other islands. In that simple meeting-house we had a good meeting, 250 present. I had full and pleasant service amongst them, enforcing freedom from sin as the Christian's experience, and that "if any man hath not the spirit of Christ he is none of His." We returned from our round of twenty-six miles, nearly the whole way by mountain paths, through a rich and beautiful country.

Mount Charles, 21*st*.—Whilst I have been writing we have had one of the grand thunder storms, shaking the wooden house. Now, heavy rain is falling, whilst a thick mist prevents my seeing objects at the distance of fifty yards. Four hours ago I saw as many miles, so wonderfully changeful is this climate!

We arrived at Oberlin just in time to witness the commencement of a schoolroom that C. S. Renshaw is erecting, with funds kindly raised by Sophia Sturge. I have drawn some plans for it, which has served the double purpose of instructing the builder, a young man of colour, in this kind of drawing.

One of the three days of our stay we had a meeting at Ramble, a coffee plantation, with about sixty people in the open air. I felt that the Lord was at work in the hearts of some present, and prayer was offered for those gathered together. During my ride thither my heart seemed full of the love of God. Under His merciful visitation my heart was softened in answer to prayer; and a willingness was then felt to serve my God to the full extent of His will. I felt that I could repose on His fresh covenant of promise, "Keep thy lamp trimmed, and I will supply the oil!" May I be faithful to my part of the covenant. We had a full meeting of 500 persons at Mount Charles, and gave notice of another.

We went to Oberlin and attended the most crowded of any meeting we have had. At first tumultuous, but a holy calm followed, and in this I felt enabled to rise with the words, "God is greatly to be feared in the assembly of His saints, and to be held in reverence of all them that are about Him." Close dealing followed with the formal professor and backslider. C. S. Renshaw at the close reminded the people that our responsibilities were increased by such opportunities.

We find Mount Charles a very congenial place. Our apartments are under the same roof as the meeting-house. Our elevation is about 2,500 feet, but it does not appear high, because many mountains around are much higher. We have abundance of rain, lightning and thunder, and require a thick quilt at night.

We had given notice of a meeting here, but the rain came down so copiously that few came. All West Indians are very careful to avoid exposure to rain, or the damp atmosphere succeeding heavy rain; so that all appointments are dependent thereon. We found this district very damp:

almost every morning we were above the clouds, which filled the valleys around us, and had the effect, beautiful beyond description, of extensive lake scenery, with wooded islets and promontories; the rising sun silvering the surface of these fairy lakes, which sometimes disappeared whilst we took one or two turns for exercise in the spacious chapel. These mists made our garments damp; shoes laid aside for two days became mouldy.

We went with C. S. Renshaw to Fernhill School, and from thence to Scots' Hall, a rural settlement of Maroons, who are negroes escaped from slavery by guile or force, who have maintained independence amongst their fastnesses. After a time the planters availed themselves of the services of the Maroons to bring back their runaway slaves, which they were willing to do for the sake of reward. In lieu of former privileges they have grants of freehold land, two acres per man, and one acre for each child.

We were at the house of Francis Ellis, a fine vigorous fellow. He had six acres given him, and was quite a rich man, intelligent and interesting. He wears the brow of a free and noble Maroon, and is, I believe, coming, if not already come, under the power of the cross. Whilst detained by rain in his commodious and clean cottage, we conversed about his dozen nice books of a serious character, kept neatly in simple book-shelves.

We returned to Mount Charles, eight miles, by moonlight, up steep rugged paths, and through defiles rich with the luxuriant plumes of bamboo.

25*th*.—We rode to Grateful Hill, where we had a good meeting with about 500. Much service devolved on J. Jesup. I felt as though many who were present could with me "drink of the same spiritual water," and "partake of the same spiritual bread."

Thomas Burrows is the pastor of Grateful Hill. He married Elizabeth Coultas, of York. She has suffered much from ill health. She says it is a very different matter to sit in a missionary meeting when young and full of vigour, and listen to the thrilling appeals to become devoted to the spread of the gospel, compared with the every-day duties and privations of the missionary's wife, remote from the friends of her youth, and precluded from the fellowship with them which had helped her in former days of discouragement.

Belvedere, an old coffee plantation two miles distant, belongs to Harriet Coryton and her brother, both young people of colour. It is let out in lots from one to four acres, at four dollars per acre, to free settlers.

Here we had a meeting with 100 or more, in and outside, H. Coryton's simple dwelling. J. Jesup and I sat out of doors amongst the people, under the shade of a spreading tree. The language of invitation and warning was addressed to these people, many of whom, I fear, are strangers to the gospel of peace. They fear the wrath, without seeking the love of the Lord.

It was not till after this meeting that I recollected that Myalism prevails: an African fiendish superstition, the opposite to Obeeism, which it is supposed to counteract. For instance, a man becomes sick, and his illness, if out of the common, is attributed to some Obeah man who has looked on him with an evil eye, or has buried something near his house which has caused the mischief by secret indescribable means. Well, his resource is the Myal doctor, who says he can disclose the cause, and effect a cure on condition of being paid for his skill. On having his fee, he goes to some spot of ground near, and digs away till he finds what he pretends did the mischief. This generally satisfies the patient and his friends, but sometimes not, and then they have often legal vengeance on the impostor.

Pleasant Hill, 30th.—We had planned to ride up into this district, when a letter came from Charles McGregor inviting us. We gladly availed ourselves of his kindness. This morning he came and breakfasted with us, and showed us the way through a beautiful mountainous country.

Pleasant Hill is a coffee plantation, under the attorneyship of Charles McGregor. It formerly belonged to Simon Taylor, who lived on his estate, and was earnest to benefit his slaves.

Ninth Month 1*st*, *First Day*.—We had a meeting at Pleasant Hill in a coffee store-house adjoining the barbicue, which is an assemblage of smooth plaistered surfaces on which the coffee is spread to dry. Many of the labouring class came, as well as planters and overseers. It proved a good season, when I felt much liberty in preaching Christ crucified, and Christ within as the hope of glory. I believe some will have cause to thank the Lord for His goodness, that He did not cut them off in their sins without afresh visiting their souls. Oh that all who have felt this power at work in their hearts may yield themselves thereto, and know the thorough change without which we cannot see the Lord.

2*nd*.—We reached Mount Fletcher and saw a school of sixty children before dinner, and at five met about 300 persons, chiefly labourers, in a new commodious chapel. There were several of the planter class present, for whom my interest increases with increased acquaintance with the mazes of Satan, who tries to spin his web around them. Under feelings of more than common strippedness I may thankfully acknowledge that I am helped to confide peacefully in the power that has constrained me thus to put my hand to the plough.

Belcour, 3*rd*.—This morning we had a pleasant ride home, calling by the way on a planter whom it seemed right to visit. I will not call this kind of service difficult, or use any term that can be construed into "I pray Thee have me excused"; but let me rather acknowledge that "help is laid upon One that is mighty."

Poor James Ritchie loses ground rapidly. I trust his soul is preparing for the change. He is grateful for the attentions we have been able to bestow, and I trust that they have not been in vain. But this, and all other labours, must be left without seeking unduly to discern the results.

Richmond Pen, Ninth Month 8th.—And so we have really quitted Belcour of pleasant memory, and came here to dine yesterday, having been kindly permitted to make this place our home during John Daughtry's absence in America.

We had our usual meeting together this morning. We rode into Kingston in the afternoon, and took tea with Charles McGregor, who accompanied us to the Wesleyan Chapel, where we found more than 2,000 persons assembled. It felt to me that most who were there had need to get deeper in spiritual things, to examine the ground of their faith.

Sligoville, 12*th*.—We left yesterday for Spanish Town, after I had spent two days in visiting schools in Kingston. This morning we rode to this very pleasant spot to a ten o'clock breakfast. Our elevation is about 2,000 feet, giving us an extensive view of the southern side of the island, from Yallah's Hill to Portland Ridge, with the ocean as the horizon. The sea is visible again in the north, about Portmarée and Annatto Bay.

13*th*.—We much enjoyed our calls at the cottages in this settlement—nice neat dwellings with brick floors and glass windows. They are built in the midst of gardens containing bread-fruit trees, mangoes, pomegranate, orange, coffee, pines, granadilloes, sugar-canes, arrowroot, onions, etc. I do not say that any one cottage has all this variety around it.

We spent half an hour at the house of Sidney Smith, who has built for himself, on his freehold of six acres, a nice four-roomed dwelling. There was a neat table, side-board and chairs. On the table lay a large octavo Bible, bearing symptoms of being daily read, a "Pilgrim's Progress," hymn-book and tracts. I opened the Bible at Psalm ciii., and it seemed so appropriate for this prosperous pair (who were liberated from their bonds in 1838) that I asked leave to read it to them. They called in their neighbours, and we had a time of spiritual refreshment together. I would that such a picture of the risen, but lately abject slave, could be seen by all our English people who have given their pence towards setting him free.

We had an interesting meeting with about 200 at Sligoville. There were many present who had partaken largely of the privileges of the gospel, and where much has been given much will be required.

14th.—We descended to Spanish Town, and called on Dr. Palmer. He has just been returned a member of the Legislative Assembly. In a very agreeable manner he said he should like to have our sentiments as to his course for the benefit of the colony. This gave us a favourable opportunity of commenting on the wisest course to be pursued by all legislators—that of making the golden rule their rule, and doing what is right rather than what is expedient.

J. M. Philippo's wife accompanied us six miles to Passage Fort, where we had a meeting with about 500 in the Baptist Chapel. It was evident to me that some present were by no means strangers to the gospel and its joys, though I believe many backsliders were amongst them.

Annatto Bay, 15th.—We had arranged to be at Jericho, sixteen miles north of Spanish Town, for a meeting at twelve o'clock; but on rising we heard that our mule had escaped from the stable-yard; so we concluded to leave Harris behind to find the mule, and for me to drive. Our road lay through the Bog Walk, one of the loveliest districts I have ever seen; but I could scarcely look at it, as the horses required my attention. The road was narrow and bad, without a fence on the side that was precipitous to the river Cabre, which ran swiftly in its rocky bed at a depth varying from 15 to 150 feet beneath us. Within a mile of Jericho we came to a standstill, and James Jesup walked forward to obtain a leader; with this help we reached our destination. I felt greatly tried at being an hour late for our meeting. As I sat stuck in the mud, some women coming to the meeting showed their kindly sympathy, and at their instigation some stout young men turned to and helped me. After a cup of coffee and a gallina's egg and toast I went to the meeting, where 500 were assembled, and where the Spirit and power of the Lord seemed to prevail as much as in any meeting we have had. Such deep, reverent stillness I have rarely known.

17th.—We proceeded on horseback for Ebenezer, calling on our way at Mount Hermon, ten miles from Jericho, to arrange for a meeting next week, and then proceeded to lodge at Elliot Station. Yesterday morning Harris arrived with our missing mule.

We have met with a cordial reception from William Lloyd, of Pembroke, now a Baptist minister at Annatto Bay, who offers us the use of their chapel for a meeting this evening. His house, where we are now, is among the mountains, five miles from Annatto Bay, overlooking the valley of the Wagwater, with the sea beyond.

20th.—Our meeting last night at the Baptist Chapel was a favoured one; I felt the great Master was amongst us, and that His power melted the hearts of many.

We had a call from two Friends; one has resided here forty-three years, and the other twelve years. We have paid them a pleasant visit this morning, enough to satisfy us for journeying many miles of rough road under a vertical sun.

Jericho, 23rd.—Yesterday morning we proceeded to Mount Hermon, where we had a kind reception from James Hume, from Berwick. We had a meeting in his chapel with about 800 persons. James Jesup had pretty much to communicate; after which I felt much enlargement in speaking on the redemption which has been purchased for us by our Redeemer's death, and is ours if we are willing to comply with the terms—obedience to His laws, and renouncing the enemy of our souls.

On arriving here we had a meeting with about thirty persons in the piazza of the house of our hostess. It is Eliza Hewitt's usual practice to assemble them on First-day afternoon, when her husband may be at a different station. On this occasion it was conducted as a Friends' meeting, and proved a good season.

The following morning we enjoyed being present at an examination of their day school. About 150 boys and girls were assembled, whose master seems to have been well qualified at the Borough Road Training College.

Phœnix Park, 26th.—We left Jericho yesterday as soon as the daily mist that spreads each morning over the face of that beautiful vale had been dispelled. With hired horses in our carriage we proceeded to encounter the ascent of Mount Diabola. J. Jesup rode on Whitefoot, Harris on Blackfoot, Edward Hewitt's man on our mule, to take back the hired horses. I had screwed up my courage to brave the dangers of a pass, but was surprised to find that I was much mistaken. The hill was long certainly, but the ascent was not greater than that of Haldon from Exeter, and the views we obtained brought that lovely valley of the Exe freshly before me. On reaching the summit we sent back the hired horses, and placed our own in harness to descend five miles to Moneague through a beautiful park-like country, reminding me of the best parts of Berkshire. It is the grazing ground of the island.

We soon reached Phœnix Park, the residence of Jonathan Edmundson. He is chairman to the Wesleyan Mission. Ten days ago we passed each other on the road, when he kindly pressed us to visit him. His house was once the residence of the Duke of Manchester, who was formerly Governor. It is situated on a conical hill, round which the broad carriage road winds, making two circuits to reach the summit.

Soon after dinner we set out for Watsonville, to attend a meeting appointed at our request. We found about 500 present. I went to that meeting under a more than usual sense of insufficiency, yet I found that nothing is too hard for the Lord.

Bariffe Hall, 28th.—We left Phœnix Park for Beechamville, where we paid a visit to a Wesleyan school, and proceeded without much delay to Annatto Bay. Our road lay along the coast. We passed an extraordinary cascade, a broad expanse of clear rushing water, fully a hundred yards wide, sweeping over a surface of rocks, out of which large trees were growing in profusion. Many other crystal streams find their way to the sea near Ocho Rios, hence called Eight Rivers.

We sent Harris on with our luggage to the house of David Day, the Baptist minister of this place, and we followed in four hours. Harris met us, and guided us two miles through the somewhat intricate wood which surrounds the house. When I saw the fort-like position of the dwelling, I queried involuntarily, "Have we got to go up there?" feeling more for the horses than ourselves, but we reached safe and well.

We had a hearty welcome from David Day and his assistant William Teill, formerly a teacher at Friends' School, Bishop Auckland.

Bariffe Hall stands on the summit of a knoll about 500 feet high, near the mouth of the Ora Cabessa river. Behind rises an amphitheatre of hills, forming three-parts of a basin, the edge of which may be five miles in diameter. On the north side, looking across the water to Cuba, a mountain is seen, which is nearly fifty miles inland and 10,900 feet high. We arrived at sunset, just at the right time to behold one of the loveliest prospects I ever saw.

30th.—Yesterday we attended a full meeting at Ora Cabessa Baptist Chapel, where from 700 to 800 were present, mostly liberated slaves. In the afternoon we went seven miles on horseback to Port Maria, to attend a meeting we had appointed. Various grades in life, and various denominations were represented there; many Jews amongst them. I felt it my duty to allude to the importance of believing in Christ, as the Shiloh to whom the gathering of the people must be.

I visited their school at Ora Cabessa, and saw the Wesleyan chapel (a simple thatched building), where Eliza A. Foster, whose memoirs have interested me, spent some of her happy days. I inquired of a negro woman whether she remembered her, "Oh, yes! the sweet minister's wife. She used to pray with me; and when she go away, she say, we meet in heaven; and when we hear she die, we cry so."

Ora Cabessa (Golden Head) the landing place of Columbus, 350 years ago, a woody rocky island, of about an acre in extent, lies about a hundred yards from the shore, and takes its name, Santa Maria, from Columbus' vessel, which was probably the size of some of the Droghers that were now lying at anchor under the peaceful lee of that islet.

Ardoch Pen, Tenth Month 2nd.—We left Bariffe Hall yesterday morning early; crossed the basin and amphitheatre of hills, and descended southwards towards Goshen, where we breakfasted on salt fish and roasted yam, with the Presbyterian pastor, William Jamieson. He is a widower from Perth, with a pleasing little daughter Kate, of six years old. His sisters Lydia and Mary now share his labours, joys and sorrows. Mary Jamieson left the breakfast table to ride to her daily duties as teacher; accompanied by the intelligent young negro Robert Jerritt, who resides with them, and is fond of reading and mathematics.

A meeting was appointed at three, but it was 4.30 before many were assembled. I had to speak on the silence of all flesh as the state best suited to discern the will of the Lord, the Spirit of God being the Guide into all truth, leading to the Lamb of God as the Redeemer from sin and the sacrifice for sin. William Jamieson commented at the close of the meeting on the words they had heard. He said that others who had recently addressed them had alluded to their moral duties, but that we had turned their attention to the source of good and evil, to the cleansing of the heart.

This morning we proceeded nine miles through fine park-like country. We found Philippa Savory (formerly a West from Wadebridge) at home. Her husband, George Savory, was gone to Kingston. She finds, as others do, that the wife of a missionary in the West Indies cannot do all she expected in this very enervating climate.

Beechamville, 6th.—We came here in rain, to the house of William Moss, who was formerly missionary on the Gambia (Africa). He had had the opportunity of observing the results of Hannah Kilham's labours, and bore a pleasing testimony to her.

Our meeting here was of a very interesting character in a large substantial stone meeting-house. With so few houses around it is surprising from whence the 1,200 persons came who were assembled there by ten o'clock. They find their way by many a devious path out of the thick woods they have chosen for their new and free locations. These people are a class that claim peculiar care as the germs of townships growing into importance.

Ocho Rios, 7th.—We dined with Benjamin Milard, the Baptist minister, and visited the schools. Both Baptist and Wesleyan ministers accompanied us to a crowded and good meeting. Rarely have I felt more cast down than on entering that meeting, but help was laid upon One that is mighty. I quoted, "Oh, wretched man that I am, who shall deliver me from the body of this death? I thank God through Jesus Christ our Lord," alluding to the importance of being delivered, and that Jesus is the only means of redemption. I was afterwards informed that many were present who rarely enter a place of worship.

St. Ann's Bay, 8th.—We attended a meeting of about 1,800 persons in the Baptist Chapel; when ability was afresh given to declare some of the unsearchable riches of Christ.

Brown's Town, 9th.—We set off from St. Ann's Bay for a ride of eighteen miles to Brown's Town. I cannot describe at length the beautiful scenery through which we passed, the long line of cocoa-nut trees on the level sea-shore, or the groves of pimento that cover the hills. The pimento tree is very handsome, reminding me of the arbutus at Killarney, with its dark green neatly shaped leaves, and bare trunk, barkless, like the arbutus. This is the pimento season; men, women and children are high busy in picking the berries that appear like black currants. These are dried and packed in bags to be used as allspice.

Brown's Town is one of the most interesting spots I have ever visited, a complete village in the mountains. We had a most kind welcome from John Clark. We met 1,200 persons in their spacious chapel, which covers dwelling-house and schoolroom, where James Jesup had good service.

10th.—We proceeded on horseback to Stewart's Town, a well-built village. We visited the schools, and though the evening was wet, we had a nice little meeting of about 200 persons.

11th.—We rode through a beautiful country to First Hill, and thence to Calabar, passing on the road the sugar estates of Bideford and Barnstaple, and far-famed Arcadia belonging to Hankey & Co., reminding me of Barbadoes in the character and extent of the cultivation.

We returned to Brown's Town in heavy rain. I felt thankful for the preservation experienced during our recent forty miles of mountain riding.

13th.—We went to breakfast at Sturge Town, two hours' ride; and at ten o'clock met a very interesting company of settlers and labourers in a large booth or thatched chapel. Five hundred must have been in and around the building. We had not been gathered long in deep reverent silence before I felt engaged to rise with the language, "If God be for us, who can be against us?" There were 300 adults and children in the school previously held. Many spectacled men and women reading little elementary books.

We returned to Brown's Town, and met by our request the First-day school teachers. But instead of thirty or forty teachers, 1,800 persons assembled, to whom the gospel message flowed freely. They were reminded of their great privileges, and the need of proving their love and allegiance by obedience, feeding the lambs and the sheep of Christ's fold. I desired to lead them to the foot of the cross, and there I believe many were left.

James Finlayson, a leader amongst the Baptists, told us that when he was a slave he went one First-day to sell honey as usual, but that day he called on the Wesleyan minister, who told him it was wrong thus to break the Sabbath. After which he stayed near the door of a Baptist Chapel, and felt refreshed by the words he heard, which sank deep in his heart, bringing him under the power of the gospel. When this island was under martial law in 1832, he was one of the objects of suspicion and vengeance, because, like Daniel, he feared the God of his life, to whom he daily prayed. He was ordered to proceed to Falmouth to be tried for his life. Whilst walking there unescorted he met some of his acquaintance. He inquired if any had been shot that day. "Yes, several; and they will shoot you if they can catch you; you had better run to the bush!" He thought within himself, "I won't deny my Saviour, I'll go on." He went on and showed himself to two officers. The same evening a gentleman called him in, and gave him a letter to take back into the country immediately. Thus he escaped.

14*th*.—At Dry Harbour we met again Thomas Robson Stark, a pleasing young man of colour. The meeting there was the third he had attended. Six hundred crowded to it. I quoted the passage, "That Jesus, by the grace of

God should taste death for every man;" and afresh declared some of the unsearchable riches of Christ. I directed them to the grace of God, the light of Christ in their hearts, and commended them to that grace, impressing the need for earnest daily private prayer.

Calabar, 15th.—We visited the Baptist and Episcopal schools, and attended a lecture on " Air " given by J. Tinson to his students, who are preparing for usefulness in Africa. I made some remarks on the steam engine with the help of a black board and a piece of chalk.

The evening reading of the Scriptures afforded an opportunity of communicating to these fine young men instruction of far more importance. I reminded them of the need there is that the ministers of Christ should be true Christians, servants of the Prince of Peace. Allusion was also made to the kindness and proper respect due to women, who were last at the Cross, and first at the Tomb. The more civilized and truly religious persons became, the higher would women be placed in the scale, and by no means be regarded as servants and slaves.

J. Tinson told us that on one occasion he had attended the interment of a young man. After the ordinary service was over, he felt a strong impulse to address the bystanders, but he let in the reasoner, who persuaded him that it was irregular and undesirable. Whilst he hesitated, the company dispersed, so that he went home oppressed with a sense of a lost opportunity and of unfaithfulness. May such cases be borne in mind by those who feel the power of the Lord at work in their hearts.

Kettering, 16th.—We reached to-day the home of William Knibb, at Kettering. He had kindly urged us to tarry here. The house was built for his wife by the liberated slaves as a mark of gratitude, in fifty acres of freehold ground, amidst a thriving village of freeholders, and is of a superior order in dimensions, design and execution.

21st.—We had an opportunity of meeting with a number

of the teachers of the First-day schools at Falmouth. They usually meet once a quarter to devise plans for carrying on this work effectively. About sixty dined together in the school-room. We joined them at this meal; William Knibb presided. I sat between him and the daughter of Lord McK., who is an efficient, useful, matronly teacher. W. Knibb addressed the teachers on their duties, and on the need of humility. His address bore strongly on our pacific principles, which were the doctrines of the same Jesus whom all Christians professed to follow. They were reminded that we had been their friends in the time of trial, advocating their cause pacifically; but if in an evil hour they took carnal weapons, then we must part.

After the Bible reading this morning I was deeply interested by listening to "the lion-hearted Knibb" reading in gentle accents,—

> "Lord, subdue our stubborn will
> By Thy modulating skill;
> Sweetly on our spirits move.
> Make the harmony of love.
> Each to each our temper suit,
> Heart to heart, as lute to lute;
> Gently touch the trembling strings,
> Music for the King of kings."

I was particularly impressed by his prayer. "We give Thee thanks that ever and anon Thou gladdens us with the sweet fellowship of Thy messengers with the gospel of peace, who seek to do Thy will in increasing the triumphs of the Prince of Peace. Father, let thy selectest influences rest upon them. Grant them the rich unction of Thy Spirit, whilst they remind those who were in thraldom of the vows they made to Thee, and that now being set free, they are bound to serve Thee. We give Thee thanks that there are those whose spirits thus feel for Thy servants, once in bondage, and we would pray Thee to soften the hearts of others who yet hold their fellows in slavery. Hasten the day when war and slavery shall cease in this Thy earth."

Yesterday we attended a meeting of nearly 2,000 persons at the Baptist Chapel, Falmouth, when the people were reminded of their deliverance from bondage and of their obligation to serve Him whose right hand had helped and delivered them.

22nd.—Whilst dressing this morning at half-past six, I felt a decided shock of earthquake, attended with a rumbling, rushing and hissing noise, lasting about five seconds. It was regarded by old inhabitants as one of the most serious shocks that has been felt for many years.

23rd.—We went to Hampden, seven miles from Falmouth, to breakfast with George Blyth, Presbyterian minister, who with his wife has laboured here for twenty years. His wife said the cruelties they witnessed during the four years of the apprenticeship far exceeded ten years of slavery.

25th.—We spent this day in visiting schools and the prison. At the prison we met Dr. Anderson, the visiting magistrate. Opportunity was given us to speak to the forty-four convicts assembled in the yard. There is a deficiency in the matter of classification.

Montego Bay, 27th, *First Day*.—We had a meeting in the Baptist Chapel with about 1,500 persons. J. Jesup was engaged in prayer that the Lord would be pleased to bow our hearts. Quoting the words, "I remember thee, the kindness of thy youth, the love of thine espousals," I reminded those present of their covenants. At our lodgings afterwards we had a precious season of retirement together.

The Wesleyan Chapel we found crowded in the evening with 1,000 inside and 300 outside. I spoke on the text, "God is greatly to be feared in the assembly of the saints, and to be had in reverence of all them that are about Him"; and I had to call on the rich young men to use the query, "What lack I yet?" and on the strong young men to see whether they had "overcome the wicked one."

Israel Levi Lewin, a Hebrew, came to see us. He has embraced the Christian faith, and is well known to many of our friends who have been here. Our conversation was deeply interesting. His mind seems remarkably open to conviction, and as though he saw many things as we do.

28th.—We had a meeting in the dwelling of Hope M. Waddell, in a hall adapted for the purpose. I had to speak on the nature of true worship, and to call on the people to give unto the Lord the glory due unto His name; appealing to some to examine the foundation of their hope, to see what they were building upon, and not to rest till they had digged deep and laid the foundation on Christ the Rock of Ages. Prayer was offered; and James Jesup called the attention of the people to the Word, of which we read in Romans x. 8, as nigh in the heart, the Teacher that cannot be removed into a corner.

H. M. Waddell is likely to proceed soon to the Calabar river, Africa, to commence a mission there, leaving his wife and children in England. He will be accompanied by a young schoolmaster who was a planter and a printer. A few negroes will also go; amongst them an African youth captured in a Spanish slave ship four years ago.

I asked this boy George Waddell a few questions to elicit his story, which was as follows: "My grandfather sold me and my mother and sister to pay his debt, walked a long way across the country and come down river in one canoe; many canoes take we, great many in the ship; give we cassava to eat, one pint of water a day, have beef once or twice a week; upon deck most day; not hand-cuffed, no use run away, only big sea jump into (said with much humour). Near Cuba when we see ship coming; all glad to see English ship; know they safe if see ship, for when in river heard Spaniard curse English ship." This was a prime cargo of slaves selected by the captain, on the voyage which he intended should be his last. He wanted them for his own use in settling down in Cuba, of which island he was within sight, when the cruiser blasted his hopes by seizing the ship, though he and some of his crew escaped in the boat.

In our intercourse with those who meditate service in Africa, the subject of pacific principles and practice has been prominently in view, and a full response has been comforting. George Blyth, of Hampden, told us he was once a missionary in the Caucasian mountains, encompassed by warlike tribes, constantly at strife with each other. He was visited by two agents of an English Society who wished to go to a neighbouring district. The Russian commander required that they should be escorted by two armed Cossacks for their protection. G. Blyth could not accompany them on this condition. He was accustomed to go unarmed, and was unwilling to exhibit distrust, being convinced of the truth

> "That man no guard or weapon needs,
> Whose heart the blood of Jesus knows!"

In this district of Jamaica, where twelve years ago there was strife, riot, confusion, fire and bloodshed, very many acknowledge that the disciple of the Prince of Peace must renounce war and strife of every kind.

29th.—We went to Goodwill, a very nice village of total abstainers under the care of G. Blyth. The large schoolroom was crowded by about 500 persons, with whom we had a meeting of deep interest. Almost every faculty seemed prostrated before I took my seat, but ability was afresh received to dispense the bread which was blessed and broken amongst us. At the conclusion one of their elders stood up and in a feeling manner expressed his thankfulness for the visit. This man was once a slave, and an apprentice. He was charged with insubordination by the bookkeeper, because he rescued his sister from infamy. Unable to brook his abject condition, he purchased the remainder of his term for £60. As a skilful mason he soon acquired property, bought land, built a house, and is now one of the rich men of this favoured land, rich also in faith and good works, and an heir of that kingdom which God hath prepared for them that love Him.

We left Goodwill at half-past four this morning by moonlight, accompanied two miles by G. Blyth, who walked by the side of my horse. We reached Cornwall just in time to have a lovely clear view of some of the mountains of Cuba, distant about 120 miles.

31st.—We went to Irwin Hill, a Moravian settlement four miles from Montego Bay, and had a kind reception from John Elliott, who comes from Gracehill, Ireland. We met about 150 persons in their spacious chapel, towards whom the language arose freshly, "This people have I formed for myself; they shall show forth My praise;" to show forth the praise of the Lord aright we must obey Him.

Salter's Hill, Eleventh Month 1st.—We had a welcome from Walter Dendy. At twelve o'clock we met by special invitation seventy teachers of the First-day schools belonging to this district. We regard this class as an important one, believing much good may result from their labours, if rightly directed, and from humbled hearts; but it is nothing new for the pride and vanity of man to exist where there is the least warrant. Three of their own ministers followed, on the subject of peace. James Jesup quoted the words, "They made me keeper of the vineyards, but mine own vineyard have I not kept."

We dined together, after which William Claydon addressed us on peace principles and practice. I alluded to the favoured condition we enjoy in having a good Queen, and a government that should be obeyed in all things that are not contrary to the will of God; but that if we resist on christian grounds it must be in a christian spirit.

In the evening we met about 1,000 persons in the Baptist Chapel; when, after a time of solemn and protracted silence, the words were addressed to them: "To be carnally minded is death, but to be spiritually minded is life and peace."

At his house, W. Dendy read a Psalm, gave thanks for the blessings of the day, and prayed for a blessing on the labourers. After a precious silence I acknowledged the unity I felt with their spirits, "One is your Master, even Christ, and all ye are brethren." There were six ministers present, besides other labourers.

Mount Carey, 2nd.—We reached our kind friends Thomas Burchall and family at Mount Carey. Deep conflict has of late been my portion, so that I have been ready to yield to discouragement, but I crave that I may be preserved in depths as well as in heights, keeping my eye fixed on Jesus, who is able to keep me from falling. At times I am ready to believe that it is for the sake of others that I am thus baptized, and that if I am faithful, this proving dispensation will be blessed to the furtherance of the gospel.

3rd.—At eleven o'clock we attended a crowded meeting; 1,700 were sitting and standing within the walls, and 200 outside. Soon after taking my seat the language arose, "When Israel went out of Egypt, the house of Jacob from a people of strange language, Judah was His sanctuary, and Israel His dominion. The sea saw it and fled; Jordan was driven back." I drew the parallel in the two conditions, and reminded them of their covenants. I called on the office-bearers to be faithful and to walk as examples to the flock. David fell by unwatchfulness; he feared he should fall by the hand of Saul, but he fell into another snare. The backsliding sinner was invited to repentance—the condition of forgiveness. Prayer was offered that the Lord might not pity nor spare till He had made us what He would have us to be.

James Jesup and I met twice to-day in private retirement, when the silent breathing of my soul was—

"More of Thy grace, O Lord, impart,
  More of Thy Spirit let me bear;
Erect Thy throne within my heart,
  And reign without a rival there."

Lucea, 6th.—We are at the point most remote from England that we expect to visit. After a meeting to be held here this evening we shall probably turn our faces homeward. We are quartered at the house of W. Henry Hann, a young Wesleyan missionary. He accompanied us to see the schools and prisons of Lucea, all of which are decidedly of a satisfactory character.

We called on Thomas Daly, who, when young, gained a good livelihood as a millwright and cartwright, but an attack of inflammation of the eyes deprived him of sight in three days, and left him destitute. Then he proved that "man's extremity is God's opportunity." From having been a careless, hardened sinner he became a humble Christian, and now he says that he can bless the name of the Lord, who has done all things well. He employs himself in plaiting grass for hats, sharpening razors, and joining and squaring shingles for roofs.

The bay of Lucea, on the western side of which the town stands, is about the most beautiful I have ever seen. It forms nearly three-quarters of a circle. The road runs near the edge of the water all round the bay, so that when we came in sight of the place we seemed within a mile, and yet we had to ride four miles to reach our destination.

Our meeting at Lucea was so crowded as to be noisy and unsettled at the commencement; but though there were many unruly spirits present, they seemed by degrees to be brought into subjection to the power that is mightier than the noise of many waters, and we felt glad that we had been led thither.

E. O. Tregelles, in a letter under date New Carmel, 13th, writes:

A week has elapsed since I penned the foregoing, and I must try and give you a sketch of our proceedings.

7th.—We left Lucea at six, travelling by starlight until

the sun arose, and had an enjoyable ride to Sandy Bay, ten miles, to breakfast. Early morning is the time for travelling in Jamaica.

8th.—I drove to Sutcliffe. Our road lay through a beautiful park-like country. Magnificent clumps of bamboos studded the undulating pastures, and a fringe of these elegant plumes shaded our road for a mile, as it wound down a lovely ravine. We had a hearty reception from J. Hutchings and wife in their simple cottage, which stands on the side of a range of hills that surrounds the extensive savannah.

9th.—Early in the morning we drove to Savannah la Mar, and at once went to some lodgings kindly provided for us by Aaron de Leon, to whom we were introduced by J. L. Lewin, of Montego Bay. Their circumstances are somewhat similar, both of Hebrew stock, and proselytes, merchants and magistrates. A. de Leon is of dark hue, with thick-set curly hair. I have rarely seen a more interesting face; every feature from the brow to the chin expressing perfect repose—not the repose of indolence, but as if he partook of that rest that is prepared for the people of God. Hitherto he has not united with any set of professors, and is pretty much alone in his views of Scripture truth, which seem closely to coincide with ours, and deeply interesting it was to me to hear his firm declaration: "Christ is the head of His own Church. Where two or three are met together in His name, there is He in the midst of them. 'God is a spirit; and they that worship Him must worship Him in spirit and in truth.' 'Ye are not your own, ye are bought with a price.'"

10th.—We had a meeting in the Baptist Chapel in the morning with about 900 persons. In the evening the Wesleyan Chapel was crowded; 100 persons outside. This proved a season blessed to several, I believe, besides myself, and I felt thankful that I had again incurred the fatigue of a second meeting.

11th.—We left Savannah la Mar at seven for Bluefields, to breakfast with John Coleman, from Leominster, once a Moravian minister, now a Plymouth Brother. He and his wife appear to live in much simplicity and usefulness.

We passed on to New Hope, a Moravian station, where we had a meeting with about 400. The school, which numbered 125, has now diminished to about thirty. The condition of nearly all the schools of Jamaica is discouraging. The universal complaint of the caretakers is, "I don't know how it is, but somehow or other our schools are falling off, partly because of the want of rain, and scarcity of provisions and employment, so that parents say they cannot afford to send their children; and partly because they do not know for themselves the value of being able to read and write." Such is just the transcript of a lamentation that I have had to listen to fifty times at least. I generally add, " and partly because the parents spend their money in rum !" To which the reply is, " Yes, indeed."

12th.—We started before breakfast for New Carmel, accompanied by Laars Kielson. He gave me an outline of his history. When young he was gay, and never read the Bible until he was twenty-one. His mind was first awakened by attendance at a reformed church in Denmark. After which his eyes became gradually opened, and he forsook the sinful path.

We proceeded on borrowed horses to New Beaufort, accompanied by a little black boy, who, as the happy owner of trousers, shirt, and hat, and mounted on our mule with the saddle-bags, seemed as pleased as a prince. My horse was "trickified," as he soon informed me, but as I had a good curb bridle I put him to rights, and when he discovered that I was master we went along as good friends, and he carried me safely to New Beaufort.

I asked a man about what time the meeting was to be held. " I can't tell; the parson is not come yet." So, as soon as we arrived the bell was rung to announce the fact to the district, and at four o'clock a large company were assembled.

13th.—We left by starlight this morning, and had a delightfully cool ride back to New Carmel in two hours. The valleys which lay stretched out beneath us were filled with mist, and it required no stretch of the imagination to be reminded of Killarney with its lower lake, and Innisfallen and other islets.

CHAPTER XIV.

WEST INDIES.

Jamaica—H. G. Pfeiffer and Martial Law—Meeting at New Bethlehem—Schools at Fairfield—Work of Moravians—Meeting with Maroons—Mandeville—Visits Prison—School—Rest at Mount Providence—Old Harbour—Spanish Town—Interview with Earl of Elgin and John Daughtry respecting Prisons—Meeting in Baptist Chapel—Penitentiary—Kingston—Silk-cotton Tree—Morant Bay—Climate—Beauty of Bath—Belle Castle—Port Antonio—Moore Town—Maroons—Fording Rio Grande—Golden Grove—Surrey Gaol—Meeting at Port Royal—Hayti—Arrival at Jacmel with J. T. Hartwell—Climate and Appearance of Town—Call on General Geffrard—Journey to Port Républicaine—Mules—Citrounier—Delmay's Hut a Bethel—Leogane—Port Républicaine—Reminiscences of S. Grellet—Meeting with American Wesleyans—Fabius Day—Prison—Lacahaye—Thomas Williams—Alexis Dupny—St. Marc—President Guerrier—Desert—Gouaives—James Osler—Coffee Sales.

ELEVENTH MONTH 14*th*, 1844.—When I was at New Fulneck Henry Gotlieb Pfeiffer, the minister of the Moravian station, gave me an outline of his sufferings in 1831, when this district was under martial law.

Some of the negroes from the north came to this parish and told the slaves they were free, and if they continued to work they would come and murder them. Pfeiffer used his influence to induce them to return to their work, which they did. On the following Seventh-day, whilst sitting musing in his study on the duties of the coming day, two officers and thirty-two soldiers came, and without warrant, apprehended him and conveyed him on horseback to the Oxford estate. The next day, being First-day, they conducted him with fixed bayonets and loaded muskets to

Mandeville, where he was lodged in the organ loft of the church, and guarded by four sentinels with drawn swords. Without bedding he lay on a bench with his bundle of clothes for a pillow, and even this was taken from him. He had no food brought him till the afternoon.

The next day two officers visited him, when he avowed his ignorance of the charge; telling them that as their prisoner he should be fed, but that he had had no food for twenty-four hours. It is difficult to believe that any person would thus treat a fellow-creature in such a place, said to be consecrated. Next day the same neglect was observed. He was then turned over to the tender mercies of the gaoler, and an officer told him his trial was to come on, but that none of his friends would be admitted as witnesses. They might give in written testimonials.

A person called and told him that his judges were determined to convict and destroy him, but that it was contrary to law to refuse any evidence he might bring. He must therefore send for his friends. "You write your letters; I will get them conveyed."

At two o'clock next morning a host of his friends were in motion from many points, and appeared at Mandeville, completely confounding his accusers. His trial lasted four days, when he was reluctantly acquitted, to the rejoicing of thousands.

Pfeiffer's witnesses were kept locked up night after night in the court-house, and two nights before his release they were engaged in prayer for him without ceasing. The release was marvellous, as his accusers were bent on his destruction, and a regiment of militia from Vere was kept on purpose to shoot him, as they could depend on them. He saw several negroes led out for trial, and in half an hour he saw them led to execution. He is convinced that many worthy, innocent men were put to death.

15*th.*—We rode from New Fulneck to New Bethlehem, twenty-four miles, over an undulating plain, through which runs the Black River, the only navigable river in Jamaica. We left our carriage at South Valley, and climbed 3,000 feet the last four miles. In the evening we had a good meeting, having the company of a few of the planters who live near, whose characters are sweetly in accordance with the gospel. We rejoined our carriage at South Valley, and drove sixteen miles to Lelitz, a Moravian station. A young schoolmaster gave us a welcome. I felt truly happy there, though without most of the comforts of domestic life.

17*th*.—To our surprise on waking we learnt that W. A. Prince, of Fairfield, had arrived. He had set out at midnight, and ridden twenty miles to meet us. He and the schoolmaster were at our meeting, which was a favoured one.

18*th*.—Busy visiting the schools of Fairfield—a day school, a good normal school, and a very interesting Orphan Refuge for poor girls. We had a large meeting, which was owned by the Lord, I believe.

19*th*.—W. A. Prince rode with us to Huntley, to breakfast with a family of the name of Tomlinson, some of whom had attended the meeting the previous evening. After the usual Bible reading I spoke on the nature of true worship as resulting from brokenness of spirit, contritedness and humility, and left them the blessing of "Peace be to this house." The master of the house remarked that his cup of blessing felt running over. He had been a persecutor, but having been smitten as Saul was, he is now engaged to feed the flock of Christ. His occupation is that of attorney and planter.

Our visits to the several stations of the Moravians have been comforting and satisfactory, causing thankfulness to arise for the mercy shown to the coloured people, amongst whom many dedicated servants of the Lord have laboured.

20*th*.—Our meeting at Nazareth was truly pleasant. We left for Siloah, and had a good meeting with the people of that district in a Church Missionary schoolroom chapel. The language arose livingly towards them, "Who is he that will harm you, if ye be followers of that which is good?" We retired to rest early. It had been a good day. I felt I was kept as in the Lord's holy hand, and that as one who was bearing precious seed, it was needful for me to have a close watch set on my spirit.

21st.—Rising early, we proceeded on our mules to Accompong, one of the Maroon stations, by a steep and intricate road. Our reception was most hearty. Soon after nine they assembled in their schoolroom chapel. Prayer was offered that the Lord would save this people, and bless their inheritance, feed them also with daily temporal and spiritual bread. After a blessed meeting we visited many of their commodious and clean habitations. We saw Colonel Rowe, a fine negro, six feet high, and eighty-six years old, grey and erect. About one hundred families are settled here, subject only to their own laws, and not paying taxes to our Government.

We repaired to the schoolroom, and heard those who were able, read in the Testament, and gave them some books and tracts. At the house of the schoolmaster a repast was prepared for us, for which he made many apologies from shortness of notice; but we made a hearty meal on a nice well-roasted pig and three wild doves. Many expressions of gratitude for the visit followed, with the wish they could have a repetition each week.

22nd.—Our meeting at New Eden proved to be a close searching season for many. We heard some of the children read in the New Testament, and departed at noon.

A warm three hours' ride over a level country brought us to Gentle Hill. Here we alighted to let our beasts rest, and I thoroughly enjoyed a piece of dry bread from my pocket and delicious water from a flowing stream. We were an hour scrambling up this hill. The road was steep and rough and stony; but when we reached the summit we found ourselves at Fairfield, from whence we rode to Mandeville.

24th, *First Day.*—We had a meeting in the chapel of the

London Missionary Society at eleven o'clock; about 400 present. J. Jesup spoke of the happy condition of those who worship God in the spirit, rejoice in Christ Jesus, and have no confidence in the flesh. Several of the planters came to the house after meeting, giving us an opportunity to converse with them, which was, I hope, profitable, though often wearying to the flesh.

25th.—We visited the prison, which is in excellent order, under the care of Thomas Wells, from Launceston. He was a tailor, enlisted as a soldier, became a sergeant, exchanged to the police, and is now governor of the prison, postmaster, and store-keeper, acquiring wealth rapidly.

After visiting a school of one hundred well-taught children, we proceeded to Porus, a large village of freedmen. Very much rain fell; however, about 500 came to our meeting, with whom we had a close, searching time.

26th.—We left Porus for Four Paths: our road to Lime Savannah was like a ploughed field. On returning a cart and mule we had hired to carry our luggage, the owner politely returned the cheque we gave him, saying he freely gave us the accommodation.

27th.—We had a kind reception from Robert and Anne Jones, at Mount Providence, where John and Maria Candler stayed six weeks, and which we find a very pleasant resting place. About one hundred of the settlers on this estate were present in the schoolroom at a meeting, and a nice season we had.

Twelfth Month 1st.—Much enjoyment has been my portion here. We read this morning in Acts v., the account of the imprisonment and liberation of Peter and John, and my mind turned to Hayti, as though bonds and afflictions awaited us there. My feeling is a desire to be found faithful, keeping in the path cast up day by day for us to walk in, not pursuing our own wills, but the will of Him who I believe is sending us. Now my prayer is, If Thy presence go not with me, carry us not up hence.

We had a good meeting at Lower Chapelton, well attended by negroes, and by some of the white class. I rose with the language, "A day is coming when the secrets of all hearts shall be revealed," and urged a change of heart.

We visited the prison, and were pleased to find but few inmates; no women. We called, on our way back to Mount Providence, on a young overseer who had been at the meeting, and had invited us to the estate where he lives. His dinner was on the table when we arrived, but when we declined partaking of it he left it untouched, had his horse saddled, and rode with us home. I was glad, as it afforded me an opportunity of having further talk with him in the garden of our host, which proved to be a confessional. He promises fairly. After taking tea with us, he returned in the dark, over a wretched road.

4th.—Yesterday we had a meeting at Lionel Town of about 200. We lodged with John Dingwall, the schoolmaster, under circumstances far below our usual comfort. I dressed at three o'clock, and by four we were ready to start for Old Harbour by the light of a diminished moon, and aided by Venus in full strength. I had an intelligent boy by my side to point out the turns in the road, and the bad places. Our progress was slow, but pleasant. We passed through an extensive district, once cultivated, but now lapsed into the wilderness state. Here wild cattle exist, that are caught by rope nooses. Guinea fowl are also wild, and are excellent for the table. Alligators abound in the waters that washed our road for miles, but we did not see any.

We had a kind reception at Old Harbour from H. C. Taylor, the Baptist minister, and a very scanty meeting in their chapel; but though scanty, I felt it worth attending.

5th.—This morning we reached Spanish Town. A kind greeting awaited us from James M. Philippo and wife. I was glad of a quiet hour or two in my chamber to read welcome letters from home, and for writing some letters for the island post, which goes once a week.

John Daughtry called to conduct me to the Governor's, to look at some designs he had obtained in America for the new penitentiary now being erected under his care. I had a long interview with Lord Elgin, with the plans spread before us on a billiard table. But these plans did not engage one-twentieth of our time. The prevention of crime, rather than its punishment, occupied our attention. Neither of us would get quickly to the end of his story when education is the theme. Schools elementary, agricultural, and normal are claiming and receiving the close attention of the Governor.

We had a large meeting in the Baptist Chapel, when I quoted the words, "What shall it profit a man, if he shall gain the whole world, and lose his own soul?" Prayer was offered for all classes in the land, the servant and the served, the ruled and the rulers, that they may be united together in the bonds of peace.

6th.—We made many calls, among them at the two prisons, and then took our leave of the Governor. He offered us letters to Hayti, but he believed we should do better with those from my cousins Fox, of Falmouth, than from him, which might excite suspicion.

7th.—Accompanied by J. M. Philippo we drove to Kingston, and took possession of a house which had been hired for us.

John Daughtry breakfasted with us, and we proceeded with him to the Penitentiary, where we saw the muster of 450 men prisoners examined by the surgeon, who passed along the ranks, giving each man an opportunity of claiming attention. One man said, "Very sick in stomach." "What did you do with your breakfast, then?" At the same moment the surgeon's eye detected a loaf of bread intended to be concealed under the arm beneath the short frock, and the loaf was forfeited, which had been reserved to purchase tobacco. The poor fellow must like tobacco better than I do; but this is one of their snares, for which they are often punished. J. Daughtry gave excellent counsel in a mild, delightful manner. To some who needed it, rebuke; to others, pleasant encouragement. Silence is enforced, though they work together as coopers, carpenters, smiths, shoemakers, tailors, and bone and stone breakers.

8th, First Day.—I rose at four o'clock to complete my letters for England. We had our meeting together in the morning, attended by Sophia Nicholson, our housekeeper, and her servants. In the evening we were at a meeting in the Baptist Chapel, when I had to call on many to forsake the broad road that leads to destruction, to come out and to be separate. "Love not the world, neither the things that are in the world. If any man love the world, the love of the Father is not in him."

9th.—Charles S. and Mira Renshaw breakfasted and dined with us. C. S. R. was once a lieutenant in the American navy. He left the service on account of its immoral tendency, not because he thought war unchristian. Four months ago we had a close discussion on this point. He now sees that all war is opposed to the will of the Lord. I was cheered by his honest avowal.

11th.—We left Kingston and had a delightful drive to Yallahs, breakfasting at a comfortable tavern eleven miles on our way. The ride is beautiful, reminding me of the ride from Cork to Glanmire. The water inside the pallisades which form Kingston harbour, of nearly twenty miles in extent, was calm with a gentle ripple, but outside, a long swell from the Atlantic broke on the rocky shore with boisterous waves.

The celebrated silk-cotton tree attracted our notice; it is a magnificent object. It covers a circle sixty yards in diameter. Each of its fifteen or sixteen arms is as large as an ordinary forest tree.

The meeting we had in the Baptist Chapel was full to overflowing; many young men of the planter class present. A man forced his way to a seat in the meeting whilst intoxicated, and had to be turned out. The disturbance fell out rather for the furtherance of the gospel.

12*th*.—We passed on from Yallahs to Morant Bay to breakfast, and visited there the schools of the London Missionary Society, the Wesleyans, and the Episcopalians.

We called on Thomas Thompson, the senior magistrate of the district; he is seventy-six, and came here from Scotland fifty-five years ago. He regards the climate of Jamaica as favourable for Europeans. His conversation was refreshing, lively, and without frivolity, intellectual without pedantry; evidently the result of reading, reflection, and good association. He lives temperately, avoids strong drink and animal food, and never lights a candle.

About 500 were present at the chapel of the London Missionary Society. Some of what I had to express seemed too close for a man of the middle class, who I believe left the meeting to stifle his convictions.

13*th*.—The road from Port Morant to Bath, seven miles, lay through a valley of extraordinary beauty. Bath is one of the most lovely spots in the Antilles. It possesses a hot spring of medicinal value; also a small botanical garden, where orange, mignonette, magnolia, and other fragrant flowers filled the air with their rich aromatic perfumes.

The rain fell copiously at intervals throughout the afternoon; so we expected no one would come to the meeting. I was glad, however, to meet 300 persons, and ability was granted me to labour amongst them to my comfort.

14*th*.—We left Bath early this morning, and drove to Amity Hall. Here we left the carriage, and mounting our horses, followed by Harris on the mule, and accompanied by William Kirkland, of Amity Hall, we jogged on over a rocky road to Belle Castle. On our way we had a fine view of the Plantain Garden river, the district we had passed through—a garden indeed! covered with cane fields in the highest state of cultivation, the high land studded with fine trees, the whole district bearing the evidence of profitable return to the capitalist.

Belle Castle, 15th.—We are made very welcome by John and Mary Kingdon, and had a small meeting with them this morning. I expressed my belief that the crumbs which fall from the Master's table would be valued by those who desire to be fed by Him alone. My mind has dwelt much on the condition of Hayti whilst looking over the channel of a hundred miles that separates us from that land.

16th.—At 5 a.m. we parted from our dear friends, J. and M. Kingdon. It was so dark as to be difficult to discover the path amidst the thick trees, so that Harris had to lead his mule before us; the light coloured bag on the saddle served as a lantern. At eight o'clock we arrived at an estate where we were kindly accommodated by a negro, once a slave, named Charles Brown, *alias* Dr. Brown, by virtue of his having been a hospital doctor; but now he works on estates. He and his wife gave us a hearty welcome; guinea grass and bamboo-tops, furnished abundantly, gave a feast to our beasts, whilst we were well supplied with coffee, hashed fowl, yam, and salt fish.

After breakfast we met an interesting company of 200 persons, who having heard that we were coming, all brought their seats and assembled in their usual place of worship, an open shed by the roadside. We had a favoured time together, which will be remembered by me, I believe, as long as some seasons in which more effort had been made to meet with thirsty souls. We passed on from this simple gathering with peaceful hearts, and at the end of three more hours of warm riding along a most beautiful sea-coast, we reached Port Antonio in safety.

We had a crowded meeting in the Wesleyan Chapel, 600 persons present. I had to allude to the broken and contrite heart as being acceptable in the Lord's sight. Before we parted they were reminded that the destruction of man is of himself, his salvation is of God.

Port Antonio, 17th.—This morning we rose early and started for Bluff Bay, but rain began to fall, and drove us back thoroughly soaked. After dining with our friend, J. Mearns, Wesleyan minister, we started again, but after riding two miles we met some negroes, who told us that the Rio Grande was so full with the heavy rain as to preclude our crossing. We therefore returned again to this pleasant home.

Moore Town, 18th.—We rode through a beautiful country, hoping to have a meeting with the Maroons, 700 of whom reside here in a fine healthy situation, climate temperate though moist. I am now writing at the house of one of them, Duncan McFarlane, an intelligent negro, a Wesleyan and a decided Christian. His wife and daughter-in-law soon provided us with a good breakfast, of coffee grown on their own ground and parched after we arrived here, ripe plantain roasted, toast and eggs.

At four o'clock we made our way to the snug sheltered abode of Mitchell Lowe Harris, an aged Maroon. A number of persons assembled, with whom we had a good meeting. A precious silence attended us on sitting down, and I called their attention to the working of their Lord in their hearts, "One Lord, one faith, one baptism, one God and Father of all, who is above all, and through all, and in you all."

We retired to rest about seven o'clock in a small bed under a leaky roof, from the wet of which we were protected by leaves of the cabbage palm laid on the tester.

19th.—The night proved restful and refreshing, and though the rain continues to fall, I bless the Lord for the light of His countenance, which pierces the outward clouds, and is better than any other gift, proving the truth of the language, "The entrance of Thy words giveth light."

Golden Grove, 20th.—The rain continued to fall after leaving Moore Town. I was well protected by the green plaid given me by William Forster, which I always carry with me, in a leather before the saddle, when riding. Our course for two hours lay along the banks of the Rio Grande, which we had once to cross, and once was enough. My grain of faith was needed and availed of, when we came to the ford and saw how wide it was; but our kind Maroon took the lead, and guided us through safely. We found pleasant quarters at a lodging-house at Bath, where I should like to stay a week; and all who come to Jamaica should spend several days there, and make excursions to districts yet more beautiful.

We saw some of the survivors of the twenty-one Scotch emigrant families that were injudiciously located at Altamont, in beautiful scenery, it is true, surpassing their loved native mountains; but every man has died excepting the one we saw at the door of his house. We talked to him and his interesting wife of the things that belong to their peace, and sent them some tracts that may point them to the balm yet found in Gilead.

I felt engaged to give thanks this evening for the preservation we had experienced. My horse fell with me ascending a steep clay bank, and again he tripped when passing along a narrow path, with a bank one hundred feet deep at my right.

Kingston, 21*st*.—Our meeting in the schoolhouse at Golden Grove was well attended by about 340 labourers, most of them recently imported Africans.

22*nd*.—We went with J. Daughtry to Surrey gaol, and addressed the prisoners. One stout black man who was overcome with grief for his backsliding, rushed from the rank in which they stood. We afterwards had separate interviews with five men charged with murder. One of these was an Irish Roman Catholic, a soldier. J. Daughtry asked him if he felt any objection to listening to me. He replied, "Not the least," and seemed glad to hear me read the tract, "Guilty or not guilty," and the fifty-first Psalm. I afterwards saw him alone, when he told me that it was all owing to the accursed drink.

27th.—We came this morning from Kingston to hold a meeting at Port Royal in the evening. We preferred crossing the lagoon harbour before the sea-breeze rose, and had a peaceful and delightful sail. About 300 attended the meeting.

28th.—Went to the Penitentiary, where we had an interview with about 450 persons as they sat in rows partaking of their breakfast of gruel and bread. I addressed them on the love of Jesus, the need and benefit of yielding to His grace in the heart, that it was by degrees they fell from grace, and by obedience to it they would be restored to the condition of believing disciples.

29th.—We attended a large meeting in the Wesley Chapel. I had to bear testimony to the need of having the heart broken and bowed before the Lord, so that true worship might be experienced.

Richmond Pen, 31st.—Came to this pleasant spot yesterday to dine. Discovered that my watch and pocket-compass had been stolen from our dressing-table whilst we were asleep.

This last day of the most memorable year of my life, proved one of fresh reduction. Through all it is a favour to feel that I am under the continued care of a merciful Father.

Kingston, First Month 1*st*, 1845.—My heart, if not my mouth, was filled with praise in the language of the thirtieth Psalm, which was read at my request by William Whitehorn, who breakfasted with us. I had a long and interesting conversation with him. On conscientious grounds he resigned the pastorate of a Baptist congregation. He seems to discern with unusual clearness the spiritual teaching of the Lord, and this subject had such hold on his mind that he regards the chief happiness of heaven to consist in knowing and doing perfectly the will of God.

4th.—James T. Hartwell, a Wesleyan missionary from Hayti, who is just now invalided, called on us. He is likely to accompany us to Jacmel.

5th.—This morning, being First-day, James Jesup and I have had a precious time together to our refreshment. I felt engaged to pour forth the tribute of praise and thanksgiving, for the mercy shown, and preservation in heights and in depths, to Him who had considered my trouble, who had known my soul in adversity, and who now had brought us into a plain path, as the future in mercy appears to me. J. Jesup expressed the belief that we might thank God and take courage. My soul was feeding so delightfully on the heavenly manna, that the abiding sense was, "Evermore give us this bread." Surely this is the partaking of the flesh and blood of our Redeemer.

Jacmel, Hayti, First Month 11*th*, 1845.—We went on board the *Severn* steamer on the 8th inst., at Kingston, Jamaica, escorted by John Daughtry, who, faithful to the last, drove me in his gig to the waterside, our carriage having been sold the day before by auction.

At daybreak yesterday morning our civil young steward came to announce to me that we were off this port. We were both ready to enter the boat before sunrise, and were rowed a mile to the pier, over some stormy seas.

A well-dressed mulatto, probably the Harbour Master, took a record of our names, and placed our luggage in his store. A police officer escorted us to La Place ; J. T. Hartwell explained to the Commandant of the port that we were members of the Society of Friends. By the same escort we were soon handed on to the Commissary of Police. I explained to him our object in coming here.

After a fruitless search for lodgings, we called to rest at the house of J. A. Frith & Co., with a letter of introduction from G. C. & R. W. Fox. After we had partaken of refreshment, an invitation was given to quarter here, which we were glad to accept, as there seemed no alternative.

The town of Jacmel is situated at the head of a bay, a mile and a half long, and two or three miles wide at the entrance. It is built chiefly of wood, on a white coral rock, which gives a clean appearance to the streets. The population is 5,000 to 6,000. It exports log-wood and coffee. The climate has been delightful since we have been here. In this district, which contains 30,000 inhabitants, there is no regular physician. A black chemist seems to supply the place of one more qualified.

In the afternoon we called on General Geffrard, a young energetic officer, distinguished in the Revolution by having entered the town of Leogane, without knowing the disposition of the inhabitants, and there planted the standard of his party. His aspect and attire was that of an accomplished gentleman, and his conversation proved that his education was in keeping. Let our pale-faced brethren who are fond of denouncing their sable neighbours spend a day with this man before they express their opinions. There exists in this country doubtless much that is repugnant to our feelings, but whilst we see this, let us remember the difficulties they have had to encounter, and the serious defects which exist in their education, and in the example set by Europeans.

First Day, 12*th*.—James Jesup, J. T. Hartwell and I had our meeting for worship together this morning, when the Lord again refreshed us with His life-giving spiritual presence. I bowed the knee in prayer, "Thou hast been our help: leave us not, neither forsake us, O God of our salvation."

I have enjoyed the repose of this day, reading Hannah More's "Practical Piety." She says, "Resignation of soul, like the allegiance of a good subject, is always in readiness, though not in action: whereas an impatient mind is a spirit of disaffection." "A sincere love of God will make us thankful when our supplications are granted, patient and cheerful when they are denied."

13*th*.—We rose at four o'clock to prepare for our departure for Port Républicaine. The horses and mules arrived at eight o'clock. A full hour was occupied in loading them in the spacious court-yard of J. A. Frith's house. When I was engaged some years ago in preparing packing cases for the loads of Mexican mules, little did I think that it would ever be my lot to have to manage matters for my own travelling. Seeing our animals with their loads standing ready to depart, I was ready to say "Poor things!" but three of them had to endure the additional weight of our three guides, who sprang lightly on their backs and moved off, each conducting another mule with luggage.

Our kind host accompanied us three miles, until the first crossing of "La grande Rivière." The road lay in the ravine through which the river runs, often almost in the river's course, and we must have crossed it sixty times. Two other roads were proposed to us, but we preferred this which took us through the district most inhabited. I was surprised at the number of cottages, and small plots of cleared ground.

After travelling for four hours and a half we left the bed of the river; and, ascending rapidly up the sides of a mountain, we halted at a cottage, where we obtained forage for our beasts, and accommodation for eating the good things provided by our kind host at Jacmel. Whilst waiting for the rain, J. Jesup remarked a bottle buried up to its neck in the earthen floor of the room. Our hostess, Josephine Pain, said it was "Eau béni." This led to discourse on the subject. The master came forward, and other listeners joined the group, whilst things that belong to their everlasting peace were spoken of, and I read to them a portion of our Lord's parables from one of the nice little books selected by Josiah Forster. The man seemed very earnest to hear the truth, and equally so to persuade the poor woman that she had been following a cunningly devised fable.

At 4.30 we proceeded to Citrounier by an exceedingly bad road. J. Jesup's horse slipped away from under him, and he came down without injury.

On reaching the cottage of a man named Delmay, it was some time before he came home, and in his absence his wife thought it right to withhold permission for us to enter. She brought us chairs, and we sat surrounded by our luggage, our horses browsing, our guides smoking. When he returned he gave us a hearty welcome. Coffee was promptly prepared, of which we gratefully partook by the light of home-made castor oil, cotton just plucked from the bush supplying a wick. After our meal, all, including our guides, collected in this hut, which I must ever remember as a Bethel, whilst J. T. Hartwell read John iii. and Psalm xci. He offered a simple, appropriate prayer, and I added a few words. We slept well on a bed of straw laid on planks raised eighteen inches from the floor. We overheard one of our guides discoursing, and expounding Christian doctrine with our host, who is decidedly one of the right sort, and was glad of our visit.

14th.—After leaving the river path we had an hour's scamper over a savannah covered with log-wood, along a broad and level road. This brought us to Leogane by ten o'clock. A shopkeeper named Bacon received us. We took a walk through the town, the streets of which are wide, clean, and laid out at right angles, and there is a spacious market square. We saw a school of seventeen boys and girls, and gave notice of a meeting in the large entrance-hall of our host. About fifty came, many stood in the verandah outside, occasioning a noise that was very trying; but much must be endured in this way. We distributed several tracts and a few books, and left with a calm sense of having done what we could, though nothing whatever to glory in.

15th.—Our road lay over the village green, the battle-field of the Revolution, at the close of which Boyer fled. After a two hours' brisk trot on a level, straight, soft road, shaded by logwood trees now in full flower, like privet hedges of giant growth, with scent resembling magnolia, we breakfasted at Grélier, a military post, and had our passport signed.

The trees and plants appear larger than in Jamaica, especially the guava and star-apple. I have recognised the mahogany, bread-fruit, mango, coffee, orange, forbidden-fruit, and cabbage palm tree which is their emblem of liberty. There are butterflies of large size, in all the varied hues of withered leaves, from bright yellow to dark orange; and dragon-flies of many brilliant colours. But if trees, plants and butterflies be larger, the men are not so; few exceed the middle stature. They ride with monstrous spurs, a curb-bit of cruel power, and almost every saddle has pistol holsters. Most men ride girt with a sword. All this looks preposterous when the horse is rarely larger than a Welsh pony. These, though small, are good, with rapid and easy paces. The horse I ride cost £13 10s., and is regarded as a *gros cheval*, though by no means large in our eyes.

We came without swords from Jacmel. I made up my mind not to proceed if I could not obtain guides who would go unarmed. I believe that gospel messengers do not need the point of sword or bayonet to make or clear the way for the Prince of Peace.

A few miles before we arrived we passed the late country seat of Boyer standing well at the foot of a range of hills, having a beautiful view of Port Républicaine, and an amphitheatre of hills and mountains behind.

The first view of Port Républicaine, a place I had for seven years desired to visit, was to me more than usually interesting. I should have liked it quite as well without having in sight six large vessels of war, one of them an American, and the rest French. If however I was pained by the ships of war, I was equally pleased with the crowd of merchant vessels lying closer to the town. Probably forty or fifty schooners, brigs, and ships were receiving their cargoes of coffee from numerous well-built stone stores.

17th.—Accompanied by Mark B. Bird we called on the Secretaries for justice, education and religion, for commerce, and for war and foreign relations. By each we were pleasantly received and welcomed.

18th.—At half-past six I started for a ride on the north road through a plain covered with logwood. As I passed out at the Barrier two soldiers were overhauling the market people coming in with their loaded beasts, a continuous stream for a mile and a half. Donkeys, horses and mules bore loads of grass, forage, charcoal, logwood for firewood, plantains and other vegetables.

A merchant named Doran from Jacmel has apartments under the same roof with us. Stephen Grellet stayed a week at his house. He says, "If that man had stopped here he would have regenerated the country by this time." S. Grellet knew better, I expect, but it is indeed sweet to hear the many testimonies borne respecting his visit here.

We have had pleasant visits to a saddler, named John Charles Pressoir. The first sound of the gospel which he heard was when Stephen Grellet addressed Pétion's army from the steps of the palace. He came there a careless listener, a soldier with folded arms, leaning with indifference against the wall, but being directed to the love of God in his heart, he had no rest until the arrival of two Wesleyan missionaries. He is now a valuable member of the Wesleyan body.

19th, First Day.—James Jesup proposed that we should ask the domestics and others of the house to join us in our reading of the Scriptures after breakfast: seven came. He read in French, Psalm i., the Ten Commandments, and John i., and added a few words.

We afterwards had our usual meeting together, in which ability was given to draw water out of the wells of salvation.

We had arranged to be at a meeting of the American Wesleyans at three o'clock. Half an hour before this we called upon Fabius Day, a man of colour, born at Pernambuco. He visited Lisbon as a servant to the Ambassador, became a shoemaker at Philadelphia, and came here a few years ago, a stranger to the covenant of promise. In this land his eyes became opened, and his heart enlarged to receive the gospel of good tidings. He has had a desire to meet with the people of God since he was nine years old, when he picked up in the street at Lisbon the leaf of a Bible relating to Peter and John healing the sick; a boy read it for him, and this simple fact smouldered in his breast till fanned into a flame by the American Wesleyans settled here. The meeting proved to me one of deep interest, and worth all the fatigue and care of riding from Jacmel. J. Jesup spoke on the rest enjoyed by the people of God. I followed, on the nature of true worship; and the close searching of heart needful for the Christian.

We had an interesting call from Henry Allen. Our conversation turned on religious doctrine, worship, and gospel ministry. He seemed pleased to hear of our practice in labouring as ministers of the gospel without payment. He is a wheelwright and blacksmith, and works industriously for his support, though engaged as the minister of the American Wesleyans.

22*nd*.—We had a call from Morinée Valcour and Thénesil Brechon. The former had read with much pleasure, in French, the tracts, "On Divine Worship," and "On War." We conversed on spiritual work in the heart, and read many portions of the Testament, the words of our Lord and His apostles.

24*th*.—We visited the prison, which is in a deplorable condition; about 140 persons waiting for trial. The President of the Tribunal attended us, and we were escorted or guarded through the three courts which contain the unhappy men by two soldiers with fixed bayonets, a lieutenant with drawn sword, and two turnkeys with stout clubs. They want a John Daughtry to enjoin silence and to practise quiet, gentle control. Two prisoners were under sentence of death. One case took such hold of my mind that I deemed it right to lay the matter before the Secretary for Justice, who said it was probable that a petition would be forwarded to the President.

25th.—I called on Dr. Smith, at whose pleasant villa I planted a cocoa-nut tree for my dear A., who is this day ten years old. May the Lord grant him of His gifts, and grace to enjoy every blessing as the gift of God.

26th.—We had so many callers that we found it difficult to obtain time for our own meeting. Amongst other visitors was Henry Allen, who returned "Tuke's Principles of Friends," and offered to buy it, he liked it so much. He never read any work he liked better. It was so fully in accordance with the Bible. He had risen at midnight to read it. We gave it to him with the understanding he should lend it to others. He wished to see our "Rules of Discipline," and if we objected to receive persons of colour as members; on this we set him right.

A meeting in the Wesleyan Chapel was well attended by Haitians, English, and Americans. Mark B. Bird very suitably assisted as interpreter, repeating sentence by sentence. I set forth the origin and power of the Redeemer; the reception He had from those to whom He was sent, His exaltation and office as our Mediator. That the disbelief of these things did not change their truth. That receiving Jesus as our spiritual King would give us power over Satan. That when we are His followers, violence will no more be heard in the land, and that these can say, "I will trust and not be afraid." The meeting concluded well, and I felt relieved of a load of exercise. May the savour of my feeling of joy of heart long be remembered with gratitude to the Giver of every good and perfect gift.

28th.—We rose at three o'clock, but it was nearly six when we passed out of the town. We were accompanied by Fabius Day. The air was so cold that we were glad to proceed at a rapid pace for many miles. Our horses were in high condition for work, the road level, smooth, soft, wide and good, shaded by fine mimosa trees, forty feet high. At eight the sun was warm, and we were glad to rest at a cottage by the road side, and partake of the provisions we brought with us. After breakfast we read some of the Psalms, and then followed discourse which seemed to interest four or five women, who listened with deep attention as they sat around us. The sound of the gospel seemed new to them, and is by some gladly received. Doubtless some of the ground will prove stony and thorny, but some seed will fall into good ground. At one o'clock we again proceeded, our hostess declining to accept any remuneration for her coffee and accommodation. The road now lay for some time near the sea-coast, on which was a large quantity of the net-work coral. The beautifully smooth sandy beach took me in thought to my children, as I knew that dear S. E. at least would like to engrave her name on the changing tablet.

At half-past four we reached the cottage of Thomas Williams at Lacahaye. He is one of a number of American emigrants, and ministers amongst them in their simple meeting-house. He had profited much by the religious care bestowed upon him whilst in the service of James Yearsley, a Friend in Maryland. We wished to have a meeting with them, and thirty or forty assembled with all the decorum of a Friends' Meeting, and the power of the Lord was felt to be among them. Our certificates were read, as they could appreciate our object, and many had been in the service of Friends in America. The time of worship with these people was one of much refreshment to me.

Thomas Williams told me that after a course of vanity and sin, he was, at the age of twenty-five, impressed with serious things, and began to learn to read. This he found difficult, but being in earnest, he struggled on. A few months ago he felt a concern to visit his fellow emigrants in the southern promontory near Jeremie. He laid it before their little church. It was approved of, and Henry Allen joined in the service.

29th.—We left before four o'clock, and had been on horseback more than an hour before the planet Venus arose above the horizon to add her brilliant light to the soft rays of a nearly half moon.

We met a company of life-guards escorting Alexis Dupuy. Though unknown to each other we were not long in discovering our respective names. We were bearers of despatches to him. I had an interesting talk with him, part of which would furnish him with subject for reflection as he rode onward. He hoped to return so as to receive us when we came back, and giving us advice as to a stopping place on the road, he passed on with his troopers. Our road lay along the sea-shore, the island of Gonave in sight. On the right was a range of abrupt hills, from which we heard the distant cry of the hunters pursuing the wild hog.

We reached Mourins at half-past nine, and stopped at the house of Joachin, a farmer. Here we concluded to rest after our six hours' ride. A great quantity of cotton is grown here; and our host had one hundred or more stocks of bees, each occupying an American flour barrel laid on its side. The wife gave us some honey in the comb, and delicious it was, extracted from the choicest flowers.

A negro, incapacitated for work, was acting as schoolmaster, teaching three little girls amid a grove of plantains. I afterwards found him and J. Jesup seated together, discoursing on points of Romish doctrine.

In this settlement of peasantry we distributed sixty or seventy tracts. All seemed to value them, and opportunity was afforded for conversing with many of the people, I hope to profit; at any rate I felt well satisfied that we had tarried here, although deprived of some of the comforts which have usually been our portion. The furniture of our room consisted of a mat to lay on the floor, three muskets and a sword. On this mat we spread our cloaks, and covered ourselves with my plaid and a blanket we carry with us. I could have slept well, being very weary, but the ants attacked me and bit me most sharply, waking me at least twenty times.

St. Marc, 30th.—We are quartered at the house of L'Administrateur Verna, to whom Dupuy had recommended us. Here we were received with much hospitality. The master was at his plantation, but his son did his part very kindly.

We visited the École Nationale, where thirty-three boys were present. We heard seven of them read John iv., their spelling was good, and writing fair, considering that the school is not yet a year old. Amongst the scholars was a son of the President, and one of a General who commands the arondissement. We called on the General and found him much gratified by the circumstance of our having given to his son a "Discours de notre divin Sauveur," a British and Foreign School writing book, and a lead pencil. The President's son being in a lower class, had only received one of Josiah Forster's "Scripture Selections." The President Guerrier is now at St. Marc, making the place very busy with military doings.

31st.—At three o'clock this morning, soon after moonrise, we were on our way. On reaching the big door which forms the Barrier we were told by the guard that we could not pass, that he would say "No" to the President. Then Chéri our guide began, "My brother, they are two ministers of the good God, who are going to preach the gospel." He then advanced to the door, unlocked the bolt, and in silence received our thanks.

In two hours we reached the rapid and deep river Artibonite, and crossed it by a floating bridge. Soon we saw the sun rise, and I believe I never saw it look more beautiful. By eight we reached another river, and crossed by a wooden bridge at D'Esterre. Here we halted, gave the horses a good feed of juicy maize stalks, and partook of coffee at a nice cottage.

It was well we stopped, for we were two hours in crossing a plain of sand. We followed the track of naked feet in the sand, which seemed, as far as eye could reach, like a desert. Clumps of mimosa, aloes and cactus were scattered about, but not a vestige of civilization. Our good horses did their work well, though weary, and were so thirsty as to be glad to drink some black water we found by the wayside. By noon we entered Gonaives, and received from James Osler a welcome worthy of a Cornishman. The country through which we have passed for 123 miles during four days is remarkably bare of population, and for hours we saw no house or vestige of cultivation, and have met very few persons on the road. Though solitary, we have both possessed a large flow of satisfying peace.

Second Month 2nd, First Day.—We had a good meeting with about fifty persons at the new Wesleyan schoolroom. The captains, and some of the crews of the vessels in port, the British Consul, and other residents were present, and more than all, we had, I believe, amongst us the spiritual presence of Him who giveth strength unto His people, and who blesseth them with peace. Although there appears but little to be done, yet it will be enough if we can hear the language, "He hath done what he could."

Accompanied by Samuel Osler we made some calls in the afternoon. Amongst these was one on James Moreau, a respectable trader. He is called in this country a "speculator," corresponding with the English broker. The Haitian law prohibits foreign merchants from buying direct from the peasantry, and therefore the merchants advance a few hundred dollars each week to the speculator, who buys coffee, cotton, and other produce.

3rd.—There was a busy scene in J. Osler's yard—two carts heavily laden with coffee, so as to require seven donkeys to each cart, all harnessed abreast. It is really cheering to see the evidence of commerce in the logs of mahogany lying in thousands on the shore, ready for shipment for England.

The first impression on entering Gonaives is not favourable. It stands on a sandy plain, with houses low and scattered. The earthquake of 1842, and the fire more destructive still which followed, destroyed more than a quarter of the town. It now contains about 4,000 inhabitants, and is badly supplied with water.

CHAPTER XV.

WEST INDIES.

Hayti — River forded thirty Times — Escalier — Plaisance — Limbe — View of Cape Haitien — Miseries from Earthquake — Visits to Lycée and École Nationale — Prison — Meeting with Europeans and Americans — Plaisance — Gonaives — School — St. Marc — Meeting at Lacahaye — Port Républicaine — Meetings — Incidents on Journey — Haitian Costumes — Miragoane — Aquin — General Lelièvre — Aux Cayes — Meeting — Prison — André Télémaque — St. Louis — Baynet — One of the Horses dies — Jacmel — Voyage to St. Thomas — Santa Cruz — Governor — Visits to Moravian Mission Stations — Schools for the "Unfree" — Fredericksted — Christiansted — Prison — Meetings at St. Thomas' — Return Voyage — Bermuda — Storm — Meeting with Passengers — Southampton — Arrival at Falmouth.

SECOND MONTH 4th, 1845.—We left Gonaives, our horses fresh, and ourselves in good spirits. For two hours our road lay over a country nearly level; it was a broad, straight, and soft road, shaded by logwood, mimosa, or cassia; then we entered a defile, through which runs a river, which we forded thirty times. We stopped to breakfast at the cottage of Jean Pierre Banania, where we could obtain forage for our horses and coffee for ourselves. After breakfast we read to the cottagers.

Continuing half an hour through the defile we reached the foot of the dreaded Escalier, a steep ascent. The road is well laid out by skilful engineers, and was once paved. It is now partly broken up. The pass is 2,000 feet high, and on each side the mountains rise very abruptly to a height of about 3,000 feet.

At three o'clock we reached the pleasant village of Plaisance, on an undulating plain that occupied an hour in crossing. Again we ascended and descended a mountain path, and at length, weary enough, reached Camp Cog at five o'clock. Grass was obtained for our horses, a chicken was slaughtered, cooked, and placed on a neat table in about an hour and a half. Our host was an intelligent man, an officer in the army; he read French fluently, and conversed a little in English. Here we distributed a few tracts, and read the Scriptures to many listeners.

Cape Haitien, 5th.—This morning our way lay for many miles by the side of a broad and rapid stream, which we had to cross twice. The road was green turf, and very beautiful, shaded with magnificent trees, and adorned with rich flowers.

The appearance of the people in the village of Limbe pleased us. The women, in black gowns with white turban handkerchiefs, were just leaving their chapel, as it was Ash Wednesday. At eleven o'clock we reached the summit of the chain of hills, whence we had a view of Cape Haitien, its surrounding plain, distant headlands and the ocean, forming one of the grandest pictures I had seen. I cannot attempt to describe the scene of misery and wretchedness and desolation that greeted us on reaching Cape Haitien. No idea that I had formed of the horrors of an earthquake equals the reality of Fifth Month 7th, 1842. Three-fourths of the houses must have been prostrated; half of the streets are yet blocked up with rubbish, in which unnumbered bodies remain undiscovered. The President Guerrier has just given a thousand dollars to assist in clearing the rubbish from the streets, and many workmen are now thus occupied.

We failed to secure lodgings until we sought counsel of our friend James Blain, to whom we had letters of introduction. He told us he would give us the key of the house of the British Consul; and within an hour of our entering the city we were admiring the clock of the consul, which has on it the motto, "There's no place like home."

During the past few days I have felt very earnest to know the will of the Lord as to our movements here. I believe there is very little for us to do. May we be faithful in that little.

7th.—We visited the Lycée, and the École Nationale, where more than two hundred boys receive a fair education, and had much intercourse with the directors or masters. On application to the authorities they readily granted us the Lycée for a meeting to-morrow. The boys of the Lycée, who write very well, prepared a good supply of notices. These we sent about the place.

9th.—I passed much of to-day under discouragement at the prospect before us, yet felt at times ability to cast my burden on the Lord. We went to the Lycée, and found none arrived. After a time of waiting about twenty came, to whom the religion of Jesus Christ was in some degree set forth, feeling myself the need of the help of Him who is mighty to save.

10th.—This morning we visited the prison, which is almost in ruins; sixty men were stowed in one yard with cells on each side; some of these men were heavily ironed.

We had a meeting with English and Americans. Marie Josephe Pequions lent her room, which was crowded, and it proved a good time. I have rarely felt more Christian liberty than whilst making known to others the glad tidings of the gospel of peace by Jesus Christ. Some of the trading class, who rarely enter a place of worship, felt I believe the power of the Lord to be over them, constraining not a few to bow at the name of Jesus. Our hearts rejoiced to feel at liberty after this meeting really to turn homewards.

Plaisance, 11th.—The rain which had fallen every day during our stay at Cape Haitien rendered the road worse on our return. The river was much deeper, but our horses kept their feet.

Bamboos grow in ground much of which is similar to

decomposed granite. No sugar is made in the French part of Hayti. The syrup is converted into tafia, a liquor like rum. Drunkenness pervades many classes, and I believe this ruinous vice contributes largely to the extreme poverty, misery and degradation of so many of these unhappy people.

We are comfortably accommodated at Plaisance at the house of widow Vastey. With her son Antenor we had very interesting converse. He read to us John iv. before we retired to rest in our chamber, where a lamp was kept burning all night before a picture of Mary, which, with a crucifix, occupied a corner of the room, screened by a pretty little canopy.

Gonaives, 13th.—We have to-day paid a visit to the school of eighty boys at this place. Many of them read to us very pleasantly; and a large number were made glad by the prizes, which, through the kindness of my generous friends in England, we have been able to carry into more than 150 schools amongst the various islands, strengthening in no trifling degree the bond of union between the children of these islands and their friends at home.

14th.—We left our pleasant home at Gonaives early, and crossed again that sandy desert. We met the peasantry, armed with swords, going to market with large bags of cotton. At the house of Etienne Roberts, at Pont D'Esterre, after breakfast we had an interesting reading of Matthew v., leading to lively conversation. At St. Marc we called on Alexis Dupuy and conversed with him on schools, religion and war, to our satisfaction.

15th.—We proceeded to Lacahaye, and had a kind welcome from Thomas Williams.

16th, *First Day.*—James Jesup and I had our meeting under the trees by a brook that runs at the bottom of the garden, and sweet was the spiritual refreshment of which I then partook in silence. At half-past two we had a meeting with the Americans who usually meet together.

I spoke on the commission Moses received at the Lord's hand when He appeared in the burning bush, and the important result of his obedience.

We dined by invitation with George Shea, and truly I was surprised at the handsome repast of roasted turkey and kid, with a great variety of excellent vegetables, which was spread for us on a well-arranged table in a very simple dwelling; after which we had a nice time together, in reading the Bible, and other religious service.

We left Lacahaye at half-past twelve by the light of a moon which set at two, and passed many groups of travellers asleep by the roadside, a blazing fire warming their feet. We watched the ascension and descension of the Southern Cross. Proceeding steadily at a walking pace we reached Port Républicaine on the morning of the 17th, glad enough to pass under the triumphal arch erected in honour of President Guerrier, which stands at the northern entrance to the town, and thankful for the guiding and upholding mercies which have been granted us during the journey of 360 miles. On telling our old serving woman that we had had a good journey, she replied, "I am glad; I prayed for you every day." We have moved faster than the slow-paced couriers who carry the letters. These, as they march along, shod with sandals, and their burdens strapped firmly to their shoulders, remind me of Bunyan's pilgrim.

23rd.—We had a meeting at the Wesleyan Chapel, of which notice had been given in English. It was well attended by a large number of the more wealthy classes, whom we much wished to see.

Third Month, 2nd.—We had a meeting in the American Baptist Chapel this morning, when J. Jesup spoke on the text, "Blessed are they which do hunger and thirst after righteousness, for they shall be filled." Prayer was offered that the Lord would create clean hearts.

Amongst a great deal that we must deplore in this city as being at variance with the gospel there is yet cause for encouragement, and at times I cherish the hope that brighter days will soon dawn on Hayti.

In one of my morning rides I visited the cemetery, which occupies a well-wooded and retired spot south of the city. Attaching my horse to the branch of a tree near the bridge which crosses the fosse at the gateway, I passed quietly and without notice amongst the loiterers. Numerous devotees appear to visit daily the graves of their departed, where they light one or more candles, and keep them continually burning.

I have felt much interest for some sick French sailors who have lodgings in this street. I handed them two French Testaments. One man rejected it scornfully, but his shipmates were grateful for it. One of the sailors clasped the book earnestly with both hands, as though it was his greatest treasure, and seemed surprised when he found it was a gift. This poor fellow had passed nine days and nights without sleep.

We have paid some little attention to the First-day schools. They are small at present, but will exercise a beneficial influence against First-day marketing, and in favour of worship and Christian practice.

3rd.—We had a pleasant ride to Leogane. We went at once to the house of our acquaintance Jean Pierre Banania. He was out, but his servant made us welcome. Her master and mistress returned in the evening from their little plantation. Our time was pleasantly spent in making some calls, and presenting tracts and books. One interesting aged black woman sat at her door busily engaged at needlework without spectacles. She had evidently a superior mind, and was delighted with "No Cross, no Crown." On inquiry I learned that she had borne an excellent character for a long time. She refrains from working on First-days, and is an example to many around her. I shall long remember our friend Fleurisaux, who is setting her face steadfastly towards Zion. Our host had much valued "Penn's Maxims," which I had given him. He carried it in his pocket to read in his intervals of leisure. I now gave him a New Testament, and Penn's "No Cross, no Crown."

5th.—Leaving Petit Goave early we saw several poor women on their knees in the street, worshipping an image of our Saviour on a cross.

We enjoyed our ride along the sea-shore for a few miles. As we proceeded to Miragoane we had for our companions part of the way a Haitian couple mounted on their lively ponies. The woman was of Mulatto complexion, with long ear-rings, a broad brimmed black beaver hat, broad figured band, fastened with a richly embossed gold-like buckle, a lilac cotton shawl with deep border of white flowers, printed cotton gown, white cotton stockings, green shoes of delicate material, sandals of green ribbon, and the left heel furnished with a brass spur of noble dimensions. Before her rode her boy with a large straw hat and blue shirt, carrying her wardrobe, and shouting to his ass, "hoo-e," the universal cry in encouraging these animals. Her spouse was attired in black hat and coat, and blue trousers, with a sword, and holsters to his saddle.

The descent by a rocky, rugged road to the little seaport of Miragoane reminded me of some of our little fishing coves in Cornwall, and our reception here from Charles Geltson and George Reed was as cordial as if they had been Cornishmen. They are American merchants. C. Geltson is coloured. Both appear decidedly serious; perhaps the result of a miraculous escape from shipwreck, when their vessel was capsized in a squall off Turk's Island. All sank but these two, who reached the boat, in which they remained without food for two days and a half. They were picked up by a French vessel, and landed at New York. They entertained us hospitably, and most readily gave up their ware-room for a meeting in the evening, which was well attended.

6th.—We left Miragoane at 5 a.m. When we were

about four or five leagues on our way, we were hailed by a voice from the wood, inviting us to partake of coffee. It was the Magistrate of the Commune, who had been at the meeting the previous evening, and having preceded us, he had prepared some excellent coffee grown on his own estate of 1,500 acres. A few bundles of grass refreshed our horses, and some raw eggs with the coffee ourselves.

Our route was over a savannah, a league in width, between ranges of hills for many leagues. This elevated plain terminates by an abrupt descent of 1,500 feet. From the brow of the hill we had an extensive and beautiful view of the southern coast towards Aux Cayes, studded with islands, wooded hills of varied outline, and an extensive plain, which we had to traverse for ten miles before we reached Aquin. Perhaps the most interesting sight of the day was the sea, of which I did not expect again to lose sight for a day, before we should be floating towards my cherished home.

During much of this journey my mind was preserved in sweet peace, reflecting often on the language, "He that dwelleth in the secret place of the Most High shall abide under the shadow of the Almighty."

Although weary with our journey of nearly forty miles we had to traverse Aquin before we found a resting-place, and then it was at the house of General Lelièvre, whom we saw seated under his verandah at the door, cleaning a beautiful double-barrelled fowling-piece. His aide-de-camp and guard were seated near him. After he had heard our letter of introduction read, he invited us to lodge and partake of their dinner of fried eggs, fried egg plant, chicken ragout, shrimps and bananas. A long bare-legged boy poured water on our hands before the meal, having a towel on his left arm.

After I lay down and reflected on the way we were surrounded by armed soldiers on duty all night, I felt less secure than when sleeping in a cottage without doors, as at

Mourins. Strange it seemed to express without reserve or fear our sentiments on Peace to the black general who sat surrounded by his officers, guards, and other less military listeners.

7th.—We proceeded by a road still beautiful, mountainous and varied, to Cavaillon, where we had a very cordial reception from André Télémaque, the Commandant, whose heart seemed remarkably opened.

Aux Cayes, 8th.—It was pleasant to be kindly greeted by Colquhoun Smith, whom I had seen at Falmouth. We boarded at his table with an agreeable circle of young men of good education connected with C. Smith's establishment.

As we passed through the country we saw and heard much of the ravages of war, from which they have suffered since 1842. Revolution upon revolution has unsettled the minds of the people, a condition that is always productive of discontent and trouble.

12th.—We went to the public school, where we found more than a hundred boys, nineteen of them reading in the New Testament.

As we lodge in a spacious house our circumstances are such as to admit of many persons having free access to us at our quarters. We borrowed chairs and benches to seat our large sitting-room, and this evening 200 assembled, many standing in the hall, to whom counsel flowed freely. Prayer also was offered for the extension of the Redeemer's kingdom in the hearts of this people, and for the spread of love which shall prevent war, so that peace may prevail.

13th.—We visited the prison, which is not apparently so bad as some we have seen. After this we had a very pleasant call from Joseph Castel, a merchant from Cuba. His mind seems alive to his eternal interests, and on behalf of the people of his country also. He is earnest to have a girls' school established.

15th.—We left Aux Cayes accompanied by Colquhoun

Smith, his brother Charles, four other young Englishmen, and last but not least, André Télémaque, the Commandant of Cavaillon, who was dressed in his regimentals as a colonel, and was preceded by a mounted soldier to clear his way. I had very agreeable conversation with A. Télémaque. He had attended the meeting at Aux Cayes, and seemed satisfied that religion does not consist in external observances, but in the dedication of the soul and all its powers to the Lord. After riding four miles, two of our companions left us, the remainder took leave of us at one o'clock. I felt reluctant to part, when the time came for them to turn their faces homewards.

The horse which we purchased at Jacmel, and which I named Carib, carried me safely and delightfully from Jacmel to Cape Haitien, and thence to Aux Cayes, but his back becoming sore with my saddle, I exchanged him for another of our horses, which from his crooked legs, the shape of his head, easy gait, and being a beast of burden, we called Camel. Carib then bore our panniers with luggage, and when within a few miles of St. Louis, the cord which bound the luggage slipped, so as to cause him to kick, and to start off at full gallop. He cast some of the luggage on the ground, which I had to watch, whilst J. Jesup and Cheri, our guide, went in pursuit of Carib, who had turned aside into a thicket of logwood, so dense as to cause us to lose sight or trace of him, except where our carpet bags were dropped. I soon gave him up for lost, and was the more surprised when the shouts of my companions announced his capture. No sooner was Carib secured, than Camel showed symptoms of spasms, and I had to mount him and ride at full speed to save his life. We certainly felt in doubtful plight, for " Haitien" (J. J.'s steed) was biting his off fore foot, as much as to say, "I can't go much further." But Camel was restored by his four mile heat, and Haitien relieved as soon as we reached St. Louis by being bled in the foot.

The town of St. Louis is of a striking character. The

streets are at right angles, thickly covered with short green grass, looking very neat and pretty. It is backed closely by high mountains; these form the amphitheatre for a calm bay, which for size and aspect reminded me of Plymouth Sound, the breakwater and Drake's Island having their counterparts in flat green islands. Instead of gulls there were magnificent pelicans.

16th.—We were kindly received by Pierre Nicolas Salien, and were well satisfied to spend First-day here. We had a meeting with some of the inhabitants at the house of our host. His gratitude for services rendered to the negro race prevented his receiving any payment for his good accommodation.

17th.—We reached Aquin to breakfast at the house of C. A. Rospide, a merchant.

18th.—We left Aquin at four o'clock, on a road destitute of water, and for ten leagues destitute of habitations. We deemed it best to hire a mule in case our beasts should fail; its rider served as our guide. We proceeded through the dark by an intricate road. Three times fallen trees intercepted our way, but by dismounting, and having on one occasion a passage cut round the tree by the guide, who, as one of the *gens-d'armes*, carried his sword, we succeeded in passing. The remainder of our road was tolerably smooth and level, through a dense forest of log-wood, lignum vitæ, and cacti. We often heard and occasionally saw the sea, and arrived very unexpectedly at a hamlet of fishing cottages. At one of these, beautifully neat and whitewashed, we made an excellent breakfast, helped out by nice sardines caught there in great abundance in nets made by the men from cotton grown and made by themselves. We were glad of a few hours' repose, and at two o'clock started for Côté de fer, where we lodged in a select chamber. Sometimes we think that an average of our accommodations would be just agreeable; we must take things as we find them, and may well be thankful for our lot.

Our Scripture reading in the evening was attended by a large company, and it proved a season for imparting religious counsel that was well received.

19*th*.—Setting off at six o'clock we pursued a rough, and occasionally beautiful, sea-side road for five hours, when we were glad to seek rest in the shade of some fine trees that grew near a clear stream, supplying us with fresh water for our chocolate, which we boiled on a fire kindled with leaves and dry sticks. Some women came with their children, and sat by us whilst we ate our breakfast, and had our usual reading. One of them had given Chéri a bunch of plantains, our bread being short. She thought herself overpaid by the gift for one of her children of one of the little garments my Aunt Fox gave me.

We reached Baynet, a small town with about one hundred houses. Jean Dominique, a trader, received us handsomely, refusing payment for the service. On the square before his door we saw his men training a wild bull, recently caught in one of the adjoining forests. The wild and tame bull were bound by their horns to the beam of a yoke, to the no small annoyance of both beasts. The wild one, unaccustomed to the restraint, dragged the other about until both were weary. Then a small quantity of forage was thrown quietly before them; such was the treatment for three or four days. Whilst they were standing quietly before the door, a sudden noise like the discharge of musketry alarmed both us and them, and they took to their heels. The noise was a part of one of the scenes acted at the Roman Catholic Chapel, by some persons who like to re-act the events of the crucifixion, and had some reference to frightening Judas out of the town. We gave our host a New Testament.

20*th*.—Leaving Baynet we reached a beautiful bay, where we stopped under some trees, and breakfasted on shaddocks, bread, and water. We passed over a steep long hill, and obtained magnificent views, but my pleasure was damped, when a league distant from Jacmel, by Chéri calling from behind, that Carib my favourite horse was ill. We soon discharged his load and took him as fast as we could towards a soft part of the road, but before he reached it he staggered and fell on a rocky part, under the influence of poison, which we conjecture he ate at the bay where we breakfasted. James Jesup went forward to procure oil and syrup. I stayed with Chéri until five o'clock, and then, as the sun was sinking, it was needful for me to proceed, leaving Chéri in charge of Carib; but all our many efforts were fruitless; he died at nine that evening. I regretted his loss much, but it teaches us that we have been mercifully dealt with in proceeding thus far without serious accident, and that it did not occur on a remote track, where help would have been out of the question.

Jacmel, 21*st*.—James Jesup and I had our meeting together this morning, when ability was given to commemorate the mercy which has been extended to us in this land, where, on landing, we sought afresh to dedicate ourselves to the service of the Lord. In our travels He has kept us as in the hollow of His holy hand. This was acknowledged, with the addition, "I will trust, and not be afraid." O Lord, I pray Thee increase my faith and dependence!

We find written here in the margin of the journal, "Amen says E. O. T., 9th of Sixth Month, 1884."

We had a meeting in the National School-room, to which we invited the inhabitants. A sense of the Lord's power was felt.

30*th*.—We reached St. Thomas at two o'clock this morning. The *Trent* steamer did not arrive at Jacmel until the 26th. We went on board, and found our friend William Knibb, who gave us a hearty greeting. Our voyage through the Mona channel to St. John's, Porto Rico, was both rough and tough, against a strong head wind that kept me very quiet. I enjoyed my berth for reading and thought, both retrospective and prospective.

Yesterday we began to bear down with a south course on the harbour of St. John's. The view of the low wooded knolls on richly wooded plains for the foreground, backed by lofty hills in the distance, reminded me more of the Isle of Wight than any other I have seen. Dangerous shoals at the entrance of this harbour are their natural protectors from invasion, but not content with these, very strong forts and batteries have been built of white stone on the east bank of the entrance. We anchored half a mile from the town of St. John's, and saw but little of it. The buildings appeared large and somewhat magnificent. Many slave ships take refuge here from our cruisers, whilst making their stealthy way to the hot-bed of slavery at Cuba.

Fourth Month, 5th.—Still at St. Thomas, waiting with a degree of patience day after day for the arrival of the *Vigilant*, a government schooner, by which to proceed to Santa Cruz. The leisure I have had has given me much time to look backwards and forwards; at times I can do so with entire calmness, which is the result of the support graciously afforded, but at other times my nature shrinks when my eyes are taken off from my Guide and Helper. I find that I am too earnest in trying to lift the veil of the future as it regards my darling children (ill with whooping cough), but through all I am constrained to say, "Oh the depth of the riches, both of the wisdom and knowledge of God! how unsearchable are His judgments, and His ways past finding out!"

Friedensfald, Santa Cruz, 8th.—On the 6th we embarked on the *Vigilant*, and soon glided rapidly out of the harbour in one of the swiftest sailers I was ever on board.

The cabin was occupied by five or six young ladies who had accepted an invitation to a ball to be given by Von Scholten, the Governor of Santa Cruz, whilst their companions and we way-worn travellers had to do as well as we could on deck, and we did very nicely. I went to sleep under my cloak just as we lost sight of the light-house, and did not awake until we were close to Santa Cruz. On landing we walked to the borders of the town of Christianstedt, and easily found Friedensfald, the Moravian Station. W. Warner went with us to call on the Governor, whose reception was most frank and cordial, placing no difficulty in the way of the object of our visit. He said he could do no less, introduced as we were by my cousin Alfred Fox and Sir Charles Fitzroy, the Governor of the Leeward Islands.

Von Scholten is favourable towards ameliorating the condition of the "unfree," the term here given to the labouring class.

We have had a kind reception from the Moravian Brethren, and this evening we had a meeting here, which was attended by about 200. Prayer was offered for that help which is needful in building the house of the Lord, and testimony was borne that the Lord would give strength unto His people, and bless His people with peace.

9th.—We visited Mount Victory school, which is under the charge of an intelligent teacher, Benjamin Fouseca, a Jew, who has embraced Christianity. Two hundred little "unfree" children are here taught; 176 were in the gallery when we arrived, receiving a lesson on Naaman the Syrian, a rich subject for such auditors; but the captivity of the little Israelitish maid was not dwelt on.

We had an agreeable call from Adam and Martha Stevenson, to whom we were introduced by letter from Joseph John Gurney, whose memory is precious with many whom we have seen. They accompanied us to the meeting at Fredericksted, which was crowded, and a good meeting, the power of the Lord being manifest in bringing many low before Him.

When the Judge of Fredericksted heard of our intended meeting, he questioned our right to hold it. It was well that the Governor was in that town at the time. He had given full permission, and there the matter ended.

Christianstedt, 10*th*.—Adam Stevenson came with his carriage to convey us to this place. We called at Diamond school, arriving before the master. A. S. with great readiness marshalled the little "unfrees" in the gallery. A little fellow of six years old was soon singled out to drill them, and interesting indeed it was to hear the questions from this infant: "Who discovered this island?" "What is the name of this island?" "What does it mean?" "Who is the king?" "What is the name of the queen?" "Where does the king live?" And after replying to all these, they sang the chorus, "Copenhagen the capital, Copenhagen the capital."

We had appointed a meeting in the Moravian Chapel at eight o'clock. Before seven it was crowded. Such packing in this climate produces a temperature that is difficult to bear. The meeting was owned and blessed by Him whom we have sought to serve. We withdrew with thankful hearts to our guest-chamber, where we read Psalm cxi., and I felt I could have testified that I was by no means weary of that work which " is honourable and glorious."

11*th*.—Before our second breakfast we were surprised by another call from the Governor, who seems much interested in our visit to these islands. At his previous visit he avowed his full intention to carry forward the work of emancipating the people to the utmost extent, and that as rapidly as circumstances would allow.

Accompanied by Alexander Tower, of Strawberry Hill, we visited the excellent gaol. It was erected in 1836 on improved principles, so as to render its arrangements the most complete that we have seen in the West Indies, but it is deficient in moral and religious care.

A. Tower is an interesting man. I plainly told him that I did not feel bound to preach liberty to the captive, but rather the glad tidings of the gospel, which should be to all people, who, if they would receive it and become disciples of the Redeemer, would obey His commands by observing the golden rule, and of their own accord would undo the heavy burdens, and let the oppressed go free. This came home to him. He desires to be a follower of Christ, and avowed his readiness to liberate his people, but he did not know how. I replied that it was no business of mine to point out the way. "Where there's a will, there's a way," and he need not be afraid of doing right. He conveyed us in his carriage to the wharf whence we embarked on the *Vigilant*.

12th.—At two o'clock we were under sail, and wafted gently out of the critical reefy harbour with a fair south wind. I slept soundly, but awoke in time to enjoy entering the harbour of St. Thomas. We landed just as the moon sank behind the Western Hills.

13th.—We had another meeting at the Moravian Meeting House. We went early, expecting it might be crowded, and met many coming away. Again were we favoured with help as from the sanctuary. Great solemnity prevailed, although many persons stood the whole time, filling every corner, the steps, and the gallery.

We called on the Governor. J. Jesup had close talk with him on emancipation, which he deems doubtful and apparently undesirable.

I was privileged to-day to have good tidings of my dear children—a cause of thankfulness which engages me afresh to enter into covenant with the Lord, desiring that my dedication of heart may be full and unreserved.

"*Tweed*" *steamer, 200 miles off Bermuda, 18th.*—We embarked at sunset on the 14th, and steamed out of St. Thomas early next morning, and took our leave of the beautiful cluster of islands, Tortola, St. John's, St. Thomas and Porto Rico at one o'clock. I have twice left my writing to go on deck and see the whales that are sporting in this vast sea, spouting up the water in their gambols.

Throughout most of yesterday we were crossing the Gulf Stream, which was running from west to east. My attention was first called to this by the sea-weed which was drawn in that direction. Through this weed we passed most of the day. This would make the stream about a hundred miles wide, but it was probably wider.

Great peace has been my uninterrupted portion since we left St. Thomas. It has flowed like a river.

19th.—We made Bermuda; and very interesting it was to skirt along the southern shore of the principal island, which is low, and in many parts covered extensively with white sand blown up from the shore. After a time it becomes covered with a slight herbage, then the cypress takes root, verdure increases, and grazing ground is formed. We had to pursue with care, under the guidance of a young negro pilot, our intricate course amongst the coral reefs and innumerable shoals that surround the 365 islands or rocks.

20th.—Our transhipment took place to-day to the *Clyde* steamer, after which J. Jesup and I had a meeting together to my comfort, when the language of thanksgiving arose to the Hearer and Answerer of prayer, for the grace which had been granted to direct and sustain.

22nd.—Yesterday, about noon, we had a storm of thunder and lightning with rain, and very serious were the feelings that came over me—such a sense of our weakness to help ourselves in the midst of this waste of waters. My soul was driven to its sure refuge, whilst the language ascended:

"Into Thy hands, my sovereign God,
I did my all resign,
In calm reliance on Thy word,
Which made salvation mine."

Fifth Month 1st.—On the 23rd the wind increased to a gale, and it was with feelings of alarm that I looked at the stupendous billows that opposed our progress, which were wrinkled and crested by the howling blast that swept over us. On First-day, the 27th, my mind participated in tossings, though from a different cause. I believed it right to propose having a meeting with the passengers. Captain Symonds read the Episcopalian service in the saloon, after which it was given up to the use of the Spanish Ambassador, returning from Mexico, who has his padre on board.

In the evening an opportunity was afforded us, when ability was, I believe, received to preach Christ crucified as the hope of glory for sinners who are repentant and reconciled.

Falmouth, 8th.—Through the continuance of the Lord's protecting mercy and care we were permitted to reach Southampton in safety on the evening of the 5th, landed at 11 p.m., and met cousin Samuel Fox and Thomas Catchpole on the pier, whence we had embarked Tenth Month 2nd, 1843. I met my sister Elizabeth at the Star Inn. We read a Psalm, at the close of which cousin Samuel knelt and offered up thanks to the God of our lives for His preserving care. I did not sleep until morning dawned. The silence of the night seemed strange to me after the chirping of insects in the islands, and the constant creaking of our mighty ship.

My companions left for London, and I departed per *Brunswick* steamer, reaching home in peace and safety, favoured to find my children and sisters well, and much cause for gratitude, although my darling Jenepher has been taken. In reference to her the language arises:—

> "Lament not your loved one, but triumph the rather
> To think of the promise, the prayer of the Lamb,
> Your joy shall be full, and I will, O My Father,
> That those that Thou gav'st Me, may be where I am!"

CHAPTER XVI.

FALMOUTH.

Yearly Meeting, 1845—Falmouth—Redruth Monthly Meeting—Goes with Sister and Children to Youghal—Death of Junia Price—Elizabeth Fry—Prospect of Service in Norway—Professional Engagements—Dartmoor—Yearly Meeting—Farewell Gathering at Samuel Fox's—Benjamin Seebohm.

EDWIN O. TREGELLES remained for a week with his sisters and his children in the changed home at Falmouth. The return there, and meeting his friends for the first time after the loss of his wife, naturally brought back the past, so as to awaken his tender feelings, of which he writes, "A sadness, not easily described, weighs down my spirits. May I learn in whatsoever state I am, therewith to be content."

He attended the Yearly Meeting in London, and there returned the certificate granted to him in 1842, giving some account of the travels and service which he and his companion James Jesup had accomplished in the West Indian Islands.

After the Yearly Meeting he went to Southampton on railway business, and returned to London, whence he writes :—

Tottenham, Sixth Month 14th, 1845.—I returned here in low spirits yesterday, under the apprehension that the various cross occurrences which seemed to thwart my movements were cause for regret; but instead of this I now feel as though the Lord had ordered all things for me in a way marvellous to myself. In the midst of my fears as to mis-stepping I was able to say, "Thou art my hiding place; Thou shalt preserve me from trouble; Thou shalt compass me about with songs of deliverance."

Yesterday morning my secret prayer ascended that the Lord would be pleased to turn the hearts of those with whom I had dealings, so that they might be favourable to me. This prayer having been granted in an extraordinary way, I desire rightly to commemorate the loving-kindness of the Lord. May my arrangements that yet remain to be made with other parties be such as may most conduce to the praise of the Lord, and be in accordance with His will.

15th.—It has been my privilege to meet several times in meetings for worship with my friends Hannah Chapman Backhouse and Lindley Murray Hoag, both of whom have ministered profitably to my state.

Hannah C. Backhouse alluded to Abraham, the father of the faithful, after having given many proofs of dedication of heart to the Lord, having been proved yet further, and manifesting unhesitating obedience by his readiness to offer up his darling child when required of the Lord.

Falmouth, Seventh Month 5th.—On reading this morning for the first time in my dear Jenepher's Bogatsky, I found that her neat mark had been placed, I suppose by her, at the 16th day of First Month, ready for the morrow which she never saw, and the last lines of the verse are:—

> "In suffering be Thy love my peace,
> In weakness be Thy love my power;
> And when the storms of life shall cease,
> Jesus, in that important hour,
> In death, as life, be Thou my guide,
> And save me, who for me hast died."

10th.—Went this morning to Perran to call on Barclay and Jane Fox. Enjoyed my visit to them, and rejoiced in the prospect for them of many happy years.

16th.—Went with Isaac Sharp to the monthly meeting at Redruth. Met there with Hannah C. Backhouse and Eliza Hunt, John F. and Hannah Marsh, and Samuel Treffry. At the conclusion of the meeting I handed back the certificate that was granted me for service in the West Indian Islands, with a brief allusion to the merciful dealings of the Lord.

23rd.—This is the anniversary of my deliverance from death, when my horse ran away with me at Belcour, and threw me on my neck. May the sense of this mercy cause me to hope, although some of the events now passing are not such as we should contrive if we had the power. The railway bill for Plymouth and Falmouth has been thwarted, to the disappointment of many besides myself; but I hope that this is amongst the all things that will work together for good.

Hobbs Point, Eighth Month 23rd.—On the 7th sister Lydia and my three dear children left home with me for Youghal, by the way of Plymouth and Cork. They proceeded with Abraham Fisher, jun., to Youghal, and I went with my dear father-in-law to Limerick to attend the interment of his sister Anne Fisher.

I had much satisfaction in revisiting haunts very dear and interesting to me, and associating with kind relations. I have been obliged to part from them somewhat abruptly, in consequence of a summons to attend to business. I feel very thankful to my heavenly Father, who, I believe, has hitherto watched over and cared for me; and not only so, but He has also helped me to keep hold of faith in His care and power, which is no small mercy. And now that He has seen meet to continue to guard and protect and provide for me, inclining the hearts of my friends to employ me, I desire to renew my covenant with Him, to be unfeignedly His on His own terms.

12th.—On the 2nd my dear cousin Junia Price passed from time to eternity, being dismissed in her peaceful sleep.

17th.—Again have the ranks of our Church been thinned by the removal of Elizabeth Fry. Her memory is truly precious to me, for I have cause to rise up and call her blessed.

Falmouth, Eleventh Month 9th.—During the past few weeks my time has been very fully occupied, so much as to preclude my giving attention to anything except positive duties. But although thus closely occupied in railway business, I trust I have not been unmindful of the renewed daily mercies of the Most High. The ruling desire of my heart is, that I may consecrate my gain unto the Lord of the whole earth. May I be preserved so fully from the din of worldly cares as to keep my spiritual ear open and attentive to know my Father's will; and when known, I hope I may faithfully obey.

16th.—I have been very closely occupied in worldly matters, and have been often ready to query, Is it right for me to be thus engrossed? The answer occurs to my mind, "Not slothful in business; fervent in spirit; serving the Lord," and I trust that this may be my case, using and not abusing, the gifts by which in mercy I am surrounded. I hope and believe that if I ever again hear the call to leave home for religious service, that I shall be as willing as heretofore to be thus engaged in spreading a knowledge of the truth.

21st.—In my retirement this evening my heart has been lifted up with thankfulness that my railway duties, which for the present closed to-day, have been accomplished without the compromise of principle, the result of sustaining grace.

Yesterday John Scoble and Thomas Spencer held an anti-slavery meeting here. J. Scoble lodged with us, and before we went to rest, prayer was offered for the entire fulfilment of the Lord's purposes over all the earth.

Twelfth Month 28th.—One of the important matters that now occupies much of my attention is further service in the gospel, if I am not mistaken in the apprehension of duty. I now seek to enter afresh into covenant with the Lord, to commit all my future to His wise government and guidance, being His on His own terms.

First Month 4th, 1846.—During the past twenty-four hours I have partaken more fully and richly of peace than I have known for a long time, and I seem to have been feeding spiritually on Christ. Such are the wages of those who seek the Lord, according to the language of Psalm xxxii., "Thou art my hiding-place; Thou shalt preserve me from trouble; Thou shalt compass me about with songs of deliverance."

11th.—Went this afternoon with Lovell Squire on board the *Grace Darling*, to see Robert and Sarah Spence, of North Shields, who are now in the harbour waiting a fair wind for Madeira, whither they are going, on account of the health of R. Spence. We stayed one hour with them, and had a season of refreshment as from the presence of the Lord. I believe this proving dispensation will be greatly blessed to them.

Second Month 16th.—Yesterday morning in meeting I was constrained to share my crumbs with others. Sometimes I am afraid I give to others what is intended only for myself, and yet I trust it is done in good degree with a single eye to the glory of God, and with the honest desire of spreading abroad the truth. If I do not starve in the act, and become a castaway, I do not mind.

17th.—I attended the monthly meeting at Redruth, and under a sense of much disqualification ventured to tell my dear friends of my call for gospel service to Stavanger, Norway. This was approved by Friends, who liberated me accordingly.

21st.—Very precious was the sense given me this morning, whilst silently waiting on the Lord in meeting, that Jesus was indeed my High Priest, who was presenting me before the throne of His Father as one who had afresh entered into covenant of servitude. Great was my peace as in the child-like state I rejoiced in the overshadowing of Divine regard, and the language flowed through my soul, "Because he hath set his love upon Me, therefore will I deliver him," and an assurance was granted me, that the Spirit of the Lord should go with me in the service I am desirous of performing in His name.

Fourth Month 9th.—Yesterday the quarterly meeting was held here. The meetings for worship on both days were favoured seasons to me, in which my great Master was pleased to commune with me; and I believe enabled me to move in His power, declaring His will. My friends liberated me to proceed with the engagement in Norway, to which I feel bound, and my dear friend John Budge also received the consent of the meeting to accompany me.

11th.—Whilst dressing yesterday morning I was engaged in considering what is the condition needful for the Christian minister. The language, "Be it unto me according to Thy word," seemed to describe the state at which we should aim; God working in us to will and to do according to His own good pleasure. Then our acts would all be in Divine ordering, and His gracious purposes be accomplished.

20th.—My only safety seems to be to cleave very closely to my dear Redeemer, who has prayed for me that my faith fail not; and when strengthened may I seek to strengthen my brethren.

> "My God, how perfect are Thy ways!
>   But mine perverted are;
> Sin twines itself about my praise,
>   And slides into my prayer."

Fifth Month 3rd.—Since I penned the last I have spent a week on Dartmoor, very closely occupied. Whilst there I was cheered in a season of waiting and worship by the language, "Thou art my hiding-place; Thou shalt preserve me from trouble; Thou shalt compass me about with songs of deliverance."

Plymouth, 15*th*.—Was at Dartmoor yesterday, in much conflict of mind as to my course in matters of business, and whilst walking over the moors near the prison, thinking intently on the best mode of procedure, the language came before me, "Commit thy way unto the Lord," in which I readily acquiesced, and soon found peace in pursuing what appeared to be the safest course. As I sat down to my simple dinner an intimation was given me that a song of praise would be put into my mouth. Before night, on coming here, I saw some persons very satisfactorily, so as to remove the load of care that had rested on me lest I should be hindered from proceeding to Norway.

London, 19*th*.—Was enabled this day to lay before the Yearly Meeting of ministers and elders the burden that has rested on my mind relative to Stavanger, and received its concurrence to proceed. May all my movements be in accordance with the Lord's holy will.

25*th*.—Attended meeting at Stoke Newington yesterday morning, and was led to minister on the subject of worship, and of yielding obedience to the will of God in order that we may be disciples of Christ, and be saved by Him. Towards the close of the meeting, in which Lucy Maw, Anthony Wigham and others had spoken, L. Maw briefly alluded to the sense given us of the overshadowing of good. I ventured to present prayer at the throne of grace on behalf of those who have not yet relinquished the gratifications of the world; and that our sons may be as plants grown up in their youth, plants of the Lord's right hand planting, and our daughters as corner-stones polished after the similitude of a palace, whilst our garners are filled according to the Lord's holy will. It was a densely crowded meeting, especially with the young, for whom my interest feels lively.

Edward Anson Crouch and I walked to Tottenham together, and met a large company at Samuel Fox's; Benjamin and Esther Seebohm, John and Eliza Allen and daughters, Anna and Rebecca Fox, William Matravers, Daniel and Sarah Wheeler, my sisters Rebecca B. Gibbons and Rachel, and Nathaniel, and many others; two dining-rooms full. After dinner cousin John Allen spoke of the cause there was for gratitude to Him who cared for those on land and ocean. Hannah Thomas addressed those who were in gospel bonds, as well as him who had returned from service. This made way for me to express my feelings for Benjamin Seebohm. Cousin Samuel Fox knelt in prayer for us, that the crooked might be made straight, and the rough places plain. B. Seebohm then handed the language of strong encouragement to me, which I gladly receive as a token of the continued loving-kindness of the Lord. Truly the season felt to me like "a feast of fat things . . of wines on the lees well refined."

CHAPTER XVII.

NORWAY.

Sets off for Norway with John Budge and Isaac Sharp—Bible Reading on Board *Caledonian*—Hamburg—Emily Sieveking—Copenhagen—Tracts—Crossing the Sound at Midnight—Gothenburg—Meeting on Board the *Tees*, Captain George Brown—Christiansand—Stavanger—Elias E. Tasted—Dussivigan—Two Months' Meeting—Yearly Meeting—Visits to Friends—One who gave up the Trade in Strong Drink—Hund Vaag Island—Crowded Meeting at Stavanger—Stransund—Conference with Elders and Overseers—Letter from E. E. Tasted—First-Day Meeting—Leaves Stavanger—Stagland—Farewells—Meeting at Olen—Bergen—F. A. Putter—Tracts—Letter from Peter Boyesen—Christiania—Gothenburg.

CHEERED by the encouragement of their friends, Edwin O. Tregelles and John Budge, with Isaac Sharp as their companion, prepared immediately after the Yearly Meeting to set off for Norway.

Sixth Month 6th, 1846.—John Budge, Isaac Sharp and I are on board the *Caledonian* steamer on our way to Hamburg. The voyage is as calm and peaceful in all respects as any voyage could be.

7th, First Day.—We applied to Captain Gibbs to know if he would allow of our reading a portion of the Bible to the company assembled in the cabin; to this he most readily assented. I read Isaiah lv. and part of lvi., and commenced the first Epistle of John, which was finished by Isaac Sharp. After which John Budge addressed us, and I revived the words of our Lord, "I thank Thee, O Father, Lord of heaven and earth, because Thou hast hid these things from the wise and prudent, and hast revealed them unto babes." It felt to me that it was a time of favour, and very peaceful were my feelings afterwards.

9th.—Our steamer came to at Hamburg within the range of wooden piles which are driven into the bed of the river to protect the extensive range of shipping that lies within this shelter, from the masses of floating ice that must come down during the winter season. Such is the intensity of the cold here at times that this mighty river is frozen so rapidly as to admit of a person walking across it on the second day after the frost commenced.

We called this morning on Emily Sieveking, a superior woman in easy circumstances, who devotes herself to charity and good works. She is engaged every day in the education of twelve girls, for which she receives no pay. She keeps them in her school from nine to fourteen years of age, when they are dismissed, and their places filled by others of the same age. Her influence is great with the wealthy merchants, who cheerfully aid her in benevolent objects. One of these is the Kinder Hospital, an establishment where forty-eight families are lodged at a very small expense, if not gratuitously, provided they claim care from the circumstance of having a sick child, or some other affliction. I am not sure that this is not more of benevolence than wisdom. We called to see this, and also the Rauhe-House, for the reception of young offenders, or those likely to become such. We saw also the extensive public hospital, where 1,700 patients may be well accommodated.

10th.—We left Hamburg this morning, arriving at Kiel in three hours.

11th.—We reached Copenhagen after a smooth voyage of nineteen hours from Kiel. We put up at the Hotel d'Angleterre, and found it a comfortable house. After breakfast we had a precious time of spiritual refreshment together, when we felt braced to go steadily forward as way might open.

We left Copenhagen in a four-wheel barouche drawn by

a pair of good horses, driven by a very civil man. The Danes now appear to be a gentle people, and they or we must have greatly changed for them to have been able to subdue our forefathers.

The fortification of Copenhagen towards the land is very strong; we passed two or three fosses with their respective drawbridges and barriers. The road to Elsinore kept a straight course without regard to hills or valleys. About six English miles on the road we stopped for a few minutes, and walked up an avenue of trees to the king's country house, a handsome old-fashioned building, though small. A few miles further on our coachman drove us without ceremony into a barn, a large door at one end being open; and after baiting the horses for fifteen minutes without unharnessing, the door at the other end was opened, and we drove out and on, enjoying our drive through a pleasant, not to say beautiful country.

We supplied very many persons as we passed along the road, much to their surprise, with Danish tracts. We were glad to have this means of diffusing truth amongst the people. The tracts were, "The Way of Salvation through Jesus Christ," "Extracts from Thomas Chalkley's Journal," "T. Chalkley's Comments on Christ's Sermon on the Mount," and others.

The clock struck ten in two minutes after we had passed through Elsinore and had reached the quay, where we were to embark to cross the Sound. Five minutes later we should have been too late, as the gates would have been closed.

At 10.30 p.m. we were seated, luggage and all, in a capital launch. We had about two tons of ballast on board, and three well-trained sailors. Though at midnight we crossed the Sound in an open boat I felt no fear, but calm confidence, as we glided along, a gentle breeze filling our sails, so as to waft us across to Helsingborg in half an hour.

12*th*.—At eight o'clock we proceeded in a nice compact four-wheel carriage, drawn by a pair of lively ponies, which were changed every seven miles, the harness being detached from the horses, and fresh animals brought to their places, to have the rope and leather trappings put about them. I pity the poor beasts; they have no portion of harness, as in England, for keeping back in going down hill, but a simple strap passed round the neck is attached to the pole, and they must get out of the way of splinter-bar and wheels as fast as they can, and consequently the speed down the hills is beyond what some nervous persons would like. Our driver was wonderfully expert; he would just bring the point of the pole to strike the centre bar of some of the many gates across our road, and throwing them open with a bound, would pass through before they had time to close again on us; and this he did by night as well as by day.

The towns we passed through were Engelholm, Halmstad, Falkenberg, Warberg, and Kongsbacka. The latter is in ruins from one of those devastating fires so prevalent in these parts. A spark from the cigar of a drunkard caused the fire.

We travelled without fear of any kind through the lonely woods and forests by night, being earnest to reach Gothenburg as promptly as possible. During the journey I have enjoyed unusual peace, whilst the prayer often rose, "Withhold not Thou Thy tender mercies from me, O Lord!" and this has been granted largely, I might almost say to the full.

Gothenburg, 13th.—On our arrival here Isaac Sharp and I made inquiry about a vessel by which to proceed to Norway. On turning a corner of the street we very unexpectedly met with George Brown, commander of the *Tees*, of Stockton. He quickly proposed having a meeting on board his vessel on the morrow. We gave no definite reply, but when we learnt that we could not proceed on our way, the weight of this duty came, and with it the language, "O Lord, truly I am Thy servant," attended by such a sense of recognition from the Holy One as to subdue all questioning, and cause more than a resignation to do His will.

Christiansand, 19th.—On the evening before we left Gothenburg we had a deeply interesting meeting on board the *Tees*, captain, George Brown. The crews of three English vessels were present, one from Stockton, one from Hull, and the other from Manningtree. Solemn silence prevailed over all for some time, when Isaac Sharp was engaged to minister amongst us. Then F. E. Kleinschmidt spoke, after which I said a few words, to my own relief, on the nature of true worship, on the need of reconciliation, and on the gospel means essential to salvation. Thus closed a long and impressive meeting, which I trust may be blessed. Several persons had come from the city, amongst them Frederick Neilson, a deeply interesting character, a Swede, who is engaged in distributing the Scriptures, and has suffered imprisonment on account of his religious opinions. He was very earnest to possess a copy of George Fox's Memoirs. He had had a Danish copy of the small edition, prepared by Edward Backhouse, jun., given him by the master of a sloop from Stavanger, and this made him desirous of knowing more about the man and his principles. Of course we gladly supplied him.

We arrived here yesterday, having voyaged on board the steamer *Christiania* as far as Sandusand, and thence per *Prince Consort*, a smaller vessel, better adapted to thread the intricate mazes of the thousands of isles amongst which we passed. The steamers were crowded; and, as this was a coasting voyage, calling at nearly every village to exchange passengers and letter-bags, an opportunity was afforded to diffuse tracts and books amongst many persons whom we could hardly have met otherwise. One of our companions was Peter Boyesen, of Porsgrund, a member of the Storthing. He told me that the address of the Meeting for Sufferings had been useful in obtaining religious liberty, not only for our Friends of Stavanger, but for all Norway.

Stavanger, 22nd.—Through continued mercy we were

favoured to reach this place last evening (First-day), and met with a kind welcome from Endré Dahl, who with three companions came off to the side of the steamer in a boat, and conveyed us ashore, where we were met by Elias Eliason Tasted, and many other warm-hearted friends. We proceeded to Endré Dahl's house and partook of a nice tea. E. E. Tasted joined us at our evening meal, and amused us by his honest and simple remarks. After querying about John Budge and myself, he turned with thorough good temper to Isaac Sharp, and said, "Thee, the little boy?" I soon set the matter right, by making known that I was the junior of the party. E. E. Tasted often pitied the poor French prisoners marching off to the desolate Dartmoor, when he was a Danish prisoner at Plymouth. He is a choice Friend, in very poor health, the result of hardships, and finds his school duties somewhat trying. We saw his school, twenty boys and seven girls, some of whom were gladdened by cousin Charlotte Fox's kind presents.

Precious was the visitation of the Lord on my spirit, sealing the evidence of His approval in my coming to this place, and causing me to rejoice in the bountiful wages He grants to His poor unworthy servant. After tea I felt bound to render praise to the Lord for mercy granted us on the way, and to crave His blessing on our visit to this place. Oh that it may be to His glory, and to my abasement in my own eyes!

23rd.—Stavanger is the most singularly built place I have ever visited. It stands on seven hills. Warehouses are built along the margin of several creeks of this extensive fiord. The whole place indicates moderate prosperity without wealth. Very few of the houses are of a superior kind, and all of wood. Fires, however, are rare, owing in part to the care taken in prevention. Fire ladders and hooks are to be seen in many streets. A watchman sits in a tower at night, overlooking all the town, or perambulates the streets, uttering a long and somewhat harmonious cry, and bearing a staff with a large knob at the top, capable of giving an unmistakable rap at the door of a house in danger.

The chief source of income is from the herring fishery. About 200,000 barrels are sold annually. Of late years the herrings have frequented this fiord in great numbers.

We have this evening attended the week-day meeting of Friends, at which about a hundred were present, being many beyond the usual number. John Budge expressed his gratitude that a people had been raised up in this portion of the Lord's heritage to bear testimony to the spirituality of the gospel dispensation, after which I revived the language, "The Lord direct your hearts into the love of God, and into the patient waiting for Christ," alluding to the worship of the Lord in spirit, the rejoicing in Christ Jesus, and having no confidence in the flesh, the need that there is for having Christ as our Instructor, our Intercessor and Sacrifice, and the terms on which this is experienced. John Budge spoke on the subject of worship, quoting a passage of Scripture from Ecclesiastes v. 1. Isaac Sharp knelt in prayer, to the comfort of those who understood the language, and influencing the spirits of many others. I felt thankful in the belief, on leaving the meeting, that we had been helped to perform the duties of the day.

24th.—This morning we proceeded to Dussevigan in a capital boat, steered by our active friend, Knûd Kaisen. We were accompanied by several Friends, and on our arrival at the place we found a crowd of persons at Endré Dahl's new house, which he had arranged for this meeting because the usual house was too small. About a hundred persons were assembled, and sat down apparently gathered individually to a deep exercise of true worship. I went in great poverty of spirit, and in this state I sought to draw nigh unto God by His dear Son ; after which I felt commissioned with the language, "Blessed is the people that know the joyful sound : they shall walk, O Lord, in the light of Thy countenance." In the ability afresh bestowed I ventured to bring this passage of Holy Writ before the interesting company, having also to speak on the blessedness of being disciples of Christ, and the awful consequences of denying Him. Soon after I sat down John Budge rose with the words of Peter, "Ye were as sheep going astray; but are now returned unto the Shepherd and Bishop of your souls." Isaac Sharp spoke acceptably. Then I quoted the words of our Lord, "I am the Light of the world: he that followeth Me shall not walk in darkness, but shall have the light of life," and, "I am the Way, the Truth, and the Life;" "I am the Door of the sheep-fold." A man spoke a few words solidly and pleasantly in Danish, to the effect that a message had this day been handed them, and they must give heed to it.

25th.—The meeting for worship was held prior to the two months' meeting; it was attended by about 150 persons, much crowded in the house which was built by E. E. Tasted at an expense of about £100. At this meeting John Budge and I had some service, and two men spoke approving of what had been expressed; neither of these were members. It was attended by a solemnizing influence.

Fifteen men and fifteen women were present at the two months' meeting. E. E. Tasted acted as clerk, read our certificate in Danish, then their minutes, two of which had reference to applications for membership. The Friends appointed gave verbal reports in a very solid manner. A note was handed to the clerk from a man once a Moravian elder, now applying for membership amongst Friends. One of the minutes referred to an application from S. S., requesting to be acknowledged as a minister. He had been received about a year ago, and had spoken occasionally during six months, I believe, to the satisfaction of Friends. This was left for the consideration of the yearly meeting. The Queries were read over, but not answered in writing, only verbally. The Advices were also read. The book they use is one that was prepared by Stephen Grellet and William Allen in 1818.

At four o'clock the Yearly Meeting commenced. Some of the minutes of each two months' meeting were read. The subjects before the meeting were, whether Friends could allow the Lutheran schoolmaster to be quartered at their houses for the purpose of keeping the rotation schools, whether they should memorialize the king for relief in the matter, and whether S. S. should be acknowledged as a minister. In this latter case the judgment of the meeting inclined to the mode of proceeding in England so far as can be practised. The other cases were referred to a committee of five men, who met us at our quarters. We concluded to recommend Friends to be faithful in refusing to have the schoolmasters (many of whom are of objectionable character), although they may offer to omit the Catechism during the time the school would be held in the houses of Friends. Also, that it is not desirable to memorialize King Oscar at present, but rather to bear for a season, with a Christian spirit, the trial which may result. To these recommendations the meeting assented when we again met. After a solemn pause we encouraged them faithfully to endure persecution in a Christian spirit. John Budge knelt in prayer, and the concluding minute was read. Thus closed this memorable day, for the mercies of which we felt grateful.

27th.—We paid fourteen visits to-day of varied kinds, amongst a very poor people, which proved deeply interesting. One was to a worthy man who was in a good business, part of which consisted in the sale of strong drink. He became uneasy with this trade, and believed it right to give up that part, after which his customers left him, and his business declined so as to reduce him to poverty. He now labours with his hands.

28th, First Day.—Another day of favour. We went at ten o'clock to meeting, very punctually to a minute. Found the house so crowded that it was difficult to pass to our seats, and yet more came in afterwards, so that nearly 200 must have been crowded together. John Budge, after a time of silence, quoted the words, we "seek not yours but you," we "have coveted no man's silver or gold," and expressed the desire only to direct them to Christ, who died for them. "Ye are not your own. Ye are bought with a price." After which I gave expression to what had rested on my mind from the commencement, "Ho! every one that thirsteth," "If any man thirst, let him come." Again we met at half-past two, with the house crowded. At the close we gave notice of a meeting in the Lutheran schoolroom for Third-day evening.

We called on Knûd Kaisen. The visit to him and his wife was of a deeply interesting character; all seemed broken before the Lord under a sense of His goodness. They were exhorted to apply to the service of the Lord the many talents which He had committed to their trust. I believe that there are good things in store for them; and very useful will they be, if faithful, for they have vigorous minds in vigorous bodies. Thus closed a day of peace and renewed favour.

29th.—Went to Hund Vaag Island in this fiord, separated by a channel about half a mile wide from the mainland. Here we visited several Friends; some rich in faith and heirs of the kingdom, although poor as to this world's goods. Our first visit was to Thore and Anna Olsen, labouring people living in a simple cottage with three small rooms, yet able to contribute to the aid of their poorer fellow-members, and that cheerfully.

A fisherman on whom we called showed us four or five live tusk fish, about two feet long, which he had swimming about in a well five feet cube, formed at the end of his stone pier; here they are fed daily, and fattened for sale. His wife is in membership with Friends, and a very pleasing woman of striking expression, and if faithful to the convictions of duty, will, I believe, be blessed to many.

From this island we took a boat to go to an islet where

lived some attenders of Friends' meetings struggling for a subsistence in fishing and farming. Much of our time was spent at the dwelling of the Huseseböes, where three families of this name live. Ole Huseseböe is a fine, promising young man. We had a meeting in their house, which was largely attended; about a hundred persons being present. We re-crossed the narrow channel, rowed very heartily by four of the men who had been at the meeting.

30*th.*—In the evening attended an appointed meeting for worship in the schoolroom belonging to the Lutherans. It was crowded with about 500 persons of various classes. So great was the earnestness to be present that some men took a plank and placed it near a window, hoping thereby to effect an entrance.

Isaac Sharp was engaged in prayer that the words of our mouths and the meditations of our hearts might be acceptable. These were the words that had been on my mind throughout the day, and which I was helped to express with some addition after John Budge had spoken on silent worship, and the efficacy of Divine grace. The gospel was freely, and I trust with some degree of fulness, preached to a very interesting audience, and I know not that I ever experienced a deeper sense of the power of the Lord being over every heart present than for five minutes of that meeting. At the close many queried when we should have another meeting; one man came to us at our lodgings, several having spoken to us before we left the schoolroom.

The Friends had chiefly remained out of meeting so as to give place to others, and when they found that they could not enter, they withdrew to their own meeting-house and sat down there.

Seventh Month 1*st.*—We had a call from Helge Ericson Hagene. He is about twenty-nine years of age, and has travelled in many parts of the country, preaching. He supports himself in part by making chains as he walks along.

We arranged to proceed to Stransund, distant about ten miles. The weather was boisterous in the morning, gusty with heavy showers from the south. Our course was north, and as our dear kind friend Endré Dahl said it was considered " beautiful weather," we concluded to go. At four o'clock we were seated in a capital boat, manned by five nice fellows, all " Friends "; and under a close, double-reefed main sail, with plenty of ballast and good hope, we slipped across one of the arms of this grand fiord. It was a much enjoyed cruise, though part of the way the sea ran high. We landed near the mouth of a river, where it falls by a cascade of eighty feet down to the sea. We had a full mile and a half to walk to our simple lodgings by the seaside, near the parish church. Before we settled for the night we read Psalm xci., having our crew assembled with us, after which Isaac Sharp addressed them on the first verse, which had been presented to his mind before I commenced reading.

2nd.—We had a beautiful cruise of nearly two miles on a freshwater lake; then we ascended a steep mountain path. But our hour of toil was well repaid by an interesting meeting with a hundred persons in a barn belonging to Thore Thorge; some of these had come ten miles.

It was nearly four o'clock when we began our descent to the lake, and we reached Stavanger by eight, having a fair wind again, though our rudder broke when we were about half-way over the fiord, and we were obliged to steer with an oar. We are thankful for the mercies of this day, and I have cause to bless His name who gave me during that visit to Stransund repeated evidence of continued lovingkindness.

4th.—This morning we had a call from Lars Larsen, of Bergen, a student in the Missionary Institute here. He was desirous of information on the subject of baptism. We gave him a copy of " Barclay's Apology," and had much interesting conversation with him.

We had a conference with E. Erasmusen, Endré Dahl, and Ole Huseseböe on the subject of elders; afterwards with them and E. E. Tasted on overseers.

After a visit to E. E. Tasted he placed in my hands a letter, from which the following is extracted:—

"DEAR FRIENDS, E. O. TREGELLES, JOHN BUDGE AND ISAAC SHARP,—

"Your dear and tender visit to us in the love of the gospel I believe has been a singular and living encouragement to our Friends in this place, as well as to many without. It will be a powerful remembrance to each of us as long as we live. Although it may be to your sensibility as bread cast upon the waters, I believe it will at the right time be found and gathered of many. Oh that we may be willing to suffer in our time of humiliation, that the true humbling may be known in us, so that the name of the Lord may be honoured in and by us. . . .

"Our love is more to you than we can express in words, and also to our dear and beloved Friends in England. They have made themselves worthy of our love in many respects for above thirty years. May this lead us to gratitude before God.

"Your sincere friend,
"ELIAS E. TASTED."

Such testimony is cheering under a sense of much weakness.

Stavanger, 5th, First Day.—In the afternoon meeting ability was given to express what I believed was the message for the large company then assembled, on the subject of the voice of the Lord being heard in the silence of all flesh. Under a solemn sense of renewed mercy the meeting separated, when we requested the members and attenders still to sit with us. I found it right to quote the words, "I have learned, in whatsoever state I am, therewith to be content," enjoining close dependence on the Lord in heights and in depths, reminding them that fishermen were called of the Lord to uphold His truth, and telling them that I believed that some present, fishermen and labourers, would be employed in His service, but that all such must remember to be subject one to another in love. John Budge took leave of them affectionately, and Isaac Sharp knelt in prayer and thanksgiving. Standing near the door we shook hands with them, some sobbing aloud, and nearly all much broken in spirit. Several Friends and attenders called this evening once more to greet us. And thus closed a deeply interesting two weeks at Stavanger.

Stagland, 6th.—When we left Stavanger this morning many Friends were assembled on the quay to bid us farewell, among them dear E. E. Tasted.

Our boat is a capital one, belonging to Endré Dahl, nicely fitted up with an awning. E. Dahl is with us, and Ole Huseseböe, Thore Olsen, Jacob Jacobsen and Andrias Jacobsen. We had light winds for about sixteen miles across the fiord, when the wind shifted and blew strongly from the S.S.W., wafting us rapidly with a heavy sea to the branch of the fiord on which this place stands. For one hour the storm seemed alarming, and Ole, our able helmsman, kept one eye to windward; but we reached in safety, and landed in the beautiful grounds of Ander Anderson, of Stodvig. After staying three hours at Stodvig we proceeded to the house of Soren Ericson, who kindly met us at the waterside, four miles from his home at Stagland, with three nice ponies, on which we rode over exceedingly rough ground, not to say road, for in some parts there was none. Our ponies passed safely over the sloping surfaces of granite and slate rocks.

Ander Anderson (the son-in-law of Soren Ericson) is the possessor of many hundred acres of beautiful land—wooded, fertile, and rocky, besides a fine luxuriant isle of forty or fifty acres.

Soren Ericson lives on his own extensive farm. He has suffered much for refusing to pay baptismal fees, for which nine of his cows were taken at once, leaving only one calf; but with all this he has prospered. I felt much peace on entering his very simple dwelling, where we sat in a nice neat garret, ten feet square, which they have fitted up for a meeting, which is regularly kept up in this house. We had a precious time there. A blessing manifestly rests on the prayers and labours of these parents on behalf of themselves and their children.

We afterwards attended a meeting we had appointed in a new house built on the farm. It was crowded with about seventy persons. The district is very thinly peopled.

Olen, 10th.—Soon after breakfast on the 7th we embarked in our boat, taking leave of our friends from Stavanger, eight of whom had followed us in a small boat. These, and seven or eight others, shook hands with us as we stood on the rock, and again we bid each other farewell with a few words, commending them to live in the unity of the Spirit and in the bond of peace.

The meeting here was attended by about seventy persons —working people and a few soldiers. It was a good meeting. Isaac Sharp, although he had been very poorly, was strengthened to speak with authority amongst us on the need of cleansing and reconciliation.

Hugleöe, 12th.—We left Olen yesterday morning. Our men had hard work to row across the fiord, and we concluded to stop at this island. This morning we met together for worship with our crew, and the members of the household. John Budge spoke on the subject of silent worship, and suggested that they might meet together in such a way to their profit.

After the meeting Endré Dahl and I were rowed across the channel, three miles wide, to call on Chatrina Hendricksen, a serious woman who had believed it right to forsake the Lutheran mode of worship. We paid her an interesting visit, when she was reminded of the language, "It is good for me to draw near to God: I have put my trust in the Lord God, that I may declare all Thy works," and that the blessing was promised to those who hunger and thirst after righteousness. Her husband and she cheerfully set out to give notice of a meeting to be held here this afternoon.

13*th*.—The meeting was well attended. I felt more openness to speak of spiritual things than for some time past, to my comfort and relief. Chatrina Hendricksen came to our room after the meeting, when we encouraged her to increased dedication of heart to the Lord's service, that so she may help others. We presented her with a large Danish Bible.

Bergen, 14*th*.—We had a very calm cruise amongst the innumerable islands of the several fiords we crossed on our way to Burgholm, where we lodged last night in quarters that appeared to us delightful after the rough and dirty accommodation we have had in some places since we left Stavanger. Whilst passing calmly along yesterday, I thought much on the prospect of a peaceful return, and of the last retreat when the everlasting doors will be opened, I trust, for me "to go no more out." Delightful as rest appears to me, I remember my covenant of unconditional allegiance,—

> "My life, if Thou preserv'st my life,
> Thy sacrifice shall be,"

and sweet peace followed even the desire after true resignation to the unfoldings of the Divine will concerning me. Oh that I may be enabled to obtain and maintain a patient, quiet spirit, leaving my every care in the hands of Him who has done all things well.

17*th*.—Meeting in the evening in Harmony Hall, which was crowded with about 700 persons. We were favoured with grateful hearts for the mercies shown. Before we left the room many came to shake hands with us. Amongst these was a venerable old man, who handed us a slip of paper, on which was written in Danish as follows: " In the year 1822, in July, about twenty-four years since, was in my house that dear Thomas Shillitoe of Hitchin, Hertfordshire; at that time I had joy in being instructed how a true Christian should follow after.—F. A. PUTTER." At tea we had the company of four or five who had been at the meeting, all of whom seemed more or less inclined to embrace the principles of our Society. After tea they were encouraged to faithfulness to apprehended duty in small things as well as great, and told that if they followed their Guide closely, with a single eye to the glory of God, they would be enabled clearly to discover the path cast up for them to walk in. A hope was expressed that they may meet together for Divine worship, in simple faith on Christ as their great Minister.

18*th*.—A closely occupied day. Very many persons called for tracts, which were distributed freely in small parcels. Not less than a hundred persons came, so as quite to prevent regular occupation. We had a very interesting call from F. A. Putter, who spoke with much interest of Thomas Shillitoe, whose last words to him were, " If we do not meet again on earth, I believe we shall in heaven." F. A. P. queried of me respecting the baptism of the Holy Ghost as the spiritual baptism that was alone efficacious; he queried whether our Lord had not commissioned His disciples to baptize. I turned to the latter part of Luke, where the commission is recorded, and reminded him that the baptism of John and of Christ were different; that the disciples of John did well to practise his baptism, but that the disciples of Christ must regard the baptism of Christ, the baptism of the Holy Ghost and of fire, as the dispensation they were instructed to set forth; and also to teach all men to observe all things that Christ hath commanded, which things were too much neglected by professors of the Christian name.

Peter Boyesen, of Porsgrund, called, with whom I had interesting conversation, remarking that no man felt true peace unless he were reconciled to God; and when this was the case, he had peace with himself and all mankind; and that such persons were far more easy to govern and control, than those who have no fear of God before their eyes; to all which he honestly assented. When he left us I followed him out of the room and said I believed he had now seen enough of Friends to convince him that Government had nothing to fear as the result of having granted them religious liberty. To this he fervently replied, "I am glad we have met; I love you all; may God bless you."

He called again soon, and spent a short time with Isaac Sharp, who was poorly upstairs. With him he left the following letter:—

"*Bergen, July* 18*th*, 1846.

"To my Honoured Friends of England,—

"I hope you will not misjudge my addressing you these, the view of which is to testify the great satisfaction it has afforded me to meet with persons of your enlightened understanding and amiable character, the first time I became acquainted with any of your confession. In matter we agree, in forms we may differ, but with God there is no difference. He will gather around Him all His children, who earnestly though faultfully seek Him, when the trial is finished.

"Each sect has its peculiar preference, so yours has the predominating doctrine of peace. I shall ever grave on my soul the Divine truths you uttered at your departure, "Let us have peace with God, and we will have peace with all the world." . . .

"Before concluding I remark, what I observed to your sick friend, that in my neighbourhood most of the poor families want a New Testament, and that their being provided with one certainly would be an act of blessed benevolence, and I take the liberty to remind him of his kind promise to exercise his best interest in behalf of this matter with the British Bible Society.

"And now I take a tender leave of you all, and pray God to guide and guard you wherever you are, assuring you that the words we have exchanged, and the moments we have spent together, will never be extinguished from my remembrance.

"Yours with regard and friendship,
"PETER BOYESEN, OF PORSGRUND."

Christiania, 24th.—We left Bergen on the 19th, in the *Prins Carl* steamer, and reached Christiania yesterday. A meeting was held in the Freemasons' Hall, and well attended by about 300 persons, chiefly of the middle and upper classes. This being the first occasion of a public announcement of a meeting for worship differing from the established form, since the law was passed that granted religious liberty, it felt to me and to all of us a very serious prospect. As the conflict is severe, so is the rejoicing the greater, when the song of praise is put into the mouth.

We dined with Hans Ericksen, at whose house we met with many persons before unknown to us. Amongst these was the Norwegian Chancellor of the Exchequer, who came to the meeting with his son, and afterwards took tea with us, when we had very interesting conversation on serious subjects.

Gothenburg, 26th.—We had a good meeting together at the Hotel here, in which prayer was offered for the land we had left, for the king, the rulers and the people, especially for those who by us had heard the sound of the gospel. The acknowledgment was raised, "We are nothing, Christ is all," "To us belongs blushing and confusion of face, but to the Lord God and the Lamb everlasting praise!"

CHAPTER XVIII.

FALMOUTH.

Return from Norway—Croydon—Prince Town—Meeting on Dartmoor—Anna Price—Distress in Ireland—Dr. Philip—Death of Joseph John Gurney—John Hodgkin—Cornwall Railway—Marriage of his Brother Nathaniel—Samuel Capper and Joseph Eaton hold Tent Meetings at Falmouth—Accident at Railway Works—Depression in Trade—Influenza Epidemic—Meeting with Sailors—Visits Prison.

CROYDON, *Seventh Month 31st*, 1846.—We were favoured to reach London safely from Hamburg this morning. In the evening I came to Croydon, and have much enjoyed a few hours with my dear friend Peter Bedford, whose welcome and counsel and encouragement were cheering.

Prince Town, Dartmoor, Eighth Month 5th.—I arrived here yesterday. The coach nearly upset at Teignmouth, but amongst some less conspicuous mercies, and many unseen, is the sense given me of my unworthiness without undue discouragement. This is in answer to my earnest prayer that the Lord would be pleased to give me humble, correct views of myself, ascribing all the praise to His power and grace. The language freshly arises, "Return unto thy rest, O my soul; for the Lord hath dealt bountifully with thee."

Falmouth, Ninth Month 15th.—The monthly meeting at Redruth liberated me to have some meetings at Princetown.

Tenth Month 18th.—We are now located in a new dwelling, Grove Place, where I crave that we may be sustained and cheered by the good presence of the Lord, who thus gives us richly all things to enjoy. May I, when yielding to calls of duty, and in so doing making sacrifices, remember that it is of His own that I thus give.

About two weeks since a meeting was held in the hospital of the war prison on Dartmoor, when more than 200 persons were assembled. The nature of true worship, the omnipresence of God, the consequence of sin and means of restoration were dwelt on.

Neath, 25th.—To-day I attended meeting here to my comfort, and again felt commissioned to take of the things of God to hand unto others. This evening has been spent in the company of my dear Aunt Price, who is in a very feeble state. Her quotations from the sayings of Catherine Philips were very interesting: "Resignation is heaven begun on earth;" also "I always feel careful not to interfere with the work which the Lord commences in the hearts of any of His children." On parting, my dear aunt said, "Farewell; may the Lord bless and preserve thee in heights and in depths, that thou mayest be kept in His fear." (This proved to be the last interview.)

Falmouth, Eleventh Month 15th.—In meeting I encouraged my friends to present their gold, frankincense and myrrh, and not to hide what they may regard as the one talent.

None know but those who have proved it, what the poor minister feels when speaking under an apprehension of duty. He may fail in delivering the whole counsel of God, or, under creaturely weakness, may substitute words or matter of his own, which is not of the Lord. What a mercy that for him, as for others, the Advocate is ever at hand.

25th.—William and Ann Tweedy, and Elizabeth and Caroline Tweedy drank tea with us very pleasantly. Our attention was much occupied by the grievous distress in Ireland in consequence of the crop of potatoes having failed. Subscriptions are being raised to supply soup and meal to the sufferers.

Prince Town, Twelfth Month 4th.—I feel thankful for the

employment here, aiding in the support of my dear family, and above all thankful for the spiritual support granted me during a season of deep mental conflict. Surely it is not by any power of my own that the peace is obtained which is granted and enjoyed. I may well say, " Being kept by the power of God;" for it is wonderful to me how the promises of the gospel are brought to my remembrance, and applied for my comfort and for the increase of my faith, so that I can trust and not be afraid, and can commit all my cares and desires to the disposal of the Almighty One.

9*th.*—Went to Teignmouth, and saw Dr. Philip of Trinidad, and his daughters at the house of Captain Reed. We had pleasant converse together.

16*th.*—Cheered last evening in reading Luke iii., by observing that after our Lord was baptized He prayed, and then the heavens were opened. Surely there is instruction for us in this, that when we experience a baptizing influence of the Lord's Spirit, then is the time to pray, and prayer will open to us all needful heavenly treasure.

Falmouth, First Month 7*th,* 1847.—I was informed this morning of the decease of Joseph John Gurney, after a very short illness. Thus has it pleased the Almighty to deprive us of one who was commissioned by Him to declare His gospel. Oh, may He be pleased to raise up others who may be faithful standard-bearers in the cause.

20*th.*—It is my firm present conviction that the principles held by our Society are the most perfect of any with which I am acquainted, and the mode of worship most in accordance with the Divine will. It appears to me highly important that the ministry should never be mistaken for worship. They are conditions separate and distinct. That ministry only can be true which leads the mind of the audience off from the creature to the Creator.

12*th.*—Completed this evening the perusal of the Old Testament of "Kitto's Pictorial Bible," which I commenced ten years ago at Exeter. The perusal of these volumes has been slow, because of my frequent absence from home. The notes please me much.

14th.—I was cheered by hearing that dear John Hodgkin is likely to visit Ireland with a certificate. The joy I feel at this is to me a strong evidence of my love to him and my dear friends in Ireland.

28th.—Went after meeting with sister Elizabeth to the workhouse. She read, "Sudden Death, sudden Glory," a narrative of T. Rogers, by Mary S. Lloyd. I read Psalm xxxi., and afterwards encouraged some to return to the Lord.

Third Month 7th.—An interesting letter from Endré Dahl was forwarded to me by Isaac Sharp, who enclosed a notice of a meeting with the railway men at New Shildon, at six this evening, just at the hour I received this letter. My first impulse was to retire to my room, and there pour out my soul in prayer for my dear friend, in the language, "Grant unto Thy servant that with all boldness he may preach Thy word, and that many signs and wonders may be done by the name of Thy holy child Jesus." And oh, may he and I be kept in our right places, walking daily in the path cast up for us.

24th.—The contract for the Cornwall Railway was taken by S. M. Peto yesterday. Cousin Maria Fox has had a meeting this evening with the inhabitants of the neighbourhood of our meeting-house, chiefly poor people. William Tanner, Eliza Allen and I took part in the service. I believe it will be blessed to some.

Sixth Month 9th.—I returned this evening from Prince Town, having experienced there in no common degree the Lord's protecting mercy, for whilst standing under the eave of the hospital, a bar of iron slipped down the roof. The noise attracted my attention, and I moved away just in time to escape being struck by the bar, which fell on the ground where I had been standing.

10th.—This evening I have received tidings of the decease

of my dear sister, Susanna Fisher, at Cork, whither she had gone on a visit prior to her proposed marriage next month. About four weeks ago she became ill with fever, which has proved fatal. Thus are we again taught the uncertainty of all earthly things.

25th.—Yesterday it was my privilege to attend the happy marriage of my brother Nathaniel, to Frances Allen, at Liskeard. On waking in the morning I was impressed and quieted by the language, "Be still, and know that I am God." At the conclusion of breakfast, when John Allen read in the Bible, my spirit was quickened into a state of prayer, under a sense of which I petitioned that the Lord would give strength unto His people, and bless them with peace. Soon after we were in meeting, Eliza Allen prayed that the Lord would be pleased to own our assembly by His spiritual presence. When dear Nathaniel and Fanny had nicely made their solemn declaration, I petitioned on their behalf the Lord who had recorded their covenant vow. Samuel Capper followed, alluding to the ability to perform these rites without human intervention.

Seventh Month 6th.—Samuel Capper and Joseph Eaton have had two meetings under their tent, which was pitched in the Bowling Green, Falmouth. They were well attended, and owned of the Lord, who enabled me to convey a message to the many hundreds assembled. Another meeting was held last evening at Penryn.

11th.—Cousin Samuel Fox came to us last Sixth-day. He cheers us by his presence, and animates me by his example. He went with us to the workhouse after meeting, and commented feelingly on Romans xii.: "Abhor that which is evil; cleave to that which is good."

27th.—Honora and Julia Philip, daughters of Dr. Philip of Naparima, in Trinidad, have been spending a few days with us. Dr. Philip was my kind attendant in fever, when I was ill there.

Ninth Month 8th.—Through condescending mercy we

have been favoured with renewed heavenly visitation at our quarterly meeting at St. Austell. Philippa Williams broke the silence: "Whatsoever thy hand findeth to do, do it with thy might." John Budge followed, on silent worship. Then I gave utterance to what I felt required of me: "Create in me a clean heart, O God, and renew a right spirit within me." Maria Fox, Ann Tweedy, and Eliza Allen also spoke.

I bless the Lord, who hath given me counsel, and inclined my heart to follow His will. May I seek increasingly to obey the leadings of His providence. I trust that I shall be made more than conqueror through Him who hath loved me, and laid down His life for me.

Some years previous to this, Edwin O. Tregelles, whilst engaged at Restronguet, supervising the repairs of the machinery of a steamer, felt his interest called out for the people amongst whom his daily occupation led him. With the concurrence of his friends he held some meetings in that neighbourhood. Again we find him applying for their approval of his holding meetings in the district between Truro and Falmouth, where much of his time had been spent while surveying for the Cornwall railway.

22nd.—I returned the minute granted me for the meetings on Dartmoor, and then mentioned my prospect as it regards the district between Falmouth and Truro, which was united in by John Budge as a coadjutor, and cordially approved by the monthly meeting, for which I feel thankful. I heard yesterday with a grateful heart that some important steps towards liberating the peasantry of the Danish West Indian Islands have recently been taken.

Tenth Month 7th.—I went with William P. Dymond to

see the proceedings of the railway at Buck's Head, and whilst we were arranging to descend one of the shafts, a man who was moving the plank of a platform fell through. Deeply painful were my feelings as I watched his body falling down the deep pit, at the bottom of which he lay for a few seconds like a lifeless corpse. We hastened to him after his companions had descended to his aid, and very thankful I was to hear him speak, after a deep groan of distress, and in a few minutes he was able to walk about.

9*th.*—I was agreeably surprised by the arrival of James Nibbs Brown, of George Town, Grenada.

10*th.*—Thomas Pumphrey was engaged instructively in ministry this morning. The transgressions of Adam and of David, with their convictions for sin, and the means of return for the sinner by Jesus, the new and living way, formed the subject of a touching address.

In the afternoon meeting I felt constrained to pray for all present that we might really bow at the name of Jesus, who was set for the fall and rising again of many in Israel. Sweet peace has been my portion this evening, the result of a well-grounded hope that all my future is safe under the guidance of our good Shepherd if I be but faithful.

16*th.*—Many are the trials that are now dispensed among the princely merchants of England. Some who have been brought up luxuriously are reduced very low. I believe that these things are in mercy permitted, if not appointed, to wean us from the glory of the world, which is as sure to pass away as ever it had any existence. It is difficult to trace the cause of this distress. Some regard it as the result of the loss of the potato crop during the past few years, but I cannot see it so. I believe the cause must be deeper and more extensive.

I saw the swallows assembling to-day at Trelerswell, prior to their departure.

30*th.*—Attended a meeting at Frogpool, which was large. Hannah C. Backhouse, Philippa Williams and John Budge were there, and they and I were employed as ambassadors for Christ.

Eleventh Month 8th.—I went to Roscrow this morning, and accompanied H. C. Backhouse and Jane Barclay Fox to call on Sir Charles Lemon, with whom the former had a religious opportunity, much to her comfort, and, I trust, to the benefit of the visited.

Twelfth Month 19th.—I heard to-day of the death of George Crosfield, of influenza, which is now carrying off many, like the fatal visitation of the cholera in a new form. More than 2,600 persons died of various complaints in London during one week recently, being 1,600 more than died in the corresponding week of last year.

25th.—For some time past my attention has been turned to the condition of sailors. Notice was given at every vessel in the port yesterday for a meeting in the Sailors' Room this afternoon. A few came; perhaps twelve besides the Friends. It was closely exercising to my faith, yet in the retrospect as much peace prevails as has been the case after meetings attended by as many hundreds. Reconciliation with God by Jesus Christ was the purport of my communication; that yielding obedience to the convictions of God's Holy Spirit is essential to the disciple, who will then experience deliverance from the thraldom of Satan, and partake of the blessing derived by the sacrifice of our Lord Jesus on Calvary.

26th, First Day.—At meeting ability was given me to rise and revive the petition, " Let the words of my mouth, and the meditation of my heart, be acceptable in Thy sight, O Lord, my Strength and my Redeemer." I went on to speak on the privilege those enjoy who have Christ as their High Priest, being fed with the bread and the water of life; such are satisfied with favour and full with the blessing of the Lord.

I called with Thomas Christy Wakefield, jun., at the town prison, and saw two men who are confined for smuggling. We sought to direct them to apply by faith in Christ to the

Lord Jehovah, not depending on their fellow men for anything they can do for them. Whilst the Bible was being read to them, the Romish priest came to see some Italians who are there for smuggling. He was very noisy, and interrupted us very unsuitably, of which we took no notice.

CHAPTER XIX.

FALMOUTH.

Meeting with Sailors at Falmouth — Call on Captain B. — French Revolution — Public Meeting in Manor Rooms, Stoke Newington — Funeral of Mary Howitt's Mother — Yearly Meeting — J. and M. Yeardley's proposed Service in Germany, Russia, and Austria — Disturbances in Paris — J. Lavin — Visits to Vessels in Falmouth Harbour — Neath, J. Rees. C. A. Price — Banbury — Ipswich — Croydon School, Peter Bedford — South Wales Railway — Holds Meeting with Navvies at Neath Abbey — Letter from A. R. Tregelles — Funeral of Elizabeth Fox of Bank House, Falmouth — Conversation with Captain B. — Banbury — Adderbury — Removes to Frenchay — Caroline Fry — Sibford and Sidcot Schools — Barnstaple Meeting — James Veale — Interview with a Swiss — Eliza Allen's Address at Liskeard Meeting — Removes to Derwent Hill, Shotley Bridge — Tin Works — Marriage to Elizabeth Richardson.

FALMOUTH, *First Month* 1*st*, 1848.—I finished to-day the perusal of William Allen's very interesting Life and Correspondence. The same grace which led him safely will be granted to me in the measure which I need. May I be found daily occupying with the talent committed to my trust.

16*th*.—This day four years the spirit of my dear Jenepher entered on that sweet rest which is the privilege of those who sleep in Jesus. By unmerited grace and mercy have I been upheld in my path, which has been far more pleasant than I had dared to anticipate. May I be encouraged to go on step by step, in faith that the staff of my Shepherd will be granted for my support, though His rod may correct.

I was this evening at a meeting for sailors, which was well attended. Rising with the words, "This is life eternal, that they might know Thee the only true God, and Jesus Christ, whom Thou hast sent," ability was given to unfold the consequences of the believing and the unbelieving state.

20th.—I attended a meeting in our meeting-house for the promotion of permanent and universal peace. James B. Cox was in the chair. Edmund Fry, as a deputation from the London Peace Society, ably stated the case, and Barclay Fox and I followed. It was agreed to petition the House of Commons, and to address the people of Brest, France.

Second Month 4th.—Under an apprehension of duty I believed it right to call on Captain B. to-day, and pay him a visit of sympathy, in consequence of the decease of his son Edward, at Agra. I felt supported under a clear sense of duty until just as I entered the gate, but I ventured onwards. When the servant returned, saying I could see him, I felt that way was made for me. Very soon he joined me in the drawing-room, and we entered into pleasant converse. Touching on the subject of his loss, a full opportunity was afforded me for setting before him all that was laid upon me. Whilst I enlarged upon the blessedness of serving the Lord, he leaned forward towards me, eager to gather all that was expressed, and very heartily did he thank me for the visit. It was truly a season of bowedness before the Lord; we wept together as we praised God for the mercy of sending His Son to be the ransom for those who obey and follow Him.

26th.—Tidings have reached us to-day that Louis Philippe has abdicated the throne of France. A strange, and marvellous, and unexpected fall from uncommon popularity and power. May the Father of mercies overrule these events for good. A Reform banquet was to have been held. The Government forbade it, and took measures to prevent the meeting. The people became incensed, and a bloody revolution has been the fearful result. Oh that all men were taught and trained to regard human life as sacred! Then would all wars come to an end.

Third Month 30th.—I received to-day a very interesting letter from Isaac Sharp, in which he hands me sweet encouragement to do the Lord's work, as though he had a sense of a requirement of which I do not feel conscious. But it is remarkable that before I opened the letter I was led to consider the wondrous mercy in my recovery from fever in the West Indies, and the language passed through my mind, "O Lord, truly I am Thy servant; I am Thy servant, and the son of Thine handmaid; Thou hast loosed my bonds," with desires after continued and increased dedication.

Fourth Month 5th.—For some days past I have felt drawn to visit the passengers about to leave these shores in the *Roslyn Castle* as emigrants to New York. Arrangements were made for a meeting this afternoon. It was difficult to obtain any quiet settlement, but at length we gathered round the capstan, and were refreshed with the "Bread which came down from heaven." Words flowed freely and fully, commencing with, "If God be for us, who can be against us?"

9th.—I have felt much impressed with the state of insubordination manifested by nearly all classes in Europe.

11th.—Information has reached us to-day that the apprehended disturbance in London yesterday was averted by the crowd of malcontents having been advised by their leader to disperse.

16th.—Read with interest in the Memoir of Elizabeth J. Fry of her first appearance in the ministry. The words she used were the same as those I first uttered in meeting at Swansea in 1827. It is strange to think that more than twenty years since I was enabled thus to avow my allegiance, and yet, instead of feeling a proficient in the Lord's service, I am but as an infant still.

23rd.—To-day I went with Thomas Christy Wakefield, jun., to the prison, where we saw a youth under punishment for a week. He was humble and contrite, in a hopeful condition. He had been a Sabbath school teacher until lately, when he gave way to temptation.

Stoke Newington, Fifth Month 8th.—At meeting yesterday morning I prayed that we might so receive the grace of God into our hearts as to become true disciples of our Redeemer, and partake of the benefits designed by His sacrifice. After this I was enabled to address the large company, and to urge on the attention of the young the importance of being reconciled to God by Jesus Christ.

11th.—I was at the funeral of Ann Botham, the mother of Mary Howitt, who, with her husband, attended the interment. At the grave I felt the spirit of supplication come over me. To this I gave way, craving that in this solemn hour, when we could acknowledge that Jehovah was God over all, blessed for ever, we might so receive His Son by His Spirit in our hearts, as to be engaged to count all things but loss, so that we may win Christ, and be found in Him. I have since learned what I did not remember at the time, that William and Mary Howitt are in the practice of attending the Unitarian Chapel.

16th.—Intelligence has reached us to-day that the mob had attacked and dispersed the Chamber of Deputies assembled in Paris. What the result may be is known only to Him who sitteth on the circle of the heavens, and sees the end from the beginning.

23rd.—At the Yearly Meeting of ministers and elders, John and Martha Yeardley laid their prospect before us of religious service in South Russia, Prussia, Bohemia, Austria, Germany, Switzerland, France and Belgium.

Just before the close of the Yearly Meeting I attended a large and deeply interesting meeting at Devonshire House for young persons, invited at the request of Cousin Sylvanus Fox, who addressed us very powerfully, commencing with the words, "I am not ashamed of my hope."

Falmouth, Sixth Month 11th.—I spent half an hour at Bristol with dear Daniel Wheeler, jun., who was very ill, and to whom I sought to hand some consolation; but frail and impotent is man for this work. May the Lord in the riches of His mercy be pleased to carry on His own work.

27th.—Tidings have reached us to-day from Paris, that a dreadful carnage took place there a few days ago. Another revolution, in which it is said 1,500 of the National Guard and some thousands besides fell in the contest. Thus grievous are the effects of war. The carnage and confusion were increased by a contest between two bodies of the regular troops.

30th.—Last evening's post brought me a letter, announcing the peaceful release of dear Daniel Wheeler on the 24th, at Clevedon. This rapid sinking is far more speedy than I had expected. I feel thankful that I went to see him on my way home from London.

Seventh Month 11th.—I called to see John Lavin at Perranwell, who is ill in consumption. He told me that if the Lord had sent an angel round to his neighbours to tell them what he wanted, he could not have been better supplied. "I must tell you," said he, "that I feel great peace. For many months past the Lord has granted me an evidence of His pardoning mercy. I used to touch my hat to you when I met you on the road, because I believed you were a traveller Zionward, and I believe I shall meet you among the 'hundred and forty and four thousand.' I have sought to serve the Lord for thirty-five years, but I have nothing to trust to but the atonement of Christ." I repeated to him, "They have a strong consolation who have fled for refuge to lay hold upon the hope set before us, which hope we have as an anchor of the soul, both sure and steadfast, and which entereth into that within the veil: whither the forerunner is for us entered, even Jesus"; in which he very heartily united. His amens were emphatic when prayer and praise were offered on his behalf.

30th.—Yesterday evening I went off with a supply of German books and tracts for the vessels now detained in our harbour in consequence of the war between Prussia and Denmark. I heard lately that the *Roger Sherman*, an emigrant vessel which sailed from this port, has reached America safely, but that a quarrel had occurred amongst the passengers, and that the steward's wife had jumped overboard and was drowned. Deep is now my regret that I yielded to discouragement, and refrained from visiting this vessel before they left.

Eighth Month 4th.—I received this morning a very interesting letter from George Richardson, with tidings from Asbjorn Kloster, from Stavanger, respecting some young men professing the peaceable principles of Friends, who are suffering imprisonment, with fear of further punishment, because they refuse to bear arms. I have written to Josiah Forster on the subject, hoping that the Meeting for Sufferings will move in the case.

I called on John Lavin to-day. He said, "I have been travelling sixty years through this world, and nothing can I bring as an acceptable offering from anything I have done to secure my acceptance with Jehovah, but I can depend on the one offering of the Lamb, the blood of Jesus. I feel sure I shall be safe in His keeping. Yes, so sure as your name is Mr. Tregelles, I shall be saved by Him!" "Yes," I said; "if thou art faithful unto death, thou wilt have the crown of life." "Oh!" said he, "I have had a dreadful struggle this morning; the enemy is still busy, but he can't prevail. He tried to persuade me that I shouldn't get home, and I had a fearful struggle, ready to give all up, but the grace of God prevailed. No passage of Scripture could afford me comfort but this, 'I am He that liveth, and was dead; and, behold, I am alive for evermore, and have the keys of hell and of death.' 'I shut and no man can open, and I open and no man can shut!' After this, for a quarter of an hour such sweet passages of Scripture flowed through my mind."

Ninth Month 24th.—Sweet and precious has been the sense

given me this evening that my soul is in the keeping of Jehovah, and that if I live and move in His holy fear, I may be persuaded that neither height nor depth, things present nor to come, will ever be able to separate me from the love of God which is in Christ Jesus.

25th.—I went this morning to the prison, and had some interesting conversation with a man who had delivered himself up as a deserter from the 80th Regiment in the north of Ireland. He told me he had had a joyful night, and was feeling full of the blessing of the Lord. I asked him if I could do anything for him. He replied, "I thank you, sir. I have need of nothing. I left my brother's house at Kentbury, a few weeks ago, believing myself called to preach repentance, and this I have done in several towns. I had a little money when I left Kentbury, and when that was expended, I lay down one day by the road side, engaged in prayer for temporal aid, when two ladies came along in a little carriage. They stopped and asked me if I was the person who had been preaching in the street lately. I said 'Yes,' and they gave me 2s., as they said, in the name of my Master."

I asked him how he expected to be supported. He replied, his life was one of faith, although he expected to have a pension of nine-pence a day from the East India Company. On taking my leave of him he said, "I thank you for your kindness; it will turn to your account at the last day. Be watchful; for your adversary the devil goeth about as a roaring lion, seeking whom he may devour, whom resist steadfast in the faith."

Neath, Tenth Month 1st.—I took tea with Jonathan Rees. We sat in his drawing-room, where I had taken tea on the evening after I first spoke as a minister. The language then addressed to me by Elizabeth J. Rees came before me to my comfort, "In quietness and in confidence shall be thy strength;" and the prayer arose that I might know this to be my case during the coming week in an especial manner, acknowledging the Lord in all my ways, and trusting that He will direct my paths.

In the evening meeting cousin C. A. Price rose with the language, "'He that goeth forth and weepeth, bearing precious seed, shall doubtless come again with rejoicing, bringing his sheaves with him'; for whom the good Shepherd putteth forth, not only does He guide, but He goeth before them." Great comfort flowed in my heart at this message.

Banbury, 15*th*.—I came to Joseph A. Gillett's yesterday. At meeting to-day, after a season of close watching, I had to rise with the words, "Without faith it is impossible to please God."

Falmouth, Eleventh Month 2*nd*.—Leaving Banbury on the 16th of last month, I went to Ipswich, where I visited dear Nathaniel and Fanny pleasantly. On the 19th I returned to London, and spent First-day at Peter Bedford's, at Croydon. The day was one of much favour. In the evening I visited the school. After John Sharp had read the history of Elijah, I spoke of the beginning and the course of wisdom, being centred in the fear of the Lord, leading step by step to true faith in the Son and Sent of the Father, who, though the Shepherd, condescended to lay down His life for the sheep.

The next day Peter Bedford and I called at Newgate, to see R. W., who is sentenced to seven years' transportation for forging a cheque for £10. He had been a "Friend." We had an interesting time with him. Peter Bedford gave him good counsel, and presented him with a Testament.

I met John Yeardley at Gracechurch Street meeting, on his return from Belgium.

The construction of the South Wales Railway brought to Neath a large concourse of navvies, for whose moral and religious benefit E. O. Tregelles' niece, Anna Rebecca Tregelles, had for some time been labouring cheerfully and successfully. Her letters descriptive of these labours were published in a little book entitled " The Ways of the Line."

Being at Neath on business for my sister, Rebecca B. Gibbins, I went with my niece, Anna Rebecca, on the line, to invite the railway men to a meeting on the following day. It was well attended. I rejoiced in having such a gospel to hand to such men. Rarely have I felt more enlargement of heart than on this occasion. After the meeting, letters were handed me from Falmouth, conveying tidings of the serious illness of dear Aunt Fox. I left Neath for London, and after arranging sister Gibbins' matters very satisfactorily, I started for Falmouth with the expectation of being too late to see my precious aunt alive. This was sadly true, as I found when I reached Truro. The loss to me is no common one.

From Anna Rebecca Tregelles.

Dearest Uncle E. O. T.,—

Much as thy mind must be occupied with the exceeding, the unrealizable loss that our circle has sustained, I do not like to refrain from offering thee the comfort of knowing how thy mission was received by my men friends. In the first place, more than eighty were present, which is a greater number than any of them ever remember to have seen in one place of worship before. They say they understood every word, . . . it was all exactly the same as they read in the Bible.

My first business on Second-day morning was to go and see the poor fellow who has broken his leg. He told me that his brother and the lodgers had come 'after the chapel' and spent the evening before with him, and they told him all they could that had been said, and they each read in the Testament in turn, and two or three tracts; and they said they would for the future manage their horses so on Sunday to be able to go to some place; and then they all said they had never spent such a comfortable evening before. And these were the 'tip-drivers,' the very pariahs of the line. 'And see,' the poor fellow said, 'I can bend my knee a little now, so I think when the gentleman comes again I'll be able to get upon crutches to hear him.' They petition for a meeting on some working-day evening, because then they won't mind their clothes; so many have no change except of shirt. One said, 'I'm sure I'll be able to rise a pair of trousers, and then Harry will lend me a clean slop, so I *will* go next time.' Thou oughtest to sing the Te Deum, dear Uncle E., for often have I heard some contract described as a 'terrible place for the bother of them parson chaps,' who were doubtless well-meaning men, but who, instead of seeking for and working on the spark of good latent in the hearts of their ignorant audience, have attacked the evil with a sweeping condemnation, repulsive of sympathy, and almost of hope. Now it is all 'more, more.' . . .

With dearest love, I am, in great haste, thy ever affectionate   A. R. T.

Falmouth, Eleventh Month 5th.—A large number of friends and relations assembled at the graveyard on the occasion of the funeral of my aunt, Elizabeth Fox, where the voice of cousin Sylvanus Fox was heard in supplication. After the coffin was lowered I too felt constrained to bend the knee, and pour forth my soul in prayer. The meeting, though densely crowded, was solemn, and this impression conveyed in the silence seemed confirmed by a sweet address from cousin Eliza Allen. Philippa Williams, William Ball, John Budge, and Sylvanus Fox also addressed the meeting.

When walking home we observed before us a frail old man, who seemed lingering to speak with us, and soon found it was Captain B., who began, "Oh, Mr. Tregelles, I am so glad to see you. I intended to have called on you long since to thank you for your visit. I have been at the meeting and in the grave-yard. Dear Mrs. Fox! Well, we had a blessed time of it." "How art thou getting on, Captain B.?" I said. "Oh, not as well as I ought to, but I hope I shall." I reminded him of some words that had been much with me in meeting. "Come now, and let us reason together, saith the Lord: though your sins be as scarlet, they shall be as white as snow: though they be red like crimson, they shall be as wool. If ye be willing and obedient, ye shall eat the good of the land: but if ye refuse and rebel, ye shall be devoured with the sword: for the mouth of the Lord hath spoken it." He replied, "Oh, that's what parson Hitchins used to say." Thus did he give an interesting proof that these words, which fell more than thirty years ago upon a heart as careless and reckless as any of his buoyant class, did not fall in vain.

Banbury, 13th.—I arrived here on the 9th, and have been closely and pleasantly occupied in my business engagements. May the Lord in His mercy direct my way, and make it prosperous. The last message that I had from my dear Aunt Fox was as follows: "She trusts that thy sole dependence will be on that Power which can preserve in heights and in depths."

19th.—I walked to Adderbury meeting to-day with James Cadbury, and had much comfort in that pleasant season for worship, when I believe many were refreshed by Divine consolations. Joshua Lamb said a few words: "Be still, and know that I am God." I encouraged mothers to bring their children to their Redeemer.

Falmouth, Twelfth Month 9th.—I spent a week at Neath, where I had two meetings with the railway men to my comfort, and I hope to their profit.

I enjoyed the perusal of John Newton's letters to J. Coffin. He says: "I have learnt from what I have written myself not to judge of others by what they write; saying or writing and doing are two things."

24th.—I read yesterday the dying words of a Christian in America. "You will not, I am sure, lie down upon your bed and weep when I am gone. You will not mourn for me, when God has been so good to me. And when you visit the spot where I lie, do not choose a sad and mournful time. Do not go in the shade of the evening, or in the night. These are not times to visit the grave of a Christian; but go in the morning, in the bright sunshine, and when birds are singing."

First Month 7th, 1849.—I wrote to Francis Tuckett yesterday, agreeing to take the house at Frenchay. This step has cost me much thoughtfulness and prayer for right direction. It matters not by what means we are brought to the mercy seat, provided we really have access there. I trust this step may have the Divine approval; the language of my soul has been, "Cause me to hear Thy loving kindness in the morning, for in Thee do I trust: cause me to know the way wherein I should walk; for I lift up my soul unto Thee." Earnest have been my petitions: "If Thy presence go not with me, carry us not up hence."

This morning I was cheered by the text for the day in "Daily Food," "In all thy ways acknowledge Him, and He shall direct thy paths."

> "Each future scene to Thee I leave,
> Sufficient 'tis to know
> Thou canst from ev'ry evil save,
> And every good bestow."

13th.—I have read this evening with much comfort the remarks of Caroline Fry on Matthew xxi. 21, "I am persuaded there is no limit to what we might have, to what we might be enabled to do, of things holy, good and desirable in themselves, if we had so much confidence in God as would enable us to expect them. But we have not! We do not ask till driven to extremity. Then we ask with very little expectation of receiving, and go away with no more calmness of mind upon the matter than we came. We do not see how our mountains can be removed; we have calculated their weight and size; we perceive all the difficulty; and God's word, His unlimited, unconditional, uncalculating promise goes with us for nothing.

"There are not wanting evidences of what God has done in answer to prayer, but no man perhaps has ever yet proved the extent of what He would do if our faith were adequate to our demand. Let us think of this; for our Father delights in a trusting, asking, expectant spirit. He likes that we set no limit to His power or His love. Let those particularly who have some mountain of spiritual or temporal evil in their way make trial of the truth and meaning of the text. It was Jesus Himself who spoke it."

15*th*.—This has been a day of deep feeling in recurring to the events of this day five years, the last day that my precious Jenepher spent on earth, and on which she wrote me her last letter, which I have again perused. Whilst I deeply feel my bereavement, I can trust in the continued mercy and providence of Him who has hitherto upheld and guided marvellously, and who, I trust, will teach me strict obedience to His holy will, and give me faith in His power and love.

Neath, Third Month 9*th*.—I attended the monthly meeting yesterday. It was that day twelve years that my friends recorded me as a minister. The recollection of the many mercies since received stimulates me to increased diligence in the service of my Master, whom to know and to serve is life eternal.

Fourth Month 2*nd*.—On the 31st of last month I was at Banbury, and in the evening went over to Sibford, where, on the following day, I attended their meeting. And in the afternoon had a religious interview with the children of the school. After going to Falmouth and attending the monthly and quarterly meetings there, I had again a meeting in the evening of First-day, the 15th, at Sibford, which was well attended, and proved a season of renewed favour. The house was packed closely, and the power of the Lord seemed to reign for a time over the hearts of all present.

I left Banbury on the 16th and went to Sidcot School, to see the children there in accordance with the certificate granted me, and ability was given to call the attention of these children, as at Sibford, to regard the fear of the Lord as the beginning of wisdom.

Frenchay, Fifth Month 20th.—This morning I was led to consider the importance to the Christian of having firm reliance, firm faith on the promises of God. Not merely to remember them, but to act as though we believed in their truth.

Barnstaple, Ninth Month 9th.—I left Frenchay yesterday, and had a very pleasant voyage along the north coast of Devon.

At meeting this morning, after close searching of heart, I felt ability to speak to the few assembled, on the importance of vital experimental Christianity, and on the only means by which it can be experienced, quoting the words of our Saviour, "I am the way, the truth, and the life; no man cometh unto the Father but by Me."

A letter to-day mentions the decease of Elizabeth Dudley and William Cash by cholera.

Liskeard, 23rd.—Much peace was my portion yesterday, when at work through the streets of this town, as the thought passed through my mind, "I will walk, O Lord, in the light of Thy countenance," which seems to be the secret and key of all true happiness.

Barnstaple, 30th.—I called this evening with James Veale to see a person named Aebli, a native of Switzerland, who resided some time in Stuttgard, where he was a teacher at a college for educating young men for the ministry. Here his mind became alive to the inconsistency of Church and State arrangements, which he mentioned to the heads of the college, who dismissed him after a fruitless attempt to alter his opinions. In Germany a person who renounces Church preferment renounces his means of living; and Aebli was obliged to seek an asylum elsewhere. Like Abraham he went forth, scarce knowing whither he went, but he believed it right, though he knew not a word of the language, to visit England, where he has found abundance of peace in fellowship with some whose eyes have been spiritually anointed. And marvellously was he led, proving the truth of that promise, "I will make darkness light before them, and crooked things straight." He has much enjoyed the perusal of Elizabeth Fry's Memoirs; and with great simplicity said this evening, "I think if I am privileged to enter the pearl gate where Mrs. Fry is, I shall thank her for having the pleasure of reading such memoirs; I shall say to her how much they were blessed to my soul!"

Liskeard, Eleventh Month 8th.—I arrived just in time for a meeting which was one of no small favour. Access was granted to the Father of spirits. Towards the close Eliza Allen rose with these words: "The apostle, in alluding to the sacred writings, said they 'were written for our learning, that we through patience and comfort of the Scriptures might have hope,' and may we not be instructed by the language of the Psalmist, 'I waited patiently for the Lord; and He inclined unto me and heard my cry. He brought me up also out of an horrible pit, out of the miry clay, and set my feet upon a rock, and established my goings: and He hath put a new song in my mouth, even praise unto our God'? And yet we find the same Psalmist saying, 'Hath God forgotten to be gracious? hath He in anger shut up His tender mercies?' Oh no, those who trust in the Lord shall want no good thing. With holy confidence they can say, 'The Lord is my Shepherd: I shall not want. Thou preparest a table before me in the presence of mine enemies. Thou anointest my head with oil; my cup runneth over. Surely goodness and mercy shall follow me all the days of my life: and I will dwell in the house of the Lord for ever.'" To all which I could reverently say, Amen. And cheered and refreshed, I felt that we had had angels' food, that God had sent us bread from heaven to eat.

Frenchay, Twelfth Month 9th.—I attended monthly meeting at Olveston last Third-day, when our certificates of removal were read. To-day John Gayner and Philip D. Tuckett have visited me thereon. May the blessing of the Lord, in the truest, fullest sense, rest upon my tarriance here, and on my efforts to provide things honest in the sight of all men.

Barnstaple, First Month 18th, 1850.—On Fourth-day at meeting I sat down alone with James Veale, and felt a sense of heavenly love immediately as we took our seats. J. Veale spoke on the words, "Truly our fellowship is with the Father, and with His Son Jesus Christ." After which I alluded to the prophecy respecting our Lord, "His name shall be called Wonderful, Counsellor, The Mighty God, The Everlasting Father, The Prince of Peace. Of the increase of His government and peace there shall be no end."

Second Month 3rd.—I enjoyed a call on Philip and Anna Tuckett this evening, when they conversed on a subject of deep interest to me.

This subject was the approaching marriage between Edwin O. Tregelles and Elizabeth Richardson, daughter of the late Thomas and Elizabeth Richardson, of Sunderland.

Shotley Bridge, Fifth Month 13th.—I went to Darlington to attend the interment of my dear friend Hannah Chapman Backhouse.

Sixth Month 26th.—I took possession of our new home Derwent Hill, which through mercy has been provided for me.

Tenth Month 1st.—In the quarterly meeting at Darlington Jonathan Priestman knelt in prayer, and almost immediately I felt required to give expression to the message laid on me. Rachel Priestman followed, and John Dodshon, also John Pease in prayer. The watchword of the day seems to be, "The work of righteousness shall be peace; and the effect of righteousness quietness and assurance for ever."

Derwent Hill, Twelfth Month 13th.—Since I last penned any memorandum one of the most important events of my life has occurred. On the 4th of this month I entered, by the good providence of God, into marriage covenant with my precious Elizabeth.

14th.—I went to Newcastle to meet my dear children, who arrived from Frenchay. The evening was wet and stormy, and rejoiced we were to have them safe in their new home.

15th.—We had a favoured meeting this morning, and spent the evening at Snows Green. On our return to our pleasant home I read to the family, the servants being present, Matthew xi. and Psalm iv., also the hymn, "How sweet the name of Jesus sounds."

Snows Green was the home from which Elizabeth Richardson had married, and where resided her brother and sister, Thomas and Sarah Richardson.

CHAPTER XX.

SHOTLEY BRIDGE.

Derwent Hill—Darlington Quarterly Meeting—London—Scotland on Business—Plants Trees on Wedding Anniversary—Newcastle Quarterly Meeting—Burning of *Amazon* Steamer—Visit from Isaac Sharp—E. O. and Elizabeth Tregelles ride to Winnow's Hill on Horseback—Yearly Meeting—Eli and Sybil Jones—Visits Scotland with Minute—Aberdeen—Lydia A. Barclay—Glasgow—Meetings at Hayden Bridge—Business Thoughts—Address from Jonathan Priestman—John Hodgkin's Address—Endré and Maria Dahl at Derwent Hill—Eli and Sybil Jones—Cholera at Newcastle—Business Changes—Goes with his Wife to Bristol—Mary Ann Schimmelpennick—Falmouth—Illness of his Sister, Anna P. Fox—Camborne—John Dunstan—Visit to his Nephew, S. P. Tregelles, at Plymouth—Family Visits from Ann Eliza Dale and Eliza Barclay—Death of William Forster—Meetings in Cumberland—Harvest Rejoicings—Loss of Mahlon Day—Death of Joseph T. Price—Newcastle Quarterly Meeting—Prospect of Peace with Russia—Death of Emperor Nicolas—Visits the Hebrides with Certificate—Meetings in North Uist, Mull, Skye, and Oban—Capture of Sebastopol—Death of Stephen Grellet—Visits Families with J. Priestman—Colliery Strike—Meeting at Darlington with Young People—Oswald Baynes—George Richardson—Narrative of Preservation from Shipwreck of Dr. R. H. Thomas—Susan Howland and Lydia Congden—Financial Panic—Failure of Bank—Visit of Sarah Squiro and Sarah Tatham.

DERWENT HILL, SHOTLEY BRIDGE, *First Month 1st*, 1851.—Another year has opened upon me under circumstances far different from what I have known. May I daily number my many blessings, and whilst I rejoice in them, receive all as unmerited gifts from Him who sendeth rain on the just and on the unjust. Let me never forget the wormwood and the gall, of which I have had to partake largely, and look unto the rock from whence I have been hewn, to the hole of the pit whence I was digged.

Third Month 16th.—Much tried of late by many things, but chiefly by the evils of my own heart. I was instructed yesterday in a low season by a sense that my "Father is at the helm," and I have felt as though in the midst of the heavy storm through which I may be passing, or may have to pass, that I am safe in being near Him, where I crave I may ever be.

Fourth Month 13th.—We attended the quarterly meeting at Darlington, where we met the Committee of the Yearly Meeting, Josiah Forster, Robert Jowitt, Samuel Capper, Barnard Dickenson, William Miller and Joseph Thorp.

Sixth Month 18th.—Sometimes a fear attends me lest I have not been careful in bringing my dear children before the mercy seat in prayer. I crave forgiveness for this, and that I may daily beg of my God, through Jesus Christ, that they may be sanctified wholly, and I with them given up, body, soul, and spirit, to His will.

Ninth Month, 29th.—This day two weeks dear Elizabeth and I went to London for ten days, kindly welcomed by Nathaniel and Fanny at Tottenham. Before I went I felt bound to crave the blessing of the Lord, to whose care I sought to commit ourselves and our home circle. A sense of His preserving care was manifest when I escaped being run over just as I was leaving Charles Gilpin's shop—perhaps the narrowest escape of that kind that I have ever known. We arrived home in a storm in which six vessels went ashore near Redcar.

Eleventh Month 14th.—I have visited Glasgow and Edinburgh on business. I had a proving time of temptation at Glasgow, being tried for an hour with some of the miseries of unbelief, which I was ready to regard as designed to enable me to enter into sympathy with some of the many thousands of that place, who I fear are strangers to peace. Through mercy the temptation passed away, and I was enabled in answer to prayer to say, " Lord, I believe ; help Thou mine unbelief."

Twelfth Month 7th.—During the past few days Paris has been in a disturbed state, causing expectation of another revolution. I crave that the horrors of war, and its desolating consequences, may be averted by Him who has the hearts of all men in His hand. The fact of my sisters Lydia and Rachel being at Nice, to companionise our invalid cousin B. Middleton Fox, makes me think more of any disturbance in France.

12th.—This day twelvemonth we took possession of our pleasant home on our return from our Scotch tour. A year of much joy and unutterable mercy it has been. I long that my dedication may keep pace with my privileges, which are very great. We have commenced this day by planting about a thousand trees in our grounds. Though thus pleasantly occupied, we have not been unmindful of the future period when we must leave this sweet spot, and whenever it may be, I trust it will be to exchange temporal and chequered joys for those that are unalloyed and eternal.

First Month 2nd, 1852.—" In the day when I cried, Thou answeredst me, and strengthenedst me with strength in my soul." It is marvellous, and the Lord's doing, that He has wrought deliverance for me from the depression which I endured yesterday and for some time past. To the Lord be ascribed the glory now and for ever.

5th.—I went to Newcastle to an interesting meeting of ministers and elders. John Pease spoke on the words, " Ye have not chosen Me, but I have chosen you ; " encouraging to a right occupation of our gifts.

7th.—Remaining at Newcastle yesterday I attended our quarterly meeting, when John Dodshon spoke on the words, "The cup which My Father hath given Me, shall I not drink it ? "

After dining at Benwell I drove home, and went in early

this morning to attend the monthly meeting, feeling very low and quiet, as though no public service was required of me. But ere we were long seated I felt the call to speak to the unconverted to arise, and after aunt Katherine Backhouse, John Chipchase, Jonathan Priestman and others had spoken, I quoted the words, "Who maketh thee to differ from another? and what hast thou that thou didst not receive?" and enlarged on the need of being not "almost a Christian," but "a soldier of the Lamb's army," that we may know the blessedness of hearing the language, "I have blotted out as a thick cloud thy transgressions, and as a cloud thy sins."

8th.—I saw in *The Times* to-day an account of the burning of the *Amazon* West Indian steamer, 120 miles off Scilly. The passengers and crew were mostly lost, and Captain Symmons with them. It was with him that we crossed from the Bermudas when we had such a fearful gale, and I well remember the care of the captain, going all through the vessel every day with a lantern in the dark places, to see that all was safe.

Second Month 9th.—On Seventh-day Isaac Sharp came to us rather unexpectedly, and paid us a truly acceptable visit; so that I feel my responsibilities are increased with my privileges. He addressed us yesterday morning on the words, "Come unto Me, all ye that labour and are heavy laden." And in the afternoon meeting he was strikingly engaged in prayer for all classes of our company. Thankful did I feel in having him under our roof.

This day has been one of comfort. I crave that in this season of peace my soul may grow in grace.

12th.—The trials of my heart, and the tendency to be encumbered with the cares of this life, are known only to the great Searcher of hearts. Ardently do I long for deliverance from undue care about things that perish with the using.

15th.—Yesterday I received a letter from John Dymond, informing me of the decease of Judith Templeman, and asking me to prepare a sketch of her history, which I shall try to accomplish from the narrative of her life which she related to me.

In accordance with the above request E. O. Tregelles wrote the tract, "Judith Templeman, or Village Piety."

24*th*.—Last week I was at Hull, Sheffield, Manchester and Leeds on business, passing very near the scene of the calamity at Holmfirth, where many lives were lost by the bursting of a reservoir, and property destroyed equal to £600,000.

27*th*.—During the past few weeks I have felt more freed from mundane cares than for a long time past; the result, I trust, of having really committed my cares to the keeping of the Shepherd of Israel, with whom I felt sweet union this evening, when the language arose,—

> "Cover my defenceless head
> With the shadow of Thy wing"—

and then I felt that I was safe in temporals as well as spirituals. Again would I pray, "Give me neither poverty nor riches, feed me with food convenient for me:" give me a competency without harassing care, so that I may feel liberty to aid my fellows and to seek their good, and also without that lavish excess that would lift up my heart to forgetfulness of the great Giver.

Fourth Month 11*th*.—We went to Durham to visit John Church Backhouse and Eliza Barclay. It was a much enjoyed season of refreshment, as from the presence of the Lord. We attended meeting at Durham, and passed on to the quarterly meeting at Darlington. James Backhouse of York was there, and spoke on faith, briefly but excellently: John Pease on seeking for heavenly riches. We returned home next day, since which I have been very closely occupied in mundane affairs.

7th.—After meeting this morning William Barkas informed me that a funeral was to take place at an old burying-ground belonging to Friends at Winnows Hill. In the afternoon dear Elizabeth and I rode there on horseback. After a very smart ride of nine miles, having missed our way, we arrived just in time to see the coffin conveyed to the ground. We had a very solemn season. I felt engaged to address the company on the importance of making and keeping covenant with the Lord, seeing that assuredly the dust must return to the dust, and the spirit to God who gave it. We rode home just in time for our evening meeting at six, which felt like a season of favour.

Stamford Hill, Fifth Month 30th.—We came here two weeks since. At Tottenham we found our sisters Elizabeth, Lydia and Rachel, and heard many interesting particulars of their recent experience in attending the sick bed of dear Middleton Fox.

We had the privilege of meeting with Eli and Sybil Jones of New England, whose ministry was very acceptable. Their exercise seemed to be strong on behalf of the ministers, that they might be faithful to their Master, especially during the Yearly Meeting.

In the meeting of ministers and elders John Yeardley was liberated to visit Pyrmont, Minden and Norway; and Robert Lindsay for South Africa, Australia, Van Dieman's Land and New Zealand.

Among the many subjects of interest before the Yearly Meeting the most prominent were, the importance of attending our week-day meetings; the state of Guernsey and Jersey meetings, for which a committee was appointed; a change in the size and boundaries of our quarterly meetings; schools for young children before they are eligible for our public schools, proposed by William Forster; the report of the Yearly Meeting's committee for visiting the counties. The meeting was visited on several occasions by women Friends; amongst them Isabel Casson, Sybil Jones and Sophia

Alexander, whose communications were, I trust, blessed to us. Eli Jones, Jacob Green, and John Pease visited the women's meeting.

Derwent Hill, Sixth Month 9th.—At the monthly meeting at North Shields I laid before the meeting a prospect of visiting friends in Scotland, which was feelingly united with, and a minute granted, liberating me for the service.

Edinburgh, Eighth Month 13th.—I was very kindly welcomed by John Wigham, who took me to his house. The next morning we set out for Aberdeen, where I was kindly received by Lydia A. Barclay, at whose simple and comfortable dwelling I lodged during the General Meeting. I was feeling very low, and this continued until after the meeting next morning, when help seemed laid on One that is mighty, and peace was the reward of simple obedience.

After the evening meeting on First-day I had an interview with James Forbes, of Stonehaven, who had come to Aberdeen to attend these meetings. I felt much interested for him as we stood on Union Bridge and looked towards the setting sun, and spoke of eternal things.

I had a pleasant time at Glasgow, two favoured meetings, and saw many Friends in their own homes.

Derwent Hill, Ninth Month 18th.—On the 12th we went to Haydon Bridge and had a very comforting meeting in the Wesleyan Chapel, well attended by earnest souls. At this place we met unexpectedly with John and Mary Mason, of Penrith, who heard of the meeting, and came from Gilsland that day.

Tenth Month 10th.—"The fear of the Lord is the beginning of wisdom;" so it is His fear that first operates in our hearts to produce the first semblance of anything heavenly. Lord, carry on this work in our hearts, and fulfil the petition raised in my soul in my quiet waiting before Thee this morning. Oh, visit me with Thy salvation! Visit me; visit my family.

22nd.—On my return home I found a letter waiting for

me from James Forbes, of Stonehaven, to whom I wrote last Seventh-day. He craves my prayers. I need more earnestness for myself, but my mind was turned towards him whilst listening this evening to reading the thirty-second Psalm.

I was interested in hearing of the persecution in Tuscany of persons who are drawn off from Romanism by reading the Holy Scriptures. Surely we should value our privileges more than we do.

28*th*.—Whilst enjoying a season of retirement at the Works this morning before I commenced business, I was cheered by a sense that the influence of the Lord's Spirit was felt, and powerfully too, though the soul framed no language in which to express its desires. This is the condition that seems to constitute true worship.

31*st*.—Yesterday I wrote to my West Indian friends Dr. Philip and John Daughtry. Sometimes I am ready to fear I give up too much time to correspondence, but when I take into account how little time I have ever devoted to what the world calls "pleasure," I may feel at liberty to take some recreation in this sort of social intercourse with distant friends to whom I am largely indebted.

We have had to-day two blessed meetings, in which I was favoured to feel the spirit of true worship, attended with the sweet belief that many present were partaking in silence of the same spiritual Bread; in this I did and will rejoice.

Twelfth Month 16*th*.—In our monthly meeting at Newcastle yesterday Jonathan Priestman addressed us at some length on the ornament of a meek and quiet spirit. And now in my sweet home I feel that the language of thanksgiving is due for the blessing of a quiet spirit, which through favour is granted me. May I remember the watchword, "What time I am afraid, I will trust in Thee."

31*st*.—The last day of an eventful year. I will now bless the Lord who hath given me counsel, and held up my goings in His paths that my steps slipped not. All the praise may well be ascribed to His directing and preserving grace. To Him who has been the guide of my youth, and my stay in riper years, I desire to commend my soul, body, and estate for the future. Lord, if Thou wilt, Thou canst make me clean and holy. Let me feel Thy unction, and hear Thy voice, "I will; be thou clean."

Derwent Hill, First Month 4th, 1853.—In the quarterly meeting I was appointed as one of a committee to visit Darlington monthly meeting, which I durst not refuse, though outwardly it may be very difficult to go.

Tottenham, 9th.—At meeting here John Hodgkin arose with the words, "What is truth?" and expressed his belief that indifference had more effect in keeping many at a distance from God than unbelief. In the afternoon meeting John Hodgkin said the further he advanced in life the greater was his sympathy with those who suffered from wandering thoughts.

Derwent Hill, Second Month 13th.—This Sabbath has been a season of close searching of heart and some conflict. I was helped this evening to cast my care on the Lord. This was promoted by listening to the account of the Madiai, as detailed in "The Prisoners of Hope" by S. Prideaux Tregelles. Their sufferings and constancy may well stimulate us to fight the good fight of faith and to lay hold on eternal life.

23rd.—I went to Newcastle on business, and to attend the monthly meeting. It was a season of profit under a sense of my poverty and nothingness, much like midwinter, corresponding with the outward season, which is now very cold and stormy, the snow lying thick on the ground. Whilst I sat in meeting I was cheered by the belief that this wintry season as to my spiritual condition would be blessed to me.

24th.—Endré and Maria Dahl, of Stavanger, arrived here this evening, also Louis Philip, son of my kind friend Dr. Philip, of Trinidad. Thus the north and south seem united in one small locality.

Fourth Month 11*th.*—Last week we attended the Darlington quarterly meeting, where we found Eli and Sybil Jones. The former spoke of the blocks of marble that were used in the temple, that they did not form, fashion, and polish themselves; and that the cedars of Lebanon were felled in the forest, and despoiled of their foliage and beauty before they were fitted for the place designed, and when hewed, planed, and polished, they were occupying a far more important position than when they were flourishing on the sides of Lebanon.

15*th.*—Yesterday evening a meeting was held at Newcastle for the youth of the monthly meeting at the request of Eli Jones, and I went to it. Eli Jones alluded to the importance of the little word "now," causing immediate attention to the Divine call, instead of delaying the surrender of the heart to the Lord; that the enemy of our soul could not induce us to give up our title to everlasting blessedness by any open, undisguised suggestion, but he adopts the system of delay, so as to beguile us from the path of self-denial and rob us of our peace.

Fifth Month 26*th.*—I have been much cheered by the words, "Thou hast beset me behind and before, and laid Thine hand upon me," which feels as much like Divine care, guidance, and protection as can possibly be experienced, prevented from going too fast, or lagging too much behind, similar to being encompassed, or the angel of the Lord encamping round about them that fear Him, and delivering them.

Eighth Month 21*st.*—More of a Sabbath than for some time past. I rose early and walked in our fruit garden, reading Gurney's hymns; felt sweet union with God by Jesus Christ, and though much assailed by irksome business thoughts, yet did I seek to go to Christ as one of the heavy laden, and found the promised rest.

Ninth Month 15*th.*—We were somewhat appalled in passing through Newcastle to-day to see the evidence of mortality in the funereal symptoms. Very awful is the visitation of cholera in that town.

Tenth Month 7th.—This awful scourge has swept Newcastle and Gateshead fearfully. Since I penned the above more than 1,700 persons have fallen victims. We have had little intercourse with these towns during this period, and trade was very much paralysed.

23rd.—I awoke this morning with a sense of serious trial awaiting me, but on seeking after best help my mind was stayed by the words, "Fear not, I am with thee; be not dismayed, I am thy God." The perusal by dearest Elizabeth, before we went to meeting, of the little book "Earthly Care a Heavenly Discipline" helped to bring sweet acquiescence with the will of my heavenly Father.

The trial which awaited E. O. Tregelles was his withdrawal from the business with which he had been connected since his marriage; on being liberated from this, he and his wife went to visit their friends in the South of England.

Frenchay, Twelfth Month 4th.—Yesterday we made several calls in Bristol; no one gave us a more hearty greeting than Mary Anne Schimmelpennick. On reaching her house the servant told us that her mistress was just going out for a drive. I gave her my card, and sent a message to say that one of her old friends would be glad to see her if for a minute only. We were shown into the dining-room, where we found portraits of Joseph John Gurney, Elizabeth Fry, William Allen, and the King of Prussia, also Penn's treaty with the Indians, with the inscription, "Blessed are the peacemakers."

We were soon asked upstairs, and found Mary Anne Schimmelpennick in her ample sitting-room. Conversation turned on the sanitary condition of the country, and she appealed to me,—

"Don't you think that great good would be done if some of your Friends would go about giving lectures on the laws affecting health? The working class seems so to need information on this point."

We replied that much was done, and that the longevity of our race was now much greater than formerly.

"But do you think," she said, "that the nervous energy is prolonged in proportion to the length of days?"

She was reminded of what Sir James McIntosh said of William Allen, that a man's life was not to be measured by length of days, but by what he had achieved.

She asked when ——'s memoir was likely to be published, and whether it was likely to be well done, that it should be the work of one mind, and not spoiled by being patched and dissected. She said, "I think he was an excellent Christian, but it always appeared to me that his sermons were the result of much reflection, and that he gave an impress of his feelings."

My reply was, "Probably he felt at liberty to bring out of his treasury things new and old."

"But don't you think William Forster was different? His communications seemed to rise spontaneously at the time. I consider —— rendered great service to the Society of Friends, and the world at large, by exalting the Saviour in His various offices; but I hope there may be always a wholesome variety among your ministers, on the principle of antagonistic muscles to keep the body straight."

Falmouth, 11th.—We called to see our dear sister Anna P. Fox, whose calm aspect bespoke a peace which the world cannot give. She said she was trying to discover if there was any condemnation, but she could not discover a single spot in her prospect that was not covered with mercy.

Penzance, 15th.—We left Truro by train; the first time I have tried this West Cornwall railway. It was very interesting to travel in this way over a country with which I was so familiar, some years ago, when engaged in surveying it.

16th.—We went to Camborne to lodge at John Budge's, and called on John Dunstan. He spoke to us very sweetly, saying, "I have for forty years known something of the Lord's goodness, and I find my all in Him. If ever I feel any straitness it is in myself, not in Him. My eyesight is gone, but I am not like one in darkness; I have a light within, which is far better than any outward light. I have also the holy Scriptures without, with the Holy Spirit to guide me within. I do mean from the very depths of my heart to do the Lord's will; if this be the case I shall find myself on a rock that can never fail. Oh, the Lord is full of mercy and goodness and love.

25th.—A blessed day! Soon after the meeting was gathered dear Cousin Maria Fox spoke on the words, "God so loved the world that He gave His only begotten Son, that whosoever believeth in Him should not perish, but have everlasting life." We called on my sister, Anna P. Fox. She had enjoyed listening to her daughter Rebecca reading in the eleventh and forty-third chapters of Isaiah, of the full and free salvation there offered. I said, "Thou art rejoicing in it on behalf of thyself and family?" "I do desire for my family that they may avail themselves of it," she replied; "but as regards myself I cannot speak much of rejoicing. I feel it no small favour to be free from condemnation, and believe the time of rejoicing will come."

First Month 2nd, 1854.—I took leave this evening of my dear sister Anna. It was a deeply proving time to me, parting without any prospect of meeting her again. She said, "Blessings on thee! I have valued your visits much, and felt cheered when I heard you were coming. Thou hast sought to comfort me by pointing to the one great Offering.

Kingsbridge, 8th.—We left Falmouth for Truro-Vean, experiencing there much kindness, as in former days. We had a hearty welcome from our cousins Allen at Liskeard. At Plymouth we spent a very pleasant evening, at S. Prideaux Tregelles', where we enjoyed looking at some of his many MSS. of the Greek and Hebrew Scriptures.

Derwent Hill, 23rd.—Through the lovingkindness of the Lord we were favoured to reach home and find our dear children well.

27*th.*—Ann Eliza Dale and Eliza Barclay, who are paying visits to the families in this meeting, sat with us. The former quoted the words, "Why art thou cast down, O my soul?" She expressed her sympathy with us in our varied exercises, and desired our encouragement. She exhorted our dear children to a steadfast walking in the fear of the Lord.

Second Month 24*th.*—William Forster has sunk under his illness in America, falling in the field of service after having diligently followed in the footsteps of His Master for more than forty years. "Whose faith follow, considering the end of his conversation, Jesus Christ, the same yesterday, to-day and for ever."

27*th.*—Our dear sister Anna passed from time to eternity on the 24th, the anniversary of her marriage day thirty-five years ago.

Fourth Month 13*th.*—I mentioned to my friends at the North Shields monthly meeting that I believed myself required to visit the meetings in the eastern part of Cumberland and the General Meeting at Edinburgh. This was united in very fully, and a minute prepared. And now I am oppressed with a sense of total unfitness and unworthiness. But as I wrote the word "oppressed" I was cheered by remembering the text, "They looked unto Him and were lightened, and their faces were not ashamed."

Allendale, 23*rd.*—I much enjoyed my ride to this place, feeling very peaceful. I had a kind reception from William Wilson, who had had no tidings of my prospect of visiting the meetings in this neighbourhood. We called on Isaac Hall in the evening, and went to see the gravestone of Thomas W. Williamson, who suffered ten years' imprisonment for non-payment of tithes.

The public meeting at Alston was very small. I doubt proper notice having been given. However, I believe there was one there for whom my message was designed, and I bless the Lord that I was not turned aside.

Derwent Hill, Seventh Month 19th.—Detained at home from meeting by a pain in my neck and shoulder, which causes me to feel how dependent I am on the Most High for health and vigour. Whilst seeking to profit by this hour of retirement and worship, I have desired that others might realize the truth of the language, "They that wait upon the Lord shall renew their strength."

Eighth Month 1st.—"Oh that men would praise the Lord for His goodness, and for His wonderful works to the children of men!" This was the text on which I commented ten years ago at Spanish Town, in Philippo's chapel. I could wish that this anniversary might have been marked by some special effort on behalf of the enslaved millions of America. At times I feel encouraged to believe that the day of their deliverance draws nigh. Lord, hasten the day when Thy fear may so possess the hearts of the oppressors that they may at once and for ever liberate from awful bondage those whom Thou hast created for purposes of Thy glory.

Tenth Month 1st.—A very bountiful harvest, gathered under unusually auspicious weather, has spread a widely diffused feeling of gratitude over this country. By government authority public thanksgiving was to be made by clergymen to-day. It would be a matter of increased rejoicing if these expressions arose with sincerity from the assembled congregations. For my own part, I have been sensible that the fulness of basket and of store which has been granted me from our farm this year is a great and unexpected blessing for which I desire to be thankful.

I had much exercise this morning with reference to an apprehended call to minister, but feared to venture without increased evidence of being divinely required, and I feel peaceful now in having kept silence.

16th.—Ten days ago an awful calamity occurred at Gateshead and Newcastle. A fire broke out at midnight at a worsted mill at Gateshead, which extended to a bonded store. Then a devastating explosion took place, which spread the fearful calamity to the Newcastle side of the river.

Yesterday we were informed that Mahlon Day and his wife and daughter were lost in the *Arctic* steamer whilst crossing from Liverpool to America. She was run down by a French steamer, the *Vesta*, in a fog at noon, fifty miles off Newfoundland. The *Vesta* is of iron, and having water-tight compartments, reached Newfoundland in safety, though her bow was completely stove in.

Eleventh Month 2nd.—I heard an interesting letter from Asbjorn Kloster to Peter Bedford, mentioning that Mathias Mathiason had been sentenced to thirty days' solitary confinement for refusing to bear arms.

5th.—I was impressed whilst reading the account of W. B. Kimber in "Youthful Pilgrims," with the need that there is for prayer if we desire that the Lord may bless our efforts in temporals or spirituals. I prayed earnestly that, if consistent with the Divine will, success may be granted me in my daily avocations, and that I may keep my mind in a state of childlike dependence on the great Giver of every good and perfect gift.

Twelfth Month 6th.—At meeting to-day much troubled by wandering thoughts. It seems as though the enemy of my soul took occasion to storm with increased energy at these seasons when I seek to draw nigh unto God.

26th.—Isaac Robson and William Rasche arrived on the 24th as our guests. On First-day morning Isaac Robson addressed us forcibly on the text, "He that believeth, and is baptized, shall be saved." He alluded to the results of belief, that we must not lower our standard to our practice, but bring our practice up to the true standard.

28th.—Yesterday tidings reached me of the decease of my much valued cousin Joseph Tregelles Price, of bronchitis.

Thus unexpectedly has closed the life of one who for many years acted towards me the part of a kind parental counsellor in matters commercial, domestic and religious.

Newcastle, First Month 2nd, 1855.—Soon after we sat down in the quarterly meeting the burden of the ministry seemed to rest on me. I felt ability given to labour for the encouragement of those who felt the love of Christ to be precious. When the query was put, "Lovest thou Me?" then we could reply, "Thou knowest all things; Thou knowest that I love Thee." Perhaps on no former occasion in this district have I felt greater liberty in preaching the gospel, and greater evidence of the Lord Jesus being near to help.

Derwent Hill, Second Month 16*th.*—This is the anniversary of my leaving Falmouth for Neath, thirty-five years ago. In the retrospect I may reverently acknowledge that goodness and mercy have followed me all my days.

The cold was very great last night. At eight o'clock this morning our thermometer was at 6°, followed by a lovely day of crystal beauty.

Third Month 1*st.*—It is cause for thankfulness that our government has concluded to depute Lord John Russell to go to Vienna to try to arrange peace with Russia. My heart has been lifted up in prayer to God for His blessing on this effort. May all men believe the truth and act on it, that what is morally wrong cannot be politically right.

7*th.*—Tidings have reached us that the Emperor of Russia died on the 2nd. Rumours have followed, announcing that his son Alexander has had the honours of emperor paid to him. This son is said to be inclined to peace, and therefore a hope is cherished that peace may be soon obtained, and thus shorten the woes of our troops that are now investing Sebastopol.

31*st.*—I went to Middlesbro' to visit dear Isaac Sharp, and spend First-day there. Our conversation turned chiefly on the distressed condition of the people in the Hebrides.

After the morning family Bible reading I felt constrained to bow the knee in intercessory prayer for these people, and to crave that our wills might be subjected to the Lord's will, that we may be willing to proceed on His errands.

Soon after this visit to Middlesbro', Edwin O. Tregelles received a minute from his monthly meeting setting him at liberty for religious service in the Hebrides. He went there, accompanied by John Richardson Proctor.

On Fourth Month 20th they started from Glasgow for Ardrishaig, and drove, *via* Oban, eighty miles to Fort William. Spending First-day and holding a meeting there, they travelled the next day forty miles through a beautiful country to Arisaig.

Part of their service in going to the Hebrides was to obtain information on the fishery question, and to investigate the success of the attempt to supply these poor people with boats and nets. Edwin O. Tregelles remarks on the great simplicity in which the people of these islands live.

At Loch Maddy they had a meeting in the Court House, lent by the Sheriff of North Uist. After visiting numerous places they returned to Portree, and had a meeting in the Free Church. Of this Edwin O. Tregelles writes,—

"It felt like a direct act of faith to appoint this meeting whilst waiting in hourly expectation of the arrival of the steamer by which we were to proceed onward. We were helped mercifully, and I felt thankful that my faith had not failed. Often during this visit have I cried, 'So will we not go back from Thee; quicken us, and we will call upon Thy name.' Early next morning the *Islay* steamer arrived, and we were on board at six o'clock; a very cold morning, with snow."

At Tobermory, the capital of Mull, a meeting was held in a schoolroom, of which he says, "It was well attended, and I felt more than usual gospel liberty to declare some of the unsearchable riches of Christ. I rejoiced to have such a message as was given me to proclaim, peace with God through Jesus Christ."

After a stormy voyage in a boat of twenty tons, they were glad to reach the shelter of Kerrera Island, and to anchor in front of the sweet little town of Oban. Here a meeting was arranged for the next day. Of this E. O. Tregelles writes:—

I felt required to press on their attention the need of the new birth, and of submitting to the guidance and rule of a meek and crucified Redeemer, whose command was, "Swear not at all," and "Love your enemies."

Derwent Hill, 11*th*.—Sustained by the Lord's power we were enabled to pursue our route in safety, and reached home in peace.

Eighth Month 20*th*.—Last Second-day was the Bible meeting, and the following day we had Samuel Bowly acceptably as our guest, lecturing in the evening.

Tenth Month 3*rd*.—On the 9th of Ninth Month the citadel of Sebastopol was abandoned by the Russians, and the allied troops took possession on a First-day. Grievous and terrible has been the conflict, and our "holy men try to give Scripture for the deed." A day of retribution is, I fear, impending over England; it may not come as the result of hostile attack, but poverty and distress of nations, the effect of misapplied resources, which have been turned to curses instead of blessings. Lord, in all seasons grant me a hiding and a dwelling place with Thee, that I may abide under the shadow of the Almighty.

20*th.*—I have felt impressed with the seriousness of having lived nearly half a century, and seem to have accomplished nothing. If guilty of duties neglected, may past transgressions be pardoned for the sake of Him who died for me, and may I be stimulated to increased diligence for the future.

30*th.*—On the 23rd I was at the Scripture reading of the girls' school at York, with sister Rachel, and reminded them of the importance of querying, "What is the object of my life?" I attended York meeting, and had to minister on the first great commandment, and the second like unto it.

Twelfth Month 11*th.*—I left my dear home to-day and rode in the coach, with the ground covered deep with snow to Newcastle, where I met Jonathan Priestman by appointment, to commence our work of visiting friends from house to house.

I heard of the death of Stephen Grellet: thus is he gathered to the company that surrounds the throne, after having faithfully served in the work of winning souls to Christ.

Leeds, 20*th.*—I called on Mary Wright, who is wanting only the few remaining days of this year to be one hundred years of age. She repeated with much force and feeling some lines written by Sarah Grubb. She knew our dear mother when a young, tall, slight woman, several years younger than herself.

Newcastle, 30*th.*—I have had an interesting day. A large and blessed meeting, in which I had to minister, "The foundation of God standeth sure, having this seal, The Lord knoweth them that are His," then the marks of discipleship, "Let every one that nameth the name of Christ depart from iniquity."

Derwent Hill, Second Month 17*th,* 1856.—This has been a

blessed day. I rose tolerably early; my mind was trustful and stayed on holy things. Before we went to meeting, and again very soon after we sat down there, I was reminded of the words,—

> "Sought me wandering, set me right,
> Turned my darkness into light."

Two strangers came into meeting, and I felt engaged to quote the above, after I had alluded to the words of an apostle, "Here have we no continuing city, but we seek one to come." I have since been informed that one of the men who came to meeting is a recently reformed drunkard, who has suffered grievously by his intemperance, and now is earnestly inquiring after the things that belong to his everlasting peace.

25th.—On going to the colliery I found the men all standing out. I felt annoyed at their folly, and apprehended some trouble, but remembered the language I used at Newcastle monthly meeting, "that if we have the best Pilot on board, we may navigate the most intricate waters." I was therefore desirous of being kept in the hollow of the Lord's hand. I feel thankful for the help afforded.

The colliery here alluded to was one which Edwin O. Tregelles worked, at Medomsley, near his home.

Sixth Month 3rd.—When at Harrogate, three weeks ago, we saw William Murray, a blind man who sits by the wayside, making cabbage nets. He has been blind twenty-five years, and a teetotaler seventeen years. With gratitude he spoke of his many blessings, and told me that the spiritual enjoyment he now often had could not be described in words.

Ninth Month 18th.—I went to meeting this morning anticipating comfort from sitting as at the feet of Jesus, and this was realized beyond my expectation.

Tenth Month 9th.—At the quarterly meeting at Darlington I felt it my duty to have a meeting for young people in the evening, which proposition met with cordial approval. It proved to be a good meeting, when I had ability given me to call on the young to surrender their hearts to the Lord, in doing which they would obtain bright hopes of an enduring substance. Thomas Pumphrey, Oswald Baynes and John Pease ministered very acceptably, and prayer was offered at the close.

Twelfth Month 30th.—Oswald Baynes came to us yesterday. We had a blessed meeting, when he spoke impressively on the words, "Oh thou of little faith, wherefore didst thou doubt?" "Said I not unto thee, that if thou wouldest believe, thou shouldest see the glory of God?" After our Bible reading in the evening, Oswald Baynes addressed me in the language of encouragement. That having laboured abundantly in the morning, I might also not withhold the evening sacrifice. "In the morning sow thy seed, and in the evening withhold not thine hand; for thou knowest not whether shall prosper, either this or that, or whether they both shall be alike good." To my dear children he spoke sweetly, "The path of the just is as the shining light, that shineth more and more unto the perfect day."

Second Month 8th, 1857.—A few days ago I received a pleasant note from Endré Dahl, with a good account of the spreading of the truth in Norway, for which I feel thankful.

Fourth Month 24th.—We attended the quarterly meeting at Darlington, when the minute of our monthly meeting respecting a proposition on the subject of Intemperance was agreed to be sent to the approaching Yearly Meeting.

At Blackwell we had a deeply interesting interview with Eliza Barclay and the two dear boys committed to her care. May the dew which descended on the mountains of Zion rest on them, and bless their spirits each day of their earthly travel.

Seventh Month 19*th.*—On our way home from Sunderland monthly meeting we took tea with George Richardson at Newcastle. He alluded to the privileges of his early life. When assisting in a shop at North Shields he filled up his leisure in business hours by reading the writings of Friends.

The aged invalid here referred to felt a great concern that the Society of Friends should take some part in foreign missions, and from his couch of suffering wrote letters to the Yearly Meeting, which awoke such an interest, that the Friends' Foreign Mission Association was formed.

George Richardson spoke of the humility of George Fox in not being carried away by popularity, or by perceiving the influence he gained over others. He thought the fall of James Naylor had been blessed to many of his fellows, who were in danger of spiritual pride.

In speaking of the change as regards the opening of the meetings of the British and Foreign Bible Society with prayer, he said that no portion of the Bible seemed more distorted than the beautiful words used by our Lord, who, in addressing His disciples, said, "After this manner pray ye," and cautioned them against vain repetitions. Now the "Lord's Prayer" is repeated in a manner almost monotonous.

Eighth Month 17*th.*—This day week we had the company of Dr. Richard H. Thomas, of Baltimore, at a public meeting, when to my comfort he addressed us powerfully on Titus iii. 3–5. He lodged with us, and gave us an interesting account of his father, who was a slave-holder, and who married a daughter of a slave-holder, so that the interest of his parents was great in the system. But they were favoured with ability to follow out their convictions of duty, and liberated all their slaves, contrary to the strong remonstrances of their connexions. This step materially lessened their wealth, but a blessing has rested on their obedience.

The deliverance of Dr. Thomas, when coming to England two years ago, was very remarkable. He came in a sailing vessel bound for Liverpool. During the voyage he had a meeting for worship with the captain, crew, and passengers, at which time he prayed for a safe landing at their port of destination, and he believed the prayer would be granted.

When near the English shore the captain used the precaution of keeping a man on the look-out all day, expecting to discover Holyhead about 4 p.m., but he omitted to take soundings. At 3 p.m. the man in the forecastle called out "Breakers ahead!" and the captain gave orders to put the ship about, so as to clear the rocks and high land which seemed just over their heads. As the ship went about they were almost close to half sunken rocks. No sooner was the course altered, than the man again cried out, "Breakers ahead!" The captain had the vessel put yet once more about, and in a moment she struck, and the captain called out, "We are lost!" Dr. Thomas was standing thoughtfully by his side, and lifted up his heart in prayer for deliverance. He thought of his son, who urged him not to take the voyage; he thought of the evidence given in answer to prayer for safe landing, and then he believed deliverance would be granted.

At this moment a gentle breeze off the land filled the sails, and quietly carried the vessel into deep and smooth water. The captain said emphatically, "Nothing but Divine interposition could have saved us." They found that the vessel had sprung a leak, but they worked the pumps all the way from Holyhead to Liverpool. On reaching the dock it was found that a piece of rock was stopping up most of the hole which was made when the vessel struck.

Tenth Month 27th.—During the past few days Susan Howland and her sister Lydia Congdon (ministers from America) have been our very pleasant guests, diligently, and I believe very acceptably, occupied in visiting the families of Friends and attenders in this meeting. They left us this morning after a precious season, when Susan Howland addressed us, encouraging me to hold fast my confidence in Him who had remarkably been my stay in seasons of deeply proving trial; my dear Elizabeth as a helpmate who must not hesitate to follow closely in the path of apprehended duty. She encouraged our dear children to be decided in their choice, and bold in avowing their discipleship, letting their light shine before men. After the usual Bible reading with the family, our servants were addressed on their privileges and cheered in their duties.

28*th*.—Tidings have arrived of the fall of Delhi after a fearful assault, lasting six days. The loss of life has been great. It is thought that the mutiny in India will soon be quelled.

New York is in a fearful condition in mercantile matters. Overtrading seems the cause. Many banks have stopped payment.

Eleventh Month 8th.—The commercial world has been much disturbed of late, and I have felt it a great favour to have been preserved in such calmness as has been my lot, but not without a sense of the perplexity which besets the path of many.

17*th*.—The events which have occurred since the last memorandum have been very distressing. Many who have been brought up in luxury are now laid low by commercial failures widespread and fearful. Such a time as I never knew before. It appears to have commenced by the loss of the *Central America* steamer, which contained a large quantity of gold going to New York. Glasgow and Liverpool soon felt the effects. Then some merchants in Manchester, London and Leeds, who have suspended payment for a large amount. The resources of the Bank of England were nearly exhausted, when our rulers allowed the Bank Charter to be altered under certain conditions, and thus apparently has been averted an overwhelming crisis.

Among the failures was that of Northumberland and Durham District Bank, which brought, through family connexions, the suffering from this commercial storm very closely home to E. O. Tregelles.

Just at this time the visit and ministry of Sarah Squire and Sarah Tatham, who were not told of the special anxiety, were very acceptable. Of this E. O. T. writes:—

At our monthly meeting at Newcastle, Sarah Squire and Sarah Tatham were present; the latter was strikingly engaged in the ministry. The passage of the Israelites through the Red Sea, "Stand still and see the salvation of of God," and then the song of triumph when deliverance was granted.

29th.—This has, I believe, been a blessed Sabbath to many. Soon after we settled in our small meeting, Sarah Tatham rose with the text, "Be still, and know that I am God; I will be exalted among the heathen, I will be exalted in the earth. The Lord of hosts is with us; the God of Jacob is our refuge," and commented on the subject very sweetly. Afterwards Sarah Squire quoted the words, "Trust in the Lord, and do good; so shalt thou dwell in the land, and verily thou shalt be fed."

Twelfth Month 20th.—A few days ago I received a precious note of sympathy from my dear sister Rebecca Gibbins, in which was the following:—

> "Oh, it is easy in life's tranquil day,
> When all around is peace, to kneel and pray
> Father, 'Thy will be done'; but when that will
> Calls us to suffer and be patient still,
> When God's mysterious ways are all unknown,
> When clouds and darkness veil His awful throne,
> Oh, how we need His all-supporting hand,
> To bow submissive to the high command!"
> G. W. FULCHER.

CHAPTER XXI.

SHOTLEY BRIDGE.

Letters from Oswald Baynes and Caroline Fox—Wet Harvest Weather—Death of Joseph Sturge—Visit of John and E. Clark from Jamaica—Gracechurch Street Meeting—York Meeting and School—Cottage Meeting—Three Colliers killed—Visits Cumberland and Northumberland—Wigton School—Attends Brewster Sessions to oppose Licenses—Marriage of Daughter—Distress from Depression of Trade—Russian Serfs liberated—Commencement of American War—Isaac Sharp goes to Iceland and Greenland—E. O. and E. Tregelles attend Yearly Meeting—With Charles Wilson visits Cumberland and Scotland—Francis Redford—Meetings at Dumfries—Port Patrick—Hebrides—Letter from James Reed of Portree—Wigton School—Exhibition—Extract from Hetty Bowman—Illness of his Sister Elizabeth—Visit of John L. Eddy—Death of Rebecca Gibbins—Letter from Mary Samuel Lloyd.

First Month 18*th*, 1858.—Anna Rebecca Tregelles tells me of the decease of our aunt Hingston, the last member of that generation of the Tregelles family. Her kindness to me was great and uniform, and I believe she has heard the blessed language, "Well done, good and faithful servant . . . enter thou into the joy of thy Lord."

Second Month 14*th*.—I received a kind cheering letter from Oswald Baynes, in which he says,—

"'The heart knoweth its own bitterness.' There are seasons when it is given us to realize this in our own experience; sometimes it may be when suffering from close and sore bereavement in the loss of those most near and dear to us, and at other times, when outward trials and disappointments overtake us; but what cause for thankfulness if at the same time we are permitted to possess a measure of that joy with which the stranger cannot intermeddle. Be not dismayed, my dear brother; remember, that with that peace which our blessed Lord left as a legacy to His followers, there was to be tribulation in this world. Faith and patience may be closely exercised by those tribulations and trials, but if rightly borne, they are not the things which separate from the love of Christ; far otherwise, they deepen the Christian in that experimental knowledge of Him and of the Father, which is life eternal.

CAROLINE FOX TO E. O. TREGELLES.

Penjerrick, Seventh Month 17th, 1858.

MY DEAR COUSIN,—

When looking in my beloved mother's desk for something this morning, I discovered the enclosed beginning of a letter to thee, written I think on the morning of Second-day, Fifth Month 31st (Maria Fox died Sixth Month 4th). It is exactly in keeping with every other characteristic of those beautiful, ever-memorable, ever-precious last earthly days. It is as follows:—

"Thy letter, my dear Edwin, awakened so many tender recollections in my very susceptible heart, of present, past and future, that I was obliged to put it aside till some ability was afforded (for of myself I can do nothing), and patiently abide under that which my dear Master knows is best for me, and when faith enables us, like Peter, to plunge into the water to meet Jesus from the love we feel to Him, it must be a total surrender of our will, or we shall hear, 'Oh, thou of little faith, wherefore didst thou doubt?' His own promise is, 'Lo, I am with you alway, even to the end of the world.'"

How perfectly that promise which she last quotes was fulfilled to her a few days later, thou wilt have heard long since, and I ought in gratitude to add that the same mercy has been wonderfully continued to us all, in a way which ought to deepen our faith and love for the rest of our days.

With much love from our party to yours,

Thine affectionately,

CAROLINE FOX.

Eighth Month 22*nd.*—For some days past our faith has been called into exercise by continued rain hindering our harvest, and causing serious apprehension of considerable loss. This subject has pressed on me much to-day in both meetings, where the cares of the world are sadly too apt to intrude. It is well, however, when they are converted into blessings, like wings lifting us to heaven, rather than as weights depressing us to earth. I was much cheered by the thought that the Lord Jehovah had had the key of my granary for many years, and I did not wish to withdraw it or myself from His keeping.

Ninth Month 19*th.*—A fine comet has been visible for ten nights just below the pointers of the Great Bear.

Eleventh Month 5*th.*—Whilst watching the sowing of wheat yesterday I was impressed with the undivided attention the husbandman bestowed on his work, keeping his eyes intent on the ground before him, and I was instructed in comparing it with the care the spiritual husbandman should bestow whilst sowing the gospel seed.

Derwent Hill, First Month 2*nd,* 1859.—Yesterday was passed very peacefully, kept in the fear of the Lord. A happy commencement of a new year. Attended a large and excellent temperance meeting in the boys' schoolroom, Black Hill.

Second Month 9*th.*—My sister Elizabeth came to us from York. To-day she ministered to us in meeting, "The name of the Lord is a strong tower: the righteous runneth into it and is safe."

25*th.*—My dear friend Joseph Sturge has been gathered to the just of all generations. After labouring abundantly for the relief of others' woes, he has been called as at a moment to cease from all his labours.

Eighth Month 19th.—My dear brother Nathaniel's birthday. Sweetly have we been united for many years. He has been a kind and helpful adviser.

23rd.—For several days we have had the company of John and Eliza Clark, of Browns Town, Jamaica, also that of James Jesup. This morning, after breakfast, John Clark knelt in prayer on our behalf, craving that the Lord's blessing might rest upon us, and that we might "finish our course with joy," which petition took deep hold of my mind; and earnest are my desires that neither heights, nor depths, things present nor to come, may be able to separate us from the love of God through Jesus Christ.

24th.—Yesterday was the anniversary of dear Henry's decease, thirty-eight years ago. I thought much of the loss Nathaniel and I have sustained by losing him, and of the strength that might have existed in the threefold cord. But I do not question the wisdom and mercy of our unslumbering Shepherd. Dear Henry was taken in youth with a heart set on heavenly things, and we have had to war a constant warfare.

30th.—On First-day John Clark and his wife accompanied us to meeting. He addressed us on the love of God manifest in creation, and visible in the outward world, and on the love manifested by sending His Son to be a propitiation for all mankind. James Jesup alluded to the sacrifice of a broken spirit being acceptable to God. I spoke on the nature of the gospel, its freeness and blessedness; after which prayer and praise were offered, and a blessing craved on our beloved Queen and Councillors.

Ninth Month 6th.—I feel sure that I miss much by not availing myself of the privilege of the Christian by praying much, in confidence that the promise will be fulfilled, "Ask, and ye shall receive."

19th.—I heard yesterday of the decease of J. K. Brunel,

at the age of fifty-four. He had been a kind friend to me, and I sincerely regret his death. Unnatural exertions, and an overwrought mind have contributed to his somewhat premature decay. He had just completed the *Great Eastern* steamship, and was taken from this vessel to his bed.

Tenth Month 5th.—We returned from Darlington to-day, where I called with William Scarnel Lean to see S. B., who is a great sufferer. It was an instructive visit to me, for I saw how he was sustained by grace to bear his trial with cheerful patience and resignation, saying, as he stretched himself on his couch, "I call this my happy home." I had to encourage him to aid his brethren by intercessory prayer, reminding him of the case of Moses on the mount praying for the success of Israel against Amalek.

23rd.—Much interested in the perusal of John Yeardley's Memoirs, and I am cheered by seeing that our young people like it.

Eleventh Month 11th.—On the 8th I went to London. After completing my business with Thomas Hawkesley, I went to Gracechurch Street meeting, where we had a very favoured time, and I felt empowered to speak to my dear young friends: "Stand fast, therefore, in the liberty wherewith Christ hath made us free, and be not entangled again with the yoke of bondage." Cousin Samuel Fox and Joseph Bevan Braithwaite were also present. I felt thankful in being there to worship with them. On my return home in peace, gratitude is due to the Lord who has preserved me, and given me to partake of His blessing. At York I saw my dear sister Rachel. After breakfast I addressed the girls on the charge of Joshua, "As I was with Moses, so will I be with thee; I will not fail thee, nor forsake thee. Be strong, and of good courage."

18th.—On reading this morning Ephesians v. 2, I was much impressed with the blessed thought that Christ hath given Himself for me. On this I would desire to build all my hopes. Lord, keep me in Thy fear, and help me to walk in humility and all lowliness before Thee.

20th.—As I entered our chamber for my evening reading, the words of fervent prayer passed sweetly through my mind, "Hear me when I call, O God of my righteousness; Thou hast enlarged me when I was in distress; have mercy upon me, and hear my prayer," and as I surrendered myself to Divine influence, I thought of the blessedness of setting the Lord always before me, and knowing that because He is at my right hand, I shall not be moved.

Second Month 5th, 1860.—Last Third-day we had a very nice meeting at Derwent Cottages. The schoolroom was crowded, and thirsty souls were there, to whom the gospel flowed freely. The hearts of many were prepared by the recent sad bereavements, when three lives were lost in Medomsley Pit, about three weeks ago. The wire rope broke, and they fell forty feet, causing speedy death. I had to speak on the words, "Oh that they were wise, that they understood this, that they would consider their latter end!" I alluded also to sudden death being sudden glory, when the soul was prepared for the change, but not else. It was a blessed meeting. The power of the Lord was over all.

Fourth Month 12th.—Yesterday we went to North Shields monthly meeting. It was an interesting time. Several spoke from the body of the meeting, tending to solemnize and benefit us; these were followed by Henry Binns and Edward Backhouse, jun. At the end of the second meeting, C. S. W. knelt in prayer, his first offering of vocal ministry in public.

Sixth Month 6th.—At meeting this evening I was led very unexpectedly to reflect on the case of Henry Bath, who used to live at Portreath, and was a clerk to my father and partners. During a storm he was swept off the pier. He was an excellent swimmer, and supported himself until a rope was thrown to him, which he grasped, and by which he was hauled up the pier. When he reached the top, it was found that the rope had nearly slipped through his hand, just enough to hold by, and not an inch to spare. Herein I saw how mercifully I too have been dealt with, marvellously preserved from a vortex, with nothing to spare.

Sixth Month 9th.—Our uncle, Edward Backhouse, died two days ago. He is the last of our uncles, and we are almost insensibly sliding into the class of the elderly, though very conscious of wanting the judgment, stability, and usefulness of many who have gone before us.

14th.—Yesterday I attended the monthly meeting at Shields, and was liberated to visit the meetings of Cumberland and Northumberland, under which prospect I feel peaceful, though seeing no way for accomplishing it easily.

Wigton, Eighth Month 17th. — I came here yesterday evening, and have enjoyed being at the house of my kind young friends William and Sarah Dodshon. To-day we attended the interment of Alexander Derkin, after which I went to Wigton school, and had an interview with the children, and also with the family. At Allonby meeting I alluded to the importance of reading the Scriptures in retirement, as a means of helping a growth in grace.

Derwent Hill, 31st.—I went to Lanchester yesterday to memorialize the bench of magistrates at the Brewster Sessions on the prevention of licenses for publicans. I saw one of the magistrates to-day, who told me they had not increased the number of licenses.

I had a pleasant walk in the fields yesterday, and a season of devout prayer in the shed of the far-field, when the language came with sweetness, "Have faith and struggle on."

Ninth Month 8th.—Continued cloudy moist weather causes considerable apprehension respecting the safety of the crops. Although at times I feel ready to tremble for the ingathering, yet do I desire to have my mind stayed on the love as well as the goodness and wisdom of Him of whom it is written, " As for God, His way is perfect; the word of the Lord is tried. He is a buckler to all those that put their trust in Him."

Twelfth Month 13th.—My dear Gertrude was united in marriage with Charles Gillett. The meeting was one which may be classed as a time of precious solemnity, for which we may well be reverently thankful. A large company assembled at tea. At about nine my sisters Rebecca Gibbins and Rachel proposed that Psalm xci. should be read. Our young guests cheerfully joined us, and the season felt to many as one of solemn worship, when ability was given to bow the knee in praise and prayer. "Hallowed be Thy great and ever excellent name!"

Derwent Hill, First Month 18th, 1861.—For nearly five weeks we have suffered from frost, at times very intense. Now it seems thawing. Great distress prevails in consequence of the number of persons out of work. Corn is scarce and dear. Every trade is depressed. Much apprehension is entertained respecting America, where the Slave and Free States are threatening each other with war.

Third Month 3rd.—I was informed by my brother, Jonathan Richardson, that the serfs in Russia were to be liberated this day. A merciful deliverance, for which many good men have laboured with the Czars for more than twenty-five years. Now that they are free from earthly fetters, may they also become spiritually free.

These are eventful times. The Bill for the Abolition of the Church Rates was read a second time in the House of Commons last week, and to-morrow is the day on which the separation of the Southern from the Northern States of America will probably take place. This is one step towards the liberation of the Southern slaves in all probability, although the leaders of the movement do not expect such a result.

Fourth Month 4th.—At a conference of men and women Friends at Darlington quarterly meeting, Isaac Sharp mentioned his prospect of visiting Iceland, Greenland, and the Faroe Islands. The meeting heartily united in approval of the concern.

22nd.—Isaac Sharp and Henry Binns left us this morning. Yesterday, after breakfast, we had a time of worship together, when Isaac Sharp addressed us individually in a memorable manner. Henry Binns quoted with reference to me, "Joseph is a fruitful bough by a well, whose branches run over the wall; the archers have sorely grieved him, and shot at him, and hated him; but his bow abode in strength, and the arms of his hands were made strong by the hands of the mighty God of Jacob."

Tottenham, Fifth Month 19th.—When at York, we were speaking of the sudden death of Thomas Harvey, of Youghal, whilst attending Dublin Yearly Meeting. My dear Elizabeth and sister Lydia agreed in the exceeding blessedness of such a transition; it may be that such a lot will be theirs.

Derwent Hill, Sixth Month 12th.—The Yearly Meeting closed on Seventh-day evening, the 1st of Sixth Month. Many Friends spoke of the comfort they had had in attending the meeting; in this I could heartily unite. I went to London with a heart sadly too fearful and unbelieving, but the nourishment granted to my almost famished soul was more than I expected.

At our monthly meeting a minute was framed liberating me to go to the Hebrides and part of Cumberland. There was much expression of cordial approval.

Seventh Month 4th.—We had a good meeting yesterday evening. I was late in arriving, and a precious evidence was granted as I entered the house that true worship was being offered, and I felt engaged to tell the company so. The committee of the Shotley Bible Association was afterwards held.

In the service described in the following memoranda

E. O. Tregelles was accompanied by his friend Charles Wilson.

We had a good meeting at Kirklington on the 21st. I felt much helped in commenting on the words, "Almost persuaded to be a Christian." The Lord's power broke some strong hearts; may the contrite feelings be enduring.

Carlisle, 22nd.—Charles Wilson and I visited the Boys' Reformatory School under the care of George Head. Of the forty-three boys several are learning to be shoemakers, some to be tailors. Six shillings per week is paid by the magistrates on committal.

The evening was wet. We went to Moorhouse, where about sixty met us. I had peace in proclaiming the gospel message.

23rd.—In the afternoon Francis Redford called, and we enjoyed exchanging thoughts on Trinidad, Jamaica, and Hayti, for which places he had given James Jesup and me letters of introduction.

F. Redford had kindly arranged for our meeting, though as a clergyman he did not feel at liberty to lend his school-house. The meeting was largely attended and the query went forth, "What thinkest thou of Christ?"

Silloth, 24th.—Charles Wilson and I went to breakfast with Francis Redford and his wife at the Vicarage. Ere we left, I alluded to the passage, "One Lord, one faith, one baptism, one God and Father of all, who is above all, and through all, and in you all;" to which F. Redford responded very feelingly, and knelt in prayer for a blessing on our labours, that we might have seals to our ministry and souls for our hire. His excellent wife begged that we would bear her and her children on our hearts before the Lord in prayer.

Dumfries, 26th.—I felt exceedingly low and depressed before the meeting, but I found that "help was laid on One that is mighty," and ability was given to take of the things of God and hand them to others. The doubting of Thomas was alluded to, and I am ready to hope that an arrow shot at a venture, shot in faith, pierced between the points of the armour of one present.

Stranraer, 27th.—We left Castle Douglas by a line of railway opened about four months ago. It passes through a varied country, in which part of the way is wooded, well watered and fertile, and part rocky and barren, with wild moors very thinly inhabited. It is difficult to imagine that enough traffic can be found to support the cost of the line.

23th, First Day.—Charles Wilson and I sat down together in my chamber, and a precious season of Christian fellowship we had. Prayer was offered that the blessing of the Lord might descend on us, and that those who tarried at home might divide the spoil.

29th.—After an early breakfast we drove to Port Patrick, and called on Andrew Urquhart, the Free Church minister, who at first was cautious, but soon expanded, and made arrangements for us to have a meeting that evening in their school-house, which was well filled. Psalm cxxxix. 23 was brought prominently forward, and the need for personal holiness, with the benefit to the world if all who named the name of Christ would depart from iniquity. At the close of the meeting Andrew Urquhart came to me and softly said, "'One Lord, one faith, one baptism.' I have rejoiced that you have brought before their minds the need of individual piety." Under very precious feelings of unity we parted, never perhaps to meet again.

26th.—Often during the day my spirit has had communion with my Lord. I believe we should thank our heavenly Father for the privilege of this spiritual communion; thus the precious intercourse would be prolonged, and, I believe, oftener renewed, until at last it would be almost constant, and thus heaven would begin on earth.

On Ninth Month 5th, Edwin O. Tregelles and Charles

Wilson again left home for a series of meetings in Scotland and the Hebrides, going over much the same ground as in the visit he paid in 1855. They held meetings at Fort William in the Free Church, at Broadford and Snizort. Writing of a meeting in the Free Church at Portree, when 600 were present, he says:—

Several tourists were there. To this class I had reference in selecting the season for our visit, and the places for our meetings on First-days.

Ninth Month 17th.—We embarked on the *Clansman*, and lodged at Tobermory. James Reid (the minister at Portree) was on board the steamer, and we parted most lovingly, he giving me a letter as follows:—

F. C. Manse, Portree,
September 16th, 1861.

My dear Sir,—

I have much pleasure in stating to you that your visit, and simple and loving addresses to our people have been much appreciated, and will, I trust, bear fruit. It was very gratifying to hear from your lips so distinctly the fundamental truths of our religion. Man's ruin is of himself, his salvation of the Lord. In other words, ruin through the fall, redemption by Christ; spiritual life and holiness through the effectual operation of the almighty and blessed Spirit of all grace. May you see the desire of your heart fulfilled in Christ reigning in the hearts of many sinners, for His own glory and their everlasting salvation; and may you be carried in safety, in good time, to the bosom of your family, and be more and more blessed and made a blessing to the Church of God in the earth.

I am, yours sincerely,
James Reid.

Ninth Month 24th.—We left Carlisle by railway for Kirkbride, a meeting having been appointed in one of our unused meeting-houses. We were kindly cared for by the station-master, and were met by a young friend from Wigton school. The meeting-house was crowded; our young friend was engaged in supplication, Charles Wilson said a few words, and afterwards I spoke on the text, "As many as are led by the Spirit of God, they are the sons of God." The people were deeply attentive, and it proved a season of true worship. At the close I observed a person sitting wrapped up in a large blue cloak; he came to me and said, "I thank you for the excellent address you have given to my people." It was the clergyman of the parish, who was there with his wife and sister.

Eleventh Month, 25th.—A very boisterous day. I met Robert Marshall, of Whitton Hall, the county surveyors of Northumberland and Durham, and several others, about a bridge across the Derwent at Ebchester.

I received from Joseph Pease by post a choice little book, "Breathings of the Soul," by P. B. Power. I have much enjoyed the beginning, which reminds me of two lines of Samuel Miller Waring:—

> "How sweet shall be the incense of my prayer,
> Since He who bids me gives the power to pray."

Twelfth Month, 14th.—At the close of this week thoughts came over me as to the close of life. It is a comfort to be able to leave all my future for time and eternity in the hands of One who promised me at Barnstaple, nearly thirty years ago, "I will never leave thee nor forsake thee."

31st.—Brought in peace to the end of the year 1861. For the mercies of the past year, and indeed all the years of my deeply proved and richly blessed life, I desire to bless the Lord.

> "We'll praise Thee for Thy mercies past,
> And humbly hope for more."

First Month 11th, 1862.—My heart has been full of praise

for the continuance of peace with America. Mason and Slidell, who were taken out of the *Trent* by the *San Jacinto*, American frigate, are to be given up by the Federals.

Second Month 7th.—I was much depressed to-day. Passing through (if I may venture to write of making any progress) a kind of winter of the soul. What the end of this dispensation may be the Lord alone knoweth. My prayer is, "Keep me, and I shall be kept!"

9th.—The depression of which I wrote above has been mercifully removed, and I think I have known something of the meaning of those words, "being filled with the Spirit."

Fourth Month 4th.—John L. Eddy, from Ohio, was present at our quarterly meeting at Darlington with certificate, also James Backhouse, who spoke on the words, "Have you received the Holy Ghost since ye believed?" J. L. Eddy spoke on the parable of the virgins. And he addressed a state of dangerous unbelief.

Fifth Month 1st.—This is the day for the opening of the International Exhibition. A mournful day to many from the absence of Prince Albert, taken from works to rewards. The country mourns his loss.

I was much pleased with the following remarks in "The Christian Daily Life," by Hetty Bowman: "You feel your disease, and you come to the Good Physician, acknowledging that your comparative insensibility to it is perhaps its worst feature; yet not wanting to have that insensibility removed before you come to Him, but coming to Him in order that it may be removed. 'Do not think,' says Dr. Chalmers, 'that it is your office to heal up one part of the disease, and Christ can heal up the remainder. I come to Him with my heart such as it is, and I pray that the operation of His Spirit and the power of His sanctifying grace may make it such as it should be.' Come to the Saviour just as you are. Let your hand of faith take the gift which He offers, while you ask not so much, 'What must I do to be saved?' as 'Say unto my soul, I am thy salvation.'" For several years past I have rejoiced in holding and proclaiming this doctrine.

Sixth Month 5th.—The meeting at Staindrop was a time of close exercise to me; on waking in the morning the language rested on my mind, "First cast out the beam out of thine own eye, and then shalt thou see clearly to cast out the mote out of thy brother's eye," which I trust was a profitable watchword for myself, whilst I sought to encourage my friends to avail themselves of the great remedy for sin and transgression. I reminded them that "all we like sheep have gone astray; we have turned every one to his own way; and the Lord hath laid on Him the iniquity of us all." "Who His own self bare our sins in His own body on the tree, that we being dead to sins should live unto righteousness."

Eighth Month, 12th.—My thoughts have been turned today to the consideration of the gift of directing and preserving grace, distinguished as it is from saving grace—redeeming grace purchased for us by the blood of Christ. For many years past I have desired much to have correct scriptural views of this subject, and I wish to give my heart more and more to be taught of the Lord.

26th.—I have been happy throughout most of this day in recurring frequently to the pardoning love of Jesus. I have dwelt much on the blessings we may derive from His mediatorial offering as a substitute for poor man. This blessed condition I regard as an answer to prayer, which I have of late often presented, that I might have a deeper, clearer, more abiding and practical sense of my obligations to Jesus, because of His atoning sacrifice.

16th.—My dear sister Elizabeth has had a very alarming attack of illness at York, where she was visiting Rachel; I have had several very precious interviews with her. When conversing of former years she told me that her first serious impressions appeared to be made by reading Law's "Serious

Call," when she was nine years old, to her great uncle Samuel Tregelles, who died in 1805.

Tenth Month 9th.—The Lord hath been mindful of us, giving us beautiful weather for harvesting our oats, and though late in the season, we are favoured beyond our expectation or desert.

31st.—In the morning meeting John L. Eddy said that it was a well-known principle of the Society of Friends that the ministry was not premeditated; and that he came feeling remarkably void of any preparation for vocal labour. He then went on to speak of our Lord's language to Peter, "Satan hath desired to have you, that he might sift you as wheat." The more we were devoted to the Lord's service, the more vigorous would Satan be in sifting us, "but I have prayed for thee, that thy faith fail not; and when thou art converted, strengthen thy brethren." J. L. Eddy rose a second time, and spoke of the need of possessing rather than professing the Truth, that birthright membership would of itself avail us nothing, and impressed on us the need of personal holiness.

Twelfth Month 11th.—Tidings have reached us that my dear sister Rebecca Gibbins was released from her state of suffering yesterday. Deeply do I feel this bereavement of one who watched over and cared for me tenderly from infancy. But sweet is the thought of her reunion with her precious husband.

MARY S. LLOYD TO EDWIN O. TREGELLES.

Woodgreen, Twelfth Month, 1862.

MY DEAR FRIEND,—

. . . We are ill prepared to part with those we have loved so long. We cling to them, because we can have none to succeed them in our heart's affections.

It is pleasant, yea, delightful to know of so many coming

up, we may hope and trust, in the renewings of heavenly light and grace to their position in the church. Nevertheless there is a void, which must be felt to be understood, that can never be supplied at my time of life. There is also this rich consolation, it cannot be, in the course of nature, for a long period we have to struggle on in the fight of faith.

My dear friend, long accustomed to think of thee as my younger brother, I was truly pleased to find I held that place in thy affectionate remembrances that led thee to recall the early seasons of our intercourse at Glenvelyn. . . . So many have been gathered home lately that we are become familiar with the messenger of death. When he comes as a herald to open the gate of life and glory, we ought surely to strive to be unselfish. Jesus wept for the sorrow that fell on his friends Martha and Mary, and we too may weep whilst we may take the comfort He administered to them, "Thy brother shall rise again." . . .

Mayst thou be strengthened by the Spirit to hold on thy way, and finally to adopt, in humble hope, the apostle's testimony when he saw the crown of glory ready for him.

      Farewell, beloved Edwin, from
                      thy aged sister in the truth,
                                    MARY S. LLOYD.

CHAPTER XXII.

SHOTLEY BRIDGE.

Visits at Newcastle Gaol a condemned Murderer—Capital Punishment—Matamoros—Answer to Prayer—William Tanner—Yearly Meetings Committee—Illness of his Wife—Death of his Sister Elizabeth—Goes with his Wife to Scotland—Holds Meetings at Perth and Inverness—Isabella L. Bird—Meeting at Oban—Derwent Hill Harvest Home — Meeting with Navvies — Rebecca Collins — Ann Eliza Dale — Loss of *The London* Steamer — Escape of Sailors from Shipwreck—Sympathy for Sufferers by Financial Failures—Death of W. Tanner—John Henry Douglas and Robert Alsop—David Hunt—Severe Winter—Death of Albert Fox—Yearly Meeting — Slave Children in Brazil set free—Marriage of Son—Sybil Jones relates Experience in the War—Falmouth—Death of John Pease—Amos and Edith Griffith—Accident at Abergele—Meeting at Blackhall Mill.

DERWENT HILL, Third Month 13*th*, 1863. In consequence of knowing that a poor felon who had been convicted of murder was under sentence of death in Newcastle gaol, I ventured to bring before Friends, at the close of the monthly meeting at Sunderland, the subject of capital punishment, and trust vigorous measures will be taken to have the law altered.

After meeting I consulted Joseph Procter, John Mounsey, and Daniel Oliver, about having an interview with the convict, of which they approved. D. Oliver kindly undertook to arrange it. He obtained the requisite order from Sir John Fife, a visiting magistrate, who said he wished to smooth the passage of the poor creature to the other world, and also expressed a desire that a longer interval should be granted between conviction and execution.

Daniel Oliver accompanied me to the prison. The chaplain and governor went with us into the condemned cell, where we found the poor man standing by the fire, guarded by a warder. The chaplain explained the object of our visit, and urged him to be earnest in making his peace with God by the alone means. When the chaplain left we all sat down. Very solemn was the silence for several minutes, when I addressed him with the language, "If any man sin, we have an advocate with the Father," and urged him to lose no time in fleeing for help to Him who came not to call the righteous, but sinners to repentance. Much more was said, but all seemed received with a stolid indifference, such as I have rarely if ever witnessed. Before we left, prayer was offered that his heart may be softened to receive the impressions of the Holy Spirit, become changed and fitted for a kingdom of purity. I crave for the poor condemned man that he may know his peace made with God through Jesus before he comes to the scaffold to-morrow.

Fourth Month 7th.—I was at Middlesbro' and heard from Isaac Sharp details about Iceland and his prospects of further service in that island, Greenland, and Labrador.

I would profit by the remark of a Friend who spoke of a case where a wealthy man was about to die, and said, "It is true I am about to die, and I leave much property: this I cannot take with me, but how I gained it, and how I spent it, I take with me."

Fifth Month 20th.—To-day the Yearly Meeting commences. My thoughts have been much with those assembled there. As I stood leaning against an oak tree in the Copse-field my heart was lifted up in prayer for the gathered assembly, that they might be found waiting for the Bread which cometh down from heaven, and realize the fulfilment of the promise, "I will be as the dew unto Israel."

22nd.—Matamoros, the Spanish Protestant who has been imprisoned for reading the Bible, is now to be banished from Spain, the sentence of imprisonment having been commuted on the presentation of a memorial from the Meeting for Sufferings.

Sixth Month 12th.—This morning I read the interesting book "Remarkable Answers to Prayer." It has helped me through the day, when considering how I could meet some heavy claims. Whilst walking in the Far-field I felt led to pray for help, and to my surprise the means were supplied by persons bringing me the needful funds. Surely we do not avail ourselves as we might of the blessing and the power of prayer.

Eighth Month 22nd.—Yesterday the railway between Falmouth and Truro was to be opened, a great event for that locality. It is now eighteen years since I commenced my engagement as a civil engineer on that line.

Tenth Month 21st.—At the quarterly meeting William Tanner quoted the words, "Make to yourselves friends of the mammon of unrighteousness, that when ye fail, they may receive you into everlasting habitations;" showing how utterly at variance with the way cast up for the redeemed to walk in, are the ways which man pleases himself by contriving for himself. "Ye cannot serve God and mammon." All the gifts and talents must be consecrated—not the tenth only—but all held subservient to the great Giver.

Twelfth Month 11th.—On the 8th we went to Newcastle to attend the meeting of ministers and elders; Josiah Forster, Charles Fox, Isaac Brown, J. Bevan Braithwaite, Samuel Bowly, and Thomas Pierce were present as part of the Yearly Meeting's committee. Much excellent counsel was given as to the care of young ministers. We do not chide our little children because they trip when they attempt to walk. At a very interesting and profitable social meeting some account was given of the First-day School by Henry Clapham and George Richardson. In speaking on reading the Scriptures, Charles Fox dwelt on the solemnity of their being read in any family for the last time. He told us of a ship foundering with the captain, whose wife and child were rescued, and how the widow delighted in re-perusing the chapter they had read together a short time before the ship went down.

14th.—Letters from my sisters at Falmouth give us cause to believe that our dear sister Elizabeth is very near her end, and her gentle spirit sustained, though in great feebleness, by a sense of Jesus being near.

16th.—The state of my dear wife's health has for some weeks been very frail. I read to my comfort this evening, " The God of all grace, who hath called us unto His eternal glory by Christ Jesus, after that ye have suffered awhile, make you perfect, stablish, strengthen, settle you."

In the winter of 1863–4 Elizabeth Edwin Tregelles was very ill. This great trial is alluded to in the diary written on Fourth Month 1st, 1864.

It would not be possible to describe the depths of anguish endured, and the strength of the support granted in our extremity by One mighty to save, and able to deliver to the very uttermost. My dear sister Elizabeth was very ill at the time my darling wife was so near the verge of eternity. Sister Elizabeth lingered until the 19th of Third Month, 1864.

The gradual return of strength of Elizabeth Edwin Tregelles was accelerated by change of air and scene to the homes of her cousin Lucy Mounsey, at Hendon Hill, Sunderland, and her friend Lydia Proctor, at Low Lights, North Shields. She was able to accompany her husband in a journey to Scotland in the Eighth Month.

Oban, Eighth Month 2nd.—On the 28th of Seventh Month we had a meeting in the evening at Perth with James

Fenwick and family. At Inverness we called on Donald Frazer at the Manse, who kindly arranged for a meeting in the Free Church, which was attended by 400 persons in great stillness. The Lord gave me ability to comment on the language, "There is none other name under heaven given amongst men whereby we must be saved."

Derwent Hill, Eighth Month 15th.—This day week we left Oban, where we had almost unmixed enjoyment. Dearest Elizabeth delighted in being in a boat, cruising on the water along the lovely coast. Our pleasure was much enhanced by meeting Dora Bird, and her daughters Isabella and Henrietta.

Isabella L. Bird is the lady so well known for her interesting travels in unfrequented places, and (as Mrs. Bishop) for her journey in 1890 through Persia and other Eastern countries in the interest of Medical Missions. For many years Edwin O. Tregelles had been a co-worker with her in assisting to supply the poor fishermen in the Hebrides with boats and nets.

On First-day we had a good meeting in the Independent Chapel, kindly lent by the minister, who being absent was glad to have it thus occupied. Our friends, I. L. and H. Bird kindly promoted this meeting, and aided in giving the notice. We called on them after meeting to take leave. It was a solemn season, when thanksgiving arose for the privileges we had enjoyed of precious fellowship. Prayer ascended that the widow and the fatherless might be comforted.

Tenth Month 22nd.—We have had a very interesting gathering of about twenty of our work-people at a harvest home tea. I read the "Autobiography of a Thief; What I was, What I am, and How I Became so;" also the remarks made on temperance, at York, by the Rector of Stilton, and finished with Psalm lxv. James Edwards (the hind) spoke very nicely on harvest homes, and on the relation of master and servant, and prayed earnestly for a blessing on all. A sweet hymn was sung,—

> "We talk of the realms of the blest,
> But what must it be to be there?"

Eleventh Month 30th.—I have been this evening to a meeting with the navvies now engaged in constructing the railway. I began by reading Psalm lxiii. May the Lord bless the few words spoken.

Twelfth Month 28th.—I have attended the reading for the navvies this evening, at the Wesleyan Chapel, Ebchester, and read in "The Light on the Line; a Memoir of T. Ward," by Catherine Marsh. More of the navvies were present this evening than on the two former occasions. A good feeling was manifest. My neighbour, John Hunter, engaged in prayer.

First Month 5th, 1865.—A letter from my friend James Jesup informs me of his being very infirm with paralysis, which grieves me.

Eighth Month 15th.—A long time has occurred without a note, embracing very varied experience; joy, peace, and comfort have abounded, but now we seem passing through a dispensation of a very proving kind. I pray that the purposes designed by my heavenly Father may be accomplished.

21st.—Tidings have reached us of the arrival of the *Great Eastern* steamer, after a fruitless attempt to lay the cable for the telegraph, which broke about 1,100 miles from Valencia.

Eleventh Month 10th.—I called to-day at Westwood Farm to see Dorothy Currie, who is sinking rapidly in consumption. She is fully aware of her critical state. I read to her the hymn in the Olney hymn-book commencing, "Come, my soul, thy suit prepare." I pointed her to Jesus, the sinner's Friend, and found much liberty in praying that her soul might be accepted for His sake who died for her, the Just for the unjust.

26th.—Yesterday my dear Elizabeth felt very low and discouraged, and during a call on Ann Eliza Dale, the conversation turned on the silence which has been my dispensation of late in our meetings. In consequence I felt best satisfied to write to A. E. Dale on the subject.

31st.—The following is a reply of Ann Eliza Dale to my note:—

"*Hurworth, Twelfth Month 29th*, 1865.

"My dear Friend,—

"Thy very kind and Christian note was as acceptable as unexpected. I ventured to express to thy beloved wife a little of the sympathy and anxiety I had been feeling for thee, under an impression of the difficulties and responsibilities of thy position in your little meeting, with so few to comfort thee under them all. Deeply unworthy as I am to convey a word of encouragement to one so much more experienced in the Divine life, yet I must entreat thee, my dear friend, to rise above all hindrances from within and without, looking unto Jesus, casting all thy cares upon Him. Remember His gracious promises. . . .

"May He who hath called and chosen thee to minister in His name, strengthen and help thee as in times past, faithfully and affectionately to do so, keeping all outward things under, that the enemy of souls may not cause them to prove stumbling blocks to thyself and others. Yet a little while and the victory will be given. 'Be thou faithful unto death.' . . .

"I am thy affectionate but unworthy friend,
"A. E. Dale."

31st.—Yesterday was a day of remarkable trial; it seemed as though my way in business matters was hedged up.

But yet there was a precious sense of calm confidence in the over-ruling power of Divine providence.

First Month 18th, 1866.—I heard to-day of the loss of the steamship *London,* from London to Melbourne, with more than 250 persons on board. She foundered, and only seventeen escaped by boat in a fearful gale to Falmouth.

23rd.—I have thought much of Thomas Harvey and William Brewin, who, with W. Morgan of Birmingham, left for Jamaica by the *La Plata* steamer. Heartily do I sympathise with them in their work, and feel for them in consequence of the gales, which have been unusually numerous and heavy this winter. In the second week of this month 400 vessels were lost with many lives, and £2,000,000 worth of property, to the ruin of many.

Second Month 19th.—The *Arago* steamer, on her return voyage from America, by some means deviated very much from her course, and when about 1,200 miles from Falmouth, found a vessel in a sinking state, which had been disabled in a storm on Christmas Day. She was laden with oil from Newfoundland to Liverpool. They had cast their cargo overboard, and, marvellous to relate, the waters had been so calmed by the oil, that the ship floated in a smooth sea, scarcely moving her position for five weeks. The man who first spied the *Arago* fainted with exhaustion as soon as the others saw her, and only recovered when they said, "She sees us, and is bearing down toward us." In two hours they were on board of her, and in two hours more the deserted vessel sank. The men had access to Bibles, and had read with earnestness in the Psalms and Jeremiah as they had never read before.

Sixth Month 26th.—On going to the Bromhill colliery to-day, the men told me that they had had a narrow escape yesterday from the roof of the headway having fallen whilst they were in the cabin at lunch. Only one hour before I had warned them of the danger I apprehended from a fault which they thought would not affect the roof.

Seaton Carew, Eighth Month 6th.—The time of retirement and prayer which my dear Elizabeth and I had before we left Derwent Hill to-day was exceedingly blessed. When bowed before the Lord, asking for His guidance, support, and blessing, an evidence was granted that the Maker and Upholder of all things would care for all our wants, and protect His own gifts. "Behold, I have graven thee upon the palms of My hands; thy walls are continually before Me."

13th.—I went to Stockton meeting yesterday morning. I was led to hand sympathy to many in that meeting in much affliction consequent on the failures which have taken place. I spoke of Job as an example of sudden and entire bereavement; his friends sitting by, speechless, seven days and seven nights. Job's resignation, "The Lord gave, and the Lord hath taken away; blessed be the name of the Lord." Consolation to be found in Christ, who came to comfort those who mourn, and give "beauty for ashes, the oil of joy for mourning, the garment of praise for the spirit of heaviness."

Derwent Hill, 21st.—I have had remarkable evidence to-day that the Lord is mindful of us. A sweet calm came over my spirit whilst I was bowed in wonder and thankfulness for His providences. Truly "those who will mark providences will not want providences to mark."

Ninth Month 12th.—Earnest have been my desires to keep very close to my Shepherd, and to know His staff to uphold me. Whilst standing in a crowd at Sunderland station, taking my ticket, the promise came sweetly before me in a way I could take hold of, "Fear thou not, for I am with thee; be not dismayed, for I am thy God; I will strengthen, yea, I will help thee: yea, I will uphold thee with the right hand of My righteousness."

Tenth Month 19th.—This day brings me to the period of threescore years—an important one in the life of man. May my descent be marked by humility, circumspection, charity, and, above all, the fear of the Lord.

Eleventh Month 11*th*.—On the 9th Isabella and Henrietta Bird came to us from Edinburgh.

Yesterday tidings reached us of the decease of dear William Tanner from pleurisy. I feel his removal deeply, remembering with pleasure the many sweet seasons of intercourse we have had, especially the walk from Sidcot to Cheddar a few months before I left for the West Indies, when a beautiful rainbow seemed to bear witness to the covenant of friendship for each other, and peace with God.

Twelfth Month 13*th*.—At our meeting John Henry Douglas, of Ohio, spoke on the case of Job, afflicted, yet with his heart stayed on God, enabled to maintain his integrity. He referred to the trials and changes of life, the trial of faith being more precious than gold which perishes. He prayed fervently for all classes, for me as the aged minister who had proclaimed the gospel in other lands, that I might be kept to the end, to which I say, Amen. Robert Alsop spoke on the text, "By grace are ye saved, through faith: and that not of yourselves, it is the gift of God." I have been considering how best to retain the benefit of such privileges, and believe it will be by yielding the heart as plastic clay in our heavenly Father's hand.

First Month 3*rd*, 1867.—I attended the quarterly meeting at Sunderland, which was large. David Hunt, Isaac Brown, and John Cowgill were present. In the evening, at Ashburne, David Hunt spoke in a calm effective manner on "the Ordinances," a kind of simple lecture. He said the Passover supper was in remembrance of the Paschal Lamb, but in its continuance our Lord, not the lamb, was to be remembered as often as the passover supper was eaten. If the rite had been effective in sealing its recipients as servants of Christ, how was it the disciples denied Him and forsook Him immediately after that rite, which surely was one calculated to make a lasting impression?

20*th*.—I struggled to meeting through deep snow, which has fallen more or less for three weeks, and found very few there. But met with the Lord on the way, and found Him also there. He comforted me, and seemed to commission me to comfort others. "The secret of the Lord is with them that fear Him, and He will show them His covenant."

26th.—Much distress prevails at Blackhill, Consett, and the other villages round. The intense and enduring frost renders work very scarce, in addition to the general slackness in the iron trade. Soup kitchens are being established, one in an abandoned brewery.

31st.—A letter from Nathaniel to-day mentions the decease of our cousin Albert Fox, at Linares, in Andalusia, of severe small-pox. Gathered promptly home.

Tottenham, Fifth Month 22nd.—We left Derwent Hill at seven this morning in a snowstorm. At Grantham two persons joined us, with one of whom I had a very interesting conversation on temperance. She queried whether Friends were Unitarians. In our conversation I endeavoured to preach Christ.

28th.—Yesterday I paid a visit to the women's yearly meeting. It was a service which seemed to be laid upon me, even before I left home. Ability was granted to give utterance to truths which I trust were sealed by the Lord on the hearts of many young mothers and sisters. Paul's obedience to the call of the man of Macedonia, the work of grace in the hearts of the visited, first giving themselves unto the Lord, were the leading features of the message committed to my trust.

An announcement was made this morning that the Emperor of the Brazils has liberated the children of slaves, born after this time, and the adults to be free in twenty years. It is supposed that two million slaves are now in the Brazils.

29th.—Joseph Thorp alluded to the cause of thankfulness that freedom was in prospect for our fellow creatures in the Brazils, but that we should bear in mind that many thousands of our fellow countrymen are in a bondage worse than negro slavery, the bondage to drink. He then spoke powerfully on the claims of this class to our care. Many Friends followed him, deploring the misery resulting from the drinking usages. It was agreed to prepare a minute of earnest counsel.

Derwent Hill, Sixth Month 19*th.*—Dear Arthur was married on the 11th to Jane M. Wright, at Darlington. They came to their home at Benfieldside this evening.

Eighth Month 9*th.*—At meeting this morning we had the company of Eli and Sybil Jones, and Sarah Tatham. Eli Jones spoke on striking hands with the world. That the religion Jesus came to establish was that best suited to the wants of man, simple, unadorned, real, not symbolic, and that it is a mistake to suppose that the mission of Friends is ended.

Sybil Jones related at "the Park" (Charles Wilson's), where we dined, some of the circumstances of the death of their son, who fell in the Northern army just after he had by his arrangements gained a victory over the Southerners. Wounded in the thigh by a stray shot, he bled to death in two hours and a half. He sent a message to his mother, saying all was well. That very evening Sybil Jones was walking under some trees, looking at the moon, thinking that her son was looking at the same moon, and an impression came to her, "Thy son is safe in heaven before thee." In agony she ejaculated, "Not so, O Lord! It must not, cannot be!" The messenger was then on his way to inform the bereft parents of their sorrowful loss. His enlistment had been a fearful grief to them. Sybil Jones could not bear the thought of being a mother of a murderer; for in that light she regarded the profession of of arms.

When Eli and Sybil Jones stopped at our door, Sybil Jones said, "We have admired the scenery of your lovely valley." I remarked, "Many parts of the way you have come are truly lovely, but the valley is far more beautiful beyond." Sybil Jones replied, "This may apply to another journey."

Falmouth, Ninth Month 22nd.—I left home at 7 a.m. of the 16th, and reached Plymouth at 12 p.m., and was off next morning before six, reaching Falmouth at 8.30. I found my dear sisters in the garden, and a joyful meeting it was. At half-past ten I went to the monthly meeting, which was very small and greatly changed. At four o'clock was the meeting of ministers and elders. Friends kindly acceded to my wish to have a meeting with sailors. The Bethel could not be obtained, and it was arranged to have it in the Friends' Meeting House. It proved a good meeting.

Derwent Hill, Tenth Month 2nd.—After a time of unusual enjoyment I left Falmouth on the 26th of last month, visiting relatives on my return journey at Liskeard, Plymouth, and Kingsbridge.

Fourth Month 26th, 1868.—On my way from meeting, when thinking of the varied besetments of my path, the language was presented to my mind, "I have arranged things marvellously for thee; wilt thou trust Me still?" to which my heart responded, "I will."

" And we know that all things work together for good to them that love God " (Rom. viii. 28).

> "All things, dear Lord! is there no thread of woe
>   Too dark, too tangled of the bright design?
> No drop of rain too heavy for the bow.
>   Set in the cloud in covenant Divine.
>
> I know that all Thy full designs are bright,
>   That darkest threads grow golden in Thy hand;
> That bending lines go straight—the tangled right—
>   The bitter drops all sweet at Thy command.
>
> *   *   *   *   *
>
> Why these enigmas? Wherefore not receive
>   Their bright solution? Then a voice drew near,
> ' Blessed are they who see not, yet believe!'
>   And One I knew approached, and wiped my tear."

27th.—Tidings have reached us to-day of the fall of Theodore, King of Abyssinia, and the release of his captives, Lieutenant Prideaux, a great nephew of my sister Dorothy Tregelles, being amongst them.

Seventh Month 7th.—A day long to be held in grateful remembrance. The Lord has been gracious to the voice of my cry, and has granted deliverance from many pressing cares and threatening trials. With reverent gratitude I may say, "Blessed be God, who hath not turned away my prayer, nor His mercy from me."

9th.—Strong were my desires that the Lord would be pleased to keep me near to Himself during the remainder of my pilgrimage, and sweet was the evidence to my soul, and comforting, that He would continue His gracious care "by the way and to the end."

30th.—This evening Jonathan Priestman informed us of the decease of John Pease. Such information coming just as we were assembling for meeting was calculated to make a deep impression. I was reminded of the words,—

> "Take no thought for the morrow, its dawning may find thee
>   A spirit at rest 'neath the altar of God,
>   The last battle fought—the last conflict ended,
>   The victory won through Emmanuel's blood."

Eighth Month 7th.—On the 4th I went to Darlington to attend John Pease's funeral. The meeting-house was filled to overflowing. J. B. Braithwaite was engaged in prayer, closing with the words, "Unto Him that loved us, and washed us from our sins in His own blood . . . unto Him be glory and dominion for ever and ever." Then Edith Griffith rose, and said that the words just used were the last she had heard uttered by John Pease before he left the shores of America. She bore testimony to his service as being blessed to many, and to herself in particular.

I went to see A. and J. after meeting, and had a precious

season of prayer with them, when we sought to commend each other to the care of Israel's Shepherd.

For several weeks we have had very hot weather. This afternoon the atmosphere became much cooler, and a strong south-west wind is bringing down the valley a large volume of smoke from the moors of Waskerley, which have been burning for several weeks, threatening much loss. The whole valley seems filled with blue smoke, scenting our house as if we were burning peat in our grates.

Eighth Month 15*th.*—On the 11th Amos and Edith Griffith came here. Our meeting, held in the evening, was a greatly favoured season.

I was led this morning to consider the blessing that attends me in having so much less of business care than heretofore, and it seems to be right for me to give up more time for retirement.

26*th.*—On the 20th a terrible accident occurred near Abergele, in North Wales, to the Irish mail train from London to Dublin. Some trucks laden with paraffin ran back from a station where they had stopped, and were met by the mail train, which was going at the rate of forty miles an hour. The paraffin took fire, consumed the foremost carriages, and burnt to death thirty-three of the passengers. Lord Farnham was one of the victims, and Judge Barwick. The post-office and letters were saved, also the Duchess of Abercorn and her family, who were in the hinder carriages. The combustion was so complete, that the relics could not be identified, and it was thought best to bury all the remains of the thirty-three persons in one large grave. The rich and great mingled their tears of unaffected sorrow with the struggling poor who mourned the loss of their life's support.

Ninth Month 2*nd.*—We had an interesting and I hope profitable meeting at Blackhall Mill. John Richardson Procter, Charles Wilson, and Francis Snaith kindly accompanied me. The meeting was held in an upper room, used by the Wesleyans as their chapel. Ability was given to set forth the means appointed by our Father in heaven for all who are in bondage to sin and Satan to be made free, and turn from darkness to light, and from the power of Satan unto God.

Tenth Month 19th.—Sixty-two years old this day. Of late my thoughts have recurred often to the times at Abersychan. Well do I remember the hour which I spent there, forty-two years since, in blessed communion with my Father in heaven. The spot was a simple rude office, made of rough planks. It stood in front of the blast engine-house which I was then erecting. The covenant made without ceremony, with no other witness than the Holy Spirit, has through mercy been kept. I then gave my heart to God, and never have I desired to draw back. Very little have I accomplished in His service. Very much has He done for me; unnumbered mercies have been granted from year to year.

CHAPTER XXIII.

SHOTLEY BRIDGE.

Yearly Meeting—Conference at Newcastle—Attends United Kingdom Alliance Meeting at Manchester—Yearly Meeting, Dublin—James Owen—Death of Sarah Richardson—Visits Scotland — Neath— Public Meeting, Cardiff — War Declared between France and Prussia—Appeal for the War Victims—Letter from Robert Alsop —Manchester Meeting—Decease of Abraham Fisher—Marriage of Daughter—Liskeard—Mirfield—Prayer for Recovery of Prince of Wales—Death of Thomas and Jonathan Richardson—Yearly Meeting — Surbiton — Esher — Alabama Arbitration — Visits Northumberland, Cumberland and Westmorland—Attends Aberdeen General Meeting—Inverness, Oban, Tobermory—Joel and Hannah Bean visit Derwent Hill—Yearly Meeting—Neal Dow and Dr. F. R. Lees at Shotley—Meeting at Nenthead—Death of Sister Dorothy Tregelles—Joins Yearly Meetings' Committee in Oxfordshire—Conference in London on the State of the Society of Friends—Speaks on Temperance at Monthly Meeting, Newcastle —Decease of his Sister Rachel—Proposition on Temperance in Yearly Meeting—William C. Westlake—Deborah Thomas and Mary Haines—Joins Yearly Meeting Committee in Visits to Ackworth School and Yorkshire—E. O. and E. Tregelles go to Neath, Plymouth, and Penzance—Meetings at Marazion and Mousehole.

DERWENT HILL, Shotley Bridge, Sixth Month 13th, 1869.—We felt it a privilege to attend the Yearly Meeting, which was a favoured time. The blessing of the Lord will rest on these gatherings so long as they meet in His fear, but if there be departure from the counsels of the Lord, and expediency be preferred to principle, the glory of the Lord will soon be removed.

Seventh Month 12th.—Robert Clarke, one of our colliers, was at work with a hay reaper, mowing a field of hay for

Roger Armstrong, and it is said that a fly went down his throat, soon after which he felt unwell; his malady increased, and he died yesterday, leaving a wife and young children. I desire that we may profit by the lesson we have had of the uncertainty of life, and the need there is to give heed to the warnings we receive. "Be ye also ready; for in such an hour as ye think not, the Son of man cometh."

Eighth Month 29th, First Day.—We had a remarkable meeting this morning. Edwin Pumphrey spoke on the liability to sudden death as claiming our notice, seeing that as in a moment the Lord could lay His finger on His servant, and call him from works to rewards, from the cares of life to the joys of eternity, either by accident or in our sleep. It was, I believe, a rightly directed warning, by which I trust we may all profit. When dear Elizabeth and I spoke to one another on the subject, she remarked that preparation for such a change was the best preparation for the right enjoyment of life.

I was impressed to-day with some remarks of John Newton, 1764: "I believe myself to possess the privileges of a child of God, yet am I lean, uncomfortable, unfruitful. Why is this? It arises from two grand causes which mutually produce and run into each other, a want of faith or a want of watchfulness. I suffer much from both, much from the latter. Self-seeking, earthly care, worldly conformity, neglect of the means of grace, or formality in their use, are the enemies to comfort and usefulness."

In the autumn Edwin O. Tregelles attended a conference of Friends at Newcastle on the best way of making a holy life attractive to the younger members. After this he spent some days at Manchester, at the annual meeting of the United Kingdom Alliance for the prohibition of the liquor traffic.

Derwent Hill, First Month 30th, 1870.—In meeting to-day I alluded to the need of each day being sanctified with prayer, and crowned with praise, walking with God, and being divinely blessed, feeding on the bread which cometh down from heaven, eating the flesh, and drinking the blood of the Son of God, thus truly partaking of the Supper (Rev. iii. 20).

Second Month 1*st.*—I sent off to-day to H. A. Bruce, the Home Secretary, a memorial from the working classes on local option in reference to the drink traffic. Lord, be pleased to grant Thy blessing on the efforts now being made to remove from this land the grievous sins that are hourly, and without number, caused by this fearful traffic.

Third Month 20*th.*—On the 26th I went to Scotby, and was kindly received by William Sutton and his wife. At their First-day morning meeting I was engaged to speak on the words, "I intend at some future time to give my heart to God."

Fourth Month 4*th.*—My dear Elizabeth and I went to Darlington quarterly meeting, which was large, solemn and profitable, chiefly a prayer meeting.

Dublin, 29*th.*—At the Yearly Meeting of ministers and elders I sat besides James Owen. It was deeply interesting to see many in this meeting whom I had known thirty-one years before as very young persons. In the meeting for worship to-day James Owen queried, "What is Christianity? What is Quakerism?" I rose with the words, "Stand fast therefore in the liberty wherewith Christ hath made us free, and be not entangled again with the yoke of bondage."

Fifth Month 2*nd.*—I went into the women's meeting. The duty had impressed me for several days, and way was readily made. Adam Woods and John B. Haughton accompanied me. The subject of my address was the absolute necessity for the new birth, "Except a man be born again, he cannot see the kingdom of God." There is no salvation without baptism, and eating the flesh of the Son of man and drinking His blood; these are not elementary, but spiritual and realized.

Sarah Richardson, the unmarried and much attached sister of Elizabeth Tregelles, had for some time shown signs of serious illness. This increased rapidly, and she passed away on the 13th of the Fifth Month, clasping her sister's hand, when the language of thanksgiving arose that the victory had been won through the blood of the Lamb, and another blessed spirit had joined the ransomed multitude around the throne. Her brother Thomas left at once his changed home at Snows Green, and came to reside temporarily at Derwent Hill.

After many weeks of pressure from anxiety and grief, and needful attention to her sister's affairs, Elizabeth Tregelles needed rest and change. She and her husband spent some weeks in Scotland. After their return home, Edwin O. Tregelles visited his relations and old friends at Neath. He attended the quarterly meeting there, and took part with Stanley Pumphrey and Henry S. Newman in a public meeting in the Victoria Hall, Cardiff.

The news of the declaration of war between France and Prussia came like a thunder-clap to grieve the hearts of millions. Under the circumstances it was not strange that many Friends, and lovers of peace, were stirred to take steps to relieve the poor innocent sufferers—the victims of war.

Derwent Hill, Tenth Month 6th, 1870.—On the 25th of the Ninth Month Arthur Albright and I were at Clementhorpe, North Shields; we discussed with John R. Procter the propriety of issuing an appeal on behalf of the peasantry who had been desolated by the armies in Europe. The measure has met with much encouragement; and we hope that the Meeting for Sufferings will take the matter up fully to-morrow.

The following " Appeal on Behalf of the Victims of the War " was written in my chamber at Clementhorpe, approved by John R. Procter and Arthur Albright, and revised by John Hodgkin.

" The condition of the peasantry whose homes have been recently devastated by the ravages of war, or who have been driven from their homes, has claimed the attention of many in this country. The extent of the distress thus occasioned can be very imperfectly known, described, or imagined. Utter destruction of homes and crops and cattle has in many cases marked the track of both armies, and many of the desolated families are wandering, seeking with difficulty to obtain a precarious existence.

" Any effort to supply their need will probably fall far short of their requirements; but, whilst we cannot doubt that the cry of the homeless and helpless will ascend to our Father in heaven, and that He will hear it, and succour them, we trust also that His servants in this and other Christian lands will do their part in mitigating the woes which may be too deep for entire cure.

" It is proposed that a fund should be raised, to provide for the victims, food, shelter and clothing, and in some cases seed-corn, and other supplies; such fund to be called " The War Victims' Fund," and placed under the care of trustees to be appointed by " The Meeting for Sufferings " in London, *i.e.*, the standing committee of the Society of Friends. . . .

" Information may be obtained from John Hodgkin,

Lewes; Chas. Lloyd Braithwaite, Kendal; Robert Foster, Newcastle-on-Tyne; John R. Procter, North Shields; Arthur Albright, Birmingham; William Ball, Tottenham; William Rowntree, Scarborough; or Edwin O. Tregelles, Derwent Hill, Shotley Bridge.

"NEWCASTLE-ON-TYNE, 27th of Ninth Month, 1870."

ROBERT ALSOP TO E. O. T.

Stoke Newington, Tenth Month 7th, 1870.

MY DEAR FRIEND,—

I send thee a hasty line to say that the Meeting for Sufferings entered with great feeling into the concern, which, I believe, owes much to thee, and took action upon it, which includes the appointment of a committee. I have seen the minute in type, and I suppose that it will reach thee as soon as this will. . . .

Thy affectionate friend,

ROBERT ALSOP.

Tenth Month 15th.—The Meeting for Sufferings took up the subject most heartily, and a lively interest is awakened throughout the country on behalf of the sufferers.

Manchester, 28th.—The Alliance Meeting on the 26th was a time of much interest. Yesterday I attended Manchester meeting. Mary Waterhouse engaged in prayer for increase in purity, holiness and dedication. Early in the meeting I had craved on bended knees for a blessing on the peacemakers, and on those now gone from amongst us to minister help to the desolate; also for a blessing on those engaged in liberating the slaves around us in a condition worse than the bondage of Egypt, through drink.

Derwent Hill, Twelfth Month 4th.—This is the anniversary of our wedding day, twenty years ago. Goodness and mercy have followed, and are still following us. May the Lord continue to guide with His counsel, and afterwards receive us to glory.

29*th.*—Dear Elizabeth and I attended a meeting on the war victims' fund, at Newcastle, when William Jones and Robert Spence Watson addressed us.

First Month 12*th*, 1871.—My dear father-in-law, Abraham Fisher, died on the 8th very peacefully. My thoughts turned towards the company met at Neath this morning, with the words, " Gathered to the just of all generations."

31*st.*—Yesterday came the announcement of the capitulation of Paris, after an obstinate resistance of more than three months. No tongue can tell, or mind imagine correctly, the amazing misery which has been caused.

Third Month 28*th.*—This has been a memorable month in the world's history. The preliminaries of peace were arranged between Thiers and Bismarck, on behalf of France and Prussia. Great efforts were made immediately to feed the starving Parisians. Many of the War Victims Committee went to the places devastated by the armies, seeking to assist the sufferers. But a grievous check has been experienced by the outbreak of revolt in Paris, when the National Guards seized the cannon, and defied the regular troops, causing much bloodshed.

Falmouth, Fourth Month 26*th.*—A favoured day, when our dear Sarah Elizabeth entered into the covenant of marriage with Joseph Hingston Fox. Cousin Samuel Fox was engaged in prayer for a blessing. I said a few words, referring to the importance of the covenant, and of the other covenant, yet more important, to be sealed with the blood of Jesus. A cheerful party met at Penjerrick in the afternoon.

Liskeard, Fifth Month 5*th.*—We went to see our dear cousin, Eliza Allen, who is wasting away, but yet rejoicing in her lot. I reminded her of her address to me in 1843, before I went to the West Indies, setting forth the importance of being daily anointed with fresh oil. This led to a precious reply from her as to the guidance she had experienced all her life long, and how she confided and rejoiced in the promise, " Even to hoar hairs will I carry thee."

Derwent Hill, Tenth Month 29th.—We went to Mirfield on the 23rd to see dear A., who was seriously ill. I reminded him of the benefit of giving the helm to Christ, and then, however fiercely the storm might blow, we were safe for time and for eternity.

Twelfth Month 29th.—I went to Newcastle, and attended the week-day meeting, where I felt engaged to bow in prayer on behalf of the Prince of Wales, who is lying extremely ill of typhoid fever at Sandringham.

Third Month 17th, 1872.—The restoration to health of the Prince of Wales has caused much expression of satisfaction throughout the country. The reply of the Queen to an address from Friends was cordial and excellent.

During the past winter and spring the two elder brothers of Elizabeth Tregelles, Thomas and Jonathan Richardson, were removed by death: in the case of the latter quite suddenly, while the former lingered for several months as a feeble invalid; for many years his health had not been strong. She had also to part with other loved relatives.

Edwin and Elizabeth Tregelles attended the Yearly Meeting, which he says "was a season of much interest; the subjects of home and foreign missions, temperance, slavery, and war claimed attention."

Surbiton, Sixth Month 2nd.—Last week I was at the Esher morning meeting; and to-day we had a public meeting there, which was well attended, and a precious time.

Derwent Hill, Seventh Month 4th.—The quarterly meeting at Newcastle, and a nice public meeting the previous evening, were both times of spiritual refreshment to my soul from the ministry of others, as well as from the blessed visitations of the Holy Ghost.

The political horizon of England has been much cleared by the proceedings of the Convention at Geneva with reference to the Alabama Question, which seems likely to be settled peacefully and honourably.

Edwin O. Tregelles had a certificate for service in Northumberland, Cumberland, and Westmorland, which he accomplished during this summer. He and his wife also spent some time in Scotland, attending Aberdeen general meeting.

Allendale, Seventh Month 13th.—Met by Isaac Hall. We had a good meeting in the morning with Friends, and a public meeting in the evening.

Carlisle, 21st.—I attended Carlisle meeting in the morning, and in the afternoon went with Robert Doeg to Kirkbride, where the old unused meeting-house was crowded when we arrived, and was intensely warm. Robert Doeg and Richard Brockbank were both acceptably engaged in ministry and prayer. R. Brockbank drove us (with his nice young horse "Robert") to Brough, where a meeting, which was owned of the Lord, was held in the Hill Barn, a large place fitted up by R. Brockbank on his farm.

Aberdeen, Eighth Month 18th, First Day.—The morning meeting was good; but that in the evening was better. The house was nearly full, without any invitation having been given. Dear Isaac Sharp was well engaged in every meeting.

Inverness, 22nd.—We called on Mary Tillman and her sister. She told me of Albert Fox, and the interest they felt in his religious engagements at Inverness, where he preached at the Market cross. I walked with my precious Elizabeth to the riverside after tea, and much enjoyed the stroll in the lovely scene at eventide.

Oban, 27th.—Went by the *Clydesdale* steamer to Tobermory to see Henrietta A. Bird—a much enjoyed visit. Her sister, Isabella L. Bird, had recently sailed in the *Ben Nevis* for Australia.

30th.—We went off in a boat to take a book entitled, "The Slave Trade in Africa, 1872," for the Duke of Argyle, and left it on board his steam yacht.

After remaining a month at home, Edwin O. Tregelles, accompanied by his wife, recommenced his service in the northern counties, visiting friends and holding meetings at Carperby, Askrigg, Garsdale and Sedbergh, Maryport, Beckfoot, Scotby, Moorhouse, Allonby, and Kirklington.

Derwent Hill, Eleventh Month 25th.—Thankful for the many mercies from our Father in heaven, and for the kindness of His children.

First Month 5th, 1873.—This day month our dear cousin, Robert Charleton, was taken from works to rewards, after a few days' illness, aged sixty-three. Many besides ourselves feel that the loss of his services in the Church is great. Deep was the impression made on myself and on the meeting when Robert Charleton spoke on the Lancashire quarterly meeting committee, quoting the lines:—

> "Oh, let me kiss Thy sacred feet,
>   And bathe and wash them with my tears;
> The story of Thy love repeat
>   In every drooping sinner's ears;
> That all may hear the quickening sound,
> Since I, e'en I, have mercy found!"

Robert Charleton was a teaching example of humility, combined with active benevolence.

On First Month 3rd we had the pleasant company of Joel and Hannah Bean, of Iowa, who attended our meeting. J. Bean commented on the words of Jesus: "I am the Vine:

ye are the branches." We greatly prize the visits of such messengers.

Second Month 2nd, First Day.—I rode to meeting this morning, and walked home in deep snow, which fell while we were there. I can look back with thankfulness to the blessed feelings I enjoyed while recently indisposed, especially when the words came with power, "Thine iniquity is taken away, and thy sin purged;" and then the sense that it was because of the cleansing efficacy derived from Christ, the great atoning Sacrifice.

Third Month 2nd.—I was troubled in meeting with business thoughts, and helped to obtain relief by the words of our Lord: "Take these things hence; make not My Father's house a house of merchandize."

Third Month 9th.—Hannah Pumphrey was engaged in prayer in the meeting this morning, beginning with the last lines composed by Jane Crewdson:—

> "O Saviour, I have nought to plead
> In earth beneath, or heaven above,
> But just my own exceeding need,
> And Thy exceeding love."

Edwin and Elizabeth Tregelles attended the Yearly Meeting of 1873, which was one of much interest. Joel and Hannah Bean, Mary H. Rogers, Robert Walter Douglas and Frederick Hansen were present from America.

Derwent Hill, Sixth Month 7th.—I took tea at Shotley Park with Neal Dow and Dr. F. R. Lees, preparatory to our Alliance meeting at the Shotley Town Hall, which was a great success, crowded and enthusiastic.

30th.—The day before yesterday dear Elizabeth and I drove, by way of Edmund-byers and Stanhope, to Nenthead, where William Dalton had made arrangements for a public meeting. It was held on First-day morning in the new school-house, a capital building erected by the London Company, who have lead mines there. The meeting was well attended, and proved a good time. A meeting at Alston in the evening was also well attended. We left Nenthead at nine this morning, and arrived here about seven o'clock. We had much satisfaction in distributing tracts freely in Wear Dale on our return home.

Seventh Month 9th.—Henry Richard carried his motion in the House of Commons approving of arbitration instead of war, ninety-eight in favour and eighty-eight opposed to the measure.

21st.—R. W. Douglas came to us, and went to a public meeting, which was a highly favoured time. He spoke on the words, "As cold waters to a thirsty soul, so is good news from a far country."

30th.—My dear sister-in-law, Dorothy Tregelles, died on the 28th. For many years our love for each other has been strong and true. She has been a dear sister, inexpressibly kind to me. I like to think of the lasting joy of her reunion with many loved ones gone before to glory; and of the words of our dear brother Samuel, when he was near his end, "Dorothy, my darling, I shall not be with thee when thou art passing over Jordan; but the eternal God will be Thy refuge, and underneath will be the everlasting arms."

In the Tenth Month Edwin O. Tregelles writes of visiting Banbury and attending meetings at Sibford, Witney, Henley, and Reading, Adderbury and Hook Norton. In some of these he had the company of Joseph Jesper, Josiah Merrick, Samuel A. Maw, and Thomas Emmott, his colleagues in the work of the Yearly Meeting's committee for visiting the quarterly meetings.

Edwin O. Tregelles, in the next month, was again in the south, having gone to London to attend the Conference on the state of the Society of Friends.

Derwent Hill, Eleventh Month 11th.—Before I left home I was very low in the prospect; but in a season of retirement I was enabled to lay hold on the promise to Abraham: " I am thy shield and thy exceeding great reward."

I have a hope that the results of that gathering will be blessed, not by widening the pathway for the followers of Christ, not by hedging up the way, or doing works of penance, but in a full surrender of our all to Him, who has a right to our powers and possessions. I kept silence until near the close, when I expressed my belief that a great blessing would rest on the conference, if all who were assembled would that day give their hearts to God, and say with the psalmist, " O Lord, truly I am Thy servant; I am Thy servant, and the son of Thine handmaid; Thou hast loosed my bonds." Then we should feel that we are not our own, that we are bought with a price, and bound to glorify God with our bodies and our spirits, which are His. The conclusion of the meeting, when Isaac Brown was engaged in thanksgiving and prayer, was a very solemn time, worth going to London for.

Twelfth Month 10th.—At the close of the monthly meeting at Newcastle I ventured to speak about temperance, the need that there is for our Society to be more earnest in the matter. The response was cheering and general. Many spoke, and all in favour of some action in the matter. A committee was named. I crave that in all such movements we may act in the Divine fear, and then we shall have the power of God on our side.

23*rd.*—When at the new cottages I am now building, "Templar Terrace," I was standing by a wall on which the men were engaged, when a thick piece of iron fell from a height, and struck the ground heavily by my side. If I had been nine inches nearer the wall it might have struck my head. This is the second escape of the kind I have had.

First Month 15th, 1874.—There was a conference on mission work at the quarterly meeting. This made way for me to bring forward the proposition on temperance, which, with a little faint opposition, was well received, and a committee appointed to prepare a draft of a proposition for our next Yearly Meeting.

Third Month 1st.—Last Third-day evening, Second Month 24th, our much-loved sister Rachel exchanged her bed of languishing for an inheritance incorruptible and that fadeth not away. Just before her death she uttered the name of her precious twin brother Henry three times, as though the vista of the celestial glory was breaking on her sight; thus in her dying moments revealing a sacred, life-long affection for this much-loved brother, who died in 1821.

For our dear sister Lydia we keenly feel. We had supposed that she was the feeble one, needing the kind nursing of her sister, who has been unremitting in her tender care of her for more than seven years of weakness; but now dear Rachel is taken and she is left.

Sixth Month 16th.—This day month dear Elizabeth and I left home for London. We esteem it a great privilege to have been able to attend and enjoy the Yearly Meeting. The burden on my spirit throughout much of the time was the temperance question, for it fell to my lot to have to say a little in support of the Durham proposition; and the fear of saying too much led me to fall short in explaining, as I desired, the measure which is so deeply important. The subject was well taken up by the meeting, a petition agreed on for Parliament, and an appeal to our members. The Yearly Meeting's epistle also contains a paragraph on this deeply important subject.

On First-day we were at Stoke Newington meeting, which was much crowded. I felt engaged to speak on the words, "We have found Him, of whom Moses in the law and the prophets did write, Jesus of Nazareth." We have found; not we expect to find, or hope to find, but we have found. Well for us if we can say this. It was a good meeting. Hannah Whitall Smith was there, also the Duchess of Sutherland, and Thos. B. Smithies.

We dined at Stafford Allen's with a very interesting company. Amongst the party who met on the lawn under sheltering trees were Theophilus Waldemier, of Beyrout; Sarah Street and Elizabeth Valentine, from America; Charles Thompson, and many others.

On reaching home we found our little dog Mora had died. She has had a happy ten years of life, beloved by all who knew her—so gentle, intelligent, and highly affectionate. She lies under the weeping ash near the arbour, by the side of her former happy playfellow, Piff, and poor Carlo.

Seventh Month 15th.—We went to the quarterly meeting of ministers and elders at Newcastle. In the public meeting in the evening Richard Ball Rutter, soon after we collected, quoted the hymn, "Jesus of Nazareth passeth by," and sat down. Elizabeth L. Comstock spoke earnestly on the same words; how He not only healed the blind man, but restored the leper, quelled the storm on the lake, and was able now to help us, and willing also.

Eighth Month 9th, First Day.—We had a large meeting this morning. William C. Westlake offered fervent prayer for the assembled company, for other companies of worshippers after our manner, and for all worshippers believing in Christ; also for the Lord's blessing on the recent First-day School Conference at Darlington. After this I spoke of one of the early copies of the English Bible calling our Lord Jesus "the Healing One," desiring that the striken ones might prove Him to be the Healing One. Then W. C. Westlake spoke on the passage in the Revelation, how "some would call on the mountains to hide them from the wrath of the Lamb, from Him who had followed them with looks of love, but now turned into wrath, although He had offered to be the Healing One."

16*th*.—Deborah Thomas and Mary Haines had a meeting with us. D. Thomas spoke on the text, "Wait on the Lord; be of good courage, and He shall strengthen thine heart; wait, I say, on the Lord."

Hull, Ninth Month 13*th*.—I left home for Ackworth on the 4th, and met there the Yearly Meeting's committee; present, Stafford Allen, William Ball, J. B. Braithwaite, James Clark, Samuel Elliott, Thomas Hodgkin, and Joseph Jesper.

The evening reading with the children was a precious season. After William Ball had spoken at some length, I referred to Moses floating on the Nile, watched by his elder sister, who was not then aware of the importance of her duties in caring for one who was to be king in Jeshurun.

On the 8th we met the Ackworth teachers, and afterwards the superintendent and students of the Flounder's Institute, amongst whom was a youth from Madagascar, Rasoamiaramanana by name.

In the evening the party from the Flounders came to the school, also Friends from Pontefract, and we had a social gathering of 117, a deeply interesting and instructive time. J. P. Braithwaite spoke on the authority of Holy Scripture, and the evidences of revealed religion in opposition to science falsely so called, illustrated by allusion to the mechanism of a watch. I rejoiced that the students were there to hear the address. Very much was said, and well said. William Ball asked me to speak. I said that I felt I must practise self-denial; but I quoted the stanza :—

> "My God, Thy service well demands
> The remnant of my days;
> Why was this feeble breath renewed,
> But to renew Thy praise?"

At a good social gathering at Wakefield J. B. Braithwaite

spoke on the importance of giving our energies to our special duties; and though we may feel pleasure at the success of Christian effort among other professors, yet, as a Church, we have our own line of service. The recorded experience of Thomas Shillitoe, William Allen, Stephen Grellet and William Forster showed how way was made for the Lord's servants.

Woodhouse, Ninth Month 20th.—Went with Joseph Jesper to Woodhouse meeting, a small but interesting gathering, to whom the gospel message flowed freely. At the close of the meeting Dr. Le Tall, by whose side I sat, said to me, "Why cannot this gospel message be made known to those outside our borders?" "By all means," I replied; "we should like multitudes to hear the message." So the neighbours were invited to an afternoon meeting. The place was full on our arrival; and a blessed time it was. At Woodhouse Daniel Wheeler first attended a Friends' meeting. He then came in his regimentals. His sister Barbara lived there.

Sheffield, Ninth Month 22nd.—At a social meeting on the school premises James H. Barber gave us a brief, interesting outline of the origin of First-day Schools. A Friend was walking one day on the sands at Scarborough with Sarah Wheeler, when she said she would willingly give £5 to promote a First-day School at Sheffield. This was the nucleus; many others aided in the work.

York, Ninth Month 28th.—We attended a social gathering in the meeting-house, at which my cousin, Alfred Lloyd Fox, was present. It was a season of renewed favour. At the close I left, and reached home at 7 a.m. next morning, with a heart full of thanksgiving for the undeserved and multiplied mercies.

Neath, Tenth Month 18th.—After paying a very enjoyable visit to our cousins, Elizabeth and Sarah Backhouse at Holgate York, Elizabeth and I reached The Craig, Neath. Having a minute from my monthly meeting for any service that opened on the journey, I was glad to appoint a public meeting here. I visited cousin Christiana A. Price at Glenvelyn. I saw her alone, and a deeply interesting time it was. Before we separated, praise and prayer were offered to the Father of mercies. Cousin C. A. Price addressed me in cheering language, animating my heart for dedication.

Plymouth, Tenth Month 21st.—We were at the Fourth-day morning meeting. "Sweet is the sleep of those who rest in Jesus," was the language that arose in my heart, and to which I soon gave utterance, followed by dear cousin Rachel C. Fox and by Helen Balkwill in prayer.

Penzance, Tenth Month 26th.—Our quarters here are at Mount's Bay House, by the sea, which is beating heavily against the sea-wall, and throwing up showers of spray. Lawrence Candler and Margaret Trembath accompanied us to Marazion, where we had a public meeting in the Primitive Methodist Chapel.

27th.—We went to Mousehole for a meeting in the Wesleyan Chapel, which was well owned, I believe, of the Lord. Our ride there was lovely. We could see the line of coast from the Lizard. Many vessels were passing, and fishing-boats going out.

CHAPTER XXIV.

SHOTLEY BRIDGE.

Snow-storm, Five Trains blocked—Isaac Sharp goes to Norway, Denmark, and Minden—Death of Dr. Tregelles—Yearly Meeting—Alteration of Queries—Care of Religious Instruction of Youth—Constitution of Meetings of Ministers and Elders—Family Gathering at Surbiton—Ira D. Sankey—At York visits Elizabeth and Sarah Backhouse—Allen Jay—Sedbergh General Meeting—Thomas Handley— Commences First-day Afternoon Cottage Meetings at Templar Terrace—Women Friends' Address to the Queen on Temperance—Kinsey and Caroline E. Talbot hold large Gospel and Temperance Meetings each Night in the Derwent Valley—Yearly Meeting—Rufus P. King, Edward Scull, and Dr. Richard H. Thomas, jun., at Surbiton—Remarkable Dream—Holds Meetings amongst the Northumbrian Colliers—Friends' Temperance Conference at Leeds—Rufus P. King—At Temperance Conference, London, read Paper, "Temperance the Ally of Christianity"—Death of Jane Fisher—Strike amongst his Colliers—Friends' Temperance Union—John Bright on Temperance—Isaac Sharp, Theodore Harris and Langley Kitching depart for South Africa.

DERWENT HILL, Shotley Bridge, First Month 3rd, 1875.—As we heard the last stroke of the clock, telling of the past year being closed, the bells of Shotley were dimly heard through the storm which raged, and which rendered nearly inaudible the "buzzer" of the Consett Iron Works, telling of the birth of another year. The gale from the south-east was terrific—the thermometer 18°. The storm continued through New Year's Day, so as to keep us all close at home. It increased and caused deep drifts of snow.

On retiring to rest that night we heard a strange noise

like some one calling earnestly for help, and soon after the short, powerful whistle of a locomotive. This call was responded to by another engine; apparently they were near each other, and seemed asking earnestly for help. We concluded they wanted aid to clear a snow-drift, but we were powerless to assist. I had been unwell all day, and even if I were well it is doubtful whether I could have reached the spot. Again next morning we heard the same earnest calls and responses, and we learnt that two trains had stuck in a snowdrift in a deep cutting. The passengers had gathered into the first and second class carriages to pass the night, and proceeded to Newcastle next morning. Five trains were thus stuck fast between Newcastle and Consett.

Fourth Month 25th.—A conference was held at the close of the quarterly meeting at Darlington last Fifth-day, when Isaac Sharp was liberated for service in Norway, Denmark and Minden, with prayer and much cordial expression of encouragement. In the same conference a testimony for John Dodshon was read. It was a very interesting sketch of a good man's life.

Fifth Month 2nd.—Our niece, Anna R. Tregelles, informs us that her brother, Dr. S. Prideaux Tregelles, sank to rest on the 24th of Fourth Month, after several days of unconsciousness following many weeks of suffering, and ten years of feebleness from paralysis. And now we may well believe that "he rests before God with the angels in light," in companionship with his Lord, whose presence he longed to behold.

Seventh Month 11th.—Since the last date Elizabeth and I have been to the Yearly Meeting, which was the most agreeable I have ever attended. Such a blessed, heavenly feeling prevalent from sitting to sitting. Allen Jay, of North Carolina, was with us acceptably. Caroline Talbot and Deborah Thomas, from America, visited our meeting. The alterations of the Queries occupied much time, and were passed to my comfort. The other subjects of the Yearly Meeting were peculiarly important and interesting. Increased care in the education of our younger members in religious matters. The report from the committee appointed in 1873 for visiting the counties. Arrangements for holding general meetings, also the question of the constitution of the meeting of ministers and elders.

I was desirous of bringing before the meeting the condition of the poor slaves in various parts of the world, but a very brief portion of time was allowed—too brief to do justice to a matter of such serious moment.

After the Yearly Meeting we went to Surbiton, joining there our sister Lydia, and Nathaniel and Fanny. It felt to me a final family gathering.

On Second-day we went to T. H. B.'s to tea, where were also Ann Gardner and E. Sarah Chalk, Ira D. Sankey and wife, and other visitors. We had tea in the garden. Afterwards we met in the drawing-room and I. D. Sankey sang the hymns, "The ninety and nine" and "Oh, think of the home over there," which seemed to solemnise us and bring us to the place of true prayer. I. D. Sankey followed me in a vocal prayer, after which Ann Gardner and E. S. Chalk ministered to us. Our very precious gathering was finished by a prayer from T. H. B., in which he quoted, "What is a man profited if he shall gain the whole world and lose his own soul?"

At York we had a kind reception from our cousins Elizabeth and Sarah Backhouse. Soon after we were gathered in the meeting I knelt in prayer, "Hallowed be Thy name; Thy kingdom come," and then spoke from the words, "Ye must be born again."

Eighth Month 11th.—We had Allen Jay's company and that of Helen Balkwill at the monthly meeting at Sunderland. It was a favoured time. A. Jay spoke of the impotent man at Bethesda's pool—his unquestioning faith. We had a conference with women Friends to consider the course to be taken in giving instruction in the sound principles of Friends to our children when young.

Dear Elizabeth and I were liberated to attend the general meeting at Sedbergh, and to hold other meetings where drawn.

Sedbergh, Ninth Month 3rd.—The general meeting was small. Isaac Brown of Kendal, Isaac Brown of Leeds, Joseph Jesper, George Satterthwaite, and Hudson Scott were present. In the evening meeting I was cheered by the dedication of dear Elizabeth, who reminded us that two hundred years had passed since that house was built, and queried, Where shall we all be ere another two hundred years have passed? This had a very solemnising effect.

On the 7th we went to Narthwaite. Dear old Thomas Handley ministered to us; both he and I are much changed since we met there thirty-five years ago.

Ambleside, 12th.—I was alone at Colthouse meeting, and spoke on "cross-bearing disciples of a crucified Lord."

16th.—We went to Kendal, and were met by Charles Lloyd Braithwaite. Kinsey and Caroline E. Talbot were at the quarterly meeting.

18th.—We left Kendal for Whinfell Hall, where we had a hearty welcome from Wilson and Elizabeth Robinson and their children.

21st.—On First-day I was at Pardshaw meeting, walking there and back, with John Wilson Robinson, in our shirt sleeves, because it was a very hot day. We saw lightning in the evening, and found there had been a fearful storm at Manchester and Liverpool. A church was struck at Birkenhead, and two persons killed.

At Beckfoot we had a good meeting, and experienced much kindness from Mary Bigland. I walked with dear Elizabeth on the sands, and after an early dinner was driven by one of M. Bigland's daughters to Allonby, where we had quarters with Ann Fearon. We met Caroline E. Talbot and others at Sarah B. Satterthwaite's. A meeting in the

Public Room was crowded, and a capital time it was. I have rarely attended such a meeting.

Derwent Hill, Tenth Month 30th.—There was a large gathering at our meeting-house, when the gospel was preached and earnest prayer offered on our behalf by our visitors, Jane Gurney Pease, Isaac Sharp, Lucy E. Mounsey, Thomas Willis and E. Robson.

Eleventh Month 7th.—Our afternoon meetings are discontinued to-day for four months, because of the smallness of our numbers. I believed it my duty to go at 3 p.m. to No. 1, Templar Terrace, where, in James Armstrong's house, I met about thirty of our colliery people, to whom I read John i., also some tracts and the hymns, "Jesus of Nazareth passeth by" and "Safe in the arms of Jesus." I feel thankful for the blessing apparent on the occasion.

14th.—The monthly meeting at Sunderland last week was very interesting. In the conference with women Friends a proposal was brought forward to present an address on Temperance to our Queen from women Friends of North Durham, which was cordially united with. At the conclusion of this conference I knelt in prayer, pleading for the removal of intemperance from our land, and asking the Lord to bless our beloved Queen, that the glitter of royalty may not dim her vision, or hinder her from laying aside every weight, and running with patience the race set before her, looking unto Jesus, and that her family may be saved with an everlasting salvation.

21*st.*—Though our meeting was small this morning, it was one of much comfort. Soon after we gathered I felt engaged to thank the Lord for the mercies of the past week and the unnumbered mercies of our lives. I went to No. 3, Templar Terrace this afternoon, and met an interesting company there, to my comfort. May it prove a blessing to some present.

First Month 9th, 1876.—A week filled with mercy and goodness has passed; Kinsey and Caroline E. Talbot being with us. The meeting for worship in the Town Hall, Shotley Bridge, was a blessed season. Caroline E. Talbot was much favoured, and the message went home to the hearts of many amongst the 700 who were present. At the close the people begged earnestly for another meeting. Next day the gospel was again preached with simplicity and power at the Templar Hall, Medomsley, we may trust to the converting of many hearts.

On the 4th there was a crowded, overflowing meeting at Ebchester Wesleyan Chapel. On the 5th the temperance meeting in the Town Hall at Shotley Bridge was crowded and very impressive; sixty-three signed the pledge. C. E. Talbot seems to look back with comfort to her visit to this valley, and said that her stay under this roof "had been as a little heaven on earth" to her. On leaving she said to dear Elizabeth, "The Lord bless thee; I know He will."

12th.—I was encouraged to apply to our monthly meeting for a minute for holding public meetings in Northumberland, which was granted me.

Just at this time Elizabeth E. Tregelles had a slight attack of paralysis. Meekly and sweetly she bore the intimation of the doctor as to the nature of the attack, and she regarded it as a decided warning of the uncertainty of life.

Fourth Month 16th.—We had a blessed meeting. The first time dear Elizabeth had been present for thirteen weeks. She knelt in thanksgiving and prayer, giving praise for the mercy shown her.

Sixth Month 10th.—Various engagements have hindered any notes being made for many weeks, during which we attended the Yearly Meeting. It was to me a season of peculiar interest. Some important changes of our constitution were arranged. We may hope that good will result. The subject of slavery claimed much attention, consequent on a proposition from Western Quarterly Meeting, and that resulting from a few words in the Epistle of 1875; so the day of small things must not be despised.

For the first First-day in the Yearly Meeting we went to Surbiton, and much enjoyed our visit to dear H. and S. E. Here we met Rufus P. King and Edward Scull, also Dr. Richard Henry Thomas, who were at the evening meeting at Kingston.

The next First-day we spent at Stoke Newington, dining with Christine Alsop, who kindly interested herself about the address to our Queen on temperance.

Derwent Hill, 14*th*.—I woke this morning after a delightful dream, when I seemed pleasantly occupied with Rufus King and Edward Scull in arranging for meetings; before I awoke I was repeating the hymn,—

> " Plenteous grace with Thee is found,
> Grace to pardon all my sin;
> Let the healing streams abound,
> Make and keep me pure within."

When I was walking to the colliery two days ago, and communing on heavenly things, I had such a clear view of Jesus as my Sin-bearer; the Lord having laid on Him the iniquity of us all. "Shall we continue in sin, that grace may abound?" By no means. I desire ever to remember the time and place. It was just as I turned the corner of Watling Street and Medomsley Road.

Eleventh Month 5*th*.—For many months I have been much hindered from making any entry in this journal.

In the Eighth Month I was engaged in holding meetings for worship amongst the collieries of Northumberland. These engagements were, I believe, blessed to my own soul, and I trust to the souls of others.

The corner stones of a Temperance Hall at Shotley Bridge

were laid by Arthur Pease, Thomas Carrick, and George Charlton. All pleaded with true eloquence for the liberation from the bondage of drink of the enthralled sons and daughters of Britain. Lord, hasten the day!

Leeds, 12*th*.—The Temperance Conference commenced by a devotional meeting. On First-day we had two good meetings for worship. Samuel Bowly engaged in prayer in the morning. In the evening I alluded to the call of Moses, "I have seen, I have seen the affliction of My people in Egypt, and I have come down to deliver them." During the three sittings of the conference great harmony and earnestness prevailed. A committee of sixty Friends of the northern counties was nominated to assist in promoting Temperance. A minute was passed encouraging support of the Irish Sunday Closing Bill, another to check the sale of liquors by grocers, another to promote the local option principles in checking the liquor traffic.

Twelfth Month 3*rd*.—The Turkish question is engrossing many minds now that the Conference of Plenipotentiaries is about to meet at Constantinople.

This morning, in our little meeting I felt constrained to pray that the hearts of the councillors at the Conference may be so influenced by the Prince of Peace, that strife may be averted by Him who is God over all, blessed for ever, and that the Lord in His mercy may repair the woes of Bulgaria caused by ruthless invaders.

10*th*.—Very beautiful weather. The barometer has been lower than for twenty-four years. Fearful storms have occurred, causing great loss of ships and life.

31*st*.—At our meeting this morning dear Elizabeth called our attention to the way in which we had been helped in many trials "to keep hold of the Rock which never moves," and desired "that remembrance of past mercies may encourage us to hope for all our future."

First Month 22*nd*, 1877.—Rufus P. King came to an evening meeting here. The silence was broken by his companion,

James Terrell, in prayer, followed soon by R. P. King on his knees, saying, "We would linger yet a little longer near Thy mercy-seat." After an earnest prayer he spoke in a way that must have impressed most hearts.

Surbiton, Second Month 18th.—I came here in order to attend the Temperance Conference in London. I met Samuel and Louisa Bowly at the Institute, and read to them the paper, "Temperance the Ally of Christianity" I had prepared, which they approved. The Conference showed a great advance in the minds of Friends on the important subject of Temperance.

I attended the week-day meeting at Kingston—a good season according to my feelings. I felt impressed with the importance of abiding in Christ, asking what we desire, and having our prayers granted.

At Exeter Hall in the evening—a large and important meeting on Moderate Drinking; excellent speeches from Dr. B. W. Richardson, Canon Farrar, and Edward Baines.

Derwent Hill, Third Month 25th.—Much interested in reading in the report of the Meeting for Sufferings, William Jones' letter respecting his visit to Bulgaria. Such pacific work is a great contrast to war.

Fourth Month 8th.—Another blessed and refreshing Sabbath, in which my soul has been fed and refreshed, of which it seemed to be in great need from perplexities with the colliers. I was engaged this morning to quote the text, "That we might have a strong consolation, who have fled for refuge to lay hold on the hope set before us, which hope we have as an anchor of the soul, both sure and steadfast, and which entereth into that within the veil; whither the forerunner is for us entered." I have remembered the lines :—

> "From every stormy wind that blows,
> From every swelling tide of woes,
> There is a calm, a sure retreat;
> 'Tis found beneath the mercy seat!"

16*th*.—A note came from dear Isaac Sharp informing us that the monthly meeting of Darlington had liberated him for a visit to Cape Town, South Africa, Madagascar, Australia, New Zealand, Tasmania, California, and other parts of America.

29*th*.—At the quarterly meeting at Darlington Dougan Clark spoke effectively on Jesus being the daysman, able to lay hold of God and man, and who addresses the Father in prayer, saying, "I will that they also whom Thou hast given Me be with Me where I am." At the conference after the meeting for worship Isaac Sharp was cordially liberated for his extensive service.

On our return home we found a telegram announcing that my dear mother, Jane Fisher, had died. She passed quietly to her eternal and glorious home.

Russia has declared war against Turkey. Yesterday we were comforted in learning that our Government has decided to be neutral, being friendly with both powers.

Fifth Month 13*th*.—The Irish Sunday Closing Bill has passed the select committee of the House of Commons, at which we are rejoiced.

I have been much perplexed by my colliers striking for higher wages, and have found it needful to move very circumspectly. I have sought to cast my cares altogether on the Lord, and can say, "As for God, His way is perfect . . . He is a buckler to all those who trust in Him."

London, 21*st*.—I attended the Temperance Conference, when it was agreed to blend the four Conferences of Friends in one, entitled, "Friends' Temperance Union."

Derwent Hill, Sixth Month 5*th*.—Each meeting during the Yearly Meeting proved to me a season of blessing, whether it were on Society matters, in committees, or the meetings for worship in Peel, Westminster, Kingston, or Stoke Newington.

Eighth Month 5*th*.—We had a meeting in the Primitive

Methodist Chapel at Cullercoats, largely attended. A very full message of glad tidings was extended. A sweet prayer from Ransome Wallis concluded the meeting.

6th.—A meeting at Shankhouse in the Wesleyan Chapel thinly attended. Thomas Pumphrey also engaged in ministry and prayer.

7th.—A meeting was held at Seaton-Delavel. Richard B. Rutter accompanied John R. Procter and me. It was to my comfort, and I hope to the edification of several present.

Darlington, Tenth Month 17th.—At the last sitting of the quarterly meeting dear Isaac Sharp bid us affectionately farewell. On parting I handed him a packet, not to be opened until he reaches 48° N. latitude. It contains a reference to some of the many providences that were shown me in my travels in the West Indies, which may tend to cheer his heart. I now feel as though I have parted for ever, as to this life, with a dear friend by whom I have regularly sat for thirty years in the meetings we have attended together. In the meeting for worship dear Elizabeth quoted the words of our Lord, "Watch ye therefore, for ye know not when the master of the house cometh; at even, or at midnight, or at the cock-crowing, or in the morning; lest coming suddenly, He find you sleeping. And what I say unto you, I say unto all, Watch." The few words were blessed to the meeting.

Derwent Hill, Eleventh Month 14th.—I attended the anniversary of the United Kingdom Alliance at Manchester. It was very enthusiastic. Every one seemed cheered by the progress of Temperance principles during the year.

On my way through Leeds I called on Langley Kitching, who was busy preparing to leave for London to join Isaac Sharp and Theodore Harris. They embarked at Dartmouth on the 2nd in the *Dunrobin Castle* steamer for the Cape of Good Hope.

A few days before these dear Friends sailed I sent them a copy of the hymn extracted from the "Book of Praise."

"Speed Thy servants, Saviour, speed them!
 Thou art Lord of winds and waves:
They were bound, but Thou hast freed them;
 Now they go to free the slaves:
  Be Thou with them!
 'Tis Thine arm alone that saves.

* * * * *

Speed them through the mighty ocean
 In the dark and stormy day,
When the waves in wild commotion
 Fill all others with dismay:
  Be Thou with them!
 Drive their terrors far away.

When they reach the land of strangers,
 And the prospect dark appears,
Nothing seen but toils and dangers,
 Nothing felt but doubts and fears,
  Be Thou with them!
 Hear their sighs and count their tears.

* * * * *

In the midst of opposition,
 Let them trust, O Lord, in Thee:
When success attends their mission,
 Let Thy servants humbler be:
  Never leave them,
 Till Thy face in heaven they see!

There to reap in joy for ever
 Fruit that grows from seed here sown;
There to be with Him who never
 Ceases to preserve His own,
  And with triumph
 Sing a Saviour's grace alone!

THOMAS KELLY.

CHAPTER XXV.

SHOTLEY BRIDGE.

Origin of E. O. Tregelles' Zeal for Temperance—Letter to *Alliance News* on Local Option—Kars taken by Russians—Dr. Temple, Bishop of Exeter—Business Trials—William Hoyle—Sudden Death of his Wife—Leaves Derwent Hill—Resides at Falmouth and Banbury—Letter of Isaac Sharp from Kuruman—Cornish Sunday Closing Bill.

EDWIN O. TREGELLES first became alive to the evils of the drinking customs of the country when a young man in Ireland. He afterwards passed through a time of suffering in the change of his business prospects, rather than in any way promote the drink traffic. In later life he became increasingly earnest to encourage others, as well as to work himself, in the Temperance reformation. He joined nine different organizations, including the Good Templars and a Ministers' Association, and entered heartily into the movement for the legal suppression of the traffic by means of local option.

TO THE EDITOR OF THE *ALLIANCE NEWS*.

Shotley Bridge, Eleventh Month 9th, 1877.

DEAR FRIEND,—

The present season is rife with political addresses. It is interesting to mark the utterances of the leaders of public thought when they touch on great social and economic questions, especially the all-absorbing Drink question. It is not a new subject, and some persons who feel constrained to say something respecting it, seem appalled by its magnitude, and the interested opposition to anything having the semblance of compulsory legislation; hence the importance that the legislation should be permissive, and not compulsory.

When gas lighting became popular in Great Britain, Ireland was long debarred from the advantage, because of the expense of procuring local Acts for each town; but relief was granted by an Act passed, 9th George IV., empowering ratepayers, by a majority in any town in Ireland, to adopt the Act, and levy rates to cover the expense of constructing the works and supplying gaslight. This was not compulsion, not oppression, but a boon, and a happy condition of "local option." Where lies the difference between a permissive or empowering Gas Act for Ireland, and a permissive or empowering Liquor Act for the British Isles? There is this difference: the one involved the outlay of an expenditure year by year, proving very beneficial to the public; in the other case leading to a saving in the annual expenditure, besides promoting the elevation, order, and happiness of the people.

The passing of that Lighting Act for Ireland was a kind, judicious, beneficial, and appreciated measure. It did not infringe on liberty; each town was free to choose, without compulsion, between darkness and light. The adoption was very gradual; one town after another elected to profit by the Act.

Here we have the epitome of the Permissive Bill, which is not compulsory; the ratepayers are free to choose between darkness and light, between bondage with poverty, and freedom with prosperity. . . .

Does any one doubt that England is sorely distressed by the losses occasioned by drink? Canon Wilberforce, in his admirable address in the Sheldonian Hall, Oxford, said,

"England was in jeopardy, and no country can receive the blessing that gained revenues from the drink traffic, and forced opium on China, and colonized with the Bible in one hand and the brandy bottle in the other!

I believe all this is true, and that we cannot break any of the laws of God without suffering the consequences.

Thy sincere friend,
E. O. TREGELLES.

Derwent Hill, Eleventh Month 25*th*.—Kars was taken from the Turks by assault of the Russians on the 18th. Easily written of, but full of woe to the sufferers.

> "Oh, when will those glad tidings
> Of mercy, love, and peace,
> Cause man to spare his brother,
> And deadly feuds to cease?"

This morning, at meeting, Elizabeth spoke of the visit of Nicodemus to our Lord by night, listening to His counsel, but ashamed to confess full belief, and yet bringing spices to anoint the body that had been "lifted up," of which He had spoken to Nicodemus, and then she quoted a stanza:—

> "Ashamed of Jesus? just as soon,
> Let midnight be ashamed of noon;
> 'Tis midnight with my soul till He,
> Bright morning star, bids darkness flee."

29*th*.—I have been reading an extract from a letter describing an address of Dr. Temple, Bishop of Exeter, to the Free School, Plymouth; nothing could be more earnest. He never says what he does not feel, and he speaks often of the doubts he has had, and as if these were all removed by giving himself to the Lord; and he says others will find their difficulties removed in the same way. His discourse was on "the consistency of the Christian life." He told his crowded audience, who call themselves Christians, that if they would be real, those who belong to Christ must depart from iniquity. And if they did not show this sign by their lives, they certainly could not belong to Him.

Twelfth Month 23rd.—When our friend, Barnabas C. Hobbs, in crossing from America, was near Liverpool, his steamer cut another vessel in two, which sank in two minutes. The crew was saved with difficulty in the dark. The cry of a cat was heard in the distance, and on seeking, it was found that a cat was perched on the head of a poor fellow who was floating on the water, but insensible. The man was rescued and restored to animation.

During the past week I have had a sore mental conflict connected with a business arrangement. In my distress I bowed on my knees in my office before the Lord, and prayed that He would keep me safe from yielding to temptation. To my comfort this prayer was answered, and since then I seem to have been kept by the power of God, relying on the promise, "Be careful for nothing; but in everything by prayer and supplication, with thanksgiving, let your requests be made known unto God; and the peace of God which passeth all understanding shall keep your hearts and minds through Christ Jesus."

First Month 13th, 1878.—An armistice between the Turks and Russians has been proposed by the Turks, which we hope may lead to an early peace after fearful conflict and misery.

27th.—William Hoyle of Tollington came to us last week. A few met him at Shotley Park to discuss the merits of the Permissive Bill; the consequences of the profuse waste of wealth by the drinking customs of Great Britain; and the part which these customs have in the deep and wide-spread distress now existing.

The Russians have been advancing towards Constantinople, after taking possession of Adrianople, and the balance of this country seems vibrating oftener than the day between peace and war.

Second Month 24th.—The fears regarding a war in the

East have very much passed away, and arrangements are making for a Conference at Baden-Baden.

On the 20th Jonathan Priestman and I went to Bishop Auckland to attend the marriage of Edward Backhouse Mounsey to Rachel A. Fryer, of Smelt House, where a large and pleasant company assembled; an occasion I much enjoyed. It seemed right for me to minister, " As ye have therefore received Christ Jesus the Lord, so walk ye in Him."

This is the last entry in Edwin O. Tregelles' journal previous to the removal of his much-loved wife.

At the quarterly meeting at Darlington Elizabeth Tregelles quoted the words, "Work while it is day; the night cometh when no man can work." The address, though short, made a deep impression, and a dear intimate friend says that "she seemed ripening for heaven."

On the night of Third Month 2nd, 1878, she retired to rest, apparently in usual health, and at half-past twelve conversed with her husband, who, on awaking an hour after, found her by his side, speechless and insensible. She continued in this state for twelve hours, when her spirit passed away to be for ever with her Lord whom from childhood she had loved.

The sudden death of his wife was a sore trial to Edwin O. Tregelles, and was followed by a severe illness. But there was still work to do for his Master, and he was restored to health, but never recovered his former vigour.

The home at Derwent Hill, which he had so much

enjoyed, was given up, mainly on account of the feeble state of his health. From this time he resided at Falmouth with his sister Lydia Tregelles, and at Wood Green, Banbury, the home of his eldest daughter.

From Isaac Sharp.

Kuruman, South Africa.
Fifth Month 16th, 1878.

My beloved Friend,—

Many words need not be penned to express my tenderly awakened sympathy on hearing of thy sore bereavement, but surely the gain should be reckoned with the loss. I have long felt we scarcely do justice to our loved ones on the other side, if we fail to joy in their joy, even while pensively stricken with grief.

Last night I was dreaming of thee as stripped and peeled, stripped and peeled, yet not overwhelmed. It may be that the Lord has thus prepared the way for thy early entrance on the unseen and eternal. . . . Earth's little while here short, then for a glorious duration untold and inexpressible. . . .

Trace from the sea upwards on the 24th degree east longitude, till Kuruman is reached, the scene of the early labours of Livingstone, and most of half a century the home of Robert Moffat, that veteran of the mission field. I write these lines in the room which was his study, now for a little space my domicile. A kindly cordial welcome has awaited us here as elsewhere. The Lord is good and gracious, and the labour in this part of His vineyard is sweet, for a sense of the nearness of the good Shepherd is, in unmerited mercy, richly with us to His praise.

My love largely to thee, from thy old and
      Ever affectionate friend,
          Isaac Sharp.

During some months of his residence at Falmouth, in 1881, Edwin O. Tregelles was very diligently devoted to the cause of the Sunday closing of Public Houses in Cornwall. He attended meetings in various towns, kept up a large correspondence, and prepared a large number of petitions, as well as coming to London, in order to support the cause. All this work told severely on his feeble frame, and it seemed best for him to retire for rest to the south of France.

CHAPTER XXVI.

FALMOUTH AND BANBURY.

Spends Winter in South of France—Justine Dalencourt—Nimes—Congenies—Lydie Majolier—First Quarterly Meeting—Protestants—L. Majolier's Illness—Aigues Mortes and Tower of Constance — Fontanès — Samuel and Clement Brun — Le Vigan — Congenies, Nimes—Returns to England—Resides at Falmouth with his Sister—Temperance Tract Distribution—Encouraged by Temperance Work at Medomsley—Death of Samuel Bowly—Isaac Sharp returns—Removes to Banbury—Dr. Gabriel S. Dobrashian—Meets old Friends from Trinidad—Journal ends—Two Years of Weakness—Letters to his Grandson and Sister—Death—Recollections by Elizabeth N. Capper.

"MY HOME IS NOT HERE."

" When I gaze on the light of yon beautiful sky,
And the curtains of azure unfolded on high,
Their glory and splendour recall to my thought
The blissful inheritance Jesus has bought.
I fancy the portals of heaven appear,
And I feel at this moment, my Home is not here.

When I see all around me those flowers so bright,
Which God hath implanted to ravish my sight,
I hail them as pledges of heavenly love,
And think of the bright ones now blooming above;
Their fragrance reminds me of hopes that are dear,
And I love to remember my Home is not here!

As I list to the song of the lark as she flies,
Still warbling her notes as she mounts to the skies,
I think of the time when my heavenward flight
Will, like hers, be directed to regions of light.
I shall sing, as I leave every trouble and fear,
My home is in heaven, my Home is not here!

Oh, land of enjoyment! Oh, home of my heart!
What blessed delights can thy image impart,
In the midst of affliction, of sorrow and grief,
One thought of thy glory brings instant relief,
And quickly the darkening clouds disappear,
As the feeling steals o'er me, my Home is not here!"

Nimes, Eleventh Month 26th, 1882.—The above was copied by my precious Elizabeth in S. E.'s MS. book, Fifth Month, 1855, and seems to form a suitable preface for the renewal of my own memoranda here in the house of Jules Paradon. May I be watchful, faithful, and obedient, especially in doing the Lord's work in a land to which, in His providence, my feet have been guided. Earnestly do I pray that my every thought, action, and word may have reference to the spread of the kingdom of Christ in this land.

When at Surbiton a few weeks ago, and contemplating a visit to France, I was somewhat alarmed at the tidings that reached us of the disturbances near Lyons, consequent on the scarcity of work. In this condition I was strengthened by the promise, "Fear thou not, for I am with thee; be not dismayed, for I am thy God; I will strengthen thee, yea, I will help thee; yea, I will uphold thee with the right hand of My righteousness."

While ignorant of these feelings of apprehension and cheer, dear S. E. repeated to me these verses of a hymn, so appropriate to my case :—

"'I will uphold thee'! Redeemed one, the greeting
Is thine from thy Father to strengthen, to cheer;
And soft chimes of promise thy list'ning heart meeting,
Re-echo His word who with blessing draws near;
'For the cross and the glory My love hath enrolled thee,
I will help, I will strengthen, yea, I will uphold thee.'

* * * * *

Oh, pilgrim, thy path through the valley may steepen,
But strong is the arm of thy God and thy Guide.
Oh, mourner, though shadows and solitude deepen,
Thou art not alone—thou hast Him by thy side;

'I am thine! thou art Mine!' there is no separation,
Thine the 'joy of thy Lord,' through the 'much tribulation.'"

I left the house of my dear friend J. B. Braithwaite, Eleventh Month 15th, accompanied by my grandson, C. E. Gillett. Our route was Folkestone, Boulogne, Paris, Lyons and Avignon. At "Hotel Normandy," Paris, we had a call of deep interest from Justine Dalencourt, who is engaged in very useful Christian work in that city, and whose labours are abundantly blessed, not only in Paris, but in other parts of France.

Twelfth Month 24th.—Very thankful do I feel that I came to Nîmes five weeks ago. The weather has been very severe in England, but here generally fair.

31*st*.—Through the mercy of the Lord brought in safety and in peace, great peace, to the close of another year.

Congenies, First Month 3rd, 1883.—I came here yesterday by invitation from Lydie Majolier, at whose house I have been very kindly accommodated.

The quarterly meeting was held at the close of the meeting for worship this morning, which was a blessed time. Mary Brown ministered, interpreted for by Marie Bernard. Jules Paradon interpreted for me. In the second meeting my certificates were read, and some minutes relative to the affairs of the Society of Friends in the South of France. The meeting was large; all the scholars from the Nîmes school were there, and many of the Congenies people. May the blessing of the Lord rest on this effort to extend the kingdom of Christ. A large proportion of the inhabitants are Protestants, this village being near the Cevennes mountains, which in the days of persecution were their stronghold.

7th.—Lydie Majolier has been so unwell with a cold and cough that we have been quite anxious about her. More than a week ago a little boy came to her house selling matches. She pitied the poor child, and gave him some food in her kitchen, leaving him there for a minute or two. When she returned, her gold watch, that was hanging on the wall, was gone, and the boy also. He was pursued and captured, and confessed where he had hidden the watch, which was restored. This circumstance has preyed on her mind, and doubtless has something to do with her being unwell. This morning she told me that she wished me to know that during the night she had felt it was uncertain how the illness might terminate, but that she was "cheered by the belief that there was no condemnation."

28*th, First Day.*—The past week has been one of no common blessing to my soul, why or how, I scarcely know, unless it be that I have sought and found more frequent communion with our heavenly Father, through the mediation of His ever blessed Son.

Second Month 11*th*.—On the 5th Jean and Marie Bernard and their daughter Blanche, with Edith and Jane Richardson of Moyallen, and I went to Aigues Mortes and saw the Tower of Constance, where many Protestants in former and evil days suffered cruel imprisonment and death. We also went to the end of the canal, and dipped our hands in the waters of the Mediterranean.

Fontanès, 26*th*.—I was met at the station by Clement Brun. Anna Vally arrived a few hours after. She interpreted nicely for me yesterday. The woman of Samaria was the subject on which I spoke. It is one of great importance, for it was on that occasion, and almost the only time, that our blessed Lord avowed Himself to be the Messiah.

Third Month 4*th*.—Yesterday was the anniversary of the day when my earthly joys were so much blighted, but, through mercy, there is still much happiness left in seeking to know and do my heavenly Father's will. On Second-Day a party went by railway to Le Vigan. We visited a silk mill, and saw a large number of women and girls winding the silk off from cocoons. Augustin Verdier, the superintendent, seems to be a serious, intelligent Christian. We had a brief season of worship together, refreshing though unexpected.

Congenies, Third Month 18th.—The record of the past week may be, "Mercies abound!" Day by day the manna has fallen, body and soul being refreshed by heavenly food, because the sustenance for the body is, as well as the spiritual food, the gift from heaven.

Fourth Month 1st.—Still at Congenies, which appears to be the allotment of my heavenly Father. Earnest have been my desires that I may seek hourly to know and do His holy will. In my waking hours my frequent query, mentally, is, "What can I do for Jesus?" There seems to be much that wants mending, but the way appears hedged up; so many of the educated class in these localities are more or less connected with the wine trade. When seeking to know my duty, the answer seems to be, "Be thou an example to the believers." In our meeting this morning the message I had to deliver was, "Blessed are they which do hunger and thirst after righteousness; for they shall be filled." Lydie Majolier followed, confirming the word.

Fontanès, 16th.—Whilst indisposed I have been most kindly nursed by Clement Brun, his wife, and daughter. Their attentions were judicious and successful.

Nimes, 29th.—Surely goodness and mercy have followed me all the days of my life, and may I dwell in the Lord's tabernacle for ever. I left Congenies four days ago by *diligence*. It felt serious work to leave a place where so much needs to be done, and where I could do so little; but my prayers were frequent that the Lord would reveal His will as to His work, and that I might do it in simplicity and with godly sincerity.

We have had a good meeting this morning. I quoted Matthew v. 23, 24; that in the evening was a refreshing season of renewed favour. Mary Brown concluded the meeting by a precious prayer, in which reference was made to my rejoicing in glory, which I trust may be realized.

At a later date he writes:—

Our journey from Nimes to London was pleasantly and safely accomplished. The stay at Avignon was specially enjoyed. Jane G. Richardson was my companion; we were going home, the scenery fine, the weather delightful, and the views of the river, bridge, and the castle very imposing.

After attending the Yearly Meeting, and staying awhile at Banbury and Surbiton, Edwin O. Tregelles visited his brothers and sisters, Edward and Gulielma Richardson, at Torquay, and Nathaniel and Frances Tregelles at Liskeard, reaching Falmouth on the 6th of the Eleventh Month, 1883. When there, his home was with his sister Lydia. For some time he was an invalid, so much so that he had to postpone intended visits amongst his relations. He was, however, much cheered when his children and grandchildren came to see him. When well enough he found opportunities for Temperance work, especially in the preparation and circulation of tracts.

Falmouth, Eleventh Month 18*th*.—The meeting this morning was largely attended, and seemed like a season of worship to many. It gathered punctually. The comfort of a meeting is much influenced by coming together at one time, and in one place.

25*th*.—I received this week an interesting note from Ralph B. Robson, once a poor boy who worked for me in my colliery at Medomsley, and now a curate at Norton Kingsley; mostly self-educated.

Twelfth Month, 9*th*.—Soon after the meeting assembled this morning I quoted the words of our Lord, "Where two or three are gathered together in My name, there am I in the midst of them": if this be our case, we shall know that in His presence there is fulness of joy, and at His right hand pleasures for evermore. Peace, and a good meeting followed.

16th.—I have enjoyed, this morning, the perusal of "Pilgrim's Progress," the view of the Delectable Mountains, and also the mention of Christian's ascending to bliss. Thankful do I feel for the glimpses of glory granted to me in my recent illness, and thankful and restful I am, in the renovation of health.

23rd.—Another week passed, with many mercies granted; the greatest of these being daily companionship with Jesus —the same blessed Jesus who said, "Lo, I am with you alway, even unto the end of the world."

We have had a favoured meeting this morning, several offerings in prayer and testimony. The prayer at the close by —— was very real. The Advices were read. I felt at the end, intimate dependence on Jesus. It is not by works of righteousness that we have done, but of His mercy He saveth us, by the washing of regeneration and renewing of the Holy Ghost.

30th.—Yesterday a note came from John Weddle, of Medomsley, informing me that the Temperance Society there had been revived. I had previously prepared some parcels of religious and temperance tracts as New Year's gifts, so I posted him one in time for the New Year's greeting. It is delightful to think of this movement among a people for whom I have been interested about thirty years. May the Lord strengthen and bless their efforts.

Second Month 10th, 1884.—Another year of mercy has been granted me. Conflict has been my portion, the flesh wanting to look into the pages of the unrevealed future, the spirit at times desiring to leave all my future in the hands of a covenant-keeping God, who long since promised, "I will never leave thee, nor forsake thee." "Behold, I have graven thee upon the palms of my hands."

Third Month 25th.—The death of my dear friend Samuel Bowly took place on the 22nd, his eighty-second birthday. In 1826 he and his wife Jane (*née* Shipley) visited us at Neath Abbey, when Sister Rebecca, Nathaniel, and I lived together. They were travelling in a gig, and I accompanied them up Neath Valley to Merthyr, and on next day to Ponty-pool and Raglan Castle. A delightful time we had, commencing a friendship that strengthened with time, and was cemented by our mutual earnestness in the Temperance cause.

30th.—Isaac Sharp arrived in Liverpool two days ago, and to-day there has been forwarded to me from Banbury, I. S.'s telegram as follows: "Please forward to Tregelles; just landed, peaceful and well. Oh, magnify the Lord with me. No equinoctial storm." What a mercy that this dear friend has returned home, after an absence of six and a half years.

Fourth Month 6th.—After our Bible reading this evening my heart and voice were engaged in prayer specially for Falmouth, that the work of the Lord might go forward in every soul, and a great blessing rest on all the people. Soon after we had finished, a young man called, asking for tracts to distribute; which felt like the budding of the answer to my prayer.

Banbury, Fifth Month, 15th.—I arrived at Wood Green yesterday week, having found the journey very trying, and more wearying than I had expected. Yesterday, to my great delight, Isaac Sharp came from London to spend four hours. Our interviews were deeply interesting and affecting; the last was while I was in bed, when dear Isaac prayed beside me.

Sixth Month 8th.—Since the 3rd of Third Month, 1878, when my precious Elizabeth was so suddenly taken from me, I have not known one day of former vigour. And now my desire is that each day I may live under a sense of my dependence for every blessing on the Lord, whose wisdom and goodness I would trust to the end. Much do I crave such meek submission that I may not be elated or depressed by fluctuations.

15*th*.—The question of salvation has been often present, and pressing; and while considering the important subject this evening, the hymn "Just as I am, without one plea," seems appropriate. I desire to have every thought brought into subjection to the Spirit of Christ.

Dr. Gabriel S. Dobrashian, of Constantinople, has been here for a week. I trust that he may be kept by the power of God, and made instrumental in spreading the knowledge of Christ in that dark land.

Seventh Month 6th.—David and Emma Horsford, of Trinidad, came to tea. We showed them the picture of Petit Bourg, where I was taken ill of yellow fever. We spoke of Dr. Johnson, and of Dr. Louis Philip. My heart overflows when I think of the Lord's dealings with me. My dear companion James Jesup lived an exemplary life, and was safely gathered to his heavenly home many years ago. Lord, keep me walking in Thy fear, and in the comfort of the Holy Ghost! Have not been at meeting to-day, not feeling strong enough.

These are the last words of the journal commenced fifty-five years previously, when in the warmth of his early love the same desire was uppermost, to be kept walking in the fear of God, and the comfort of the Holy Ghost.

On the 12th of Seventh Month Edwin O. Tregelles was taken seriously ill with cramp and sickness, and was much prostrated for several weeks. After this he was frequently subject to attacks of indisposition which gradually reduced his strength. He attended meetings only a few times, and that mostly on the week-day mornings. In a memorandum dated Eighth

Month 5th, 1885, he writes, "Had a time of favour this morning while others were at meeting."

The following twelve months he continued in much weakness, often engaged in numbering his blessings, and seeking patiently to wait until the summons should come. A friend who frequently saw him when he was in this feeble state, writes as follows, of conversations she had with him :—

Banbury, Ninth Month 18th, 1884.—Something was said about several of his grandchildren returning next week to school. He remarked, "I do not expect ever to see them again." I said, "There is a land where there will be no more parting." He said, "Yes, and a far more exceeding and eternal weight of glory. What should I do now without the consolations of the gospel? I have not followed a cunningly devised fable, but a great reality. 'God was in Christ, reconciling the world unto Himself.'"

Seventh Month 14th, 1885.—Called to see dear E. O. Tregelles. He alluded to his increasing weakness, and how different it was in old age to the time of youth, but said he did not wish to have his life to live over again, that he felt thankful for the mercies of the present. I said, "It is a comforting thought that we are nearing the Haven." He said, "Yes; and with the good Pilot on board, as I believe I have. He knows all the hidden dangers. He is almighty to save. Him first, Him last, Him midst and without end."

The following note to his grandson, Edwin H. Tregelles, refers to a visit paid by the latter to the grave of Elizabeth Tregelles.

> 1st of Eighth Month, 1886.

". . . Thy mention of thy visit to Consett is interesting.

> "Not to the grave, my soul, descend to contemplate,
> The spirit is not there."

Interesting as it is, and should be, to visit the resting place of those we loved who are gone before, I often think of those lines in reference to the deeply interesting subject— a subject which I have to contemplate with fixedness, but without fear; trusting in the mercy of God through Christ Jesus, who said, "I am the Way, the Truth, and the Life. . .

E. O. T.

To LYDIA TREGELLES.

> Banbury, 31st of Eighth Month, 1886.

MY DEAR SISTER,—

For several days I have been meditating on taking up the pen and acknowledging thy welcome note, but I do not find it easy to write at the right time, and indeed at no time is it easy, for my writing powers have become very frail and defective. . . . I like to think of thee enjoying the privilege of good companionship on thy Homeward way. The angel of the Lord encampeth about them that fear Him, now and for ever. That this may be thy blessed portion, is the prayer of

"Thy affectionate brother,
"EDWIN O. TREGELLES."

On the 16th of Ninth Month, 1886, in one of his attacks of sickness, with its attendant weakness, he passed away to his home above; unconscious, it is believed, that the time had come for the great and glorious change, though he had lived for years in expectation of it. A few days before his death he had alluded to it in the words, "I am going home, to a bright and glorious home; it is a going home which has no fears for me, but I look forward to it with joy."

It may not be out of place here to insert a few recollections penned by Elizabeth N. Capper.

22nd of Ninth Month, 1886.

My first recollection of Edwin O. Tregelles was, I think, in the year 1831; I am not quite sure whether it was not a year later. He and Jenepher Tregelles came, very soon after their marriage, and stayed a few days at our house. I do not remember much about her, except her very sweet and attractive appearance; but I never lost the reverence which impressed me for him, and which now seems to me wonderful for so young a man to inspire.

It was, perhaps, seven or eight years later that he came to Bristol, I think only for the purpose of having a meeting for the young men, about which I heard something, enough to make me feel much admiration for the devotedness and single-eyed faithfulness which must have been his for such a service. He evidently felt it very deeply, as he did not remain in Bristol for any ordinary meeting. Doubtless a rich blessing rested on this faithfulness, and thus he was made a blessing all his life long.

I longed that all the dear young people present (at the funeral) could have seen, as it were, that long life of dedication spread out. If they could see it even in the small degree that I see it, they would feel animated with a fresh sense of the blessedness of an early and full surrender.

www.ingramcontent.com/pod-product-compliance
Lightning Source LLC
Chambersburg PA
CBHW051859300426
44117CB00006B/466